Witchcraft in Tudor
and Stuart England

Alan Macfarlane

Witchcraft in Tudor and Stuart England

A regional and
comparative study

WAVELAND

PRESS, INC.

Prospect Heights, Illinois

For information about this book, write or call:
 Waveland Press, Inc.
 P.O. Box 400
 Prospect Heights, Illinois 60070
 (708) 634-0081

For my father, mother, and sister
who contributed so much . . .

ISBN 0-88133-532-0

Printed in the United States of America

7 6 5 4 3 2

Contents

Besides, when any Errour is committed
Whereby wee may Incurre or losse or shame,
That wee our selves thereof may be acquitted
Wee are too ready to transferre the blame
Upon some Witch: That made us doe the same.
It is the vulgar Plea that weake ones use
I was bewitch'd: I could nor will: nor chuse.

But my affection was not caus'd by Art;
The witch that wrought on mee was in my brest.

The Poems of Sir Francis Hubert,
ed. B. Mellor (Oxford, 1961), pp. 59–60

For example, what were the social conditions in
seventeenth-century England that produced beliefs
so very similar to contemporary beliefs in Pondoland
. . . and what were the effective causes of the decline
of these beliefs? I long to read an adequate analysis
of this problem by some social historian aware of
anthropological theory.

M. Wilson, 'Witch Beliefs and Social Structure',
American Journal of Sociology, 56, No. 4 (1951), p. 313

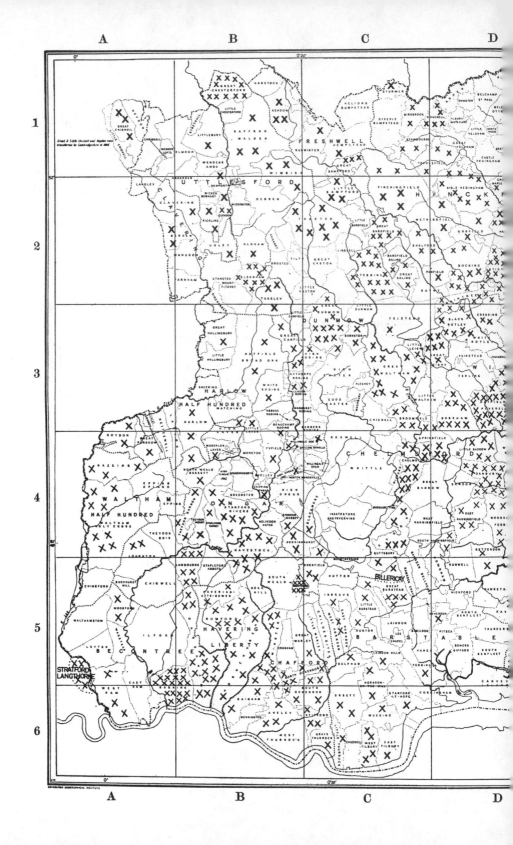

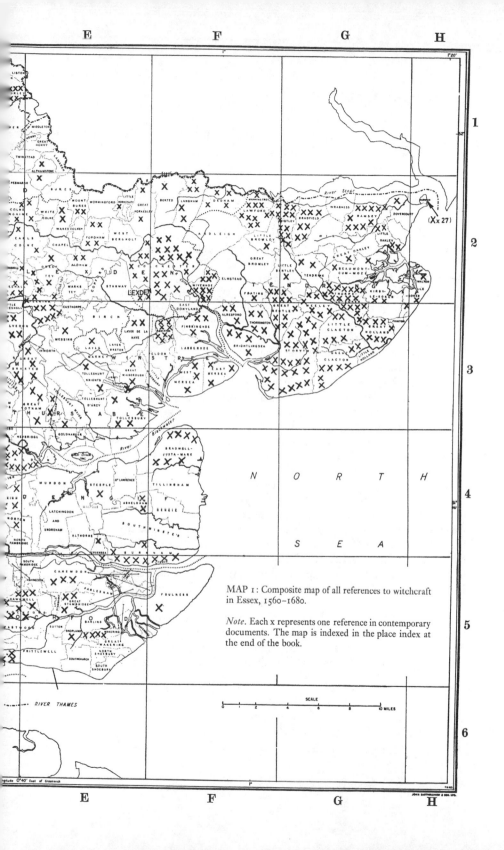

MAP 1: Composite map of all references to witchcraft in Essex, 1560–1680.

Note. Each x represents one reference in contemporary documents. The map is indexed in the place index at the end of the book.

Acknowledgements

This work is a considerably modified version of my Oxford D.Phil. thesis (1967) entitled 'Witchcraft Prosecutions in Essex, 1560–1680; A Sociological Analysis'. To the supervisor of that thesis, Mr. Keith Thomas of St. John's College, Oxford, both book and thesis owe an incalculable amount. Only a few of the many references and ideas contributed by Mr. Thomas have been explicitly acknowledged in the text; without his enthusiasm, criticism, and wisdom the book would never have been written at all. Many of the topics raised in the following pages will receive much fuller treatment in his forthcoming work on 'Primitive Beliefs in Pre-Industrial England'.

A considerable part of the documentary research upon which this work is based would have been impossible without the superb facilities offered by the Essex Record Office. Indexes, transcripts, and, above all, the generous help of Miss Hilda Grieve and her charming assistants, made research at Chelmsford far more profitable and pleasurable than it would otherwise have been. I thank the County Archivist, F. G. Emmison, and all the staff for this assistance and for permission to quote from the Essex records. Permission to quote from documents at the Public Record Office was also generously given.

A number of people kindly read part or all of the thesis and made helpful comments; Norman Cohn, Mary Douglas, Christopher Hill, Lucy Mair. Professor Evans-Pritchard, whose pioneering work on witchcraft among the Azande was the starting-point for this study, not only read the thesis and book, but also added a preface. I am most grateful to him for these kindnesses. My friends at Oxford, particularly Lady Rosalind Clay and Harry Pitt, gave me helpful advice and moral support during the writing of the original thesis. Finally, my own nuclear family are to be thanked. They not only provided the background of a restful year in a garden shed in the Lake District, but also expert assistance in the analysis of the social background to witchcraft prosecutions in the three Essex villages used as a sample. In many ways the work was a co-operative one, although I, alone, am responsible for the remaining mistakes. I am deeply grateful to those who made it possible, above all my wife Gill.

Preface

Witchcraft beliefs and the practices arising from them have been a prominent topic in anthropological monographs because they frequently, but by no means invariably, are a dominant interest for the primitive peoples whose institutions anthropologists have mostly studied. Historians of pre-industrial European society have also, it is true, written about the subject but they have seldom attempted to make it, as Dr. Macfarlane has done in this book, a central theme in their descriptions of the thought of a period. Indeed this is, I suppose, the most detailed, as it is also certainly the most sociological, inquiry into witchcraft yet made by an historian.

Now it is evident that the anthropologist and the historian should in this matter be of help to one another, mainly in the pointing to major problems that have arisen in the course of their researches. Each has advantages and disadvantages on his side. The historian's chief advantage is, of course, that he can study witchcraft beliefs over a long period of time, and so Dr. Macfarlane has been able to ask himself why prosecutions for witchcraft appear to rise steeply in the fifteenth and sixteenth centuries and then fall in the seventeenth and eighteenth centuries; even if the circumstances are too complex to enable him to give a certain answer to his question. The anthropologist who, like myself, has studied witchcraft in a primitive society is here handicapped by the absence of records; though it might now be possible to discover whether belief in witchcraft increases or declines with the breakdown of tribal society and the growth of Christianity, literacy, knowledge, urbanization and industrialization. If this can be discovered—it has not yet been—it would throw light on the almost complete disappearance of witchcraft beliefs in the England of today.

The great disadvantage for the historian is obviously that he cannot discover what is not in the documents, and even sometimes determine the accuracy of what is in them, by making his own inquiries, for the people who might have helped him died long ago. So he can only guess why the curve of witchcraft accusations rises and falls. Nor can he be certain why it is that there are, as Dr. Macfarlane has shown, so many prosecutions in Essex compared to the rest of England and why in some parts of Essex more than in others. Nor can we know for sure to what extent do the number of recorded prosecutions, even supposing that the records are complete and trustworthy, reflect the number of accusations and suspicions not brought to court. Here anthropological evidence would suggest that the prosecutions indicate a general belief in witchcraft. As the author says, before Notestein and Ewen wrote on the subject witchcraft beliefs were portrayed as sporadic and sudden epidemics instead of everyday fears.

Perhaps the most valuable contribution made by anthropologists has been in the plotting of the social relationships involved in accusations— what kind of person is believed to have bewitched what other kind of person in societies of one or other type. Here Dr. Macfarlane, guided I think by his anthropological reading, has unearthed some very interesting facts. Anthropologists have further, and time and again, shown that witchcraft accusations are usually a function of misfortune, as the author has also abundantly illustrated, though it is a problem why in Tudor and Stuart England some misfortunes are attributed to witches and others not. Anthropology has also to its credit that it has shown that while a witchcraft outlook in social relations may be unscientific it is far from being irrational. This is demonstrated also in the present study where it is shown that people of undoubted intelligence accepted without question that people can bewitch. Born into and enclosed in a narrow world of thought it is difficult for even the most enlightened not to accept what all around them believe and have believed; and granted the axiom that certain misfortunes can be caused by witches, then those misfortunes are, or may be, evidence of witchcraft and proof of its action. It is not clear, however, since some of these misfortunes must have been very frequent events, why they so seldom led to legal action. Dr. Macfarlane makes a significant observation which may explain, at least to some extent, why this is so in his discussion of the cumulative manner in which a person got the reputation of being a witch. He points out that whereas it is common in primitive societies that an event harmful to a person precedes and leads to identification of, and action against, a witch, it would appear from the Essex records that a person first became regarded as a witch and then the event was attributed to her, or his, malice. I think also that it would be true to say that anthropology has shown that where religious beliefs, whether those of spiritual cults or of ancestor cults, are strong, witchcraft beliefs are relatively weak, a point which has some bearing on the possible relevance to witchcraft beliefs of the religious upheaval in England in the period under survey.

In spite of the difficulties confronting the student who has only literary records to guide him and cannot consult men of flesh and blood, this book shows that many answers can be obtained if only one knows the right questions to ask; and it is clear that Dr. Macfarlane has been able to ask them, and I hope I may be allowed to say that he has been able to ask them largely because they have arisen in the course of his reading of anthropological writings on witchcraft. When the study of witchcraft has been continued, on the lines pursued by him, for other parts of Great Britain and elsewhere in Europe, and the conclusions reached are collated with those reached by anthropologists for the simpler societies we may hope to be able to decide what are the conditions which favour the growth and the decay of belief in witches.

E. E. EVANS-PRITCHARD

Abbreviations and conventions

ABBREVIATED TITLES

Ady, *Candle* Thomas Ady, *A Candle in the Dark: or A Treatise Concerning the Nature of Witches and Witchcraft* (1656).

Bernard, *Guide* Richard Bernard, *A Guide to Grand Jury Men* (1627).

Davids, *Annals* T. W. Davids, *Annals of Evangelical Nonconformity in the County of Essex, From the Time of Wycliffe to the Restoration* (1863).

Ewen I C. L. Ewen, *Witch Hunting and Witch Trials* (1929).

Ewen II C. L. Ewen, *Witchcraft and Demonianism* (1933).

Gaule, *Select Cases* John Gaule, *Select Cases of Conscience Touching Witches and Witchcraft* (1646).

Gifford, *Discourse* George Gifford, *A Discourse of the Subtill Practises of Devilles by Witches and Sorcerers* (1587).

Gifford, *Dialogue* George Gifford, *A Dialogue Concerning Witches and Witchcrafts* (1593; the Shakespeare Association Facsimile edn., 1931, was used).

Hopkins, *Discovery* Matthew Hopkins, *The Discovery of Witches* (1647; the 1928 edition by M. Summers was used and references are to this edition).

Kittredge, *Witchcraft* G. L. Kittredge, *Witchcraft in Old and New England* (New York, 1929).

Morant, *Essex* Philip Morant, *The History and Antiquities of the County of Essex* (1816), 2 vols.

Newcourt, *Repertorium* Richard Newcourt, *Repertorium Ecclesiasticum Parochiale Londinense* (1708–10), 2 vols.

Perkins, *Damned Art* William Perkins, *A Discourse of the Damned Art of Witchcraft* (Cambridge, 1608).

Scot, *Discovery* Reginald Scot, *The Discoverie of Witchcraft* (1584; all references are to the 1964 reprint. Preface by H. R. Williamson).

Stearne, *Confirmation*   John Stearne, *A Confirmation and Discovery of Witch-craft* (1648).

Venn, *Alumni*   John and S. A. Venn, *Alumni Cantabrigiensis* (Cam-
Cantabrigiensis   bridge, 1922–7), 4 vols.

ESSEX PAMPHLETS

1566 Pamphlet   *The Examination and Confession of Certain Wytches at Chensford in the Countie of Essex before the Queens maiesties Judges, the xxvi day of July Anno 1566* (1566: the only copy is in the Lambeth Palace library and there is no consistent foliation; page references are therefore to the reprinted version in Ewen I, pp. 317–24).

1579 Pamphlet   *A Detection of damnable driftes, practized by three Witches arraigned at Chelmisforde in Essex, at the late Assises there holden, which were executed in Aprill. 1579* (1579; a copy is in the British Museum, and Ewen II, pp. 149–51, prints abstracts).

1582 Pamphlet   *A True and Just Recorde of the Information, Examina-tion and Confession of all the Witches, taken at S. Oses in the countie of Essex* (1582; abstracts in Ewen II, pp. 155–63, and a microfilm copy in the Bodleian Library, Oxford, Films S.T.C., 1,014), by W.W.

1589 Pamphlet   *The Apprehension and Confession of three notorious Witches. Arreigned and by Iustice condemned and executed at Chelmesforde, in the Countye of Essex, the 5. day of Iulye, last past, 1589* (1589; the only copy is in the Lambeth Palace library; abstracts are printed in Ewen II, pp. 167–8, and there is a microfilm copy in the Bodleian Library, Oxford, Films S.T.C., 952).

1645 Pamphlet   *A True and Exact Relation of the Several Informations, Examinations, and Confessions of the late Witches, arraigned and executed in the County of Essex* (1645; there are several copies and abstracts are printed in Ewen II, pp. 262–77).

OTHER ABBREVIATIONS AND CONVENTIONS

D.N.B.   *Dictionary of National Biography*, ed. Leslie Stephen and Sidney Lee (1908–9).

E.R.O.   Essex Record Office, Chelmsford, Essex.

g.c.   gaol calendar.

K.B.   King's Bench.
P.R.O.   Public Record Office, Chancery Lane, London.
Q/SR.   Quarter Sessions Rolls.

All references to unpaginated material are to the *recto* side, unless 'v' for *verso* is specifically indicated.

Place of publication of books and pamphlets is London, unless otherwise stated.

All dates are in new style. When a double date is given—for example, 15 January 1578/9—the latter is the modern dating.

Footnotes containing references to 'Case 152', or another number, refer to the numbered witchcraft cases in Appendix 1.

The meaning attached to the word 'witchcraft' is explained in the introductory chapter. The use of this word, and of the word 'witch', does not imply any belief in the actual existence of witches or in the power of witchcraft. To speak of someone as a 'witch' is merely a contracted way of saying 'a person suspected to be a witch by her accusers'.

Two technical terms used are 'cunning folk' and 'familiars'. The former were magical practitioners who possessed 'cunning' or knowledge and who could heal animals, detect witches, and find lost property. A witch's familiar was a small creature of diabolic origin, often in the shape of a cat or a toad, which was believed to carry out the wishes of the witch.

Quotations are kept in their original spelling and punctuation, unless indicated otherwise. 'Yt' always means 'that'.

Where anthropological writings are frequently cited a convention unfamiliar to some historians, but utilized by anthropologists, has been adopted whereby an abbreviated reference (consisting of the author's name, the date of publication, and page number) is given. Thus, for example, E. E. Evans-Pritchard, *Witchcraft, Oracles and Magic among the Azande* (Oxford, 1937), p. 100, would be abbreviated to Evans-Pritchard (1937), p. 100. The full titles of all such abbreviated books and articles are given on pp. 323–4 of the Bibliography.

Part one
Sources and statistics

Chapter 1

Problems and sources
in the study of witchcraft

It is not surprising that the history of witchcraft should have attracted considerable attention.[1] Nor is it difficult to see why such a subject should have aroused so much emotion in those who studied it. Trials for witchcraft contain much that is brutal, much that is sexually perverted, and much that seems at first sight either ludicrous or fantastic. There are disagreements among authorities over all the fundamental problems concerning the history of this phenomenon: when witchcraft accusations and beliefs began and ended; what caused the apparent increase of accusations during the fifteenth and sixteenth centuries in Europe; what led to the apparent decline in the seventeenth and eighteenth centuries; whether there really *were* 'witches'; whether any particular group of people can be held responsible for the prosecutions and beliefs. Among the subjects upon which there is most disagreement, although this is usually implicit rather than explicit, are the very terms 'witchcraft' and 'sorcery'. Since many subsequent arguments have arisen from divergence of definitions, it is important to state as early as possible the meaning ascribed to various words.

The terms 'witchcraft', 'sorcery', and 'magic' are notoriously difficult to define. There is no consensus of opinion on their meaning, either among present-day historians and anthropologists or among writers living in the sixteenth and seventeenth centuries. Various attempted definitions and the overall state of confusion are discussed elsewhere.[2] Here we merely state quite simply how various words will be used in the following analysis while recognizing that such usage does not entirely reflect all shades of opinion in either the past or present. It has been remarked that, 'No social phenomenon can be adequately studied merely in the language and categories of thought in which the people among whom it is found represent it to themselves'.[3] This has been found to be especially true in the study of the history of English witchcraft beliefs.

The word 'witchcraft' has, in fact, been used in this book in two ways. Firstly, it has been employed as an undifferentiated term to cover all the activities which came within the scope of the English Witchcraft Statutes of 1542, 1563, and 1604, or the ecclesiastical visitation articles which enquired about 'witchcraft, conjuring, southsaying, charmes'. In this broad sense a 'witchcraft prosecution' might as easily be for looking in a crystal ball to discover where lost goods were as for supposedly injuring a person by evil and supernatural means. Witches, in this sense, are merely those called 'witches' in a society. The second use of the word 'witchcraft' is more precise. It is supernatural activity, believed to be the result of power given by some external force (for instance, the Devil) and to result

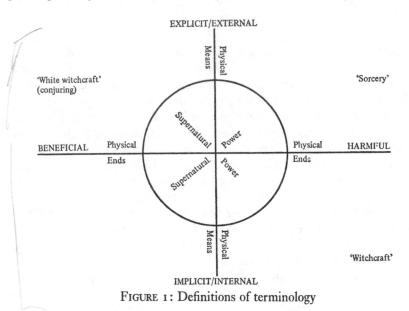

FIGURE 1: Definitions of terminology

in physical injury to the person or object attacked by it. There is not necessarily any outward action or words on the part of the 'witch'. It is basically an internal power. The opposite to this is 'white witchcraft', which is the reverse, both because its ends are 'good' rather than 'bad', healing rather than hurting, and because it employs outward means—for instance, gazing into a crystal ball. In this sense some of the offences in the Witchcraft Acts were 'white witchcraft'. Between these two terms lies a third, 'sorcery'. This combines the explicit means of 'white witchcraft'— for instance, a sorcerer makes an image of his enemy in wax—with the evil *ends* of witchcraft: he sticks pins into the image to cripple his victim. The relevance and detailed application of these distinctions will emerge during the analysis of witchcraft prosecutions. It is hoped that the context will indicate whether 'witchcraft' is being used in its general or specific sense. Both definitions are left wide enough to allow comparison between 'witchcraft' in sixteenth-century England and that in modern societies.[4]

The phenomena broadly labelled 'witchcraft' may be studied at a number of levels. The geographical and temporal unit selected for study will obviously be interrelated with the type of questions asked by the investigator and the nature of the sources he uses. If very detailed questions are asked about particular individuals accused as witches, the records used will be of a different nature to those employed by the historian who seeks to cover the whole of European witchcraft over several centuries. The following study has expanded the area of investigation in one direction—by posing questions uninvestigated by previous historians and by using sources untapped for the history of witchcraft. But a new intensity of investigation has forced a narrowing of the geographical and spatial horizon. As we will see, instead of the majestic sweep through hundreds of years of European history, we are confined often to one English county, or even one village.

In recent years the sources available to the historian of witchcraft have increased dramatically. Such an expansion is well illustrated by research in England. Until the publication of Wallace Notestein's *History of Witchcraft in England from 1558 to 1718* in 1911, studies of English witchcraft had been based almost exclusively on two types of record: literary accounts and descriptions of witchcraft trials in contemporary pamphlets. Notestein not only provided a far more detailed description of the literary controversy and of the famous trials, but also made an attempt to use other legal records. Since he tried to cover the whole of England for 160 years, he was, on the whole, only able to look at cases already in print. These included witchcraft prosecutions from a number of central and local courts, yet he admitted that 'no history of the subject has the right to be called final' until someone had been round English counties and searched 'the masses of gaol delivery records and municipal archives'. His prediction that 'it seems improbable that such a search would uncover so many unlisted trials as seriously to modify the narrative'[5] was shown to be incorrect in 1929, when C. L. Ewen published the Home Circuit Assize court indictments for witchcraft.[6] Of the 790 indictments Ewen listed, only a few had been discovered by Notestein. The difference made can be seen from the fact that, from all sources and for the whole of England, Notestein had only been able to compile a list of approximately 400 references. In Essex, for example, this meant that, instead of the fifteen trials listed by Notestein, in which there are references to about forty individuals, Ewen provided some 473 indictments, referring to 299 persons. These indictments usually included crucial details, such as the exact nature of the offence and the place of residence of both 'witch'[7] and victim. These facts were often unobtainable from many of Notestein's references. In his second work on the subject, Ewen supplemented Notestein's list by adding further cases from other printed and unprinted legal records.[8]

The first aim of this study is to extend the work of Ewen and Notestein on the sources for the study of witchcraft. They made it clear that no adequate history of the subject could be written without a detailed analysis of the actual prosecutions, and Ewen provided a review of one important and unused source, the Assize records. Yet printed cases in Ewen's works suggested that material from at least three other types of court, borough, quarter session, and ecclesiastical, needed investigation. The first part of this book is therefore a survey of all the possible sources for the study of the history of witchcraft. The jurisdiction and procedure of the various courts are analysed so that the actual prosecutions can be more easily understood and the relative value of statistics derived from different sources can be estimated. Furthermore, the accuracy of the impression derived from literary sources is tested.

Witchcraft beliefs and accusations occurred throughout most of Europe in the sixteenth and seventeenth centuries. The major figures in Continental witchcraft—for instance, the authors of the *Malleus Maleficarum*, Weyer, Bodin, Del Rio, Boguet, and Balthasar Bekker—as well as the general outline of the prosecution of witches, have already received considerable attention from historians.[9] One reason for limiting this study to England is that English witchcraft appears to be very different from that on the Continent and in Scotland. The methods of detecting and trying witches differed from country to country and, partly as a result of this, the type of person believed to be a witch, the numbers accused, the punishments inflicted, and the myths which surrounded their activities differed. As we will see, witches in the county of Essex were not believed to fly, did not meet for 'Sabbats' or orgies, dance and feast, indulge in sexual perversions, like some of their Continental counterparts. There were, in Essex, no possessed convents, no financial profits to be made from witch-hunting, no professional inquisitors. Only during the year 1645, when the witch-hunter Matthew Hopkins was active, do the Essex trials bear a resemblance to the more sensational descriptions of French or German witchcraft trials.[10] An account of English witchcraft which draws information from European records would soon become distorted.

For a number of subjects—for instance, court procedure or legal enactments on witchcraft—England is a convenient unit for study. As a result there are already a number of general studies of witchcraft in England which describe the more famous trials, some of the legal background, and some of the political and religious conflicts with which prosecutions coincided. The best of these accounts, that by Notestein already mentioned, makes more than a very general survey of the literary and legal controversies unnecessary. For this reason alone it is not worth writing another general account of English witchcraft until far more local research has been undertaken.[11] But there are also other reasons why a geographical area smaller than a nation which contained several million people, over 150 years, is the subject of this study. English historians are increasingly aware of the importance of regional variations and the consequent necessity for regional studies in topics ranging from agrarian to political history.[12] The same is patently true in the history of witchcraft and for the same reasons. Until the area for investigation is narrowed it is impossible to make a thorough use of local records or to answer with certainty a whole new range of questions. Although use has been made of most of the printed and some of the unprinted records of witchcraft for England, whenever a detailed, and often statistical, analysis is needed to provide an answer to a particular problem, evidence will be drawn from the county of Essex. Even limiting ourselves to one English county, we will be dealing with a population of roughly 100,000 people over a period of 150 years. This is a far larger unit than that normally studied by social anthropologists in their studies of witchcraft or other phenomena. Often they concentrate their attention on one or a group of several villages, numbering roughly a thousand people.[13] When even more detailed material than that provided by a county study is required this more microscopic analysis will be undertaken. A group of three neighbouring villages within Essex have been selected for intensive study for a period of forty years.[14] The method, as will be seen, is that of a sample within a sample, within a sample.

The county of Essex was chosen as a sample for several reasons. It possesses very good series of all the important court records. While it is one of the five counties in England which have sixteenth-century Assize records, it surpasses the other four in this class in the early commencement of its Quarter Sessions material; this starts in 1556, some thirty-three years before that of any of the other four. Essex has excellent Elizabethan ecclesiastical court records, and adequate borough archives. Furthermore, its records are made easily accessible by the excellent indexing and other facilities of the local Record Office. This easy accessibility is especially important in the second and third parts of this study. Having discovered the names and locations of Essex witches from all sources, an attempt has been made to relate some of the people involved in the witchcraft prosecutions to their social background. Essex is particularly suitable for such an attempt, because the names and villages of more suspected witches and their victims are known for this county, largely because of Ewen's research on Assize indictments, than for any other. How far Essex was exceptional will appear from the chapters on sources. As well as an intensive investigation into the direct records of witchcraft cases, an attempt has been made

to use the rich resources utilized by local historians—for example, wills,
manorial records, parish registers, and subsidy assessments—in order to
learn more about the background to prosecutions.

The unit chosen for more detailed study, the county of Essex, is situated
to the north-east of London. It is bordered by the sea on the east and south,
and the counties of Hertfordshire, Cambridgeshire, and Suffolk on the
landward side. Approximately forty miles long and forty miles wide, it
had a population of around 100,000 inhabitants in 1638, the only date for
which we have an estimate.[15] They lived in some 425 villages and seven
chartered boroughs; the largest of the latter was Colchester, followed by
Chelmsford, Maldon, and Harwich. This flat county was still predominantly agricultural, but the late sixteenth century witnessed the growth of
an important cloth industry in the north-east of the county. In the opposite
corner, around Epping and Waltham in the south-west, was the bulk of
the remaining forest, most of which had disappeared before our period.
Most of the county, with the major exception of the north-west, had been
enclosed before the sixteenth century. Five major geographical and agricultural regions can be distinguished: the Thames terrace, a district of
light soil close to London; an extensive belt of London clay, including all
south and south-eastern Essex, the latter particularly noted for its marshes;
the lighter soils of the north-east; the region of chalky hills on the north-
west, the main arable farming area; and the boulder-clay plateau of
northern and central Essex. Contemporaries thought that Essex ranked
with Kent and Suffolk as one of the most advanced and prosperous
counties in England during this period. Among the reasons for this may
have been the demand for Essex supplies from the swiftly growing
metropolis. Both politically and religiously it had a reputation for radi-
calism. It was in this county that Puritanism and the opposition to the
Stuarts found their strongest backing.

The same sampling approach is necessary with the dimension of time
as with that of space. Although it is possible to make some conjectures
about witchcraft beliefs before and after the Tudor and Stuart period, it
is only during the second half of the sixteenth and the seventeenth
centuries that the court records, upon which any thorough analysis of
witchcraft accusations must be based, are sufficiently numerous and
concerned with this offence. Before and afterwards it is largely a matter of
speculation.[16] Even within the years 1485–1688, during which Tudor and
Stuart monarchs were on the throne, a more delimited period, roughly
from 1560 onwards,[17] will be of central interest, for it was during these
years that the majority of the known prosecutions for witchcraft occurred.

A more extensive use of all the sources for the study of witchcraft
prosecutions and a narrowing of time and space dimensions allows a new

range of questions to be asked. Until legal and local records were used, only very broad problems about the nature of witchcraft beliefs could be studied. Literary accounts are more sensational than court cases, and earlier historians were clearly horrified and disgusted by their subject. Their major problem was how to explain the flourishing of this apparently absurd 'superstition' in the sixteenth and seventeenth centuries. The subject was usually studied on the European level and correlations between the degree of 'persecution' and the differing political, religious, and legal systems were sought. Often an attempt was made to locate the 'blame' for the prosecutions in certain groups—for instance, the clergy[18] or the Puritans[19]—or to see the whole episode as an 'epidemic' arising out of a struggle between progress and reaction, science and religion.[20] Notestein and Ewen themselves, while modifying such theories, accepted the general assumption that witchcraft was an illogical 'superstition' which would die before the onset of modern experimental science and better living conditions.[21] Although they produced a mass of new evidence, they asked few significantly new questions, and therefore provided no new general explanation of the phenomenon.

The advantages and defects of such an approach have been well illustrated by a recent essay on witches by Professor Trevor-Roper.[22] Here we see a study based on the great literary figures, covering the whole of Europe from the Dark Ages onwards. The questions asked are those that exercised nineteenth-century writers: Were the Protestants or Catholics to blame? Were the clergy to blame more than the laity? How was such a superstition upheld in the age of the Renaissance? Were torture and financial gain the main cause of the 'craze'? The footnotes show that the evidence used is the same as that employed by Lea, Soldan, Hansen, and other late nineteenth-century authorities who are so constantly cited. The theories about the 'mountain origin' of witchcraft or the coincidence of religious war and witchcraft prosecutions are impossible to prove or disprove, for they assume that we know much more than we really do about the geographical and temporal distribution of witchcraft prosecutions in Europe. It is naturally impossible when undertaking such a vast survey actually to do any research on primary sources, on the actual records of witchcraft trials. The essay has nothing to say which is helpful in explaining English witchcraft, for, as the author readily admits, England proves an exception to almost all the theories. Here there were witchcraft trials without sadistic clergy, without torture, and without mountain passes whose 'thin air [apparently] . . . breeds hallucinations'.[23] The real defect of the essay is that its tone implies that we now know a great deal about 'witchcraft' and all that is needed is synthesis. In fact we know far too little.

The most radical attempt to provide a new explanation of the history
of witchcraft prosecutions was made by Miss Margaret Murray.[24] Her
work was based on the two assumptions that witchcraft beliefs cannot be
profitably examined in isolation from other systems of ideas and that they
cannot be dismissed as mere nonsense. These convictions were shared by
G. L. Kittredge, whose wide learning illuminated the subject.[25] Having
decided that quite reasonable people really did fear witches and that
others, without torture, freely confessed to this crime, Margaret Murray
took what, in many ways, was a logical step and argued that there really
must have been witches. They were, however, not the evil creatures
described by their persecutors, but a highly organized pagan cult. She
applied a number of Sir James Frazer's theories to English witchcraft—for
instance, the idea of the importance of rituals for increasing fertility in
primitive religion—and thereby constructed a detailed picture of this
'witch-cult'. Witches, she claimed, met regularly at their 'Sabbats', they
formed 'covens' of thirteen, each of which had a leader dressed in animal
guise. They feasted, danced, and sang. This she termed 'ritual' witchcraft.
Then the Christian Inquisitors, in their attempt to stamp out paganism,
turned this cult of pre-Christian gaiety into a deadly onslaught on the
values of society. The leaders of the covens were transformed in their
hands into the Devil, the innocent meetings were described as orgies. The
'witches' were believed to have made a secret or open compact with the
Devil whereby they exchanged their souls for transitory power and plea-
sure.

Miss Murray's work was immediately criticized and has continued to be
attacked.[26] The major objection is that by extracting and quoting out of
context from the whole of European folklore she created a totally false
picture. She mistook what people *believed* to be happening for what
actually *did* happen. Though she showed that people thought there was a
witch-cult, she failed to demonstrate that there actually was one. Her thesis
will not be examined directly in the following pages. There are very few
descriptions of the phenomena which she discussed in Essex witchcraft—
for instance, the 'Sabbat', coven, and diabolic compact are absent, except
in the exceptional trials of 1645.[27] Nor does more detailed examination of
those accused of witchcraft in Essex lend any support to the argument that
there really was an underground pagan cult. Probably there were those
who came to believe themselves to be witches, but there is no evidence
that they formed a self-conscious organization. This is a negative conclusion and impossible to document. All that can be said is that the
Essex evidence does not support her conclusions and, indeed, makes her
picture of the witch-cult seem far too sophisticated and articulate for the
society with which we are concerned. Yet her assumptions about the

necessity to treat accusations as something more than intolerant superstition are subscribed to.

The major development in witchcraft studies in the last thirty years has occurred outside the field of English or European history. Anthropologists and sociologists, enabled to ask new questions by their personal contact with people who still believe in witchcraft, have provided analyses and explanations of this phenomenon which suggest many new problems for the historical student. Many of their themes will appear in this study. Attention in the following account is primarily focused on the persons actually involved in prosecutions, rather than on the philosophical background to witchcraft beliefs. Rather than asking, 'Why did people believe in witchcraft?' this study attempts to explain what types of people were the accusers, victims, and suspects, given such a framework of beliefs. Obviously, no rigid distinction can be made between these two approaches. Nevertheless, it is important to state that this is only one of several feasible ways of analysing the problems posed by witchcraft accusations; for instance, inquiry into the philosophical basis of witchcraft beliefs and their relation to the religious and scientific ideas of the times might be a better approach if the primary aim was to show why witchcraft beliefs subsided in the seventeenth century. This study is mainly concerned with showing how witchcraft functioned, once the basic assumptions about the nature of evil, the types of causation, and origins of supernatural 'power' were present.[28]

Individuals involved in prosecutions are analysed by geographical area, temporal distribution, class, age, sex, occupation, kinship, and other criteria. As in the studies of social anthropologists, not only have the victims and witches been examined in isolation, but also in their relationship to each other. Since social scientists increasingly try to see witchcraft accusations as the product of certain situations, analyses have also been made of such problems as the process by which a person became suspected of witchcraft, and the types of injury or tension which were related to prosecutions. Particular studies are made of a witch-finding movement and the English equivalent of the witch-doctor. Attempts to correlate the changes with other factors, such as medical change, religious groupings, types of social conflict, and economic organization, are also made. In all these analyses it is the questions which sociologists have posed, rather than the explanations which they offer, which have proved to be of prime value. While their conclusions, derived from other cultures and other centuries, may be inapplicable, their interests and general approach have been a most stimulating influence in the study of English accusations.[29] An outline of anthropological analyses of witchcraft will conclude this account. It will provide not only a general comparison for the Essex material, but also a general framework for future analysis. The sources for the study of witchcraft are outlined in the first part of this study. Then some of the results of applying anthropological questions to these sources are outlined in the second and third parts. Finally, the anthropological framework is revealed. It is hoped that this regional study will provide a 'model' for other students and that we will soon be able to compare Essex with other English counties.

NOTES

1. Only a few of the more important or controversial historians of English witchcraft are discussed below. For other writers see the Bibliography, p. 321.
2. See Appendix 2.
3. G. Lienhardt, *Social Anthropology* (2nd edn., Oxford, 1966), p. 123.
4. Some writers would argue, however, that European witchcraft was something special, a Christian heresy. For example, see R. H. Robbins, *Encyclopedia of Witchcraft and Demonology* (New York, 1959), p. 17.
5. Notestein, *Witchcraft*, p. x.
6. Ewen, I. Without Ewen's accurate and energetic work in transcribing witchcraft cases, much of the forthcoming analysis would have been impossible.
7. As explained in a prefatory note, the word 'witch' will be used for the longer phrase, 'a person thought to be a witch by her contemporaries'. The use of the word in no way implies that there really *are* or *were* witches.
8. Ewen, II.
9. See, for example, the works by Lea and Robbins listed on p. 322 of the Bibliography.
10. For a description of the Hopkins trial, see ch. 9, p. 137, below.
11. For this reason E. Maple, *Dark World of Witches* (1962) is unable to add to the information provided by Notestein until he reaches the nineteenth century, which Notestein omitted.
12. Above all, the work of Professor W. G. Hoskins on Leicestershire and Devon (e.g. *Provincial England*, 1963) has stressed the importance of regional variation and local studies.
13. Anthropologists, we are told, usually select two units, the first the tribe (numbering up to tens of thousands) and then the 'unit of personal observation', usually consisting of less than 1,000 persons (R. Firth, *Elements of Social Organization* (1951), pp. 48–9).
14. These villages are described in ch. 6, below.
15. The following description is primarily based on two unpublished theses: F. Hull, 'Agriculture and Rural Society in Essex, 1560–1640' (London Univ. Ph.D. thesis, 1950) and B. W. Quintrell, 'The Government of the County of Essex, 1603–1642' (London Univ. Ph.D. thesis, 1965). I am most grateful to both authors for their permission to use their unpublished work. Some of the geographical features are illustrated on Map 8, p. 146, below.
16. For a brief survey of some of the earlier and later cases see ch. 16, p. 200, below.

17. Although the first Act dealing with witches was in 1542, the records of prosecutions do not commence until the Act of 1563.
18. For example, Preserved Smith, *History of Modern Culture* (1930), i, 437 and ch. 14 *passim*; W. E. H. Lecky, *History of the Rise and Influence of the Spirit of Rationalism in Europe* (1865), i, 8.
19. R. Trevor Davies, *Four Centuries of Witch Beliefs* (1947), *passim*.
20. E.g. A. D. White, *History of the Warfare of Science with Theology* (New York, 1896), i, 350–63; R. H. Robbins, *Encyclopedia of Witchcraft and Demonology* (1959), p. 3.
21. Ewen, I, pp. 113–15. Notestein, *Witchcraft*, pp. 309–10, still speaks broadly in terms of 'superstitions', yet, on pp. 114–19, he makes a preliminary sociological analysis which anticipates, in certain ways, the approach in this study.
22. H. R. Trevor-Roper, 'The European Witch-craze of the Sixteenth and Seventeenth Centuries', in *Religion, the Reformation and Social Change; and other essays* (1967).
23. Ibid., p. 106.
24. M. A. Murray, *Witch-cult in Western Europe* (Oxford, 1921).
25. Kittredge, *Witchcraft*. On pp. 372–3 Kittredge states his premises.
26. Among the many criticisms are those of G. L. Burr in a review article in the *American Hist. Rev.*, xxvii, No. 4 (1922), pp. 780–3; C. L. Ewen, *Some Witchcraft Criticisms: a Plea for the Blue Pencil* (no place, 1938); E. E. Rose, *A Razor for a Goat* (Toronto, 1962).
27. Described in ch. 9, p. 135 below.
28. The general philosophical and religious framework within which witchcraft beliefs occurred will, it is hoped, soon be provided by the forthcoming book of Mr. Keith Thomas. I am deeply grateful to Mr. Thomas for permission to read his unpublished draft, which offers a back-cloth to this study, both complementing and expanding many of the following hypotheses.
29. This approach was foreshadowed by G. Parrinder, in *Witchcraft* (Penguin edn., 1958).

Chapter 2

The legal background
to witchcraft prosecutions
at the secular courts

The first English Statute concerning witchcraft was enacted in 1542.[1] The position before that date is not altogether clear. Although Britton and Fleta declared that 'an inquiry about sorcerers is one of the articles of the sheriff's turn',[2] most authorities suggest that witchcraft was treated as a branch of heresy, an ecclesiastical offence which was later punished by the State under the writ *de haeretico comburendo*.[3] The general impression is that prosecutions were scarce before 1542.[4] In 1547 all the new Henrician Statutes were repealed, including that of 1542 concerning witchcraft. Until the passage of a new Statute in 1563 the legal situation reverted to its pre-1542 state. Bishop Grindal in 1561 wrote to William Cecil asking for punishment of a magician because 'My Lord Cheif Justice sayeth the temporal law will not meddle with them'.[5] Meanwhile, the Queen's Attorney had to send some London conjurers to the Bishop for punishment.[6] Yet, despite the absence of any relevant Statute, two people are known to have been accused of witchcraft at the Essex Assizes in 1560.[7]

In March 1563 an 'Act agaynst Conjuracions Inchantments and Witchecraftes' was passed. This was repealed by a more severe Act in 1604. The Act of 1604 continued in force until 1736.[8] An important factor in encouraging the 1563 Statute was the concern of the Government at the amount of contemporary treasonable activity which took the form of false prophecies, astrological predictions, and other amateur conjuring.[9] The increased harshness of the Statute in 1604, when it was redrafted by Sir Edward Coke and others, was, at the most, only partly the result of James I's interest in the subject.[10]

The Act of 1563 laid down the death penalty for 'Invocacon of evill and wicked Spirites, to or for any Intent or Purpose', and for using 'Witchecrafte Enchantment Charme or Sorcerie, wherby any p[er]son shall happen to bee killed or destroyed'. Both those who offended and 'their Concello[u]rs & Aidours' were to die. Imprisonment for one year with four appearances in the pillory for the first offence, and death for the second, was the punishment for injuring people or their property by witchcraft. Similar imprisonment for the first offence, but life imprisonment and forfeit of goods for the second, was the punishment for using witchcraft to declare where treasure or lost property might be found, and for intending 'to provoke any p[er]son to unlawful love, or to hurte or destroye any p[er]son in his or her Body, Member or Goodes'. In 1604 this Act was replaced by a more severe one. The invocation of spirits was elaborated: men were forbidden to 'consult covenant with entertaine employ feede or rewarde any evill and wicked Spirit'. A new offence was added: dead bodies were not to be taken out of their graves 'to be imployed or used in any manner of Witchecrafte, Sorcerie, Charme or Inchantment'.[11] Injuring a person or his property was now punished by death for the first offence instead of the second. In all the above offences, where the first offence was now punished by death, 'Ayders Abettors and Councellors' were likewise punishable. All the offences which under the Act of 1563 had been punished by life imprisonment for the second offence were now punished by death on the second. Greater stress was laid on the punishment of intention to use witchcraft as well as its actual use: intending to hurt or destroy people or property was punishable 'although the same be not effected and done'. Put into tabular form, the punishments were as follows:

TABLE I
Punishment in the Witchcraft Statutes, 1563–1736

Offence	First conviction		Second conviction	
	1563	*1604*	*1563*	*1604*
Using witchcraft to search for treasure or lost property	1 year	1 year	Life	Death
Injuring people or property by witchcraft	1 year	Death	Death	Death
Causing the death of a human being by witchcraft	Death	Death	Death	Death
Taking dead bodies out of graves	—	Death	—	Death
Conjuring evil spirits	Death	Death	Death	Death
Intending to :				
Injure people or property by witchcraft	1 year	1 year	Life	Death
Cause the death of a human being by witchcraft	1 year	1 year	Life	Death
Provoke a person 'to unlawful love' by witchcraft	1 year	1 year	Life	Death

Note : 1 year = a year's imprisonment; Life = life imprisonment; Death = capital punishment. 1563 and 1604 refer to the Statutes of those years.

Although, as Coke pointed out,[12] felons usually forfeited their goods, the rights of wives and successors were specifically safeguarded in the 1604 Act, just as they had been by that of 1563. The only offences for which goods were forfeited were those in the 1563 Act, which incurred life imprisonment accompanied by loss of goods for the second offence. Both Statutes stated that those guilty of a capital offence lost the rights of clergy and sanctuary. Likewise, general pardons—for instance, those of 23 Elizabeth and 21 James—excepted witchcraft.[13]

The least severe punishment for witchcraft was a year's imprisonment, during which, 'once in every Quarter of the said yere [the prisoner] shall in some Market Towne, upon the Marcket day or at suche tyme as any Fayer shall bee kept there, stande openly upon the Pillorie by the space of Sixe Houres, and there shall openly confesse his or her Erro[u]r and Offence'.[14] The conditions of gaols frequently made such imprisonment equivalent to a death sentence.[15] Death was by hanging unless 'petty treason' had been committed, in which case the convicted person was burnt.[16] Nevertheless, it seems to have been a popular belief that witches were burnt. An Essex Justice threatened in 1582 that those witches who did not confess 'shall bee burnt and hanged'.[17] An Essex author illustrated the hatred against witches in the same county by making a country-woman say: 'If I had but one fagot in the world, I would carry it a myle upon my shoulders to burne a witch.'[18] A number of other examples exist of this interesting confusion between what was believed to occur and what actually did.[19] The idea of burning possibly reflected memories of the medieval burning of witches as heretics or the punishment of Continental witches in this manner.

Witchcraft, like murder by poison, was considered a crime apart. As M.B. pointed out in Gifford's *Dialogue*, the secret nature of the crime made normal legal evidence, confession and two direct witnesses, most unlikely. Consequently, in his opinion, 'if there were any likelihood, and suspicion, and common fame' that was 'proof ynough'.[20] It was only possible to testify to motives and effects, not to witness the actual act of witchcraft or the invisible way in which this force operated. If direct witnesses had been demanded, many argued that 'it will be then impossible to put any one to death . . . [for] . . . hardly can a man be brought, which upon his owne knowledge, can averre such things'.[21] For this reason it was stated in the leading contemporary manual for Justices of the Peace that, in cases of witchcraft and poisoning, 'half proofes are to be allowed, and are good causes of suspition'.[22] The extreme difficulty of providing evidence meant that special provisions were made. For instance, it was 'lawful to give in Evidence Matters that are no ways relating to that Fact, and done many Years before'.[23] Moreover, the peculiar nature of the crime precluded the possibility of an alibi. Absence from the scene of the crime was immaterial. The offence occurred within the individual. A person could be many miles from the victim and yet responsible. In this way witchcraft was similar to murder by poison, but differed from all other crimes.[24] In all criminal investigation during our period there was a far greater stress on assessing the character of the suspect than in modern proceedings. In a witchcraft case, however, where especial emphasis was laid on indirect evidence concerning the motives and possible hostilities of the suspect, such examination was especially important. The methods of examination recommended to Justices of the Peace in all cases of felony were particularly relevant in witchcraft examination. Justices were directed to discover the following facts about a suspect.

> His parents, if they were wicked, and given to the same kind of fault. . . . His nature; if civill, or hastie, wittie and subtill, a quarreller, pilferer, or bloudie minded, &c. . . . His trade; for if a man liveth idly or vagrant . . . it is a good cause to arrest him upon suspition, if there have been any felony committed. His companie; if Ruffians, suspected persons, or his being in companie with any the offendors. His course of life; *sc.* if a common Alehouse-ha[u]nter, or ryottous in dyet, play, or apparrell. Whether he be of evill fame, or report.[25]

In witchcraft suspicions, therefore, as in other felonies, the likelihood of guilt was related to the whole social background of the accused: his parents' character, his friendships, drinking habits, and general reputation.

The difficulty of proving a person guilty of witchcraft meant that extraordinary witnesses were permitted. Although at least two witnesses were still required,[26] no class of person was debarred. Bernard, in his *Guide to Grand Jury Men*, gave the following list of suitable witnesses: the 'afflicted party'; the friends and relations of the afflicted; 'indifferent neighbours' ('fearfull, superstitious, or children, or old silly persons' were to be examined, but their testimonies treated with caution); 'suspected adversaries, either to the afflicted, or to the suspected Witch', for, as the author remarked, such people 'pry very narrowly into every thing'; the physician, if one had been called; 'the report of a *White or good Witch*'; 'the *suspected Witches whole family* able and fit to answer . . . also such as be known to have had inward familiarity with the suspected'; the suspected witch.[27] Also of importance were other suspected witches.[28] Not only was the accused person's spouse allowed to witness, contrary to normal rules,[29] but children, also, were permitted to give evidence against their parents, clearly an unusual proceeding.[30]

The kinds of evidence to be used to prove a person guilty of witchcraft were based on the current ideas concerning the nature of witches' activity.

There were three degrees of evidence. There was that evidence which
was strong enough for the suspect to be examined before a magistrate;
that which was a 'strong presumption', several of which presumptions
taken together might lead to a conviction; and conclusive 'proofs'.[31] The
following 'evidence' was enough to bring a person to court on a charge of
witchcraft: notorious reputation as a witch; cursing followed by an injury
to the person cursed; known malice followed by a misfortune to the object
of the malice; a relationship by blood or friendship to a proven witch; the
victim's recovery after the suspected witch had been scratched or some of
her property had been burnt; failure of the suspect to sink when immersed
in water; an implicit confession by the suspect ('you should have left me
alone then', in answer to an accusation by a neighbour, is an example);
over-diligent interest in a sick neighbour on the part of a suspected witch.
The 'strong presumptions', several of which could lead to conviction,
included accusation by a 'white witch' and a deathbed accusation by the
supposed victim of witchcraft. The 'sufficient proofs', any one of which
could lead to conviction, were as follows: accusation by another witch; an
unnatural mark on the body supposedly caused by the Devil or a familiar;
two witnesses who claimed to have seen the accused either make a pact
with Satan or entertain her familiars. Other adequate 'evidences' were:
the discovery of pictures or images of the victim in the suspect's house;
the bleeding of the corpse when touched by the suspect; a gift from the
supposed witch followed by the injury of the recipient; and the confession
of the suspect herself. The type of evidence required for conviction as a
witch can be illustrated by one example: Bernard urged that if a woman
gave a child an apple and the receiver became ill soon afterwards, as long
as there was known malice between them, this was proof enough for the
execution of the accused.

Only a selection of these types of evidence was actually used in Essex.
An examination of the Elizabethan trial pamphlets for that county has
revealed no use of the water ordeal, no witnessing to the Satanic pact, no
hunting for pictures or images of the victim, no bleeding of the corpse at
the touch of the witch.[32] These same pamphlets show that the greatest
stress in the earlier trials was put on showing that known malice had been
followed by an injury. There was also much description of the activities of
the witch's familiar. An excellent outline of the type of evidence on which
most of the Essex prosecutions rested is given by the Essex clergyman,
George Gifford.[33] One of his characters is made to say:

> I was of a Jurie not many yeares past, when there was an old woman arrained
> for a witch. There came in eight or ten which gave evidence against her. . . .
> One woman came in and testified uppon her oath that her husband upon his
> death bed, tooke it upon his death, that he was bewitched, for he pined a long

time. And he sayde further, he was sure that woman had bewitched him. He tooke her to be naught, and thought she was angry with him, because she would have borrowed five shillinges of him, and he denyed to lend it her. The woman tooke her oath also, that she thought in her conscience that the old woman was a witch, and that she killed her husband. . . . There came in an other, . . . He tooke his oath directly that she was a witch: I did once anger her sayde he, but I did repent me: for I looked somewhat would follow. And the next night, I saw the ugliest sight that ever I saw: I awaked suddainely out of my sleepe, and there was me thought a great face, as bigge as they use to set up in the signe of the Saracens-head, looked full in my face. . . . Then followed a man, and he sayde he could not tell, but he thought she was once angry with him because she came to begge a few pot-hearbes, and he denied her: and presently after he heard a thing as he thought to whisper in his eare, thou shalt be bewitched. The next day he had such a paine in his back, that he could not sit upright: he sayd he sent to a cunning woman, shee tolde he was was bewitched, and by a woman that came for pot-hearbes. . . . Then came in two or three grave honest men, which testified that she was by common fame accounted a witch. We found her giltie, for what could we doe lesse, she was condemned and executed: and upon the ladder she made her prayer, and tooke it upon her death shee was innocent and free from all such dealings.

We see in the above passage that there was no necessity for the accused to admit her guilt. The opinion of her neighbours, who drew a link between her supposed malice and an observed illness or strange event, was enough to lead to a conviction of witchcraft. Injuries and personal tensions were interwoven as cause and effect.

There were slight changes in the nature of the evidence used over the period 1560 1680. The water ordeal spread as a method of proving a witch in the seventeenth century,[34] although there is no evidence that it was used in Essex before 1645. Probably increasing stress was laid on finding the witch's mark, though such marks had been used as evidence from the very first Essex trials.[35] Meanwhile, no major types of evidence approved of at the beginning of the century had been eliminated by 1680.[36] In theory, the proof that a person was a witch was the same in 1680 as it had been in 1600.

Since a confession by the accused was one of the few absolute proofs of guilt, there was considerable pressure to secure such evidence. Moreover, if a person confessed, she became a powerful witness against others. Confession was also enjoined as an acceptance of society's verdict. In both ecclesiastical and secular courts public confession was a stipulated part of the punishment. Nevertheless, confessions do not seem to have occurred in the majority of the Essex prosecutions. For instance, at the Essex Lent Assizes in 1582, five women confessed, but nine denied the charge of witchcraft,[37] despite the browbeating of the Judge who warned that 'they

which doe confesse the truth of their doeings, they shall have much
favour; but the other they shall bee burnt and hanged'.[38]

Torture, both physical and mental, has been suggested as an explanation of some of the confessions. There is no evidence that physical torture
was ever officially allowed in England, except where treason was involved.[39]
If no other methods worked,[40] 'then such as have authority to examine,
should begin to use sharp speeches, and to threaten with imprisonment
and death. And if the presumptions bee strong, then if the Law will
permit (as it doth in other countries in this case) to use torture'. The
activities which came closest to torture in England occurred in the Essex
trials of 1645; they included keeping the suspects awake for several
nights, immersing them in water, and continuous questioning. Probably
of much more general importance were indirect pressures: the mounting
suspicions of neighbours, the persuasive advice, threats, and promises of
clergy and justices. A witch, said the witch-finder Matthew Hopkins, was
kept in solitary confinement and

> so by good counsell brought into a sad condition, by understanding of the
> horribleness of her sin, and the judgements threatened against her; and knowing
> the Devill's malice and subtile circumventions, is brought to remorse and
> sorrow for complying with Satan so long, and disobeying God's sacred
> Commands, doth then desire to unfold her mind with much bitterness.[41]

There is little evidence, in Essex, that mental breakdown led to voluntary
confessions.

NOTES

1. 33 Henry VIII, cap. 8; all the Statutes against witchcraft hereafter cited are printed
   with only punctuation and spelling modified, in Ewen, I, pp. 13–21, 44–5.
2. Sir F. Pollock and F. W. Maitland, *History of English Law* (2nd edn., Cambridge,
   1898), ii, 554.
3. Pollock and Maitland, *History of English Law*, ii, 555; H. G. Richardson, 'Heresy
   and the Lay Power under Richard II', *English Historical Review*, li (1936), pp. 4–5;
   Edward Coke, *Third Part of the Institutes of the Laws of England* (1644), p. 44.
4. Pollock and Maitland, *History of English Law*, ii, 555–6. See p. 206, note 3, below,
   for some medieval cases.
5. *Calendar of State Papers, Domestic, 1547–1580*, p. 173.
6. *Acts of the Privy Council*, n.s. vii (1893), p. 22.
7. Cases 1 and 2.
8. 1 James I, cap. 12; 9 George II, cap. 5.
9. There is a useful discussion of the background to the 1563 Act in Kittredge,
   Witchcraft, pp. 255–61.
10. Statistics in Ewen, I, showing that prosecutions in the Home Circuit declined under
    James I, as well as an excellent defence of James by Kittredge (*Witchcraft*, ch.
    XVII), have undermined the King's reputation as a witch-finder.

11. Mere intention to use such bodies for witchcraft, Coke stressed (*Institutes*, iii, 45), was a felony.
12. Edward Coke, *Third Part of the Institutes of the Laws of England* (1644), p. 47.
13. References, and some exceptions, are given in Ewen, I, pp. 19, 21, 39.
14. 1 James I, cap. 12.
15. The condition of gaols and the number of accused witches who died of gaol fever are discussed on p. 77, below.
16. 'Petty treason' occurred when a woman killed her husband or a servant his master. No definite cases of this kind, in which a woman was accused of killing her husband by witchcraft, have been discovered in Essex court records.
17. 1582 Pamphlet, sig. B6ᵛ.
18. Gifford, *Dialogue*, sig. Dᵛ.
19. 1582 Pamphlet, sig. E5ᵛ; J. O. Haweis, *Sketches of the Reformation and Elizabethan Age* (1844), p. 220. I owe the latter reference to Mr. K. V. Thomas. Reginald Scot (1538?–99), a Kentish squire educated at Hart Hall, Oxford, and notable for his sceptical attitude to witchcraft (Notestein, *Witchcraft*, devotes ch. 3 to his work), suggested the same thing, *Discovery*, p. 259.
20. Gifford, *Dialogue*, sig. H2ᵛ.
21. Perkins, *Damned Art*, pp. 214–15. William Perkins, the famous Puritan divine and preacher, was a fellow of Christ's College, Cambridge. He died in 1602 and his work on witchcraft was published posthumously.
22. Michael Dalton, *Countrey Justice* (1618), p. 268. John Gaule, Vicar of Great Staughton in Huntingdonshire after 1646 and supporter of both Royalists and Commonwealth men, would also have allowed circumstantial evidence (*Select Cases*, p. 194).
23. Francis Hutchinson, *Historical Essay Concerning Witchcraft* (1718), p. 58. Hutchinson was born in 1660 and therefore wrote when the worst of the trials were over; he was made Bishop of Down and Connor in 1721.
24. Ibid., pp. vi–vii.
25. Michael Dalton, *Countrey Justice* (1618), p. 266.
26. Perkins, *Damned Art*, p. 213; Gifford, *Dialogue*, sig. H2.
27. Bernard, *Guide*, pp. 228–38.
28. This is clear from the Essex trials; see also Scot, *Discovery*, p. 39, although it is based on Continental demonologists.
29. M. Dalton, *Countrey Justice* (1618), p. 261.
30. Idem, where Dalton implies that such procedure was unusual and only cites precedents from the Lancashire witch trial of 1612. Gifford was clearly shocked at such occurences in Essex (*Dialogue*, sig. L).
31. The following account is based on Perkins, *Damned Art*, pp. 200–18; Bernard, *Guide*, pp. 204–24; Gaule, *Select Cases*, pp. 75–88. This leaves Elizabeth's reign without an authority. Unfortunately, Scot's *Discovery*, Book II, which alone treats this subject, is too heavily based on Continental demonologists to be anything except misleading for an analysis of English procedure. None of the above, of course, was an official guide.
32. For a discussion of the evidence in these pamphlets see ch. 5, p. 81, below.
33. Gifford, *Dialogue*, sigs. L3–L3ᵛ.
34. Scot, *Discovery*, p. 255, implied that the water ordeal was not used in England in 1584, while Perkins in 1608 (*Damned Art*, p. 206) only referred to its use 'in other countries'. Yet it seems to have been in fairly widespread use by 1616, according to John Cotta, *Triall of Witchcraft* (1616), p. 104.

35. At first they were merely spots on the face; later they probably became protruding lumps. The Queen's Attorney discovered such spots in 1566 (1566 Pamphlet, p. 323), and a group of women searched for the mark in 1582 (1582 Pamphlet, sig. D4). There is a detailed description of such a search, carried out in 1650, in case 843.
36. For instance, the wording of the 1697 edition of Michael Dalton's *Countrey Justice* is exactly the same as the 1630 edition, which, in turn, had been based, at least in its description of how to find a witch, on Bernard's *Guide*.
37. 1582 Pamphlet, *passim*.
38. Ibid., sig. B6ᵛ.
39. Perkins discussed its use in witchcraft cases and concluded that it could only be used on the Continent (*Damned Art*, p. 204).
40. Bernard, *Guide*, pp. 239–40.
41. Hopkins, *Discovery*, p. 59.

Chapter 3

The intensity of witchcraft prosecutions: evidence from Assize and Quarter Sessions records

Some 314 people are known to have been prosecuted under the witchcraft Statutes between 1560 and 1680 at the Essex Assize and Quarter Session courts. Since this figure represents more than two-thirds of those known to have been accused of witchcraft in Essex, it is necessary to say something about the procedure of the two courts.

The Quarter Sessions, as their name suggests, were held four times a year. They were an inferior court to the Assizes, and so felony could not be tried at them, yet they were empowered to examine felons.[1] Witchcraft is mentioned in presentments by panels of jurors to this court; if the presentment was found to be accurate, the indictment was sent to the next Assize. Recognizances for the appearance of the accused, accuser, or witnesses at the Assizes, as well as examinations of those involved, sometimes mentioned witchcraft, as did gaol records kept with Quarter Session archives. Thus, while no accused witches were judged at this court,[2] witchcraft is mentioned on many occasions in the remaining records.

The Assizes met twice a year, in the Hilary and Trinity terms, usually at Brentwood or Chelmsford. There were two judges.[3] At the start of the Assize a calendar of prisoners in the gaol was read out; often this included the name of imprisoned persons accused of witchcraft.[4] Presentments from the Quarter Sessions and elsewhere were then examined by the Grand Jury, mainly chosen from the minor gentry.[5] The presentment was either dismissed as '*ignoramus*' or passed as a 'true bill', in which case it become an indictment. It is these indictments which form the bulk of the evidence for Essex witchcraft prosecutions. The first indictment was then read and the named accused called to the Bar. The prisoner was asked if he pleaded guilty or not guilty, and the next was summoned. Those who confessed were put on one side until the time of judgment. The Petty Jurors were then called by the Sheriff, their names read, and the prisoners given a chance to challenge them. A group of middling yeomen and artisans,[6] it was they who decided the guilt or innocence of the accused. Witnesses against the accused were then publicly called for, and examinations of the accused taken before the Justices of the Peace were read to the jury, if they were evidence for the Crown. The accused could call witnesses but not on oath unless the crime was a felony.[7] When the group of prisoners was large enough, the jury retired with a list of prisoners 'for their better direction and help of their memory to know who they have in charge'.[8] Finally, they returned and gave their verdict of guilty or not guilty, whereupon the Judge passed sentence. Largely formal inquiries were also to be made as to the felon's goods and whether he or she had fled after committing the crime.

There were over 500 indictments for witchcraft at the Essex Assizes. A typical one will show the nature of prosecutions at this court. At the Essex Hilary Sessions in 1579, Ellen Smyth of Maldon, spinster, was accused of bewitching Susan Webbe, aged about four years. The bewitching was said to have occurred on 7 March 1579 and the child to have died at Maldon on the 8th. The presentment was found to be a 'true bill' by the Grand Jury and the defendant was found guilty and judged according to the Statute.[9] It will be immediately seen that such indictments provide information on a number of problems: the place of residence, age, sex, and marital position of witch and victim; the duration and nature of the bewitching; the verdict of the two juries. Nevertheless, it is important to remember that indictments only give a summary of the outline of the prosecutions. The examinations and evidence at the Assize are omitted. The occasional contemporary account of an Assize trial preserved in a witchcraft pamphlet corrects the distorted effect of such indictments.[10] Ellen Smyth's case is among those described at greater length in a pamphlet.[11] We learn that Ellen was the daughter of Alice Chaundeler, previously executed for witchcraft; that Ellen quarrelled with her stepfather over an inheritance and that he subsequently became ill; that she was believed to own a toad familiar which, when burnt, caused its mistress pain; that her child-victim's mother was sent mad by the sight of another familiar like a black dog; that Ellen's son described his mother's three spirits called 'great Dicke', 'little Dicke', and 'Willet', and that the bottles and wool-pack in which they were supposedly housed were discovered after a search of her house. Thus we see that the evidence written down in the Assize and Quarter Sessions records is only the barest outline of a mass of beliefs and suspicions.

References to witchcraft occur on seventy-four occasions in the Quarter Sessions records belonging to Essex. Most of these occur in the Sessions Rolls, which are almost complete after 1556.[12] Of the forty-eight accused persons, thirty-five were at the court for 'black' witchcraft—that is, for hurting people or property. The other cases concerned treasure-seeking, trying to find lost goods, gain money, or tell fortunes by the aid of witchcraft. Thus three-quarters of the cases which are recorded at the lower court were for harmful witchcraft; most of these occurred before 1603. Of the thirty-five women mentioned as black witches, all but eight appear in the Assize records: but only five of the thirteen cases of conjuration appear in the higher court. A comparison with those accused at the Assizes reveals that the Quarter Sessions witnessed only a very small percentage of the Essex witchcraft prosecutions. Of over 300 people accused under the Witchcraft Statute at the Assizes, less than thirty are noted in the Quarter Sessions records. Quarter Sessions documents cannot, by themselves, be taken as an accurate index of the amount of witchcraft prosecution in a county.

The Essex Assize records contain some 503 indictments for offences under the Witchcraft Statutes in the years between 1560 and 1680; an average of over four cases a year for 120 years.[13] In these indictments some 303 persons were accused; their offences were as follows:

TABLE 2
Types of offence under the Witchcraft Statutes tried at the Essex Assizes

	Number of cases	Number of persons involved
Injuring/killing people or property	462	271
Invocation of evil spirits	28	29
Treasure or lost goods sought by witchcraft	9	11
'Intent' to murder or injure	2	2
Using dead bodies for witchcraft	1	1
Fortune-telling	1	1
'Consulting' witches	1	1

Note: Some of the cases and persons overlap from different categories; for instance, half those accused of invoking evil spirits were also accused of particular injuries inflicted on people or property. The totals of Table 2 are, therefore, larger than the actual totals of persons and cases.

Thus, all but eleven of the 503 cases were for 'black' witchcraft: it is with this offence that we will be primarily concerned. By far the largest category was 'for injuring or killing humans or their property'. Indictments for entertaining evil spirits, eighteen of twenty-eight of which occurred in 1645, differ from these in that it is impossible to analyse the relationship between the accused and her victim. Nevertheless, whenever it is possible to use these twenty-eight indictments—for example, when maps of the distribution of witches are being drawn—they will be treated as statistically equivalent to accusations of causing injury or death. The justification for

26

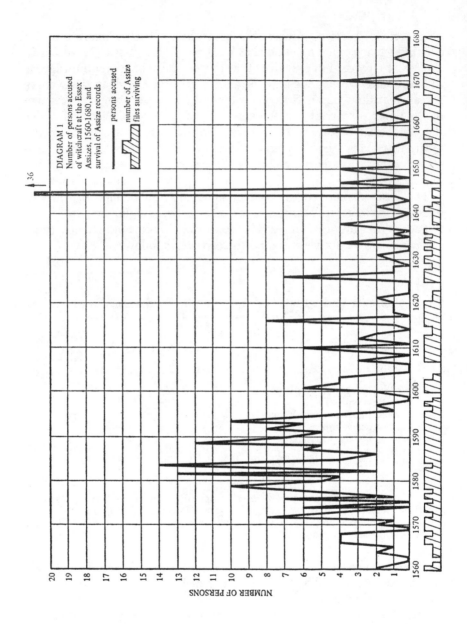

DIAGRAM 1
Number of persons accused
of witchcraft at the Essex
Assizes, 1560-1680, and
survival of Assize records

——— persons accused

number of Assize
files surviving

27

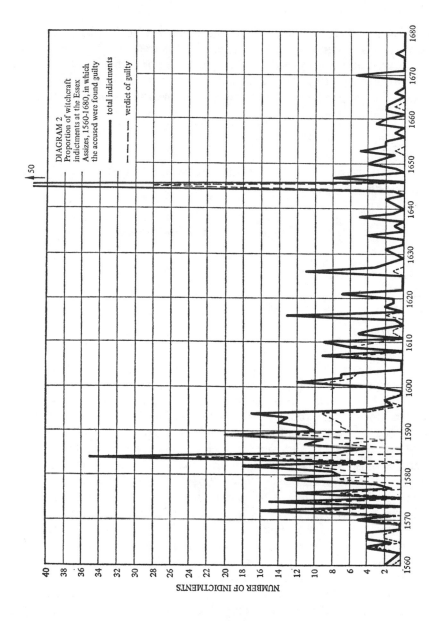

DIAGRAM 2
Proportion of witchcraft
indictments at the Essex
Assizes, 1560-1680, in which
the accused were found guilty

———— total indictments

– – – – verdict of guilty

NUMBER OF INDICTMENTS

this is that where people accused of invocation of evil spirits were also accused of another offence, as happened in thirteen of the twenty-eight such cases, all were accused of bewitching men or animals.

The majority of the prosecutions for black witchcraft occurred before 1600. The comparative density of cases in six twenty-year periods is shown in the following table:

TABLE 3
Temporal distribution of witchcraft prosecutions at the Essex Assizes, 1560–1680

Years	Number of persons	Number of indictments
1560–79	52	82
1580–99	111	195
1600–19	44	78
1620–39	25	35
1640–59	63	83 (50 of them in 1645)
1660–79	12	14

This can be demonstrated graphically, as in Diagram 1. This first graph also shows the survival of Assize records, a factor which must obviously be taken into account when discussing changes in the rate of prosecutions. For instance, we can account for the absence of prosecutions in 1562, 1599, and 1604–6 by the loss of records for those years. Often only one of the two Assize files has survived. It is clear from the diagram that records survive most fully between 1570 and 1595 and after 1646; the most extensive losses are in 1595–1600, 1604–6, and throughout the period 1620–40. Yet the graph of persons indicted does not merely reflect the survival of records. It shows a number of interesting features quite unrelated to the above. The numbers rise from fairly low figures in the 1560's to a peak in 1584. The 1580's and 1590's are consistently the highest years. Though there were peaks in 1601, 1612, 1616, and 1626, the forty years after 1600 were freer from accusations. There is the one towering figure in 1645 and then intermittent accusations petered away in 1670. The last case occurred in 1675. This shows the preponderance of the Elizabethan period as a time of accusations. It also demonstrates that prosecutions were not occasional and sporadic occurrences. Year by year accusations appeared. Though there were high peaks there were many years when three or more people were accused of witchcraft. Of the ninety years between 1560 and 1660 for which there are surviving Assize records, only seventeen have no indictments for this offence. Diagram 2 shows the number of indictments for witchcraft each year; it emphasizes the impression gained from the first graph, that Elizabethan prosecutions were much more frequent than later indictments and that the 1620's and 1630's were a quiet period.

The geographical distribution and spread of witchcraft prosecutions at the Essex Assizes are shown in Maps 2 to 4. Map 2 outlines the distribution of all the prosecutions at the Assizes between 1560 and 1680. Significantly, there are no parts of Essex without any prosecutions, although the density varies. The most intensive prosecutions seem to have occurred in two areas; in the north-east, mainly in the Tendring Hundred, and in a central belt some twenty miles wide and thirty miles high. This latter area stretched from Thaxted on the west to Colne Wake on the east, from Borley in the north to Danbury in the south. The centre, around Braintree and Halstead, was particularly heavy in the number of indictments. On the other hand, the western regions of Essex had only scattered accusations. Some 108 villages in Essex witnessed one or more indictments, almost exactly a quarter of the 426 villages in the county.

Map 2, a static representation, is misleading in a number of ways. The distortions emerge when we look at Maps 3 and 4. From these it will be seen that the two densest areas were very different in the pattern of the accusations. The high number of prosecutions in the central area arose out of a constant flow of cases, most marked in the 1580's and 1590's, but continuing until 1640. But nearly all the prosecutions in the north-eastern tip of the county occurred in two years, 1582 and 1645. These two years were different from all the other years of numerous indictments in their concentration on one small part of the county. Thus, while the density in the central area reflected continued prosecutions over a period of eighty years, the density in the north-east arose out of massive prosecutions in 1582 and 1645, with scattered cases in other years.

Map 3 also helps us to trace the spread of witchcraft accusations over the years. In the first decade they were entirely concentrated in a wide belt in the centre of Essex. In the next ten years they had moved farther north, south, and west, but there had still been no accusations in the north-eastern area. As in the first decade, the area around Hatfield Peverel and Danbury was especially notable for the number of accusations. In the 1580's the whole of Essex was covered, although the western border was still fairly free from indictments. The west was again only thinly represented in the 1590's, as was the south-eastern marshland. The central belt was again predominant in this decade. The south in the first decade of the seventeenth century, and then the north-east and north-west in the next decade, were clear. In the following twenty years the prosecutions lessened in number and the distribution grows less significant. The preponderance of the north-east in the 1640's was almost entirely the product of the 1645 trial. In the 1650's the north-west, for the first time, assumed relative importance. There were only a few prosecutions in the following twenty years; apart from an isolated central case, they occurred in the north-east.

The various yearly distributions shown in Map 4 are important because they show that prosecutions were very widely scattered. Accused witches from many miles apart were summoned to trial at the Assizes in any one year. This indicates that such accusations were the product of both general factors and local pressures. It suggests that similar causes were working in different villages, although those cases were unrelated at a personal level. For instance, if we look at the distribution of accusations in 1579 or 1584, it is difficult to believe that these prosecutions were directly interconnected; there seems to be no question of suspicions spreading from place to place. There are no grounds for using terms like 'epidemic' to describe the growth of accusations. It would be more realistic to see prosecutions as eruptions in separate communities, the products of particular and local conditions, which in turn acted on more generalized factors. If this is the case in eleven of the thirteen years included in Map 4, there were, as we have said, two important exceptions. They were the years 1582 and 1645; in both cases the prosecutions occurred in a small group of neighbouring villages. Here it would be justifiable to look for some outside agent; in both, it will be shown, there was present a man of more than ordinary energy, skill, and interest in finding witches. Yet the exceptional nature of these trials constantly needs to be stressed. The normal pattern in the geographical distribution of prosecutions, like that in the temporal distribution, was far more widespread than one might expect. Witchcraft prosecutions did not occur as occasional eruptions, abnormal reactions to particular crises. They seem to have been a normal part of village life, widespread and regular.

The frequency and importance of accusations of witchcraft at the Assizes is well demonstrated if we compare them to indictments for other offences. From Table 3 we can see that between 1580 and 1599 an average number of five or six people a year was tried at the Essex Assizes on a charge of witchcraft. Over the whole period 1560–1680 witchcraft indictments constituted some 5 per cent of all the criminal proceedings at this court.[14] In the years 1580–9, 118 of the total 890 indictments for all offences concerned witchcraft, approximately 13 per cent of all the prosecutions. The trial of witchcraft was second only in its frequency to the trial of thieves at the Essex Assizes. It was no peripheral, abnormal crime, but of central importance. As has been demonstrated, there were few years when indictments did not occur. When we remember that

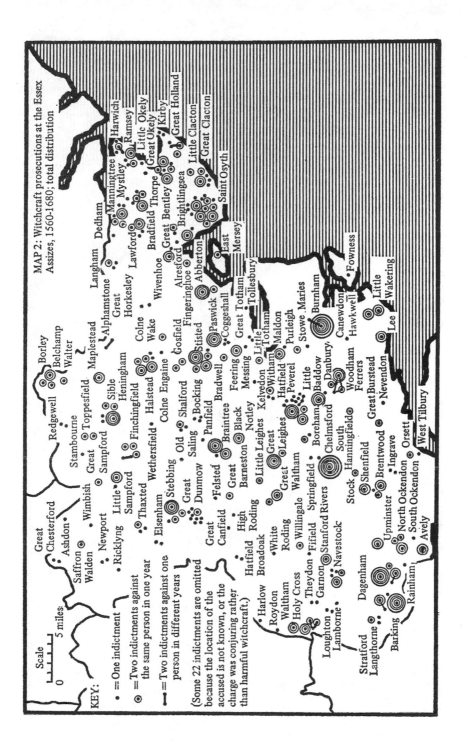

MAP 2: Witchcraft prosecutions at the Essex Assizes, 1560-1680; total distribution

Scale
0   5 miles

KEY:

• = One indictment

◉ = Two indictments against the same person in one year

◉─ = Two indictments against one person in different years

(Some 22 indictments are omitted because the location of the accused is not known, or the charge was conjuring rather than harmful witchcraft.)

32

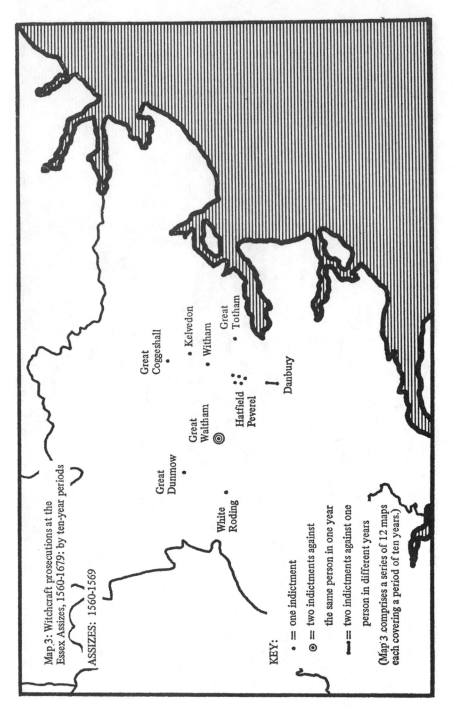

Map.3: Witchcraft prosecutions at the
Essex Assizes, 1560-1679: by ten-year periods

ASSIZES: 1560-1569

Great
Coggeshall

• Kelvedon

Great
• Witham

Great
• Totham

Danbury

Hatfield
Peverel

Great
Waltham

Great
Dunmow

White
Roding

KEY:

• = one indictment

◎ = two indictments against
     the same person in one year

▮ = two indictments against one
     person in different years

(Map 3 comprises a series of 12 maps
each covering a period of ten years.)

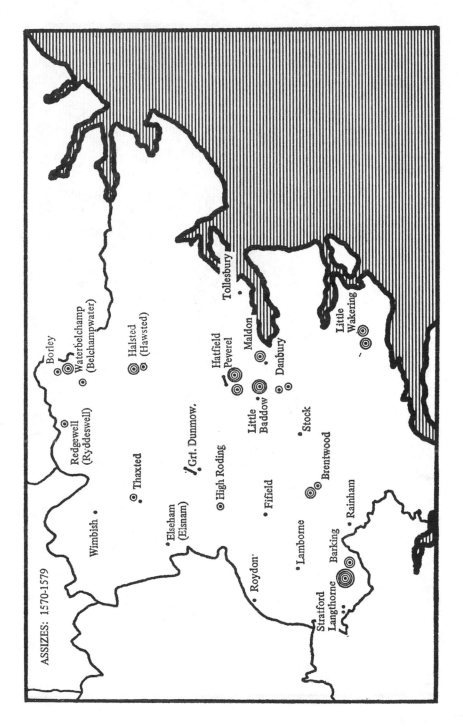

ASSIZES: 1570-1579

Borley
Waterbelchamp
(Belchampwater)
Halsted
(Hawsted)
Tollesbury
Little
Wakering
Hatfield
Peverel
Maldon
Danbury
Redgewell
(Ryddeswell)
Little
Baddow
Stock
Thaxted
Grt. Dunmow.
High Roding
Brentwood
Wimbish
Elseham
(Elsnam)
Fifield
Rainham
Roydon·
Lamborne
Barking
Stratford
Langthorne

33

34

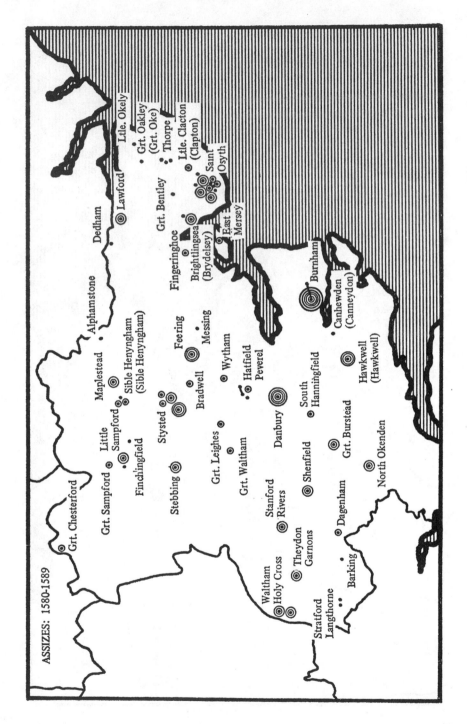

ASSIZES: 1580-1589

Grt. Chesterford

Waltham Holy Cross

Theydon Garnons

Stratford Langthorne

Barking

Stanford Rivers

Shenfield

Dagenham

North Okenden

Grt. Sampford   Little Sampford

Finchingfield

Maplestead

Alphamstone

Sible Henyngham (Sible Henyngham)

Stebbing

Stysted

Grt. Leighes

Grt. Waltham

Danbury

Feering

Bradwell

Messing

Wytham

Hatfield Peverel

South Hanningfield

Grt. Burstead

Hawkwell (Hawkwell)

Canhewden (Canneydon)

Burnham

Dedham

Lawford

Grt. Bentley

Fingeringhoe

Brightlingsea (Brydelsey)

East Mersey

Saint Osyth

Ltle. Clacton (Clapton)

Thorpe

Grt. Oakley (Grt. Oke)

Ltle. Okely

35

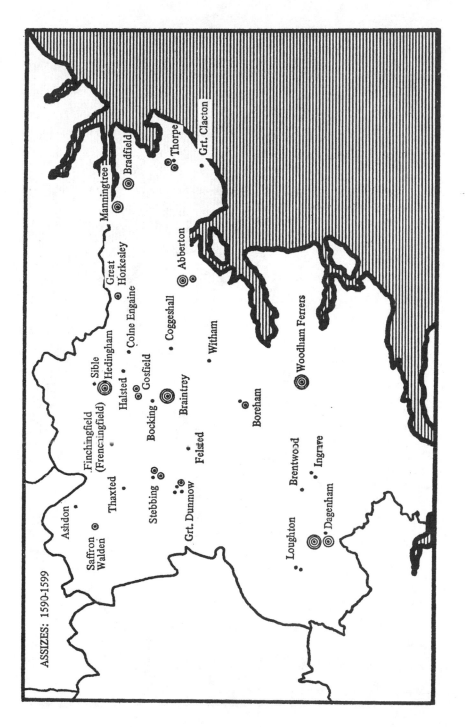

ASSIZES: 1590-1599

36

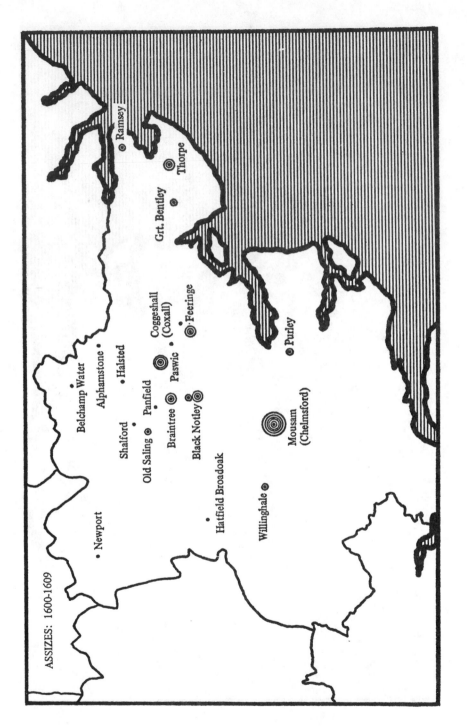

ASSIZES: 1600-1609

Newport •

Belchamp Water •

Alphamstone •

Shalford •

Halsted •

Old Saling ◉ Panfield

Braintree ◉ Paswic ◉

Black Notley ◉

Hatfield Broadoak •

Willinghale ◉

Coggeshall ◉
(Coxall)

◉ Feeringe

Mousam ◉
(Chelmsford)

◉ Purley

Grt. Bentley •

Thorpe ◉

Ramsey ◉

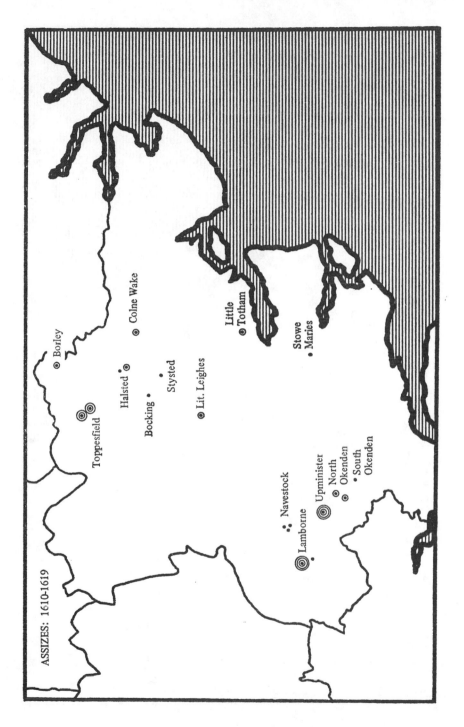

ASSIZES: 1610-1619

Borley

Colne Wake

Little Totham

Stowe Maries

Halsted

Stysted

Lit. Leighes

Bocking

Toppesfield

Navestock

Upminister

North Okenden

South Okenden

Lamborne

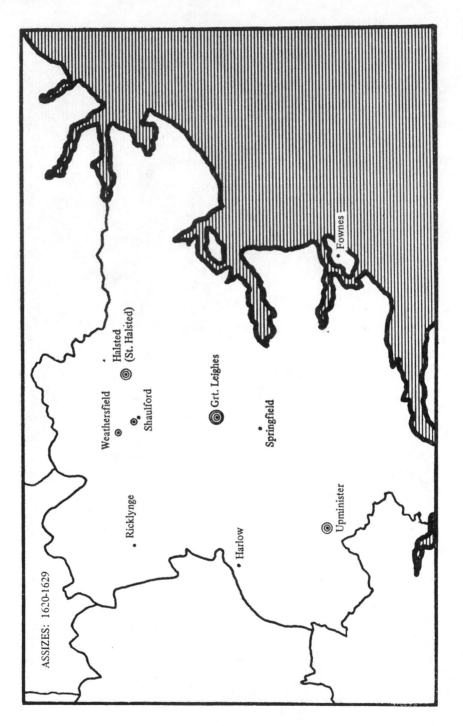

ASSIZES: 1620-1629

39

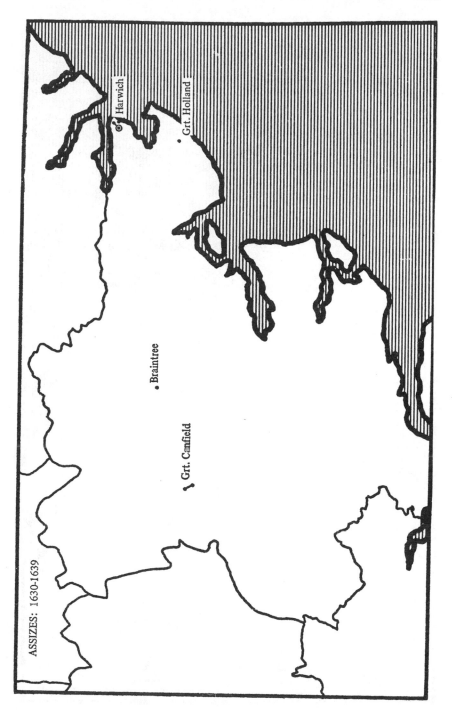

ASSIZES: 1630-1639

Harwich

Grt. Holland

Braintree

Grt. Canfield

40

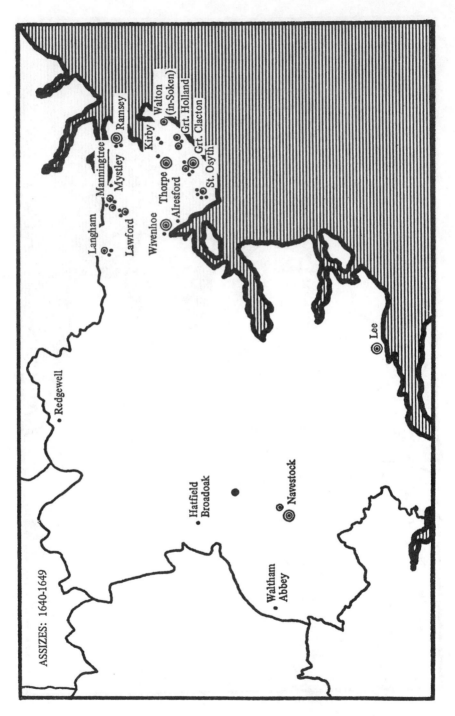

ASSIZES: 1640-1649

Redgewell

Langham
Manningtree
Mystley
Ramsey
Lawford
Walton
(in-Soken)
Kirby
Grt. Holland
Grt. Clacton
Wivenhoe
Thorpe
St. Osyth
Alresford
Grt. Osyth

Lee

Hatfield
Broadoak

Navestock

Waltham
Abbey

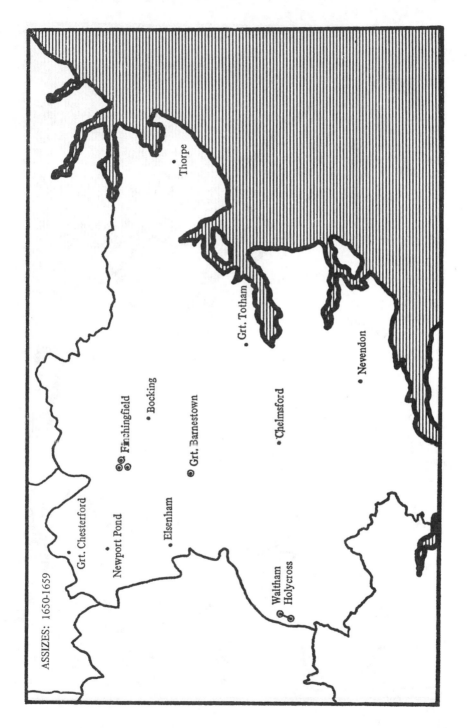

41

ASSIZES: 1650-1659

Grt. Chesterford

Newport Pond

Elsenham

Finchingfield

Bocking

Grt. Barnestown

Thorpe

Grt. Totham

Chelmsford

Nevendon

Waltham
Holycross

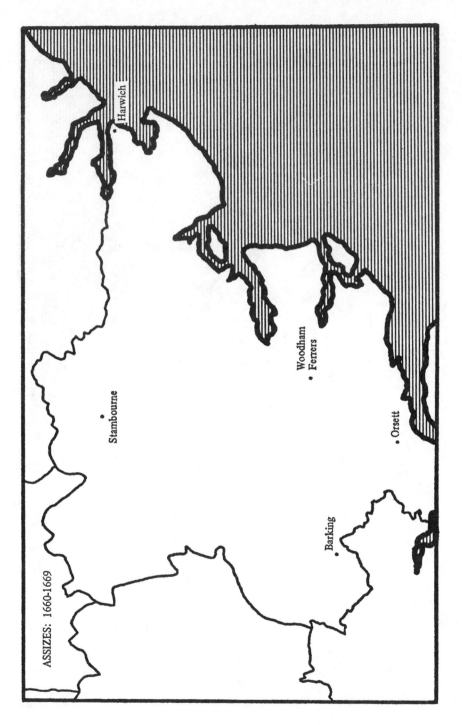

ASSIZES: 1660-1669

Harwich

Stambourne

Woodham
Ferrers

Orsett

Barking

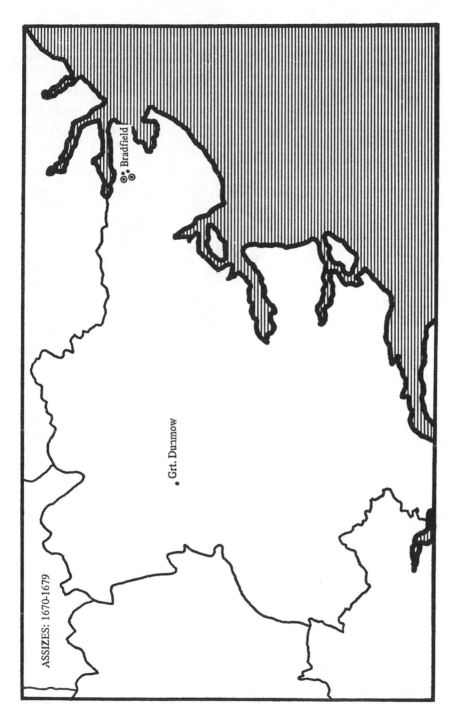

ASSIZES: 1670-1679

Bradfield

Grt. Dunmow

44

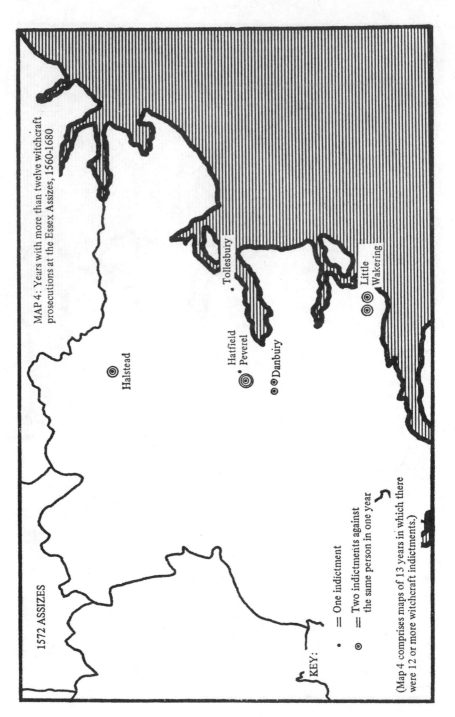

MAP 4: Years with more than twelve witchcraft prosecutions at the Essex Assizes, 1560-1680

1572 ASSIZES

Halstead

Hatfield
Peverel

Tollesbury

Danbury

Little
Wakering

KEY:

• = One indictment

◎ = Two indictments against
 the same person in one year

(Map 4 comprises maps of 13 years in which there
were 12 or more witchcraft indictments.)

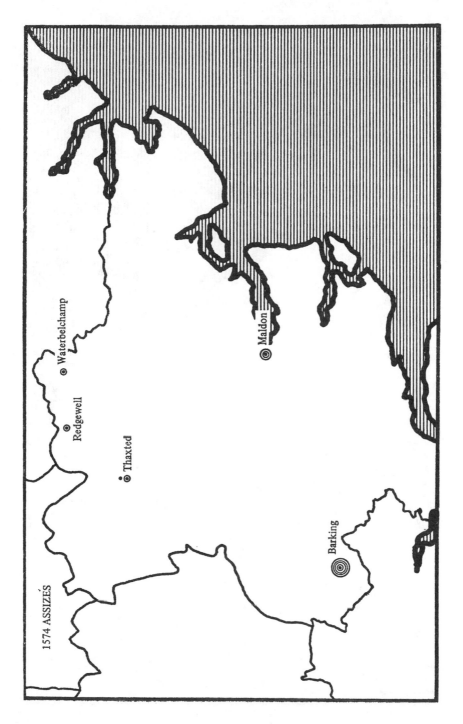

1574 ASSIZES

Waterbelchamp

Redgewell

Thaxted

Maldon

Barking

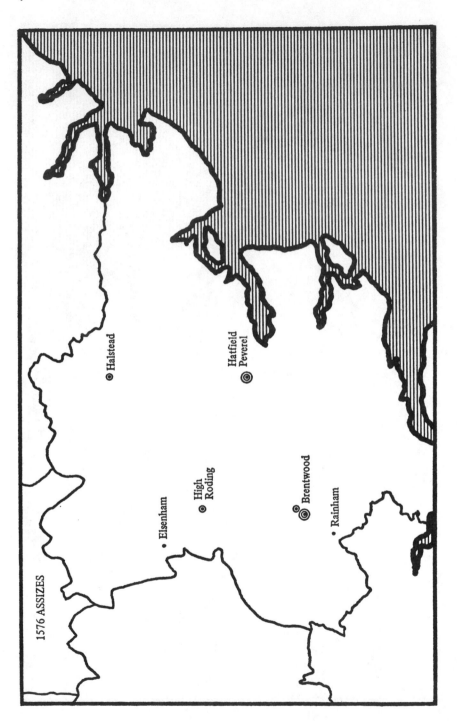

1576 ASSIZES

Halstead

Hatfield
Peverel

High
Roding

Elsenham

Brentwood

Rainham

47

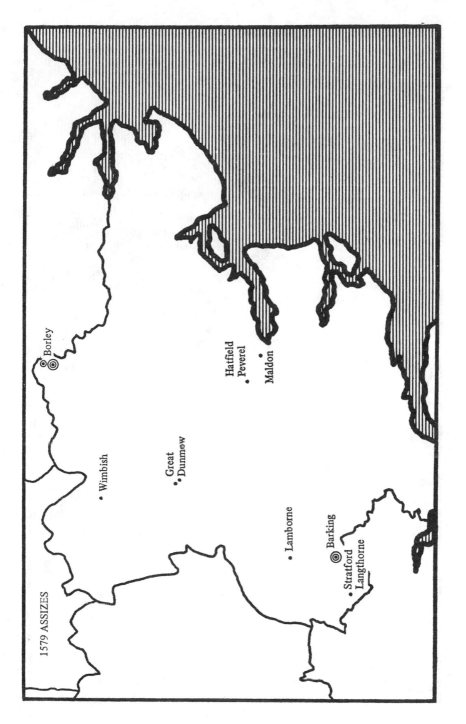

1579 ASSIZES

Borley

Hatfield
Peverel
Maldon

Wimbish

Great
Dunmow

Lamborne

Barking

Stratford
Langthorne

48

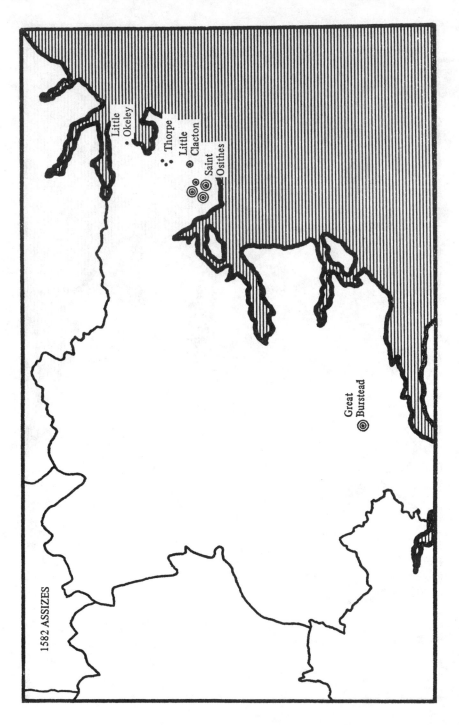

1582 ASSIZES

Little
Okeley

Thorpe

Little
Clacton

Saint
Osithes

Great
Burstead

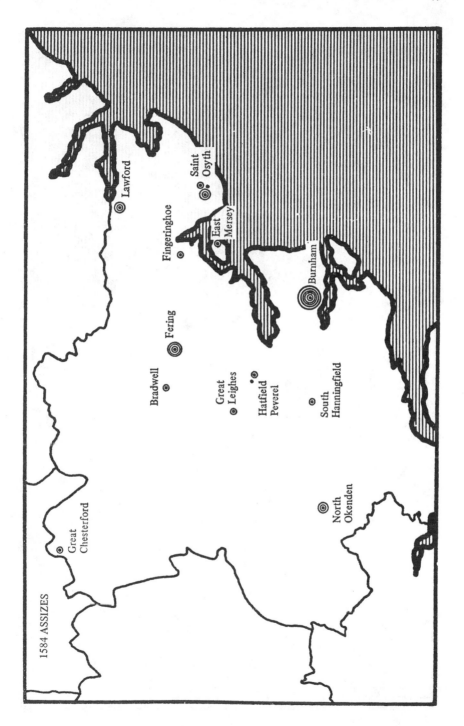

1584 ASSIZES

Great Chesterford

Lawford

Bradwell

Fering

Great Leighes

Fingeringhoe

East Mersey

Saint Osyth

Hatfield Peverel

South Hanningfield

Burnham

North Okenden

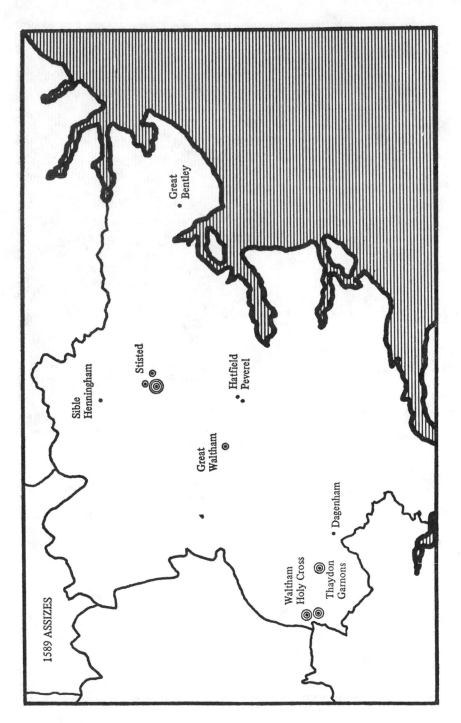

1589 ASSIZES

Great Bentley

Sible Henningham

Stisted

Hatfield Peverel

Great Waltham

Dagenham

Waltham Holy Cross

Thaydon Garnons

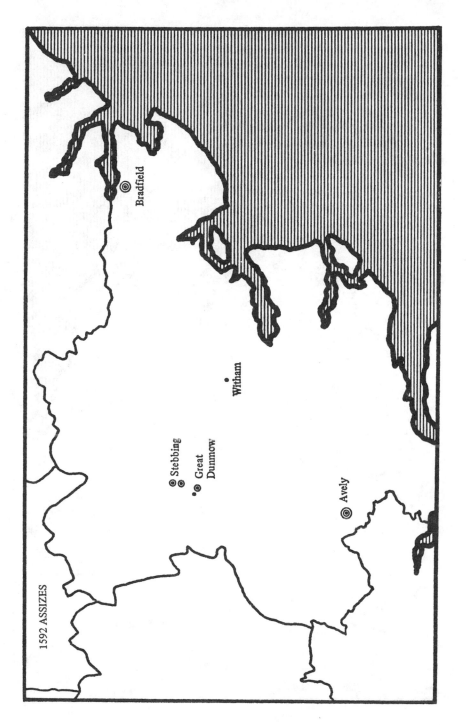

1592 ASSIZES

Bradfield

Witham

Stebbing
Great
Dunmow

Avely

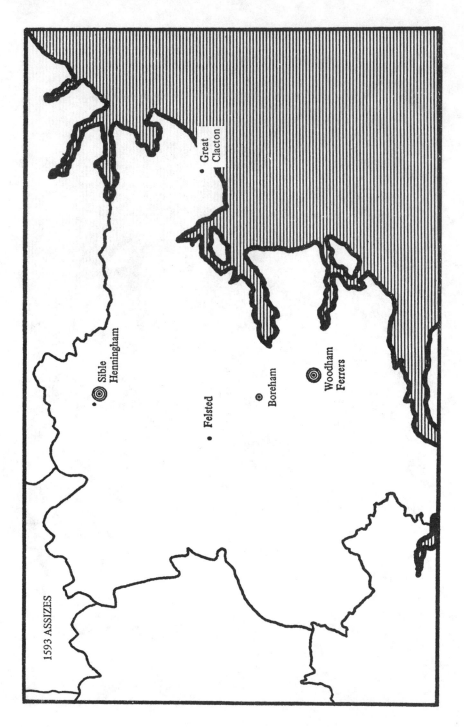

1593 ASSIZES

Great Clacton

Sible Henningham

Felsted

Boreham

Woodham Ferrers

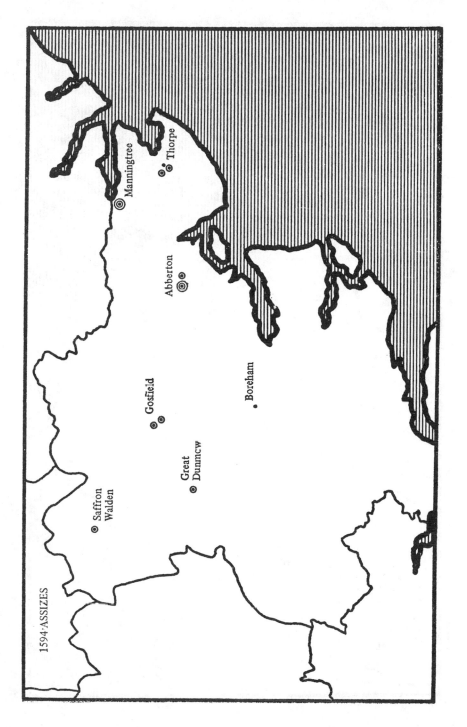

1594:ASSIZES

Saffron Walden

Great Dunmow

Gosfield

Boreham

Abberton

Manningtree

Thorpe

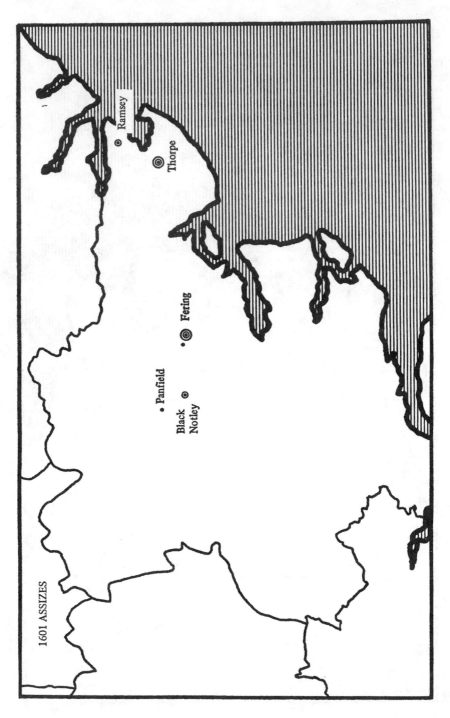

1601 ASSIZES

Ramsey

Thorpe

Fering

Panfield

Black
Notley

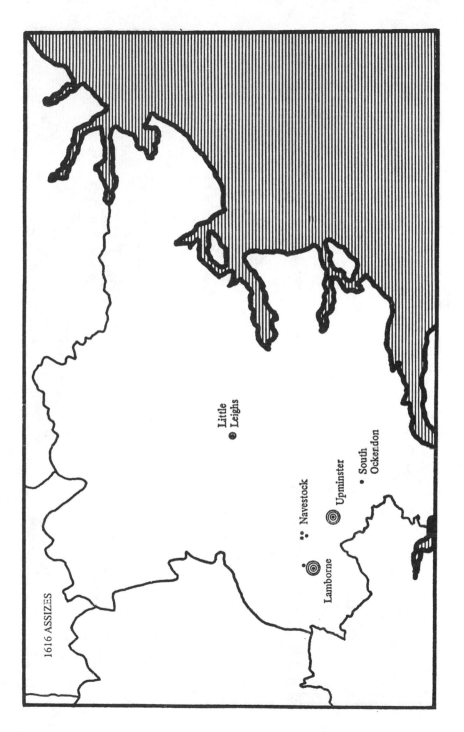

55

1616 ASSIZES

Little
Leighs

Navestock

Upminster

South
Ockendon

Lamborne

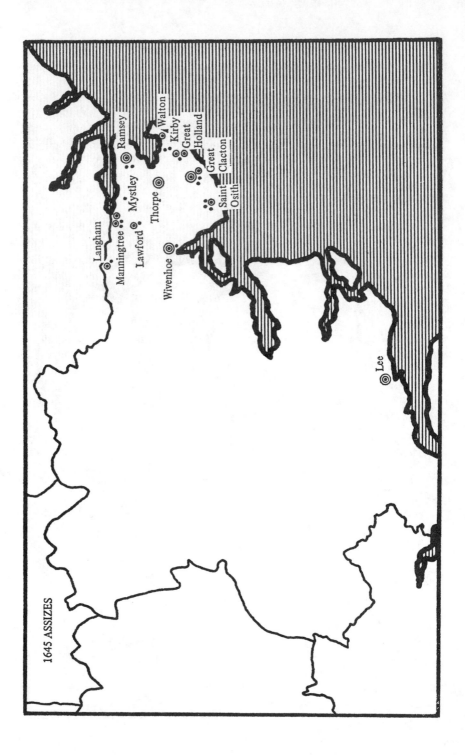

1645 ASSIZES

Langham
Manningtree
Mystley
Lawford
Thorpe
Wivenhoe
Ramsey
Walton
Kirby
Great Holland
Great Clacton
Saint Osith
Lee

Assize prosecutions were only the barest summary of the suspicions, it will be realized that witchcraft ideas were of considerable everyday importance in Essex.

Not all those accused of witchcraft were found guilty. On twenty-four occasions the Grand Jury refused to 'find' the bill of presentment and returned a verdict of *Ignoramus*. No complete rejections of bills occurred before 1647.[15] In the years after 1647 the total number of presentments for witchcraft decreased rapidly; altogether there were only thirty-nine between 1647 and 1680. Yet twenty of these were rejected as *Ignoramus*. This reflected a great change in the attitude of the minor gentry, of whom this jury was composed. Though, as we shall see, this was paralleled by a growing reluctance on the part of the Petty Jury to find accused persons guilty of witchcraft, it was, in itself, an important factor in the decline of witchcraft prosecutions in Essex.

Unfortunately, it is impossible to assess from the Assize records how many people confessed or pleaded guilty. From the indictments we learn of only seven who confessed,[16] but comparison with the witchcraft pamphlets reveals that a much larger number of suspects admitted their guilt.[17] Probably more accurately recorded were the cases where the accused pleaded pregnancy. Theoretically this only delayed the execution of the sentence. Only five women are known to have made such a plea when charged with witchcraft at the Essex Assizes.[18]

Witnesses to the indictments are named from 1600 on. From that date they appear on nearly all the bills, varying in number between one and six. Occasionally the surname of a witness is the same as that of the accused,[19] and there seems to have been a preponderance of male witnesses. Only in 1645 is there evidence of 'professional' witnesses—that is, of a group of individuals who recurred in indictments against a number of different individuals. The majority of these were women, and they may have been official 'searchers' for the mark supposed to be hidden in the body of a witch.[20]

Of the 291 people accused at the Essex Assizes for witchcraft, 151 were found not guilty or the bill of presentment against them dismissed. Of the remaining 140, 129 were found guilty, some seventy-four were executed and another fifty-five imprisoned.[21] The number imprisoned or executed per year over these 120 years is shown in Diagram 3. From this it will be seen that the percentage of persons found guilty of capital offences was highest in the period 1570–9 and again in 1601–4 and 1645. Between 1580 and 1595 a growing proportion of guilty persons were imprisoned rather than executed. The most dangerous time for accused persons was therefore 1570–1605, and again in 1645. The last execution for witchcraft in Essex, if 1645 is excepted, took place in 1626, and there were only three

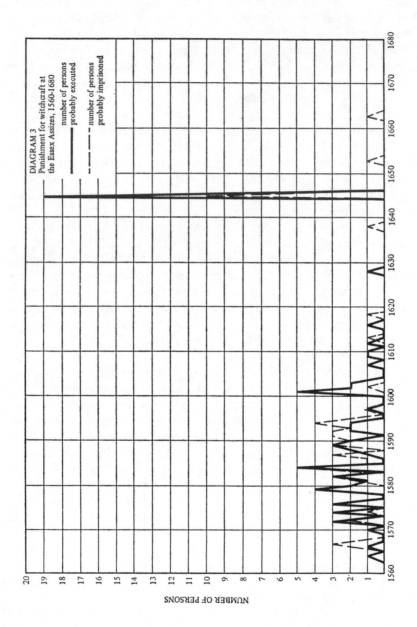

58

DIAGRAM 3
Punishment for witchcraft at
the Essex Assizes, 1560-1680

———— number of persons
probably executed

– – – – number of persons
probably imprisoned

NUMBER OF PERSONS

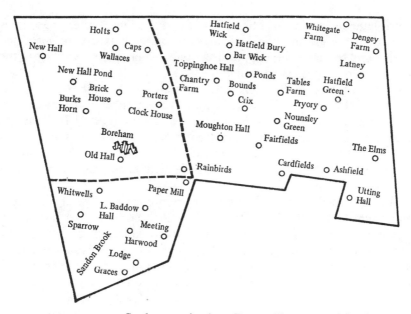

DIAGRAM 4A   Settlements in three Essex villages containing
accused witches (see chapter 6).

DIAGRAM 4B   Relative size and position of sample Essex villages.

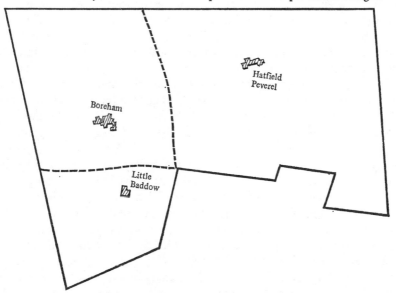

imprisonments, again excepting 1645, for this offence, after 1620. This tends to emphasize the Elizabethan period as the harshest for suspected witches and to isolate the 1645 trial as quite exceptional.[22] After 1620 the percentage of acquittals rose enormously.

Imprisonment of guilty witches theoretically lasted a year.[23] The dismal conditions of the prisons, however, meant that a number of those serving a prison sentence, or awaiting execution, died of gaol fever.[24] In Essex we know that at least thirty-six accused witches died of illness in gaol. This added another thirty-two to those already condemned to die by execution. In all, some 110 people are known to have died on an accusation of black witchcraft tried at the Essex Assizes.

Although enough of the Essex Assize records remain for the statistics from them to be reasonably helpful,[25] it may be wondered how many people tried for witchcraft at this court are not known to us through the loss of documents. More generally, there is the problem of what percentage of the suspicions in the Essex countryside grew so strong that people took the matter to court. A comparison of Assize records with other evidence provides a rough answer to these questions. The Quarter Sessions records, we have seen, include eight black witches who do not appear at the Assizes: in other words, just over three-quarters of the suspected black witches appear at the higher court. Coroners' inquisitions on deaths in Colchester Gaol give the names of twenty-one persons accused of witchcraft dying in gaol between 1560 and 1603. Of these, some fifteen appear in the Assize records. If we include four women who were almost certainly in prison on a charge of witchcraft,[26] we find that Assize records only contain some two-thirds of those who were actually imprisoned for witchcraft and died of plague. From the above comparisons, and from incidental references to people sent to the Assizes who do not appear in the surviving documents,[27] it would be a conservative estimate to suggest that the 291 people whom we know were prosecuted at the Essex Assizes for black witchcraft were only some 75 per cent of those actually indicted. We might therefore expect a total of nearly 400 black witches in Essex. Furthermore, a comparison with those prosecuted at the other Essex courts, particularly the ecclesiastical ones,[28] and with the witchcraft pamphlets, considerably extends the actual number of witches believed to live in Essex. Comparison with the pamphlets, for example, suggests that one in four of those strongly suspected of witchcraft in Essex villages were never taken to court at all. Furthermore, it becomes evident that the more than 500 indictments, or over 650 if these are only three-quarters of the actual total, are only some one-third of the actual accusations made at the Assize court.[29] A speculative total of 400 accused witches, charged with over 1,500 crimes, of which some 650 were turned into indictments, seems probable for the

Essex Assize courts as a whole. Even this was only the projecting surface of far more widespread suspicions.

We may well wonder how these Essex figures compared with those for other parts of England. At first it was hoped that it would be possible to make a statistical comparison of witchcraft prosecutions in different counties on the basis of legal records. It soon became obvious, however, that records for various counties have survived and been made accessible to such an unequal degree that this is not at present feasible. The following comparisons, therefore, are merely designed to indicate in a general manner the English background to the Essex statistics, and to stress that wherever there are surviving court records of the right type, there witchcraft prosecutions will be found.

Assize records survive for all parts of England from the seventeenth century onwards, but as part of the Home Circuit, Essex witchcraft indictments may most fairly be compared to those in the other counties comprising that circuit. This comparison has, in fact, already been made by C. L. Ewen and his figures are as follows:[30]

TABLE 4

Witchcraft indictments in the Home Circuit, 1560–1700

County	Persons indicted	Indictments	Executions
Sussex	17	33	1
Surrey	54	71	5
Hertford	52	81	8
Kent	91	132	16
Essex	299	473	82
Total	513	790	112

From this, as Ewen remarked, 'a glance leads to the immediate conclusion that the belief in witchcraft was much more pronounced in Essex. . . . The Essex indictments actually outnumber those of the four counties of Herts, Kent, Surrey and Sussex combined.'[31] This cannot even be partly explained by the better survival of Essex Assize rolls, despite Ewen's suggestion to this effect.[32] Within the Home Circuit, Essex was exceptional, though other counties all had their prosecutions.

Detailed comparisons with other Assize records cannot be made, since no other circuits have Elizabethan survivals; only the Palatinates of Durham and Chester have such documents.[33] Apart from the Home

Circuit, the Palatinates, Middlesex, and scattered Northern Circuit documents, there are no surviving indictments for England until 1654, when they start for the Oxford, Norfolk, and Northern Circuits. After that date there were eighty indictments in the Home Circuit, eighteen in the Norfolk, thirty-nine in the Northern, and four in the Oxford. If we are prepared to compare the Home Circuit indictments to the Western Circuit gaol books, which start in 1670, we find that after that date there are thirty-three indictments for the Home, and sixty-nine references to witchcraft in the Western Circuits. Thus, for the only period when records remain for the Western Circuit, they show a doubled incidence when compared to a different type of record for the Home Circuit. In all, Ewen added a little over 450 Assize cases from outside the Home Circuit.[34] He guessed that the number of executions for witchcraft in England from 1542 to 1736 would be less than 1,000.[35] In the Home Counties the average number of persons indicted per county between 1560 and 1706 (if we leave Essex on one side as exceptional) was a little over fifty; the number of executions slightly over seven per county. Middlesex, with forty-eight persons indicted,[36] supports this average. If this is the survival from some 77 per cent of the records, and these counties are at all representative of England as a whole, we might expect something like a total of 2,000 persons tried during the whole period in all the Assize courts, and some 300 executed. Seen in this framework, Ewen's figures for Essex, of 299 persons indicted and eighty-two executed, appear exceptional. Yet the rest of England is far from free of prosecutions. Thomas Cooper, writing in 1617, hardly exaggerated when he inquired rhetorically, 'Doth not every Assize almost throughout the Land, resound of the arraignment and conviction of notorious Witches?'[37]

Quarter Sessions records are less useful than Assize documents for showing the comparative density of English witchcraft prosecutions. Not only do counties vary widely in the date and volume of their records, and the degree to which these records are accessible in printed form, but Essex cases suggest that over 90 per cent of those tried at the Assizes did not appear at the Quarter Sessions. Yet it may still be asked how the seventy-four references to witchcraft activity discovered in the very extensive Essex Quarter Sessions records compare to those of other counties. Witchcraft references in records of this court were found for the following counties:[38] Lincolnshire (1), Northamptonshire (1), Worcestershire (2), West Riding of Yorkshire (3), Norfolk (4), North Riding of Yorkshire (6), Nottinghamshire (10), Somerset (10). The only two counties which can, at all fairly, be compared to Essex in their printed sessions records are Hertfordshire and Wiltshire. There are nine Hertfordshire cases after 1589, including some long depositions. Wiltshire records, starting in 1563, include twenty-three references to witchcraft. Again the impression is that Essex is exceptional: there are more references for this county than for the rest of England, excluding Wiltshire. But this impression is partly the result of the splendid survival of Essex records and the fact that they alone have been searched in the original. If Essex, as was the case with other counties, had only been judged from its printed Quarter Sessions records, few witchcraft cases would have been discovered.[39]

Despite their deficiencies, witchcraft prosecutions at Assize and Quarter Sessions courts are our best statistical source. They enable us to plot the geographical and temporal distribution of witchcraft cases and provide us with a list of suspects and their victims essential in further analysis. It is hoped that future researchers will not only test the maps and graphs of Essex prosecutions by making similar analyses for other counties, but will also locate further cases in two classes of records which are still not completely explored. In this work the prodigious and pioneering efforts of C. L. Ewen will provide an indispensable aid.

NOTES

1. J. C. Cox, *Three Centuries of Derbyshire Annals* (1890), ii, 88; Ewen, I, p. 46; William Lambard, *Eirenarcha: or of the Office of the Iustices of Peace* (1582), ii, 447, 320.
2. A possible exception is case 849.
3. For the names and dates of the Essex judges see Ewen, I, pp. 102–8; Ewen provides a brief description of some of these on pp. 50–2.
4. Ewen omitted gaol calendar references to witches in his abstracts of Assize witchcraft cases, except in 1582 and 1645 or when they added new names.
5. For the gentlemanly status of the Grand Jury in Essex see B. W. Quintrell, 'The Government of the County of Essex, 1603–1642' (London Univ. Ph.D. thesis, 1965), p. 82.
6. Bernard (*Guide*, p. 25) described the Petty Jury as 'a Jury of simple men, who proceed too often upon relations of meere presumptions'. Gaule (*Select Cases*, pp. 194–5) argued that 'these Twelve good men and True' should not be 'Impannelled of ordinary Countrey People', but of learned physicians, lawyers, and divines. It seems that, contrary to theory, jurymen were often 'picked up in court as they might be needed' (*Minutes of Proceedings in Quarter Sessions held for Parts of Kesteven*, ed. S. A. Peyton (Lincs. Rec. Soc., xxv, 1931), p. lxxii).
7. W.T., *Office of the Clerk of Assize* (1676), p. 14. Pp. 6–17 of this work contain a good outline of the procedure at the Assizes. It is upon this and the introduction to *Somerset Assize Orders, 1629–1640*, ed. T. G. Barnes (Somerset Rec. Soc., lxv, 1959), that the above account is based.
8. W.T., *Clerk of Assize*, p. 15.
9. Case 119.
10. For an analysis and description of these pamphlets see ch. 5, p. 81, below.
11. 1579 Pamphlet, sigs. Av^v–Av1^v.

12. For a description of the type and survival of Quarter Sessions records see Bibliography, p. 314, below; for abstracts of all these cases see Appendix 1, Nos. 791–855. Cases have obviously been lost, see cases 1,204–5.
13. For simplicity's sake, and following Ewen, indictments, inquisitions and references to otherwise unknown witches in gaol records have all been grouped under the term 'indictment'. In fact, the gaol records, which mention twenty-three otherwise unmentioned suspects, are less useful than indictments, since they usually omit the offence, victim, and village of the accused.
14. The number of indictments for all offences at the Essex Assizes varied between twenty and eighty per Assize; it averaged about ninety per year to 1600, 100 per year to 1680.
15. One bill was rejected as 'insufficient' in 1579; three others were pronounced *Ignoramus* with regard to one of the two people jointly prosecuted, but found to be true concerning the other. The cases are 122, 227, 272, 403.
16. Cases 17–19, 165, 201, 683, 742; Ewen, I, pp. 59–60, discusses confession.
17. For example, the Assize indictments only note one of the women as confessing in 1582 (case 165), yet the pamphlet of that year shows that at least five confessed at the Lent Assizes.
18. Cases 3–5, 61, 286–7, 347–8, 493–6.
19. For example in case 499.
20. For a discussion of the 1645 witnesses, see p. 135, below.
21. If gaol records are inadequate, it is often impossible to be certain that the statutory punishment was carried out; the above figures, therefore, partly represent an estimate based on what *should* have happened. Ewen, I, p. 98, calculated that eighty-two Essex witches were executed, an overestimate arising from his neglect of the gaol calendars, which occasionally show that a person was not executed, but was still in prison a year later, as in cases 220–1. In twelve cases the accused died before judgement, or the verdict is unknown.
22. For a graphical demonstration of the verdicts and punishments in Assize witchcraft cases, see Diagram 3, p. 58, above.
23. Sometimes they seem to have been in prison longer; for an imprisonment lasting up to six years, see case 160.
24. Ewen, I, p. 27, discusses the conditions in an Elizabethan gaol; for a more general description see *Shakespeare in His Own Age*, ed. A. Nicoll (Shakespeare Survey, 17, 1964), ch. 7.
25. Forty-three out of 240 Essex Assize files between 1560 and 1679 are completely missing; for their comparative survival see Diagram 1, p. 26, above.
26. Cases 1,187–90.
27. For example, case 1,134: see case 1,122 for a woman who died on the way to the Assizes.
28. See p. 81, below.
29. For the evidence for this statement, see p. 86, below.
30. Ewen, I, p. 99 (table).
31. Ibid., p. 100.
32. Ibid., pp. 97, 99, suggested that Essex records, especially gaol records, were better preserved than those of the other four counties. But analysis of the files at the P.R.O. shows that the number lost per county in the period 1560–1660 was as follows: Surrey (36), Kent (42), Essex (43), Sussex (51), Herts (65).
33. For the statistics on which the following account is based, see Ewen, I, pp. 109–11; Ewen, II, appendices; Ewen, *Witchcraft in the Norfolk Circuit* (n.p., 1939), *passim*.

For a description of the circuits and the survival of records, see *Guide to the Contents of the Public Record Office* (1963), i, 127–31. Some further cases in the Northern Circuits, fourteen set of recognizances for the years 1649–59 were discovered in P.R.O., Assizes 47, 14–15.

34. Nearly all are printed in summary form in the appendices of Ewen, II.
35. Ewen, I, p. 112.
36. The cases are printed in *Middlesex County Records*, ed. J. C. Jeaffreson (Middlesex Co. Rec. Soc., i–iv, 1886–92), and *Calendar to the Sessions Records*, ed. W. Le Hardy (Middlesex Co. Rec. Soc., n.s., 1–4, 1935–41); most of the cases are listed in Ewen, II, Appendix J. For a description of the exceptional nature of the Middlesex records, see E. D. Mercer, 'The Middlesex County Record Office', *Archives*, vi (1963), 30–1.
37. Thomas Cooper, *The Mystery of Witchcraft* (1617), p. 15.
38. The numbers in parentheses refer to the number of cases of witchcraft. Many of these cases are printed in the appendices to Ewen, II; see also the asterisked secondary works in the Bibliography, p. 321, below, which contain witchcraft cases; page references are given there.
39. *The Historical Manuscripts Commission, 10th Report*, Appendix, Part iv (1885), pp. 466–513, printed extracts from the Essex Quarter Sessions records; yet examination of these extracts would lead one to suppose that only three cases of witchcraft or conjuring (pp. 473, 476, 511) appeared before the Essex Justices of the Peace.

Chapter 4

Witchcraft accusations in other legal courts

EVIDENCE FROM THE ECCLESIASTICAL RECORDS

Between 1560 and 1680 some 230 men and women from Essex are known to have been presented at the ecclesiastical courts for offences related to witchcraft and sorcery. Few of these cases have previously been printed. Altogether they constitute more ecclesiastical cases than have been discovered in printed sources for the whole of the rest of England for that period. Evidence from ecclesiastical cases provides important information on a number of problems: the efforts to counter the power of a witch and the methods and numbers of cunning folk or witch-doctors; the characters and motives of suspected witches; the geographical and temporal distribution of accusations against suspected witches. Most of these problems will be discussed later. The aim of this section is to give a brief account of the jurisdiction and procedure of ecclesiastical courts in witchcraft cases, and a broad outline of the types of offence and number of cases which came before such courts.

There were several overlapping ecclesiastical jurisdictions in Essex. The more important were those of the Bishop of London and the Archdeacons of Middlesex, Colchester, and Essex.[1] The Bishop had two courts, that of his Commissary in Essex and Hertfordshire, and his Consistory. The former covered about 100 villages in Essex; only eight witchcraft or sorcery cases were discovered in this source, but growing accessibility of the material will almost certainly furnish new cases. Similarly, the nineteen cases so far encountered in the Consistory Court records probably only constitute a fraction of all the witchcraft and sorcery cases tried there.[2]

A north-western strip of Essex, covering a little under a quarter of the county, lay within the Archdeaconry of Middlesex. Unfortunately, no pre-1660 court records have survived for this area. Consequently, a region which was one of dense prosecutions, according to the Assize records, has few relevant archdeaconry records. There are no recorded witchcraft cases from this source. Much more fortunate in the survival of its records was the Archdeaconry of Colchester, which covered the north-east, and a small strip in the north-west, of Essex. The records start effectively in 1575 and 117 cases of witchcraft and sorcery have been discovered in them. Likewise, the Archdeaconry of Essex, covering the southern part of the county, has many surviving records for this period. They start in bulk some ten years before those of Colchester Archdeaconry and there are 126 cases of witchcraft and sorcery in them.[3] In both these archdeaconries, almost without exception, the cases are to be found in the detection or 'Act' books, arising out of churchwarden's presentments in answer to articles of visitation from the archdeacon or bishop.

Inquiries concerning suspected witchcraft and sorcery were included in both the Royal Articles of 1559 and Archbishop Parker's Articles for the Province of Canterbury in 1560.[4] Within the Diocese of London, in which Essex was situated, it was usual to make such an enquiry in the second half of the sixteenth century. In 1554 the Catholic Bishop, Bonner, had enquired 'whether there be any that do use charms, witchcraft, sorcery, enchantments, false soothsayings, or any such-like thing', and similar questions were asked in 1571, 1577, and 1586. In 1571 Bishop Sandys asked for the presentment of 'any that useth sorcery, witchcraft, enchantments, incantations, charms, unlawful prayers, or invocations in Latin'.[5] This was repeated, word for word, in 1577 and 1586, with the addition of 'and namely midwyves in the time of womens travayle of childe. And whether any do resort to any such for helpe or counsayle, and what be their names.' Such wording suggests that the authorities were especially interested in white witchcraft. In 1601 a new formula was used in which reference was made to witchcraft 'punishable by the ecclesiastical lawes', thereby implying that ecclesiastical and secular courts dealt with different branches of witchcraft. Such a division was explicitly stated in the 1628 set of Articles, after witchcraft had been omitted entirely from those of 1612 and 1615. In 1628 the Bishop enquired: 'Have you any in your Parish, which have used any inchantments, sorceries, witchcrafts, or Incantations, which are not made Felony by the Statutes of this Realme, or any Charmes; or which do resort to any such for helpe or Counsell?' Six years later this was repeated in a new set of articles, but it was for the last time; in 1640 and 1664 there was no mention of witchcraft. Nor was witchcraft mentioned in the articles for the Bishop's Commissary in Essex and Hertfordshire in 1625.[6]

The only surviving Elizabethan archdeaconry articles covering Essex are for the Archdeaconry of Middlesex in 1582. In Article 27 it was asked

> Whether there bee anye man or woman in your parish that useth witchcraft, coiniuring, southsaying, charmes, or unlawful Prayers or invocations in Latin or English for or upon any Christian bodie, or beast, and what be their names, or anye that do go or seeke for helpe at such sorcerers handes?

None of the three early sets of articles for Colchester Archdeaconry, issued in 1607, 1631, and 1633, contain anything concerning witchcraft. Likewise, only the first of the Archdeaconry of Essex articles, lists of which survive for 1610, 1615, 1635, 1636, 1639 and 1672, mentions this offence; the wording is exactly the same as that in the 1582 Middlesex article quoted above.[7] The impression is, therefore, that it became increasingly unusual to inquire about this offence some time in the early years of the seventeenth century, and that there was a recognition of the jurisdiction of the secular courts in offences laid down by the Statute of 1604. It will be seen that such a change in the inquiries exactly coincided with a rapid decline in presentations for witchcraft and sorcery after 1605.[8]

Accusations of alleged witchcraft might appear before the ecclesiastical courts in two forms.[9] Firstly, there were causes of 'office', disciplinary proceedings usually resulting from the presentment of offenders by incumbents and churchwardens. These 'detections' were written in an 'Act' book, as it was called in Essex, before the court sat, and were in answer to the sets of visitation articles discussed above. If the accused appeared, a scribbled summary was made by the clerk. Witchcraft might also appear in 'instance' cases—that is, in prosecutions directly between plaintiff and defendant, equivalent to modern civil suits. In the latter, witchcraft appeared infrequently and indirectly as one of the forms of libel in the frequent defamation cases. Defamation cases have been included in this study since they extend our knowledge concerning witchcraft beliefs. In some respects, however, they are the reverse of normal prosecutions, since it was not the suspected witch but her accuser who was presented at court.

Nearly all the known Essex witchcraft and sorcery cases in ecclesiastical records arose out of churchwardens' presentments at the Archdeaconry courts. This court met at intervals of just over a month. The first recorded stage was the detection, usually on the basis of 'common fame' or rumour, by incumbent and churchwardens. Thus the attitude of the churchwardens to witchcraft and sorcery was of considerable importance in determining the extent of presentments. If the accused repeatedly refused to appear at the court, he or she was pronounced contumacious and was excommunicated.[10] Usually those accused of witchcraft or sorcery denied the accusation and were ordered to 'purge' themselves.[11] Purgation consisted of a process whereby the accused brought a number of 'honest neighbours', usually three or four, who swore an oath that the denial of guilt by the accused was true. Successful purgation meant that the accused was restored to his or her former good reputation. This occurred in six Essex witchcraft cases, while ten suspected witches failed to purge themselves through the refusal of their neighbours to support them.[12] Thus a person's guilt or innocence depended largely on the attitude of his or her neighbours.

Presented because of a general rumour, the individual could only be cleared if supported by a group of fellow villagers.

If the offence was admitted or purgation failed, the accused was ordered to do public penance—that is, to confess and promise amendment of life in front of the other villagers. This was usually on a Sunday in the parish church and the accused wore a white sheet and carried a white wand. For example, a woman was ordered to 'penitentlie confesse that she is hartelie sorrie for that she hath geven vehement suspicion of wichecrafte and wicherie'.[13] Having asked for the forgiveness of God and of her neighbours, the accused was dismissed after payment of fees and production of a certificate of a completed penance.[14]

↳Three major types of offence may be distinguished from the presentments: those accused for 'witchcraft and sorcery', those for white witchcraft, and those for defaming a person as a witch‖It is not always possible to distinguish with absolute certainty between types of case or to fit cases neatly into these categories, but Table 5 indicates the general pattern:

TABLE 5
Offences related to witchcraft at the Essex ecclesiastical courts, 1560–1680

Type of offence	Total	Example[15]
'Witchcraft and sorcery'	135	922
Being a sorcerer		
working with a 'sieve and shears'	5	964
'casting a figure'	1	1,042
'soothsaier, forediviner'	1	865
finding lost goods by magic	4	1,079
healing by magic	6	873
unspecified	8	977
	25	
Going to sorcerers		
for bewitched humans/animals	5	957
for lost goods	12	898
for help in sickness	5	875
unspecified	16	1,073
	38	
Individual sorcery		
being present at a magical ceremony	1	991
anti-witchcraft magic (burning an animal)	3	983
love magic	2	1,025
	6	
Miscellaneous		
'wishes herself a witch for revenge'	1	984
calling her vicar a witch	1	1,135
defamation	22	959

70

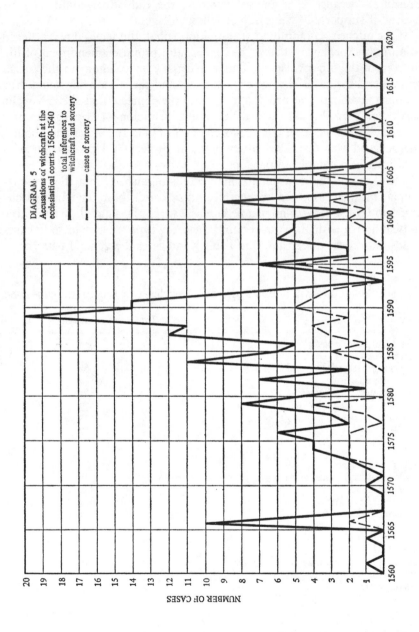

DIAGRAM. 5
Acusations of witchcraft at the
ecclesiastical courts, 1560-1640

——— total references to
witchcraft and sorcery

– – – cases of sorcery

NUMBER OF CASES

71

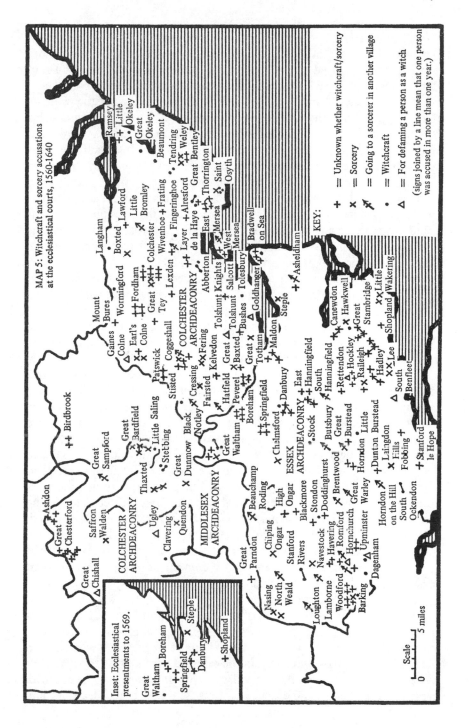

MAP 5: Witchcraft and sorcery accusations at the ecclesiastical courts, 1560-1640

KEY:

+ = Unknown whether witchcraft/sorcery

× = Sorcery

✗ = Going to a sorcerer in another village

• = Witchcraft

△ = For defaming a person as a witch

(signs joined by a line mean that one person was accused in more than one year.)

Inset: Ecclesiastical presentments to 1569.

Scale
0   5 miles

In all, if we count persons rather than cases, some 230 people are known to have been accused of some activity related to witchcraft. Of these, more than half were accused of the ambiguous 'sorcery and witchcraft'. From other court records we learn that at least twenty-five of these were suspected 'black' witches,[16] and in some other cases the wording of the presentment suggests that the accused was thought to be an evil witch—for example, Joan Page was admitted to be 'develishe of her tonge'.[17] Although this cannot be proved, the general impression is that over half the cases that came before the ecclesiastical courts concerned women suspected to be maleficent witches. The actual number of persons accused, rather than those discovered in the surviving records, must also remain at a speculative level. Taking into account the missing and inaccessible records, it would probably be no exaggeration to suggest that upwards of 350 persons were accused of activities connected with witchcraft and sorcery at the Essex ecclesiastical courts between 1560 and 1680.

The temporal distribution of ecclesiastical court accusations is plotted in Diagram 5. From this diagram it will be apparent that nearly all the cases occurred between 1572 and 1602. More than half of them occurred between 1580 and 1592. No cases after 1611 have been discovered in the Colchester Archdeaconry records, though there are five cases after 1620 in the Essex Archdeaconry and Consistory Court records.[18] It has already been suggested that a major reason for this rapid decline in the early seventeenth century was the recognition that most witchcraft offences came under the 1604 Statute, and should therefore be tried at the secular courts. To a certain extent, the diagram is influenced by the comparative survival of records; for example, the peaks in 1566 and 1605 reflect the survival of two detailed court books. Nevertheless, there can be no doubt that the peak of accusations was in the later part of Elizabeth's reign and that there was a rapid decline after 1605. The proportion of definite cases of sorcery also increased as time went on; this may reflect the growing recognition of secular jurisdiction over black witchcraft already suggested. The peak of accusations was in 1589, with twenty witchcraft and two sorcery cases. Since cases were deferred from one court to the next, the general impression is of an even greater amount of interest in witchcraft presentments. At the peak period, witchcraft and sorcery were among the most common ecclesiastical offences.

The geographical distribution of cases is shown in Map 5. From this it can be seen that presentments are to be found wherever records have survived. If there is any pattern at all, it is one of an emphasis on sorcery in the south-west and on witchcraft in the east and north. Over 125 places, or more than 25 per cent of all Essex villages, were involved in some way with presentments, despite the absence of early Middlesex Archdeaconry and other records. From the inset to Map 5, which shows the distribution of presentments until 1569, we see that cases first appeared in the area near Chelmsford, as in the early Assize records.

There does not seem to have been any obvious correlation between the amount of presentments for witchcraft and sorcery and the personality of the ecclesiastical judges. For example, in the Archdeaconry of Colchester the last presentment occurred in 1611, yet George Withers remained Archdeacon until 1617, a position he had held since 1570. Thus the considerable variations in the presentments all occurred within the time of his appointment. Although the most notorious male witch in Essex lived in Danbury, of which George Withers was Rector, there is nothing to connect Withers with this or any other witchcraft case.[19] Similarly, presentments for witchcraft and sorcery in the Archdeaconry of Essex were made before six different archdeacons. The first of these, Thomas Cole, who held the office from 1559 to 1571, is known to have examined witches and even presided at a trial of witches at the Assizes.[20] A Marian exile and reformer, it might be argued that he had a special interest in witchcraft, but presentments did not subside, but, rather, increased, under his successors, John Walker and William Tabor. These two held office from 1571 to 1585 and 1585 to 1602 respectively, and were followed by Samuel Harsnet. Harsnet may have been a moderating influence, since he was currently engaged in a controversy with the exorcist John Darrell and is known to have had extremely sceptical views on the possibility of witchcraft. During the period 1603–9, when he was Archdeacon, four cases, all concerning supposed black witchcraft, were presented; three of them were dismissed.[21] But, as we have seen, the Essex Archdeaconry was not peculiar in witnessing a decline of presentments at this period. In fact, under Harsnet's successors, George Goldman and Edward Layfield, presentments continued to appear long after they had ceased in the Archdeaconry of Colchester.

Throughout the period there was a certain amount of overlapping of witchcraft and sorcery cases between the ecclesiastical and secular courts. Twenty-two of those accused at the ecclesiastical courts appeared charged with witchcraft at the Assizes, another three in the borough and Quarter Sessions records. One person accused at an ecclesiastical court died on the way to the Assizes.[22] Usually the accused appeared at the Assizes between three and twelve months after appearing at the ecclesiastical court, though we cannot be certain that they were sent from one to the other. On three occasions the ecclesiastical presentment took place after the secular trial had finished; in two of these the gap of twenty years and ten years suggests that suspicions had re-emerged and a new case had been opened.[23] On only one occasion did the accused appear simultaneously at both courts.[24]

Equally rare was the case of a transition from an accusation for 'healing sorcery' at the ecclesiastical courts to an indictment, six years later, for bewitching humans tried at the Assizes.[25] A comparison of Assize and ecclesiastical courts, and those presented at them, confirms the view that witchcraft beliefs and prosecutions were far more widespread than any one set of records would suggest. Only about one in fifteen of those accused of witchcraft at the Assizes appeared at the ecclesiastical courts and approximately only one in eighteen of those accused at the ecclesiastical courts appeared elsewhere. Despite the fact that we have two long lists of people suspected in connexion with witchcraft, there is little over-lapping.

In comparing the more than 220 persons in Essex accused at the ecclesiastical courts of witchcraft, black and white, to the rest of the country, the same difficulties occur as in a comparison of Assize prosecutions. The survival of records is uneven, the availability of printed material varies, the type of record for each area, as well as the comparative size of the popula-tion of each, differs enormously. Printed extracts from Winchester, Sussex, Oxford, Nottingham, and Durham ecclesiastical court records only yield twenty-one cases of witchcraft.[26] The only printed documents which contain a considerable number of cases are the Churchwardens' Present-ments for the Archdeaconries of Norwich, Norfolk, and Suffolk in 1597; witchcraft was presented fifteen times.[27]

If we turn to unprinted sources, however, we become aware of many more prosecutions. Some forty-six cases have been either printed or alluded to in the Diocese of York. On the basis of these it was concluded that 'for the laity it ranks as one of the major offences . . . about on a level with scolding and more frequent than drunkenness'.[28] A more detailed search of the unprinted cases has revealed a much larger number of cases, at least 111 between 1561 and 1637.[29] Of these, seventy-two were for 'white' witchcraft, thirty-four for the ambiguous 'witchcraft and sorcery' and only five for definitely maleficent witchcraft. The largest number of cases occurred in 1590 and 1598 (seventeen in each year).

An impression based on the printed extracts from Essex ecclesiastical records would not suggest anything exceptional about this county. Arch-deacon Hale, using the Act Books of the Archdeaconry of Essex, printed seven cases for the years 1564–1632.[30] Andrew Clark noted another nine cases from the same source:[31] but a total of sixteen is completely misleading. A more thorough search of the documents used by Hale and Clark has revealed over 126 cases: more references to witchcraft in one archdeaconry than could be gleaned from the printed ecclesiastical sources for the rest of England. This warns us not to trust printed extracts. It also suggests that, even compared to what we know of Yorkshire, Essex was exceptional. In one county there are a good many more cases than those surviving for the whole of the Diocese of York.

The widespread nature of witchcraft prosecutions in Essex villages has already been demonstrated. It remains to be seen how far such prosecutions were a rural phenomenon, or whether suspicions were just as strong in the towns of Essex whose borough records survive. Some twenty-five persons are known to have been accused in the borough courts of Maldon, Colchester, and Harwich. Several other towns—for instance, Chelmsford, Brentwood, and Braintree—had no borough courts: the number of witchcraft prosecutions from them, tried at the Assizes, does not suggest that witchcraft accusations were different in intensity according to the size of the town.

A number of Maldon witchcraft cases appeared at the Assize and ecclesiastical courts.[32] The borough court records add details concerning the activities of a group of treasure-seekers in 1591 who used magic and consulted Dr. Dee. The combined information concerning Maldon witchcraft to be derived from a pamphlet account and the informations against Margaret Wiseman in the borough records gives us a considerable insight into the situation in this town. Apart from the reference to a broom which mysteriously swept by itself, it seems that beliefs about witches were not essentially different here to those in near-by villages: there were the same fears of being cursed after quarrelling with a neighbour, and the same small, evil looking animals. Maldon has an especial interest as the home of George Gifford, whose works are of such importance for the study of Essex witchcraft. Gifford was Vicar of All Saints' only from 1582 to 1584, though he was a preacher there for most of the period until the end of the century. There is nothing to connect him directly with the prosecutions of 1574, 1579, and 1592. Nevertheless, it seems more than likely that some of his material was drawn from these accusations, and it may be more than a coincidence that his greatest work on the subject, the *Dialogue Concerning Witches and Witchcrafts*, should have been published in 1593, the year after the long and controversial trials of Margaret Wiseman, both at the borough and ecclesiastical courts.[33]

Roughly similar to Maldon, both in size and in its coastal position, was Harwich. There is no evidence that its borough court was active before 1601, but between that date and 1645 at least thirteen Harwich residents, two of them men and the rest women, are known to have been accused of witchcraft there.[34] The five accusations which took place in 1601 all ended in verdicts of guilty and an order that the suspects be executed.

Other women were sentenced to execution in 1606 and 1619. Unlike Maldon, therefore, the borough authorities inflicted the death penalty. As well as the indictments and recognizances there are two long depositions against suspected witches in 1618 and 1633. Both show that behind the prosecutions lay the same beliefs as we shall find in the villages: that the witch acted out of malice after being refused something, that she employed small animals to carry her evil power, that she caused violent and sudden illness. Reflecting the position of Harwich as a port, there was a preponderance of sailors as victims of witchcraft.

Only a third of the Elizabethan sessions rolls for Colchester borough court have survived. Some eight suspected witches, all but one of them women, were discovered in these records.[35] None of these appears to have been sentenced to execution, though at least two were imprisoned for a year and made to appear in the stocks. Three of these eight had previously been accused at the ecclesiastical courts, though none of them appears in the Assize records. There is a reference, however, in an Assize trial pamphlet of 1582, to a Colchester man who received a familiar from another witch.[36] The examinations of witches and witnesses reveal many interesting details, among them the suspicion of Alexander Bradock, surgeon, and Marcel Goodwyn, physician, of Colchester.[37] The fear of witches, and beliefs concerning their familiars and their evil activities, seem to have been both widespread and very similar to those in other parts of Essex.

A search of Essex borough records produces a total of twenty-five accused witches. Similar records from other counties remain to be searched in detail, but it seems likely that a considerable number of such cases were tried in them. Wallace Notestein listed over three dozen witchcraft references in borough records from all over England, among them, for instance, five from Great Yarmouth, four from King's Lynn, and five from Newcastle.[38] In his list there were only two Essex cases. Search of unprinted Essex material multiplies this by a factor of twelve. If this is a fair sample, we might expect over 400 cases for the whole of England, though it is probable that the total will be a good deal less than this. Again, witchcraft prosecutions are seen as a widespread phenomenon, with Essex heading the list.

CENTRAL COURTS

Only four witchcraft cases from Essex have been discovered in the Star Chamber records; these are all from the reign of James I. The practically unexplored Elizabethan records almost certainly contain a few more cases, but the bulk of such a source makes search impracticable until there is an index.[39] Only one of the four Essex cases appears in other Essex records: this concerned Edwin Haddesley who, a year after being accused of trying to use his 'magik glasse, or familier and conjuring glasse' to secure his release from a charge of deer-stealing, was accused at the Assizes for bewitching two people.[40] In none of the cases was the charge merely witchcraft. For example, in the first, the charge was fraud, counterfeiting the symptoms of being bewitched to earn money from sympathizers. The second case, we have seen, mainly concerned deer-stealing and assault. In the third, the Vicar of Radwinter believed that his enemies, in an attempt to oust him from his living, had conjured up 'fearfull and uglie shapes and formes of evill spiritts or divills'. The final case was a dispute over property; witchcraft only appeared incidentally as one of the means whereby a man was driven mad and hence gave away his land.

The records of the King's, or, in the Elizabethan period, Queen's, Bench are primarily of interest to the student of witchcraft because they contain coroners' inquests. These inquests were often on prisoners who had died in Colchester Gaol, and among them are a number of suspected witches. Some fourteen persons whose indictments are to be found in the Assize records died in prison between 1560 and 1603, but we also learn the names of six witches who do not appear in other records and another four who were also, almost certainly, incarcerated for witchcraft. Of the thirty-five accused women in 1645, at least nine had died of gaol fever or old age by 1647. As well as the inquisitions, we find three more obvious witchcraft cases. One, already in print, was a slander case in 1612, but the other two are identical to cases at the Assizes. The first, in 1561, concerned John Samon of Danbury and was transferred by writ to the Assizes, where it was tried in the same year. The second case was that of Edmund Mansell, accused at the Assizes in 1584 of burning a barn by 'magic art', a charge which came up in identical form at the Queen's Bench the following year; there is no recorded verdict.[41]

Only infrequently do we find references to witchcraft in the State Papers. In the seventeenth century there are a number of pardons granted to suspected witches in various parts of England, but none of these are from Essex. The only two Essex cases concern a Roman Catholic priest, who, in 1561, was examined for taking masses in Essex and for love magic in Hampshire, and a case of treasure-seeking by magic in 1577.[42] From another source, the papers of the House of Lords, we learn of a petition for the pardon of nine accused witches in 1645.[43] This petition may have saved some lives, but five of the accused were still in prison in 1648 and the rest had died in gaol.

The Privy Council only intervened in witchcraft cases where there was also a suspicion of treason, coining, prophesying, or other affairs of State.

This intervention was infrequent before 1560, reached a peak between 1578 and 1581, and terminated in 1589.[44] All seven Essex cases concerned sorcery, rather than that bewitching of one human by another which, we have seen, formed the bulk of the Assize cases. The first Essex case occurred in 1577, when Henry Chittam was sought and captured for the offences of coining and conjuring; the verdict is unknown, nor has Chittam's case been found in the Assize records, the court to which he was ordered. Another case of conjuration was ordered before the Privy Council in 1580; this overlaps with the treasure-seeking case of 1577 in the State Papers. In the same month a letter was sent to Mr. Darcie of Tiptree, soon to become notorious as a judge in the trial of witches, to apprehend Humfrey Poles 'for conjuration'; nothing more is known of this case. Within two months another letter was sent by the Privy Council, this time ordering that the boy accomplice of William Randell, committed with his master for conjuration, was to be released unless a serious charge could be brought against him. Randell was executed in 1581.[45] Again, in 1580 Nicholas Johnson was ordered to be released and examined concerning his sorcery, especially the 'making of her Majesties picture in wax'. The final group of letters written by the Privy Council, in 1580 and 1581, concerned the escape of Robert Mantell alias Bloise from Colchester Gaol. His crime, that of pretending to be King Edward, would not concern us if it had not been for the activities of his accomplices in the escape; they were accused 'with lewde practises of sorceries and conjuracions'. Mantell was sentenced to execution at the Hilary Assizes, 1581.[46]

It is possible that cases of slander which involved calling a person a witch may be found in the Courts of Requests and Common Pleas. Sampling of these extensive records has not, so far, produced any Essex cases.[47] On the whole, however, it seems fair to say that an analysis of witchcraft as represented in records deposited at the Public Record Office, excepting the Assize records, would give a very distorted and limited impression of Essex witchcraft. Very few of the more than 500 Essex individuals known to have been accused of witchcraft or sorcery appear in central records. No accurate study could be based merely on such sources. Nor can a comprehensive list of those suspected of witchcraft and sorcery be made until the massive central records are fully indexed. Cases are still being discovered —for instance, the names of three otherwise unknown Essex conjurers who were pardoned in 1568 have only recently appeared in a Calendar of Patent Rolls, and it seems likely that new cases will emerge as the Calendar proceeds.[48] Comparison of Essex cases to those for other parts of England suggests that Essex was again outstanding. In the State Papers Domestic there are two references to Essex witchcraft in the total of more than thirty cases for the whole of England.[49] After 1560 there were twenty-five references to witchcraft and conjuring in the Privy Council Acts, all occurring before 1589. Of these twenty-five, seven were Essex references, an exceptional proportion.

NOTES

1. These are shown on Map 5.
2. The Consistory and Commissary material is given in cases 1,111–27 and 1,128–38.
3. Cases 991–1,108 and 861–986. ⟶
4. *Visitation Articles and Injunctions of the Period of the Reformation*, ed. W. H. Frere (Alcuin Club Collections, xvi, 1910) 5, 85.
5. *Articles and Injunctions*, ed. Frere, vol. xv, 353 and vol. xvi, 313.
5. British Museum, 5,155.c.10.
7. The location of these sets of articles is given in the Bibliography, p. 318.
8. Some offences—for instance, attempting to heal a person by magical means—remained within the jurisdiction of the ecclesiastical courts after 1604, since they were not made offences by the Statute of that year.
9. This account of ecclesiastical court procedure is based on the following authorities as well as the actual court records: E. R. Brinkworth, 'The Study and Use of Archdeacon's Court Records', *Trans. Roy. Hist. Soc.*, 4th ser. xxv (1943); John Addy, *The Archdeacon and Ecclesiastical Discipline in Yorkshire, 1598–1714* (Borthwick Institute publications, 24, 1963); Kathleen Major, 'The Lincoln Diocesan Records', *Trans. Roy. Hist. Soc.*, 4th ser., xxii (1940).
10. For example, in case 931.
11. An exception was case 920, where a man was detected 'to be a Witche by his own confession'.
12. In all, we know of some forty-two accused witches who were ordered to purge themselves, but in only these sixteen cases has the result been found.
13. Case 910; details of the confession have been omitted in Appendix, that in 1,001 being particularly long and interesting.
14. Purgation could be costly—for instance, in case 917, after successful purgation, a woman owed 7s. 9d.
15. This refers to the number of a case in the Appendix.
16. For example, cases 947/1,143, 1,084/167, 1,049/269 are pairs from ecclesiastical and other sources.
17. Case 1,024.
18. Cases 983–5, 1,126–7.
19. The Danbury male witch appears, for example, in cases 241, 250, 253. This account of the ecclesiastical officials is based on Newcourt, *Repertorium*, i, 73, 92.
20. In case 794 a witch was said to have fled 'upon her confessyon before Mr. Archdeacon Cole', and the 1566 Pamphlet states that some of the Assize cases were tried before Cole.
21. Cases 970–4.
22. Case 1,122.
23. The twenty-year gap was between cases 22 and 1,035 (Joan Osborne): that of ten years between cases 157 and 1,084 (Agnes Heard).
24. Cases 269 and 1,049 (Joan Pakeman).
25. Cases 46 and 873, noted in Ewen, I, p. 125.

26. The sources for these cases are asterisked, and the page references to witchcraft cases given, in the Bibliography, pp. 319.
27. *Bishop Redman's Visitation, 1597*, ed. J. F. Williams (Norfolk Rec. Soc., xviii, 1946), p. 26.
28. J. S. Purvis, *Tudor Parish Documents of the Diocese of York* (Cambridge, 1948), pp. 198–9.
29. Dr. Philip Tyler, late of Magdalen College, Oxford, kindly lent the writer his abstracts of witchcraft cases. Mr. K. V. Thomas has found some further cases in the York Diocesan Archives.
30. William Hale, *Series of Precedents and Proceedings in Criminal Causes, 1475–1640* (1847), pp. 147, 148, 157, 163, 185–6, 219, 254.
31. *Lincoln Diocese Documents, 1450–1544*, ed. Andrew Clark (Early Eng. Text Soc., 1914), pp. 108–10.
32. The following Maldon cases occurred in other than borough records: 67–9, 119, 870, 947, 949, 1,200. The Maldon borough cases are 1,141–3.
33. There is a description of Gifford's works on witchcraft on p. 89, below; for Wiseman, see cases 947, 949, 1,075, 1,143.
34. Harwich cases are listed as numbers 1,144–63. Other Harwich women were sent to the Assizes in cases 580 (*a–d*), 586, 588, and in case 1,219 we hear of a woman in Harwich Gaol on suspicion of witchcraft in 1645.
35. Cases 1,164–76.
36. 1582 Pamphlet, sig. D2.
37. The latter was almost certainly the cunning man 'Goodin of Colchester', to whom a man sent in 1598 (case 1,096), and whose will is to be found at Chelmsford (E.R.O., D/ACW, 7/125). There is no reference to magical equipment in the will.
38. Notestein, *Witchcraft*, Appendix C.
39. Essex cases are 1,181–4. There are no sorcery cases in the selections and calendars for the period 1477–1603 listed in the Bibliography, p. 318.
40. Cases 488–9.
41. For John Samon see cases 1, 2*b*; he appears in P.R.O., K.B. 9, 600, m. 149–51 and 602, m. 209. Mansell was accused in cases 224, 225; see P.R.O., K.B. 9, 662, m. 48.
42. Cases 1,196–7. The second of these is continued in case 1,199.
43. The details are included in cases 613, 618, 624, 629, 637, 639, 645, 647, 648.
44. For Essex cases see Nos. 1,198–1,203. Notestein, *Witchcraft*, Appendix C, cites most of the English cases from this source.
45. R. Holinshed, *Chronicles* (1808 edn.), iv, 433.
46. P.R.O., Assizes 35/23/H, m. 48, 49.
47. No cases were found in *Select Cases in the Court of Requests*, ed. I. S. Leadam (Selden Soc., xii, 1898) or *Proceedings in the Court of Requests, 137–203* (P.R.O., Lists and Indexes, xxi, 1963). Ewen found a slander case in the Court of Common Pleas (Ewen, I, pp. 271–6).
48. Case, 1,206. I owe the reference to Mr. K. V. Thomas.
49. The *Calendar of State Papers, Domestic*, for the years 1547–1660 was searched; most of the references have been collected in Notestein, *Witchcraft*, Appendix C, as are Privy Council cases.

Chapter 5

Literary sources for the study of witchcraft

THE BACKGROUND TO FORMAL PROSECUTIONS: EVIDENCE FROM THE WITCHCRAFT PAMPHLETS

Reports of the depositions of witnesses and the examinations of suspects have occasionally survived in the form of popular pamphlets whose titles suggest that they were written for the sensation-loving London literary market. It will be one of the major tasks of this chapter to discuss how reliable these accounts are. This is possible, since they often describe trials at the Assize courts, which can be checked against the actual indictments. The comparison of these two sources also allows an estimate to be made concerning the fullness of the Assize indictments. The pamphlets themselves provide three principal kinds of information of value for this study; they give added information about those involved in prosecutions, their age, wealth, personality, and relationships: they indicate how witchcraft was believed to work, the power of cursing, the use of spells and familiars; they reveal the motives ascribed to witches and the actual incident which was believed to have prompted the bewitching. As such they are of vital importance in the subsequent analysis.

Essex is fortunate in possessing five detailed pamphlets.[1] These did not necessarily mirror the actual number of prosecutions, as may be seen in the following table:

TABLE 6

Assize prosecutions and pamphlets compared, Essex, 1560–1680
(Years with twelve or more indictments, a pamphlet or both)

Year	Number of Indictments	Pamphlet	Year	Number of Indictments	Pamphlet
1566	4	P	1589	19	P
1572	16	—	1592	14	—
1574	15	—	1593	13	—
1576	12	—	1594	17	—
1579	13	P	1601	12	—
1582	18	P	1616	13	—
1584	35	—	1645	50	P(×2)

Thus we see that the year 1584, with thirty-five indictments, has no surviving pamphlet, while 1566, with only four indictments, has a pamphlet account. Another point to emerge from Table 6 is that the state of affairs revealed in the pamphlets is not extraordinary, though it may appear so to us. Taken by themselves, pamphlet accounts might appear to describe isolated outbreaks of prosecutions, perhaps encouraged by some particular crisis or witch-hunter. Yet, when they are compared to the known Assize indictments, they come to be seen as only a minute sample of what was occurring at the time. Of 163 men and women who are known to have been indicted for witchcraft at the Essex Assizes between 1560 and 1600, only twenty-three were described in the Elizabethan pamphlets, detailed though they are. Another 140 trials are not described. Nor, if we compare the descriptions in the pamphlets to those in accounts which are as detailed, do we find them to be unrepresentative of current ideas.[2]

As indicated in Table 6, there are Essex pamphlets for 1566, 1579, 1582, 1589, and two for 1645. At least one further pamphlet is known to have existed, but appears to have been lost. This described the activities of a notorious Essex witch executed in 1575; five indictments against her have survived in the Assize records.[3] The first Essex pamphlet, therefore, describes the Assize trial in 1566. The cases, involving three women, all from the village of Hatfield Peverel, came before a distinguished panel of judges, including the Queen's Attorney, a later Chancellor of the Exchequer, and a justice of the Queen's Bench. The whole pamphlet gives the impression that witchcraft beliefs were already complex and widespread.[4]

Ten people were prosecuted at the Essex Assizes in 1579. They came from widely-spaced villages and there is no evidence that any of the cases were linked.[5] This, therefore, can be used as a sample year; it has neither a concentration of cases in one area, nor an extraordinary number of prosecutions. It seems fair to assume that if we can gain a more detailed account of some of the cases so barely set out in the indictments we could apply conclusions drawn from them to other years with a similar pattern. Fortunately, such an account is available because the Lent Assizes were described in a contemporary pamphlet. Of the seven women against whom indictments were made, only four appear in the pamphlet account.[6]

Ellen Smythe, spinster, was prosecuted at the Assizes for bewitching a child, Susan Webbe, on 7 March so that it died on the next day; she was found guilty. This bare outline is filled in by the pamphlet. Ellen confessed that, after a quarrel between her daughter and the daughter of Widow Webbe, she met young Susan and, being angry, 'gave here a blowe on the face, whereupon so soone as the child came home she sickened, and languishyng two daies, cried continually, awaie with the Witche, awaie with the Witch, and so died'. Immediatcly after this Widow Webbe saw 'a thyng like to a blacke Dogge goe out at her doore, and presently at the sight thereof, she fell distraught of her wittes'. This second bewitching, like two other suspicions, did not appear as an indictment. We also learn that Ellen Smithe was the daughter of an earlier Maldon witch, Alice Chaundler,[7] and that among the witnesses was Ellen's own son, aged thirteen years, who described his mother's familiars in great detail.

Another woman described in the pamphlet was Margery Stanton of Wimbish. In 1578 she had been found guilty at the Quarter Sessions of bewitching a gelding. The case was later tried at the Assizes, but the indictment, probably because it failed to name the owner of the bewitched gelding, was found insufficient.[8] From court records alone this would appear to be a mild prosecution, but the pamphlet reveals a web of suspicions behind this one official accusation. Among the misfortunes supposedly inflicted by Margery's witchcraft were: tormenting a man, killing chickens, causing a woman to swell so that she looked pregnant and nearly burst, making cattle give 'gore stynking blood' instead of milk, making a child ill, and tormenting another so that it 'fell into suche shrickyng and staryng, wringyng and writhyng of the bodie to an fro, that all that sawe it, were doubtful of the life of it.' Perhaps the most peculiar effect of her wrath occurred after she had been denied yeast. After her departure:

> a child in the Cradle was teken vehemently sicke, in a mervelous strange maner, whereupon the mother of the childe tooke it up in her armes to comforte it, which beyng done, the Cradle rocked of it self, sixe or seven tymes, in presence of one of the Earle of Surries gentilmen, who seying it stabbed his dagger three or fower tymes into the Cradle ere it staied: Merily iestyng and saieyng, that he would kill the Devill, if he could bee rocked there.

This type of witchcraft act was hardly likely to appear in a formal indictment. Nor did the motives of the witch. In Margery's case she quarrelled with a man who cut her face, later he grabbed some corn she was carrying and threw it to his chickens; these promptly died. In another case she 'came often to the house of one John Hopwood of Walden, and had continually her requestes, at the laste beyng denied of a Leathern thong she went her waie offended and the same night his Geldyng in the stable ... died sodainly'. She did not employ familiars, but her suspicious behaviour aroused comment. When asked what she was doing making a circle in front of a house and digging it full of holes, she replied that she was making 'a shityng house for her self after that sorte': the next day the goodwife fell sick on the spot. Perhaps most interesting of all was the fact that among her victims was the Vicar of Wimbish's child, the child recovering on the godly man's return. The Vicar was no other than

William Harrison, who had two years earlier published his famous description of England.[9]

The final case concerned Mother Nokes of Lamborne, the Alice Nokes who was found guilty of bewitching Elizabeth Barfott to death.[10] This case is a little different from the others in that the motives for the supposed bewitchings were not refused loans, but rudeness, sexual jealousy, and quarrelling. In one instance Mother Nokes's daughter had her gloves snatched away by a youth and her mother was angry: the unfortunate young man was paralysed soon after and had to be carried home in a wheelbarrow. In another case she was angered by the refusal of a plough-man to answer her questions, or so the ploughman conjectured when he ascribed the swelling on his horse's head to her witchcraft rather than to his own carelessness. This act of witchcraft, as well as the bewitching of the youth, were not recorded in the indictments.

Even a lengthy summary of the 1579 trial does not do justice to the wealth of detail provided by the pamphlet, but it does indicate how limited an impression the actual indictments provide. A comparison of the 1589 pamphlet with the indictments for that year emphasizes this point. In the Assize indictments we learn that Joan Cunny was suspected of bewitching four people.[11] To this the pamphlet adds a lengthy description of how Joan obtained her power. She had been taught her witchcraft by one Mother Humfrye of Maplestead,[12] who told her 'that she must kneele down upon her knees, and make a Circle on the ground, and pray unto Sathan the cheefe of the Devills'. She tried this and was rewarded with two spirits like 'two black frogges', to whom she promised her soul. Nor does the single indictment against Joan Prentice give any hint of the long struggle with the Devil which Joan underwent before becoming a witch. While sitting in her chamber one night the Devil appeared to her 'in the shape and propor-tion of a dunnish coloured ferrit' and demanded 'Jane Prentice give me thy soule' to whom she answered, 'In the name of god what art thou?' to which, in hideous parody, the ferret replied, 'I am satan, feare me not.' The most unusual feature of the pamphlet, however, was the final description of the scene at the scaffold. First the circuit judge commended the illegitimate children for their depositions and then 'one Maister Ward a learned divine' exhorted the women to repent. The convicted women then said a few prayers with the preacher and admitted that they deserved to die. Joan Upney was especially penitent, crying out that 'she had greevously sinned, that the devill had deceived her ... asking God and the world forgivenes, even to ye last gaspe'.

In the number of indictments at the Assizes, the year 1582 was not exceptional. Two years later there were twice as many. On the other hand, both 1582 and 1645, the years of the remaining three pamphlets, can be seen to be exceptional from Map 4. Unlike other trials, they were concentrated on a small area, in both cases the north-east tip of Essex. Another common feature was the presence in each year of a man more than normally interested in the trial of witches—in 1582 Justice Darcy, in 1645 Matthew Hopkins.[13] Unfortunately, it has been on accounts of these somewhat exceptional trials, with their long pamphlets, that most descriptions of Essex witchcraft have been based.

Another possibly exceptional feature of the 1582 pamphlet is that it may have been written by Brian Darcy, the Justice who examined the suspects before the Assize trial, under the initials 'W.W.'[14] Brian Darcy certainly took particular pains in examining the suspects and his methods included much cajoling and bullying. Some of the confessions, as Reginald Scot argued, were 'wonne through hope of favour, and extorted by flatterie or threats', and the trial contains the first Essex evidence of a jury of women systematically searching for the witch's mark.[15] Darcy's interest is further explained by the fact that his family owned property or Church presentations in all the villages from which suspects came. He himself was lord of one of the manors in St. Osyth's, the pivot of the prosecutions. Lord Darcy, his father, was believed to have been bewitched to death,[16] and Ursula Kempe, the woman whose confessions formed the backbone of the prosecutions, bewitched Grace Thurlowe's child—Grace being a servant of Lord Darcy.[17] On the other hand, there is no simple correlation between Darcy property and the prosecutions. The family was powerful in a number of villages in which there were few or no prosecutions during Elizabeth's reign.[18]

Comparison of indictments and pamphlet accounts supports the general accuracy of both sources. Although there is not always exact overlapping, since each source contains material not found in the other,[19] when they are describing the same event there is little direct contradiction. When there is disagreement, it is on minor matters and supports the general impression of accuracy. For instance, the indictment against Annis Herd in 1582 declared that she had bewitched one cow, ten sheep, and ten lambs of John Wade: the pamphlet said that John's bewitched livestock were all lambs.[20] Or there were slight disagreements over dates; for example, in the 1579 pamphlet Elizabeth Francis confessed to bewitching Poole's wife 'about Lent last (as she now remembreth)', while the indictment stated that she bewitched Alice Poole, wife of Richard, on 26 June—a little late for Lent.[21] It can, therefore, be confidently stated that those who wrote the pamphlets were accurate and almost certainly eye-witness reporters.

A comparison of the pamphlets and indictments further shows that the 487 indictments for black witchcraft which reached the Assizes court were only a small portion of the actual suspicions against witches. Comparison of the 1579 indictments and pamphlet have shown how much lay behind each indictment, and if we look at the other pamphlets we find further evidence that prosecutions seriously understress the actual accusations made at the courts. There are surviving indictments in the Assize records for eighteen women who were also described in the pamphlets. In these indictments they are specified as having thirty-one victims. From the pamphlets, however, we learn the names of another fifty-seven victims not mentioned in the indictments, yet suffering from the witchcraft of these eighteen women.[22] Thus it would appear that approximately one in three of those believing themselves to be bewitched went as far as making a formal charge in the courts, registered as an indictment. Thus for each witch there were roughly four victims. Instead of the impression created by the indictments of a direct quarrel between two persons, witchcraft begins to emerge as the result of a person being suspected by a number of village families, all of whom felt themselves to have been injured. Further, it appears that, just as only one in three suspicions became formulated into an indictment, possibly more than one in four suspected witches were never openly accused in court at all. In the four pamphlets twenty-seven witches are named, but only eighteen appear in the indictments.[23] Pamphlets, therefore, are a vital and reliable source, providing otherwise inaccessible material and correcting the somewhat narrow impression of witchcraft prosecutions given by indictments.

Notestein has provided a general account of the pamphlet literature in England throughout this period.[24] From his list we can see that the detailed evidence available for Essex survives for many other English counties. Although, as we have seen, the existence of pamphlets is a far from accurate index of the amount of prosecutions, it is still worth recording the impression that Essex pamphlets are unusually early. Five of the twenty-eight 'Major English Witch Trials as Recorded in Contemporary Pamphlets'[25] were from Essex. Of these five, four were in the period 1560–90; the rest of England only contributed two. But of the twenty-two pamphlets which are listed between 1590 and 1682, Essex witchcraft only inspired one.

CONTEMPORARY COMMENTS ON WITCHCRAFT PROSECUTIONS:
EVIDENCE FROM LITERARY SOURCES

English diarists of the sixteenth and seventeenth centuries seldom mentioned witchcraft trials; in Essex only three diaries contain such references.[26] Although there were many witch trials in neighbouring villages, Richard Rogers, preacher at Wethersfield from about 1575 to

1618, showed no interest in the subject in his diary, which covers the years 1587–90.[27] The next diarist of interest to us, Arthur Wilson, was an extreme Protestant like Rogers. As steward to the Earl of Warwick he was present at the sensational trial of witches in 1645. He showed considerable scepticism in his later comments on the trial, arguing that he 'could see nothing in the evidence which did perswade me to thinke them other than poore, mellenchollie, envious, mischevous, ill-disposed, ill-dieted, atrabilius constitutions'.[28] Covering the same period as Wilson's account is the diary of Ralph Josselin, Vicar of Earl's Colne from 1641 to 1683. No prosecutions for witchcraft or sorcery after 1587 have been discovered for this village, yet Josselin twice noted informal suspicions of witchcraft.[29] In 1656 'one J. Biford was clamoured on as a witch, and Mr. C. thought his child ill by it', but Josselin believed the 'poor wretch innocent as to that evil'. On the second occasion the case was reported by the minister of Gaines Colne and concerned one Anne Crow, who was suspected as a witch and was discovered acting suspiciously beside a grave. These two suspicions never seem to have grown into formal prosecutions, reminding us that the court cases upon which statistics are based only represent a fraction of the actual witchcraft beliefs. The final diary account describes the ducking of a witch in 1699. Some very extraordinary details are given but the case is not known to have come before the courts.[30]

The minute books of religious and political bodies are even less informative about Essex witchcraft. Among the many matters discussed at the Dedham Classis in 1588 was the question, moved by Mr. Salmon, of how a witch might be known:

> it was thought fittest to geve it over to some Justice to examyne it, and that there must be some usuall experience of evell effects to ensue of their displeasure and some presumption of the death of man or beast: some said she might be found out by serche in her bodie, some thought that to be fancy in the people easilie conceiving such a thinge and to be reproved in them.[31]

Thus this group of Puritan ministers showed a mixture of credulity and caution. In a minute book of another kind, that of the Parliamentary County Committee during the Civil War, there is no reference to witchcraft at all, although there is such a reference in the equivalent records for Suffolk.[32]

There are no references to Essex witchcraft in contemporary newspaper accounts, though they refer to witchcraft trials in near-by counties.[33] Only slightly more helpful are contemporary biographies, one of which refers to some examinations in two witchcraft prosecutions at the Quarter Sessions in 1570. These were held before Sir Thomas Smith, and include fascinating details concerning anti-witchcraft charms, familiars, the motives of witches, and other matters. Smith showed no particular scepticism at the extraordinary accounts.[34] None of the individuals concerned appear in other records; without this accidental reference, we would never have known that Theydon Garnon was the scene of witchcraft suspicions.

The activities of seventeenth-century astrologers occasionally provide evidence about Essex witchcraft. There is a letter to Richard Napier from Matthew Evans, requesting the return of various books mislaid by Evans when he was accused of conjuring. Two years after this letter, in 1623, Evans was again in trouble, and was examined in connexion with the supposed bewitching of the Countess of Sussex in Hampshire. The ancestral home of the Earl of Sussex was at Boreham in Essex, but nothing concerning Evans or the bewitching of the Countess has been discovered in Essex records.[35] In the same Richard Napier's case-book there is a very detailed and interesting account of the supposed bewitching of the house, grounds, and persons belonging to the Aylett family of Magdalen Laver.[36] The case started in 1633 and continued until at least 1646, in the later part in the case-books of the astrologer William Lilly. None of the possible total of fifteen suspected witches appear in the court records, although the whole case may overlap with some strange magical rites occurring in 1643.[37]

As in other counties, references to witchcraft continued to appear in literary sources throughout the eighteenth and nineteenth centuries. These illustrate that beliefs did not immediately evaporate the moment official prosecutions ended. Old women were still informally tried by being immersed in water. Nevertheless, it is clear that this is a different phenomenon from the universally approved and widespread prosecutions of the earlier period. No references to Essex witchcraft were found in either family papers or the poetry and drama of the period.[38]

A number of writers included Essex examples in their general works on English witchcraft. It is possible that Reginald Scot was goaded into writing his classic work by the 1582 Essex trial. Certainly he alluded to it with scorn and may be describing the same trial, though his evidence is not from the pamphlet, when he described an Essex justice who 'thought he was bewitched, in the verie instant whiles he examined the witch; so as his leg was broken thereby'.[39] The next Essex reference occurs in a work by the exorcist John Darrell. Although this purported to be an actual trial at the Quarter Sessions, no record of the case has been discovered in the actual rolls of the court.[40] One of Darrell's major critics was Samuel Harsnet, the author of a number of works on witchcraft and Archdeacon of Essex from 1603 to 1609. Harsnet does not, however, refer to any specifically Essex cases in his works.[41] It is just possible that Darrell's case of possession is the same as that referred to in the following year by Dr.

Jorden. As an example of a womb disease, he cited 'an Essex Gentlewoman of good note' who was convulsed and distracted over a period of fifteen years and was persuaded 'by a stranger Physition' that she was bewitched.[12]

It is not until 1627 that there is another Essex reference. In that year Richard Bernard narrated how he had a long discussion at Castle Hedingham in Essex with a penitent white witch, one Edmunds of Cambridge.[43] Three years later a young man at Colchester was molested by the Devil, according to a subsequent account by Nathaniel Crouch. The same author described the 1645 Essex trial of witches, but added no fresh details to the pamphlet account.[44] More important for the history of Essex witchcraft is the work of Thomas Ady, published in 1656. He drew examples of old spells, the discovery of fraudulent cunning folk, and the use of ventriloquism to counterfeit possession, from Essex, and it is probable that he lived at Wethersfield in that county.[45]

The 1645 trial in Essex attracted the attention of Richard Baxter at the end of the century, though he added no significant details, despite his talks to 'many Understanding, Pious and Credible Persons' who witnessed the trial.[46] Nor does Francis Hutchinson, writing in 1718, add any new details in his descriptions of the famous 1582 and 1645 trials. He makes three allusions to the latter trial, but muddles up the Essex and Suffolk confessions.[47] One other writer with general Essex connexions was Thomas Pickering, who wrote a long introduction to William Perkins' *Damned Art of Witchcraft* in 1608. Pickering made no specific references to Essex witchcraft cases, but he was Minister of Finchingfield in Essex at the time. His presence at Finchingfield had no recorded effect on witchcraft prosecutions; there were no cases during the years of his residence. Two other writers who concentrated their attention on the 1645 Essex trial were John Stearne and Matthew Hopkins.[48] Both were resident in the county and both took a leading part in the actual prosecutions. It is in large measure their works which have been the basis for the reputation of Essex as a centre of prosecution. Neither, however, discussed any other Essex trial.

The most valuable authority for Essex witchcraft is George Gifford. Because of his supreme importance, discussion of his work has been reserved to the end of the chapter. Gifford was a leading Essex Puritan, and minister and lecturer at Maldon for most of the time after 1582 until his death in 1620. His two books on witchcraft, written in 1587 and 1593, provide a wealth of personal observation which will be incorporated in subsequent chapters.[49] Comparison of these works with the descriptions of actual prosecutions shows that Gifford was a keen and accurate observer. Unfortunately, however, it has been impossible to relate the various narratives of witchcraft cases included in the books to actual cases. For

instance, when Gifford speaks of a witch being executed who lived at
'W.H.', seven miles away, it is tempting to deduce that this is West
Haningfield, eight miles from Maldon;[50] but there is no known prosecution in that village. Again, 'old mother W of great T' fits no one living in
either of the Essex 'great T's', Great Totham and Great Tey.[51] There is
no known 'Mother Barlie of W', nor have any familiars with the names of
'Lightfoot', 'Lunch' or 'Makeshift' emerged in any of the pamphlets.[52]
Thus Gifford either altered initials and names or invented fictitious, if
typical, cases. A third, though less likely, possibility is that all the records
for these cases have been lost. The general impression from Gifford's
works is that witchcraft was a familiar and pervasive force; as one speaker
put it, 'They say there is scarce any towne or village in all this shire, but
there is one or two witches at the least in it.'[53]

If we except Gifford, the literary evidence for Essex witchcraft would
give an entirely distorted impression of prosecutions. It would leave us
with the opinion that there were only three trials of any consequence in
Essex, in 1570, 1582, and 1645, the last of these being by far the most
important. We would also know of a few instances of trickery and fraud,
some charms, and two suspected witches recorded by a mid-seventeenth-
century vicar. If we compare this with the actual pattern of prosecutions
and beliefs revealed in legal records, we see what a distortion and under-
estimation this would be. Yet, as was pointed out in the Introduction,
until the work of Notestein on pamphlet literature and, even more
importantly, Ewen on court records, all histories of English witchcraft
were of necessity based on these slight and distorting sources. It is hardly
surprising if the picture produced was of sporadic and sudden 'epidemics',
outbreaks of 'superstition', instead of the everyday fears and constant
accusations revealed by court records.

Literary sources on their own do not create the impression that Essex
was substantially different in its witchcraft fears from other parts of the
country. Contemporary writers did not comment that this county was in
any way exceptional in the intensity of its prosecutions. For instance,
Reginald Scot, in his *Discovery of Witchcraft* of 1584, drew most of his
examples of witchcraft from his native county of Kent. Gifford alone
remarked that, as far as witchcraft was concerned, Essex was a 'bad
countrey, I think even one of the worst in England'.[54] Since he had lived
in this county practically all his life, his opinion, though interesting, is
impressionistic. Of the twenty-seven 'major writers on English witchcraft'
listed by R. H. Robbins, some four had Essex connexions: Gifford,
Harsnet, Hopkins, and Ady, although Harsnet wrote when absent from
the county.[55] Once again Essex appears to lead the field, but there are
many representatives from other counties.

¶A true and iuſt Recorde, of
the Information, Examination
and Confeſſion of all the Witches, taken at
S. Oſes in the countie of Eſſex: whereof
ſome were executed, and other ſome en-
treated according to the determi-
nation of lawe.

Wherein all men may ſee what a peſtilent
people Witches are, and how vnworthy to lyue
in a Chriſtian Commons
wealth.

Written orderly, as the ca-
ſes were tryed by euidence,
By W.W.

¶Imprinted in London at the
three Cranes in the Vinetree by
Thomas Dawſon
1582.

1 Title page of *A true and just Recorde, of the Information,
Examination and Confession of all the Witches, taken at S. Oses
in the countie of Essex*, 1582
(British Museum)

2 John Norden's map of Essex, 1594 (Essex Record Office)

All the comparisons of Essex and other counties show that witchcraft beliefs were widespread through England. Leaving aside Ewen's work on Assize records, we would have received no impression of a particular Essex bias. In his second book Ewen quotes some eighty-three depositions and confessions.[56] Seven of these come from Essex and seventy-six from other parts of the country. These include six from Somerset, Suffolk, and London, five from Yorkshire and Kent, and two or more from Northumberland, Cornwall, Dorset, Huntingdonshire, Staffordshire, Bedfordshire, Worcestershire, Middlesex, Leicestershire, Lancashire, Wiltshire, Norfolk, Devon, Hertfordshire, and Northamptonshire. Another five come singly from counties. If Essex leads here, it is by a narrow margin. Notestein's study of the whole of England does not give the impression that witchcraft prosecutions were localized. His 299 placed references in the appendix of cases indicate that in witchcraft we are dealing with a widespread phenomenon.[57] The list shows Middlesex (51 cases), Yorkshire (32), and Norfolk (21) to be areas of apparently intense prosecution, with Northumberland (19), Kent (18), and Wiltshire (15) next; Lancashire (14), Essex (14), Somerset (13) and Suffolk (11) also have over ten references. There are thirteen other counties with over four references and another fifteen with between one and three. The only county not mentioned is Westmorland. These figures have been given at length because they show that, until intensive research was undertaken on Essex legal records, that county did not appear exceptional. They also show how much material is already available for other local studies of witchcraft prosecutions.

NOTES

1. Titles and location of the Essex pamphlets are given on p. 317, above.
2. For instance, the depositions in cases 1,163, 1,170, 1,173, and 1,204 are very similar, as is the whole of Gifford's *Dialogue*.
3. The pamphlet was entitled *The Examination and Confession of a notorious Witch named Mother Arnold, alias Whitecote, alias Glastonbury, at the Assize of Burntwood in July, 1574; who was hanged for Witchcraft at Barking, 1575*. Notestein, *Witchcraft*, p. 386, wrongly ascribed this 'Burntwood' to Staffordshire, but there can be little doubt that, as Ewen (I, p. 129) noted, this refers to Brentwood in Essex and the indictments to Cecilia Glasenberye of Barking, cases 75–9. The title is mentioned in W. T. Lowndes, *Bibliographer's Manual* (1834), iv, 1967, but no further trace of it has been found.
4. Those involved in this pamphlet are described in ch. 6, p. 94, below.
5. See Map 5, p. 71 above, for distribution of prosecutions at the various trials.
6. Cases 118–23. Elizabeth Frauncis, described in the 1566 pamphlet, is omitted in the ensuing description.
7. Alice Chaundler appeared at the Assizes in 1574, cases 67–9.

8. Cases 122, 810.
9. William Harrison, *An Historicall Description of the Island of Britayne*, first published in Raphael Holinshed, *Chronicles* (1577), vol. i. Harrison was vicar of Wimbish from 1571 to 1581, and the bewitched son was almost certainly Edmund. There is no known reference to this affair in his writings. Newcourt, *Repertorium*, ii, 674.
10. Case 120.
11. Cases 288–91.
12. Possibly the cunning woman 'Mother Humfrey' in case 992.
13. The 1645 trial is so complex that it has been described separately in ch. 9, p. 135, below.
14. A detailed knowledge of what happened both in the court-room and in private conversations between Darcy and various suspects, added to a tendency to lapse into the first person singular, suggests that Brian Darcy was the author. For example, the pamphleteer wrote, 'These aforesaide 5 last recited matters, being confessed by the saide Ursley privately to me the sayde Brian Darcey' (sig. A8^v). The pamphlet was dedicated to Brian Darcy's father.
15. 1582 pamphlet, sigs. D4 and E5^v.
16. Ibid., sig. C8.
17. Ibid., sig. A^v.
18. For instance, Tolshunt Darcy, Brightlingsea, Great Wigborough, and Weleigh. For the Darcy family, see Morant, *Essex*, i, 457–9, 476–88, and ii, 111, 139–40.
19. Usually the pamphlets were much more detailed, but occasionally, as in cases 17, 18, an indictment contained information omitted in the pamphlet account.
20. Case 167.
21. Case 123.
22. 'Victim' is used here to mean either the actual human being maimed or killed or the owner of bewitched property. These four 'pamphlets' used to compare with the indictments are, in fact, those of 1566, 1579, 1589, and a set of ecclesiastical depositions summarized in the Appendix as case 861. The latter is included rather than the very detailed 1582 pamphlet because, for the reasons explained, the 1582 trial seems exceptional.
23. The suspected witches mentioned in pamphlets, but omitted from court records, are listed as cases 1,208–16.
24. Notestein, *Witchcraft*, Appendix A.
25. The list of 'Major English Witch Trials' was made by R. H. Robbins, *Encyclopedia of Witchcraft and Demonology* (1959), pp. 168–9.
26. English diaries, generally, are not known to contain many references to witchcraft; for example, Notestein, *Witchcraft*, Appendix C, only cites one extra-Essex diary.
27. *Two Elizabethan Puritan Diaries*, ed. M. M. Knappen (Chicago, 1933); nor does the other diary, that of Samuel Ward, contain any witchcraft reference.
28. Francis Peck, *Desiderata Curiosa* (1779), ii, 476.
29. The first extract comes from the printed, the second from the unprinted, part of the diary; they are reprinted in H. Smith, *Ecclesiastical History of Essex* (n.d., about 1932), pp. 222, 417.
30. William Gilbert, 'Witchcraft in Essex', *Trans. Essex Arch. Soc.*, n.s., xi (1911), 211–18; E. L. Cutts, 'Curious extracts from a MS. diary, of the time of James II and William and Mary', *Trans. Essex Arch. Soc.*, i (1858), 126–7.
31. *The Presbyterian Movement in the Reign of Queen Elizabeth*, ed. R. G. Usher (Camden Soc., 3rd Ser., viii, 1905), p. 70.

32. There is no reference in the Romford Committee's Order Book as described in B. W. Quintrell, 'The Divisional Committee for Southern Essex during the Civil War' (Manchester Univ. M.A. thesis, 1962), and Mr. Quintrell has kindly informed the writer that he has not come across witchcraft in any other Committee records, or in the Colchester Civil War papers. For Suffolk see Alan Everitt, *Suffolk and the Great Rebellion, 1640–1660* (Suffolk Rec. Soc., iii, 1960), p. 73.

33. For newspaper references to witchcraft in other counties, including a description of the Essex witch-finder Matthew Hopkins when he was in Suffolk, see Notestein, *Witchcraft*, Appendix C, under the years 1643–52.

34. See case 1,204. Smith had earlier examined William Wycherley concerning sorcery, Kittredge, *Witchcraft*, pp. 211–12; neither incident is mentioned in Mary Dewar, *Sir Thomas Smith: a Tudor Intellectual in Office* (1964).

35. Bodleian Library, Ashmole MS. 421, fol. 170; I owe this and the following reference to Mr. Keith Thomas. For the 1623 case see C. L. Ewen, *Robert Ratcliffe, 5th Earl of Sussex: The Witchcraft Allegations in his Family* (n.p., 1938).

36. See case 1,207.

37. Case 840.

38. Except for some verses on the subject in the 1597 edition of the *Poems of Sir Francis Hubert*, ed. B. Mellor (Oxford, 1961), pp. 58–60. It is interesting that this Essex gentleman should have omitted the verses in a later edition of 1629. I owe this reference to the kindness of Mr. Christopher Hill. Neither Notestein, *Witchcraft*, nor K. M. Briggs, *Pale Hecate's Team* (1962), the latter an excellent description of literary sources, contains any specifically Essex references in poetry or drama.

39. Scot, *Discovery*, pp. 37, 62, 236; see also *A Discourse upon divels and spirits*, appended to the 1584 edition of Scot's *Discovery*, but omitted in later editions, pp. 542–3.

40. Case 1,205.

41. For a discussion of Harsnet and his works, see Notestein, *Witchcraft*, ch. 4.

42. Edward Jorden, *A Briefe Discourse of a Disease Called the Suffocation of the Mother* (1603), pp. 6ᵛ, 17, 22. A passing reference to a possession case at Colchester at the turn of the century is made in John Swan, *A True and Briefe Report of Mary Glover's Vexation* (1603), p. 70.

43. Bernard, *Guide*, p. 137. Edmunds does not appear elsewhere in Essex sources.

44. R.B., *Kingdom of Darkness* (1688), pp. 21, 22, 148–59.

45. Ady, *Candle*, pp. 58, 62, 79, 101, 109.

46. Richard Baxter, *The Certainty of the Worlds of Spirits* (1691), pp. 52–3.

47. Francis Hutchinson, *An Historical Essay Concerning Witchcraft* (1718), pp. 29, 61, 70.

48. Stearne, *Confirmation*; Hopkins, *Discovery* (1647). For their activities see ch. 9, p. 137, below.

49. Gifford, *Dialogue* and *Discourse*.

50. *Dialogue*, sig. D4ᵛ.

51. Ibid., sig. C4.

52. Ibid., sig. C; no cunning woman at 'R.H.' (sig. B) was located. Thus it seems a little premature to include Gifford's cases in a list of actual prosecutions, as did Notestein, *Witchcraft*, pp. 394–5.

53. *Dialogue*, sig. A4ᵛ.

54. Gifford, *Dialogue*, sig. A4ᵛ.

55. R. H. Robbins, *Encyclopedia of Witchcraft and Demonology* (1959), p. 167.

56. Ewen, II, in the text; other cases are printed in his appendices.

57. Notestein, *Witchcraft*, Appendix C.

Chapter 6

The background to witchcraft prosecutions in three Essex villages, 1560–99

Previous chapters have discussed the location and distribution of witch-craft prosecutions throughout Essex. Many of the most important problems facing the historian of witchcraft can, however, only be solved after very intensive research. Such research is only possible at the village level, because the task of discovering everything about the social background to witchcraft accusations necessitates detailed local knowledge. Among the questions that such a study would hope to answer, a few may be singled out as illustrations: the proportion of all misfortunes in a village which were attributed to witches; the frequency with which suspected witches were also suspected of other offences—for instance, adultery or scolding; whether people were believed to bewitch their relations by blood or marriage or non-relatives; to what extent accusations were confined to groups of neighbours living in the same street or the same manor. A detailed analysis of three villages within which there were a number of witchcraft accusations has been undertaken. The results of this analysis will be incorporated in subsequent chapters on specific problems. In this chapter the sources and methods of study will be outlined and the villages will be described generally.

The three villages chosen were the adjacent ones of Hatfield Peverel, Boreham, and Little Baddow. They were selected because Hatfield Peverel is the earliest Essex village to be described in a witchcraft pamphlet, that of 1566.[1] The two neighbouring villages, both of them containing prosecuted witches, were selected as a balance to the clearly exceptional Hatfield Peverel. The group lies some five miles to the east of Chelmsford, in the area where prosecutions first emerged in Essex.[2] In all, there were fourteen persons prosecuted at the Assizes from these three villages. If we compare this to the total of 291 persons for the whole of Essex, it is clear that this is a small sample of the widespread suspicions in the county. Table 7 lists the names of suspected witches in the three villages.

In none of the villages were there prosecutions after 1594. A comparison of the dates of the accusations suggests that the pressures behind them

TABLE 7
List of suspected witches in three Essex villages, 1560–99

Name	Dates of Trials	Courts	Case number
HATFIELD PEVEREL			
Lora Winchester	1566	Assize	16
Elizabeth Fraunces	1566, 1572, 1579	Assize, Quarter Ss.	17, 50, 123
Agnes Waterhouse	1566	Assize, Quarter Ss.	18, 793
Joan Waterhouse	1566	Assize, Quarter Ss.	19, 793
Joan Osborne	1567, 1579, 1587	Assize, Archdeaconry	22, 1,035
Agnes Francys	1572	Assize	58–61
Agnes Bromley	1576	Assize	97–99
(Elisabeth Lorde mentioned as a witch in 1579 Pamphlet)			
Agnes Duke	1584, 1589	Assize	203, 272
Joan Cocke	1584	Assize	208–9
Elizabeth Pillgram	1587	Archdeaconry	1,030, 1,034
Mary Godfrey	1587	Archdeaconry	1,032
John Gosse and wife	1587	Archdeaconry	1,033, 1,036
John Heare/Jenny	1589	Assize	272
BOREHAM			
'Mason's wife'	1566	Archdeaconry	863
Mary Belsted/ Middleton	1566, 1576, 1594	Archdeaconry, Assize	862, 890 892, 393
Margaret Poole	1576	Archdeaconry	889
Agnes Haven	1593	Assize	357, 358
LITTLE BADDOW			
Alice Bambricke	1570	Assize	33
Alice Swallow	1570	Assize	29–32

were very localized. Even in three neighbouring villages witches were accused in different years. It would seem that it was particular pressures within the village, rather than an external event, such as the arrival of a witch-hunter, a general economic recession, or political uncertainty, which led to accusations. This table also clearly illustrates how some people were accused of witchcraft on several occasions and over a long period of time. Thus Elizabeth Fraunces, Joan Osborne, and Mary Belsted were each accused over a period of more than ten years.

The sources for studying the background of village life, out of which the accusations emerged, are immense.[3] All three villages provide Elizabethan wills, over 120 in all, which can be used to reconstitute the kinship structure and, through the witnesses to them, groups of friends. Parish registers have survived from this period for Boreham and Little Baddow, and this enables us not only to add to our knowledge about kinship, but also suggests years of heavy mortality which can be compared to deaths by witchcraft. In Boreham we have an Elizabethan churchwardens' account book and a very rare set of Elizabethan 'Overseers of the Poor' accounts. These enable us to see who were the poorest in the village and how serious the problem of poverty was at different periods; this again can be compared to the prosecutions. Subsidy assessments for all three villages during the whole of the sixteenth century enable us to check the economic level of victims and witches; they also provide information on the amount of migration from the village. Manorial records, including an excellent court leet roll, have only been examined for Hatfield Peverel; from these we can judge whether witchcraft was restricted to the inhabitants of a particular manor, and whether suspected witches were also involved in petty quarrels settled at this court. A similar use can be made of the court records of the Assize, Quarter Sessions, and Archdeaconry courts. Since all these exist from the beginning of Elizabeth's reign for all three villages,[4] we can see how far witchcraft overlapped with other offences. A number of other records—for instance, those kept by coroners on sudden deaths— have also been used. The result is that witchcraft prosecutions, too often seen in isolation from their background, can be related to other religious, economic, and social factors.

Another use for the local records is as a check on the accuracy of the witchcraft prosecutions recorded in court records. A comparison of Assize indictments and pamphlets describing the trials suggested that both sources, independent yet agreeing, are accurate. This impression is substantiated from a comparison with local records. Though there are divergencies, it is the similarity that is striking. In Little Baddow three people were said to have been bewitched to death. These can be compared to entries in the parish register. Richard Hawkes was supposedly bewitched at the age of seven days on 9 October 1568, and then died on 1 September in the following year. The register noted the marriage of his parents in October 1567, then the birth of Richard on 14 October 1568, some twelve days from the time specified by the indictment. His death, however, is not recorded. In the case of Elizabeth Goores, supposedly bewitched to death on 2 March 1568, there appears to have been a slip with the regnal year, since the register notes her death on the 10 February 1567.[5] The most accurate indictment concerned the bewitching to death of Elizabeth Bastwick on 1 May 1569. Perhaps because she was not buried for a few days, the register gives her burial on the 11th instead of 1 May. In Boreham, Edith Hawes was bewitched to death on 20 December 1587, according to the indictment; the register noted her burial on 25 December 1587. In Hatfield Peverel only wills can be used to check the indictments, since the parish register is missing. Thus John Baker was bewitched to death on 17 September 1575, according to the indictment; on 26 November in the same year he was noted as dying intestate by the officials of the Archdeaconry Court.[6] John Bird died of supposed witchcraft on 23 February 1584, six days after he had made his will. Walter Wilmott made his will on 1 April 1572, the same day as that on which he was alleged to have been bewitched to death. Both Bird and Wilmott admitted in their wills to being 'sick in body', but neither suggested that this was due to witchcraft.

It is difficult to obtain more than a rough estimate of the total population of these three villages. Yet some general total is necessary in order to see how important witchcraft beliefs were in village life. The Boreham church-wardens' accounts provide the only clear figures. In 1575 there were seventy-eight households, which suggests a population of between 350 and 400. Over a period of thirty years some four people were suspected as witches and another six people, whose names are known, were related directly as either victims or husbands of witches. The population of Hatfield Peverel can only be guessed from comparing its total records to those of Boreham—for instance, the number of wills, persons listed in subsidy returns, court cases; all these suggest that Boreham was roughly two-thirds the size of Hatfield Peverel. If we assume that the latter contained between 550 and 650 people, we can see that the fifteen suspected witches and thirty named victims or husbands represented a reasonable proportion of the total village population. The same method applied to Little Baddow, itself some two-thirds the size of Boreham, means that a village of about 250 people contained two known witches and four known victims.[7] Naturally, this only shows the surface of suspicions. Many others in the villages would be connected to witchcraft prosecutions through links of blood or co-residence. For example, we would never have known that John Pilbarough of Hatfield Peverel was aware of witchcraft suspicions if he had not specified that no charity was to be given to witches; his is the only will, of more than 190 examined for the three villages, to mention the subject.[8]

Another way of testing the relative importance of witchcraft prosecutions in everyday village life is to compare the number accused of this offence with those accused of other offences. The results of such a comparison are set out in Table 8.

From the table we can see that witchcraft was a less common offence than theft and assault, but more frequent than murder. Compared to ecclesiastical offences, it was less common than sexual misdemeanours and failing to attend church, but more often presented than breaking the Sabbath, drunkenness, marital disputes, quarrelling, and misbehaviour on church

premises. Thus it seems clear that witchcraft prosecutions were of central
importance in village life in these three villages. Their importance will
emerge even more clearly in subsequent analyses of those involved as
witches.

TABLE 8
Witchcraft and other offences in three Essex villages, 1560–99

Offence	*Number of persons offending*		
	Hatfield Peverel	*Boreham*	*Little Baddow*
Assault	26	5	8
Murder	2	1	1
Theft	11	20	9
Witchcraft	14	4	2
Breaking the Sabbath by working	2	2	1
Non-attendance at church	52	29	23
Drunkenness	2	2	1
Marital disputes	4	6	—
Misbehaviour in church/yard	1	2	—
Quarrelling/scolding	—	4	1
Refusing to pay church rates	8	9	3
Sexual offences	80	46	30

Note: The figures are, as yet, only approximate. They are based on Assize, Quarter
Sessions, King's Bench, and Archdeaconry records. Offences are divided into those at
secular and those at ecclesiastical courts; witchcraft, however, is treated under one head
only. Total for sexual offences include both offenders.

Previous chapters have outlined various types of source which will give
us direct information about witchcraft. From these we can construct lists,
graphs, and maps of those who were accused and their accusers. Possibly
the most important expansion of sources in the study of witchcraft, however, will prove to be in what we may term 'indirect sources'. That is to
say, the huge volume of local records which help us to recreate the context
of village life within which witchcraft suspicion occurred. Not until we
know far more about such problems as movement between villages,
tensions between different groups within the village, and beliefs about the
supernatural world at the village level will we be able to understand the
part played by witchcraft. A study of witchcraft accusations, on the other
hand, provides us with an unique entry into the mental and social world of
sixteenth- and seventeenth-century villagers. We learn of some of their
fears and of the types of conflict which occurred in areas otherwise too

remote for historical investigations. We may now turn to an analysis of some of the forces in Tudor and Stuart England with which witchcraft prosecutions were linked.

NOTES

1. The whole of the 1566 Pamphlet is concerned with Hatfield Peverel; the 1579 Pamphlet also contains on sigs. Aiv–v the confession of a Hatfield witch.
2. See Map 1, p. 10, above.
3. The sources are described in the Bibliography, pp. 314–25. The extremely time-consuming work of analysing the huge amount of material was only made possible through the generous assistance of the writer's family.
4. Except, as noted in the Bibliography, the Archdeaconry records for Hatfield Peverel; these commence effectively in the late 1570's.
5. Here, as elsewhere, dates have been made uniform, starting the year on 1 January.
6. E.R.O., D/ACA/6, fol. 267.
7. The density of witchcraft thus seems roughly similar to that in the African Cewa tribe, where a village of 200 has at least three suspected witches (M. G. Marwick, *Sorcery in Its Social Setting* (Manchester, 1965), p. 272).
8. Having left various sums of money to be distributed among the poor of the three villages, the testator added: 'reproving mien [*sic*] executors that none which ar[e] or shalbe then any waye suspected or detected in the develish art of sorsery and witchcraft may have no parte of these my saied legasies or bequestes' (E.R.O., D/ACW, 4/182).

Part two

Countering witchcraft

Chapter 7

Informal counter-action against witchcraft

/It has already been suggested that witchcraft prosecutions in Essex were only the final stage in a far more complex series of suspicions. The methods employed to battle against the power of witches illustrates this contention. Such counter-action may be usefully divided into three stages, mutually interdependent yet distinct. Before the witch attacked, certain precautions could be taken to safeguard likely victims of witchcraft; once witchcraft was believed to have been used, cures could be sought; finally, attempts could be made to locate the witch and either force her to withdraw her power or have her punished. Thus the prosecutions were merely one possible method in the final reaction./ Such counter-action has been termed 'informal' to distinguish it both from the court prosecutions and also from the activity of specialized people, cunning folk, and witch-finders, who were employed to deal with witchcraft. Among the more general problems illuminated by the methods employed to ward off witches are two of particular importance. The first is the process by which suspicions became focused on a certain individual in a village. The second is the degree to which belief in witchcraft, by providing a set of magical and other activities in cases of misfortune and anxiety, provided an attractive response to the problem of suffering. Unfortunately, the informal nature of the remedies has meant that no quantitative estimate can be made of the amount of such activity. In fact, much of the evidence for counter-activity comes from literary evidence, and it is only occasionally that we learn about it from prosecutions.

There were two principal methods of avoiding being bewitched: taking magical precautions or regulating one's life so that a witch was unlikely, or unable, to attack. There is considerable literary evidence for the impression that people surrounded themselves with a wall of magical objects and gestures, intended to ward off evil generally and a witch specifically. Hanging holy writing around the neck, especially the first chapter of St. John's Gospel, was much favoured.[1] The Essex writer George Gifford told how a woman 'haunted with a Fairy' was rumoured to wear 'about her *Sainct Johns Gospel*, or some part of it'.[2] Charms were either worn around the neck or carried in the pocket: they might be certain plants, roots, or stones, or the holy objects which the pre-Reformation clergy had advocated as amulets against evil.[3] Among the most common of these objects were a holed stone, salt, communion wafers, holy water, and the sign of the Cross.[4] Unfortunately, we cannot go further than to say that it seems likely that these were commonly employed in Essex, for when we turn from the generalizations of contemporaries to the legal records we are left with a gap in the evidence. A few buried bottles with curious contents have been discovered; these were probably used to prevent or cure witchcraft.[5] We know that the use of plants and other objects to ward off witchcraft was widespread in the nineteenth century, and there are scattered instances from all over England for the sixteenth century. Nevertheless, specific cases in Essex are scarce.[6]

Another preventive against witchcraft was to behave in such a way that a witch could not or would not attack one. The most extreme solution was to move from a particularly witch-infested area. There is only one known reference to such an action in Essex. Gifford made one of his speakers say, after a long description of the witchcraft in his village, 'I had no minde to dwell in that place any longer'.[7] It is also possible that people tried to prevent witchcraft by refusing to have witches living near them. A witness in the 1582 Assize trial told how her husband was asked for the sale of a house and acre of land by a witch's husband; he refused to sell because 'he would not have him his neighbour'.[8] Better documented is the belief that a witch might be placated and witchcraft avoided if no motive for hatred was given. 'These miserable wretches', wrote Scot, 'are so odious unto all their neighbors, and so feared, as few dare offend them, or denie them anie thing they aske.'[9] Another writer noted that people 'for feare doe give something unto them', but he also remarked that those who gave in this way were the most likely victims of witchcraft.[10] This double idea, that an attempt could be made to avoid the anger of the witch by kindness, but that such an effort usually broke down as the victim's patience cracked or the demands became more extreme, is vividly illustrated by the Essex writer, Gifford. One of the speakers in his *Dialogue*, asked why he should have been bewitched, replied:

> Trust me I cannot tell, but I feare me I have, for there be two or three in our towne which I like not, but especially an old woman, I have been as careful to please her as ever I was to please mine own mother, and to give her ever anon one thing or other, and yet me thinkes she frownes at me now and then.[11]

The same author gave another example of this attempt to humour the suspected witch: a man, asked why a certain woman should have bewitched

him, replied that it might have been because he and his wife asked her to
keep her chickens out of his garden and she took offence at this, although
'Wee spake her as fayre as wee could for our lives'.[12]

It seems that, up to a point, the fear of the witch acted as a sanction in
enforcing neighbourly conduct; that people gave to others because they
feared their evil power. A conflicting idea, however, also existed. This was
that the best way to prevent witchcraft was to sever all connexions with
the suspect. Since witches often worked through physical objects, it was
best to avoid all borrowing from, and lending to, suspects. The Continental
Malleus Maleficarum warned people not to give or lend butter, milk, or
cheese to a begging witch,[13] and English authorities agreed that witches
sometimes worked 'by leaving something of theirs in your House' or by
'getting something of yours into their House'. It was even dangerous to
co-operate with them in everyday activities, since they also worked
'ingratefully, and by occasion of good turnes'.[14] If they loitered near one's
house they should be warned off, since they might be burying their magic
under the bedstraw or threshold.[15] Joseph Glanvil agreed with Scot that it
was commonly believed to be dangerous to receive an apple or similar
gift from a witch.[16] There are a number of occasions in Essex when gifts
from a witch caused the downfall of the recipient, though there is only a
little direct evidence of the article lent to the witch being bewitched. Many
must have found it attractive to combine Christianity with prudence,
shunning the emissaries of the Devil by refusing to give them neighbourly
support. The way in which this fitted in with the contemporary attack on
indiscriminate charity is well illustrated in the words of a Puritan writer
in 1617. To avoid witchcraft, he told his audience, we should:

> be wise in our Liberalitie, and Almesdeedes, not distributing to each sort of
> poore, because many times Witches go under this habite . . . especially, to
> take heed if any such suspected seeke unto us; to bee straight-handed towards
> them, not to entertaine them in our houses, not to relieve them with our
> morsels.[17]

That the witch was believed to be responding in fury to such a breach in
neighbourly relations is clear from the pamphlet accounts discussed in the
previous chapter.

The writer who counselled Christians to avoid giving to begging witches
offered one other preventive, 'to renue our right in Christ daily by
unfained repentance'. He also suggested that houses should be spiritually
protected by dedication and prayer, by a virtuous family life, observation
of the Sabbath, and other similarly Christian conduct.[18] This was the
normal remedy suggested by writers. Gifford stressed that faith alone was
a shield against witchcraft, and Stearne quoted the Psalms to the effect

that the godly need not fear witchcraft, since they were protected.[19] One writer even tried to argue that the religious were less subject to attack than other people: 'Though God may try his dearest children this way, yet it is very seldome, and upon their goods rather then upon their bodies'. Nevertheless he was forced to admit that 'sometimes it hath beene found, that they have prevailed to the taking away of the life of some, who have been reputed religious'.[20] A similarly ambivalent attitude was shown by William Perkins, who remarked that 'Though the godly man be not exempted from Witchcraft, yet he is a thousand folde more free from the power thereof, then other men are'.[21] This double idea is reflected in the actual Essex cases. On several occasions the devoutness of the hoped-for victim baffled the witch. A witch in 1566 admitted that she was unable to bewitch a man because he 'was so stronge in fayth',[22] and in 1589 another Essex woman confessed that:

> she sent her saide sprites, to hurt Master Kitchin Minister of the saide towne, and also unto one George Coe of the saide towne . . . but they could not, and the cause why they could not, as the said sprites tolde her, was because they had at their comming a strong faith in God, and had invocated and called upon him, that they could doo them no harme.[23]

Among the conclusions contemporaries could draw from this apparent immunity of the godly was the fact that one method of avoiding physical disaster was to be ardent in religion. This was implied by John Gaule when he made a list of godly actions—for instance, prayers, thanksgiving, and purity of thought—which were the real answer to a threat of witchcraft.[24] Unfortunately, the Essex evidence cannot help solve the problem of whether, in real life, fear of witchcraft led to increased outward religious devotion. One reason for doubting whether this was so is the suggestion that people, in fact, realized that godliness was no protection.

George Gifford was sensitive to the fact that among his Essex congregation an obsession with witchcraft counter-action undermined 'true faith'. He wrote that:

> many nowe doe even quake and tremble, and their faith doth stagger. Hathe hee power (thinke they) over such as be cunning in the scriptures, then what are they the better for their profession? the witch is on their bones as well as upon others. By this it might seeme, and so they take it, that other helpes and remedies are to be sought than by the scriptures. And so they run and seeke help where they ought not.[25]

Such disruptive effects on conventional religious attitudes are graphically illustrated in the struggle of an Essex minister to save his dying wife. She believed herself to be bewitched and, in considerable pain, told her

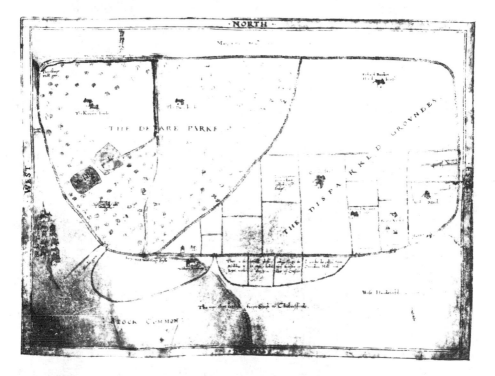

3 An indictment by the Grand Jury of Essex from the Lent assizes of 1580
in Colchester. Rose Pye, a spinster of Canewdon notoriously living as a witch,
was accused on charges of bewitchment and murder after a one-year-old
child in the same village, Johanna Snow, had died in August 1575.
Rose Pye was acquitted of both charges. Case 141
(Public Record Office)

4 Map of Stock Common, 1575, showing on the far right, the house of
widow Sawel, a witch, and next-door that of her victim's father
Roger Veale. Case 804
(Essex Record Office)

6 An extract from the Quarter Sessions Roll, 9 July 1566. A woman of Kelvedon, being refused butter, bewitched three cows belonging to 'Belfilde's wyfe of Infforde', one of which died and the others gave 'milke of all colors'. Case 796 (Essex Record Office)

5 An extract from the Act Book of the Archdeacon of Essex, 26 April 1585, concerning the case of John Shonk of Romford who had consulted the witch Father Parfoot for help for his wife. It was believed that Father Parfoot was a good witch and Shonk confessed and was 'hartelie sorie for sekinge mans helpe and refusinge ye helpe of god'. Case 911 (Essex Record Office)

husband of her fears. As befitted his position as Parson of Beaumont, he answered:

> I pray you be content and thinke not so, but trust God and put your trust in him onely, and he will defend you from her, and from the Divell himselfe also: and said moreover, what will the people say, that I beeing a Preacher shoulde have my wife so weake in faith.

However, the situation grew graver, and after his wife had threatened to seek help from her father if her husband would not co-operate, the parson began to waver, still exhorting her to pray to God, but saying that he would hang the witch if he could prove her guilt. When he encountered the suspect over the garden fence, he shouted at her:

> I am glad you are here you yield strumpet, saying, I do think you have bewitched my wife, and as truly as God doth live, if I can perceive yt she be troubled any more as she hath been, I will not leave a whole bone about thee, and besides I will seeke to have thee hanged.[26]

Given the combination of a painful and prolonged illness and a notorious witch, faith was of little avail.

The Parson of Beaumont was dealing with witchcraft already, so it was believed, at work. This second stage in the counter-action against witches could lead to several types of activity. One choice was between private action and consulting an expert. For instance, one of Gifford's characters was in a state of indecision because of conflicting advice from his friends. Finding his animals dying at an unprecedented rate, he stated anxiously that, 'Some of my neighbours wishe me to burne some thing alive, as a henne or a hogge. Others will me in time to seeke helpe at the handes of some cunning man, before I have any further harme.'[27] The first alternative, using fire as a cure or preventive, was obviously widely employed in Essex. Gifford told how a woman on the scaffold admitted that after a pig had been burnt alive 'her cat would never go thither any more'.[28] In 1582 we hear of a pig cured of witchcraft by having its ears cut off and burnt, and in the trial of 1579 a man stated that he had lost twenty hogs before he burnt one, 'whereby as he thinketh, he saved the reste'.[29] Since such incidents are only casually recorded, it is impossible to tell whether it was normal for a villager to burn parts of his property when he noticed a high level of death or disease among his animals. There are two cases in the church courts of animals being burnt alive and their owners being presented,[30] but normally it is only by accident that we hear of such incidents. Thus another man was presented in the same court, not because he 'did burne a lambe on o[u]r common w[hi]ch he sayth was bewitched', but rather because he was foolish enough to do this on a Sunday, during

evening service, and 'so set fire on the common' which drew the congregation 'w[i]th amazement from the church'.[31] Other private remedies
were employed in Essex in the attempt to cure animals, among them certain prayers and ritual actions.[32]

Animals, however, were not the only agricultural property whose
safety depended on anti-witchcraft spells and actions. Butter, cheese, and
beer were especially vulnerable to attack, and we consequently learn of
spells and activities to make them free from witches.[33] The attempt of a
woman in 1582 to make butter illustrates one of the most common of the
anti-witchcraft cures, the red-hot horsehoe. It also shows how a person
went through several possible explanations for a strange phenomenon
before deciding whether witchcraft was at work. Unable to turn her milk
into butter, the woman thought that this might be because of:

> the feeding of her beasts, or els that the vessels were not sweete, whereupon
> she saith, she scalded her vessels, and scoured them with salt, thinking that
> might helpe, but it was never the better but as before: then she saith, shee was
> full of care . . . then shee saith it came into her mind to approve another way,
> which was, shee tooke a horse shoe and made it redde hot, and put it into the
> milke in the vessals, and so into her creame: and then she saith, shee coulde
> seath her milke, fleete her creame, and make her butter in good sort.[34]

The theory behind this, as well as the assumption that such methods were
commonly employed in Essex, is illustrated by Gifford, who asked in the
person of 'M.B.' how metal stuck into cream could hurt the witch, 'You
did not thinke she was in your creame, did you?' To this it was replied,
'Some thinke she is there, and therefore, when they thrust in the spitte
they say, If thou beest here have at thine eie'.[35] Similar methods were
employed, according to an Essex pamphlet, to save bewitched beer.[36]

Burning part of the victim and using pieces of red-hot metal were
possible responses to attacks on livestocks and dairy-product, but they
were obviously impracticable in the majority of Essex cases, where the
attack was on a human being. A few of the spells and methods actually used
to cure a bewitched person have been preserved by chance in the Essex
records; in most cases such methods are not recorded. One woman,
examined in 1570:

> bore her husband in hand that he was bewitched: and as a remedy thereof, she
> caused a trivet [i.e. metal frame for a fireplace] to be set, and certain pieces
> of elder and white hazel wood to be laid upon the trivet across, with a fire
> under it; and then him, who was at that time not well in his wits, to kneel
> down and say certain prayers, as she taught him; and thereby, she said, he
> could be delivered of his bewitching, or his witch should consume as the fire
> did.[37]

Another woman, the most notorious witch in the trial of 1582, told how she:

> was troubled with a lamenes in her bones, and for ease thereof, went to one Cockes wife of Weley, nowe deceased, who telled this examinate that shee was bewitched, and at her entretie taught her to unwitche her self; And had her take hogges dunge and charnell, and put them together and holde them in her left hand, and to take in the other hande a knife, and then to cast the said into the fire and to take the said knife and to make three pricks under a table and to pricke the medicine three times, and to make three pricks under a table, and to let the knife sticke there: and after that to take three leves of sage, and as much of herbe John [alias herbe grace] and put them into ale, and drinke it last at night and first in the morning, and then shee taking the same, had ease of her lamenesse.[38]

As can be seen in both quotations, it was essential to be certain that it was witchcraft that was responsible for the death or illness; it was also important to find out the name of the witch. Nearly all the methods of curing bewitched humans depended on being certain of these two facts. 'Burning of the thatch of the suspected parties house', which is 'thought to be able to cure the partie bewitched';[39] 'daring and defying the Witch',[40] or threatening her;[41] 'Banging and basting, scratching and clawing, to draw blood of the witch',[42] and making her touch the victim[43]—all these methods were probably employed in Essex.[44] All required knowledge of who was the likely culprit.

A further implication is that all these methods helped to make a hitherto hidden tension into an open breach, often with a considerable show of hostility. If such action failed, and the suffering person died, the counter-action might be taken a stage further: the suspect was taken to the law courts. There a new set of tests, to prove or disprove the suspicions, were employed. But in a large number of cases the informal reactions to suspected witchcraft probably dealt with the problem: the victim recovered, the butter churned, the suspect moved or died. When the cases came to the courts it meant that the informal solutions had failed and that nothing less than the death or complete confession and reconciliation of the suspect were acceptable. Seen in this way, the punishment of witches was not merely for past offences. It was part of the whole graded series of counter-actions and was regarded as a prerequisite for healing from witchcraft and an insurance against future disasters. For example, Bernard stated that healing sometimes required the death of the witch.[45]

To find a witch one could either use private magic, go to a cunning man, or both. Since witchcraft was such a mysterious force, a series of tests were employed to confirm that current gossip and suspicions were correct. A person suspecting witchcraft to be at work might burn something belonging

to the supposed witch, or part of the object bewitched, and would then
wait to see if the suspect came hurrying round.[46] Ellen Smith, of Maldon
in Essex, was among those caught in this manner.[47] Not only did such a
method confirm and clarify previous suspicions, allowing the individual
an opportunity to seek the opinion of his neighbours on the matter, but it
was also connected with the idea that witches were people who were
always dropping in for small loans, or to inquire about personal affairs,
such as the health of the family. There are a number of excellent contemporary accounts of how suspicions focused on a certain person in a village.
They show how a person became increasingly disliked, the part played by
gossip and rumour, and the pooling of opinions. Richard Bernard, for
instance, divided the growth of suspicions into eight stages. First, there is
fear of witches in general; then this becomes localized and 'if any thing
happen amisse, hee [the Devil] suggesteth a suspition of this or that party
to be a Witch'. Thirdly, the individual communicates his fears to a
neighbour, who then divulges that he, himself, has his own fears. In the
fifth stage all the gossips get together and the rumour spreads right round
the village until 'it is taken for granted, that such an one is a Witch'. Once
a person is a known witch she becomes generally disliked, 'so as others
upon any ill hap, begin likewise to blame the same partie for that ill
accident'. From then on every word or deed of the suspect is interpreted
to fit the conviction of her guilt, people become 'suspicious to marke all
the words and deeds of the suspected and to interpret the worst of them'.
Just to confirm their suspicions, they go off to a cunning man, who tells
them 'that they are bewitched, that they live by ill neighbours'. The final
stage, which leads to an accusation at the courts, may be initiated by one
of a number of villagers: 'the Divell stirreth up some impatient, more fiery
and inraged then the rest, to seeke revenge, to hale the suspected before
Authoritie'.[48] In this description we see that witchcraft suspicions tended
to move in an ever-widening ripple through the village, the final accusation
being based on a general consensus of opinion which rested on the mutual
exchange of fears through gossip. Such a consensus is most obvious in the
presentments at the church courts. These were made by the churchwardens on the basis of 'common fame' in the parish. Thus counter-
action against witches was a village affair in its later stages. Not merely the
concern of an individual, it mobilized a number of emotional forces in the
parish.

The way in which people connected certain events with a woman whom
they disliked is well illustrated by Reginald Scot. He wrote that the process
occurred over a 'tract of time' and that 'the witch waxeth odious and tedious
to hir neighbors; and they againe are despised and despited of hir'. She
then went round cursing them and, some time later, strange deaths and

sickness visited the village. Not only the suspecting villagers, but also the suspected witch herself, interpret the malice and misfortune as being somehow interrelated.[49] The way in which the first stage in the growth of suspicions, the individual reaction, occurred is described by Thomas Ady. Seldom is a person hurt, Ady wrote, without crying out that he is bewitched:

> for, saith he, such an old man or woman came lately to my door, and desired some relief, and I denied it, and God forgive me, my heart did rise against her at that time, my mind gave me she looked like a Witch, and presently my Child, my Wife, my Self, my Horse . . . or somewhat was thus and thus handled.[50]

This suggests that an individual first angered another and then, expecting retribution, suffered some misfortune. This is similar to the description of a man who angered a woman, but repented, 'for I looked somewhat would follow. And next night, I saw the ugliest sight that ever I saw.'[51] Possibly the sequence was sometimes reversed. Thus one man seems to have suffered an injury, and then cast round in his mind, examining his neighbourly relationships, to see who might have had the motive to bewitch him.[52] In many cases it is impossible to tell whether the injury or the specific realization that one was likely to be bewitched came first. Thus a woman was detected at the Archdeacon of Colchester's court as a quarreller 'And because some of hir neighbours after she hathe fallen out w[i]th them have had evell successe w[i]th the Cattell therfore they have conceived an opinion that she ys a witche'.[53] What seems evident from Ady's description, however, is that it was the social relationship which determined the selection of a likely witch. Though witches may also have been ugly, poor, or old, it was not primarily this that was likely to lead to suspicion. Essex evidence clearly shows that it was the motive for bewitching which was most strongly stressed.[54] A person came to look like a witch when they acted like a witch; as Ady put it, 'my mind did give me she looked like a witch' when turned from the door.

One final description of the way in which suspicions grew, were pooled, and finally exploded into a charge, deserves full quotation. It was written by George Gifford, who, with his Essex background, is particularly well placed to understand the informal activity which took place in a village before a prosecution was made:

> Some woman doth fal out bitterly with her neighbour: there followeth some great hurt. . . . There is a suspicion conceived. Within fewe yeares after shee is in some iarre with an other. Hee is also plagued. This is noted of all. Great fame is spread of the matter. Mother W is a witch. She hath bewitched goodman B. Two hogges died strangely: or else hee is taken lame. Wel, mother W doth begin to bee very odious and terrible unto many. her neighbours, dare

say nothing but yet in their heartes they wish shee were hanged. Shortly after an other falleth sicke and doth pine, hee can have no stomacke unto his meate, nor hee can not sleepe. The neighbours come to visit him. Well neighbour, sayth one, do ye not suspect some naughty dealing: did yee never anger mother W? truly neighbour (sayth he) I have not liked the woman a long tyme. I can not tell how I should displease her, unlesse it were this other day, my wife prayed her, and so did I, that shee would keepe her hennes out of my garden. Wee spake her as fayre as wee could for our lives. I thinke verely shee hath bewitched me. Every body sayth now that Mother W is a witch in deede, and hath bewitched the good man E. Hee cannot eate his meate. It is out of all doubt: for there were [those] which saw a weasil runne from her housward into his yard even a little before hee fell sicke. The sicke man dieth, and taketh it upon his death that he is bewitched: then is mother W apprehended, and sent to prison, shee is arrayned and condemned.[55]

The Essex pamphlets corroborate this description of the gradual growth of suspicions, a process in which no event was ascribed to the evil will of the witch for several years at a time, and then more and more disaster was laid at her door. Gifford suggested that, by the end, 'every body' agreed that a certain person was a witch, that she became 'very odious and terrible to many', that 'great fame is spread of the matter'. This supports the impression from Essex legal records that a large number of village families became involved as victims, relatives, or friends. As we might expect, it seems that the whole village population became involved in the subsequent tension and gossip. Gifford's description also shows very strikingly how a man cast round in his mind, encouraged by his neighbours, to see who might have bewitched him: in this case he selected a person with whom he felt uneasy and against whom he had offended. The popular attitude to witches, they were 'odious and terrible', became more bitter because it had to remain unreleased: her neighbours 'dare say nothing but yet in their hearts they wish shee were hanged'. When enough proof was accumulated, and the village was united, the prosecution could occur.

Unfortunately, the Essex records do not allow any quantitative measure to be made of the amount of counter-witchcraft activities. Yet it seems that the prosecutions at the law courts were only the final, and necessarily partial expressions of far more widespread suspicions in the villages. One accusation, as has been seen from other evidence, might emerge from a complicated background in which the whole village, through rumour and gossip, took part. Thus witchcraft does not appear as some random outburst on the part of an individual, but rather as a phenomenon arising from the roots of society. It would thus be fair to suggest that, since 229 Essex villages are known to have been connected in some way to witchcraft prosecutions and 291 people were accused of black witchcraft between

1560 and 1680 at the Essex Assizes, the amount of gossip, rumour, and tension in this county must have been immense. Though it cannot be proved, it seems likely that villagers were constantly engaged in contending with, or discussing, witches. Through counter-action against witches, sufferers were united with their neighbours in a series of magical and other activities which not only brought present relief and some sort of explanation, but also hope of eradicating future misery.

NOTES

1. Among those who referred to it were Scot, *Discovery*, pp. 212, 230, and Bernard, *Guide*, p. 135.
2. Gifford, *Dialogue*, sig. B^v.
3. For example, see Ady, *Candle*, p. 47; Perkins, *Damned Art*, p. 149.
4. Examples may be found in Kittredge, *Witchcraft*, p. 220; Perkins, *Damned Art*, p. 245; Scot, *Discovery*, p. 236.
5. R. Merrifield, 'The Use of Bellarmines as Witch Bottles', *The Guildhall Miscellany*, i, 3 (1954), 3–15; for Essex examples see *Memorials of Old Essex*, ed. A. C. Kelway (1908), p. 252.
6. There is a vivid account showing the enormous preoccupation with counter-witchcraft in a nineteenth-century Yorkshire village in J. C. Atkinson, *Forty Years in a Moorland Parish* (1891), pp. 91–102. For a sixteenth-century example, see *Churchwardens' Presentments, Part 1 : Archdeaconry of Chichester*, ed. H. Johnstone (Sussex Rec. Soc., xlix, 1947–8), 92. A possible Essex case is No. 1,170. Charms to be hung in a barrel were prescribed in case 1,207(*b*).
7. *Dialogue*, sig. C.
8. 1582 Pamphlet, sig. F6^v.
9. Scot, *Discovery*, p. 29; see also Bernard, *Guide*, p. 184.
10. Bernard, *Guide*, p. 184.
11. *Dialogue*, sigs. A4^v–B.
12. *Discourse*, sigs. G4–G4^v.
13. Cited in Scot, *Discovery*, p. 238.
14. Gaule, *Select Cases*, p. 129.
15. Ibid., p. 144.
16. Joseph Glanvill, *Some Philosophical Considerations Touching the Being of Witches and Witchcrafts* (1667), p. 25; Scot, *Discovery*, p. 62.
17. Thomas Cooper, *Mystery of Witchcraft* (1617), pp. 287–8.
18. Ibid., p. 290.
19. Gifford, *Discourse*, sigs. 13–13^v; Stearne, *Confirmation*, p. 3.
20. Bernard, *Guide*, p. 182.
21. *Damned Art*, pp. 223–4.
22. 1566 Pamphlet, p. 324.
23. 1589 Pamphlet, sig. A3^v.
24. Gaule, *Select Cases*, pp. 151–3.
25. *Dialogue*, sig. D4.
26. 1582 Pamphlet, sigs. F2^v–F3. If, as Newcourt suggests, Richard Harrison was Parson of Beaumont from 1566 to 1591, except for a short deprivation in 1586,

Venn is wrong in identifying him with the Richard Harryson who matriculated from Christ's in 1575. Newcourt, *Repertorium*, ii, 41; Venn, *Alumni Cantabrigiensis*. Harrison does not appear in the Puritan survey of 1586, where Beaumont is omitted.

27. *Dialogue*, sig. B.
28. *Dialogue*, sig. E; there is another case at sig. L4^v.
29. 1582 Pamphlet, sig. F^v; 1579 Pamphlet, sig. B1. A number of similar cases from all over England are listed in Kittredge, *Witchcraft*, p. 96.
30. Cases 1,128 and 976, though in the former it was actually the churchwarden who was presented for not presenting the offender.
31. Case 983.
32. Case 1,007; possibly in this category was the man who could not approach his bewitched cow until he had kissed under its tail (Gifford, *Dialogue*, sig. L4^v).
33. Ady, *Candle*, p. 59; Scot, *Discovery*, p. 238.
34. 1582 Pamphlet, sig. E8^v.
35. Gifford, *Dialogue*, sigs. M3^v–M4.
36. 1582 Pamphlet, sigs. E3, F^v, F2.
37. Case 1,204.
38. 1582 Pamphlet, sigs. A7–A7^v.
39. Perkins, *Damned Art*, p. 206.
40. Gaule, *Select Cases*, p. 144.
41. As in the case of Richard Harrison, Parson of Beaumont, or, more successfully, in the 1582 Pamphlet, sig. E2^v.
42. Gaule, *Select Cases*, p. 144; Gifford, *Dialogue*, sigs. B^v, E3^v described this.
43. Bernard, *Guide*, p. 193.
44. For example, in the 1582 Pamphlet, sig. C3; 1579 Pamphlet, sig. Avii; case 1,170.
45. Bernard, *Guide*, p. 146.
46. Among the property of the witch most valued in counter-witchcraft was urine, thatch, and articles of clothing: Perkins, *Damned Art*, p. 206; Stearne, *Confirmation*. p. 34; Kittredge, *Witchcraft*, pp. 102–3, 428.
47. 1579 Pamphlet, sig. Avi.
48. Bernard, *Guide*, pp. 81–3.
49. Scot, *Discovery*, p. 30.
50. Ady, *Candle*, p. 114.
51. Gifford, *Dialogue*, sig. L3.
52. Ibid., sig. B.
53. Case 1,046.
54. See p. 158, below.
55. Gifford, *Discourse*, sigs. G4–G4^v.

Chapter 8

Cunning folk and witchcraft prosecutions

In the previous chapter, it was seen that one step in the procedure towards prosecuting a suspected witch was the consultation of a cunning man, witch-finder, or witch-doctor.[1] Analysis of the activities of cunning folk is therefore necessary before we can understand the pressures behind accusations at the Essex courts. Furthermore, cunning folk were themselves prosecuted as 'witches', especially at the ecclesiastical courts. Indeed, it is arguable that it was primarily against cunning folk that the visitation articles were directed.

There were clearly a considerable number of magical practitioners throughout England in our period. One sorcerer asserted in 1549 that there were over 500, and some seventy years later Robert Burton argued that 'Sorcerers are too common, Cunning men, Wisards and white-witches . . . in every village'.[2] Table 9 lists sixty-one possible cunning folk named in connexion with Essex. Some of them lived outside the county; in a few cases we cannot be certain that those accused or referred to were really magical practitioners. But we can be fairly sure that at least forty-one both lived in Essex and acted as cunning folk.

This list represents only a fraction of those who actually were cunning folk in Essex. As Stearne pointed out, 'not many' cunning folk were brought to court because 'men rather uphold them, and say, why should any man be questioned for doing good'.[3] One example of how much has been lost through the absence of records can be seen by comparing court records to depositions recorded in the pamphlets. There is only one prosecution during the whole period in Essex in which a person was accused of curing bewitched cattle or humans;[4] thus we would have been left with little indication that it was a common part of a cunning man's trade to detect and battle with witches. Yet chance references suggest that it was normal to send to cunning folk to inquire about possible witchcraft. In 1564 a 'women under Munckewoode' and 'the woman of Paswic' were consulted; in 1582, Mother Ratcliffe, Ursley Kempe, 'Cocke's wife', 'one Herring', a cunning man at Ipswich and a man 'of skill' were all instructing people on how to deal with witchcraft; in 1589 and 1645 other cunning

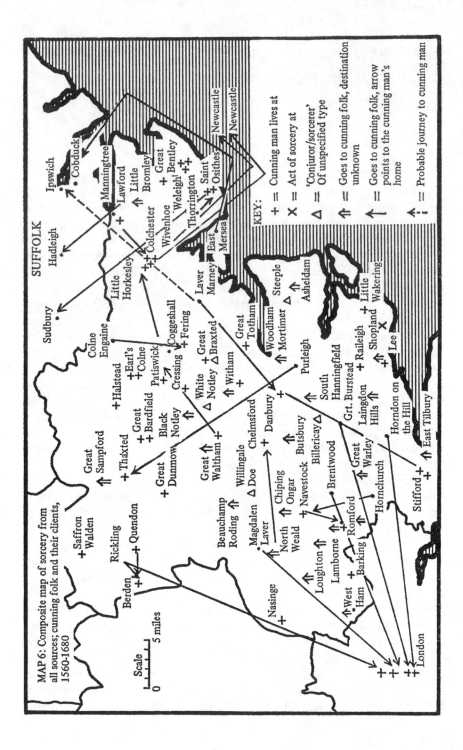

MAP 6: Composite map of sorcery from all sources; cunning folk and their clients, 1560-1680

SUFFOLK

KEY:

+ = Cunning man lives at

✕ = Act of sorcery at

△ = 'Conjuror/sorcerer'

△ = Of unspecified type

⇑ = Goes to cunning folk, destination unknown

⟵ = Goes to cunning folk, arrow points to the cunning man's home

⟵┄ = Probable journey to cunning man

Scale
0   5 miles

Saffron Walden

Rickling
Berden
Quendon

Great Sampford

Thaxted

Halstead

Great Bardfield

Colne Engaine
Earl's Colne
Patiswick
Coggeshall
Fering

Sudbury

Hadleigh

Ipswich
Cobduck

Manningtree
Lawford
Little Bromley
Great Bentley

Weleigh
Wivenhoe
Thorrington
Saint Osithes
Newcastle
Newcastle

Colchester

Little Horkesley

Laver
Marney
East Mersea

Steeple

Asheldam

Woodham Mortimer

Great Totham

White Notley
Great Braxted
Witham

Black Notley
Great Dunmow

Great Waltham

Chelmsford

Willingale

Beauchamp Roding
Magdalen Laver

Danbury

Purleigh

South Hanningfield

Great Burstead
Laingdon Hills

Raileigh
Shopland
Lee
Little Wakering

North Weald
Chiping Ongar
Navestock
Butsbury
Billericay

Horndon on the Hill

Loughton
Lamborne

Brentwood
Great Warley
Hornchurch
Romford

West Ham
Barking

Nasinge

East Tilbury

Stifford

London

TABLE 9 Cunning folk whose names are mentioned in Essex records, 1560–1680

Name	Sex	Place of residence	Type of activity	Occupation	Date	Case number
†Margaret Hosie	F	Shopland	?	—	1561	1,128
'one Richmond'	M	—	soothsayer	—	1566	866
Mr. Hawes	M	Steple	soothsayer	?cleric	1566	866
Margery Skelton	F	Little Wakering	healer	—	1566	873
'Cobham'	M	Romford	anti-witch	—	1570	1,204
Mother Humfrey	F	—	anti-witch	—	1573	992
†Robert Wallys	M	(wandering)	soothsayer	—	1574	799
Alice Reade	F	Lawford	lost goods	—	1574	1,130
(John Thomas	M	London Bridge	lost goods	astrologer	1575	886)
†John Plummer &c.	M/F	Great Totham	divination	—	1576	993
Mother Persorne	F	Navestock	anti-witch	—	1576	893
†Henry Chitham	M	Great Bardfield	conjuring	—	1577	1,198
†Miles Blomfield	M	Chelmsford	lost goods	churchwarden	1578	809
†Thomas Barker	M	Gestingthorpe	healing	surgeon	1578	807–8
Joan Michell	F	Walden	healing	—	1579	995
†Humphrey Poles	M	Maldon	conjuring	—	1580	1,200
Ursley Kempe	F	St. Osithes	anti-witch	—	1582	1582 Pamphlet A3
Mother Ratcliffe	F	—	anti-witch	—	1582	1582 Pamphlet sig. A3
Cocke's wife	F	Weleigh	anti-witch	—	1582	1582 Pamphlet sig. A7
('Herring')	M	Sudbery, Suffolk	anti-witch	'cawker'	1582	1582 Pamphlet sig. C2ᵛ)
Goodwife George	F	Abberton	anti-witch	—	1582	1,007
Catherine Reve	F	Colchester	anti-witch	—	1582	1,007
Henry Gower	M	Quendon	'sorcerer'	?cleric	1584	1,115
William Asplin	M	Great Bardfield	healing/fortunes	schoolmaster	1585	1,019
Edward Mason	M	Great Bardfield	healing	yeoman	1585–8	267, 1,021, 1,040
Father Parfoothe	M	Romford	healing	—	1585, 92	911, 944
Thomas Smith	M	Earl's Colne	'sorcery', 'cast a figure'	schoolmaster	1574, 85	1,129, 1,037
†Mr. Fountayne	M	Great Braxted	'cast a figure'	?cleric	1588	1,042
'one Brian'	M	St. Osithes	anti-witch	—	1588	1,047

* Remainder of this table continues on next page.

Name	M/F	Place	Activity	Occupation	Date	Reference
'Wilcockes'	F	Cressing	lost goods/fortunes	—	1589	1,060
†Mr. Shereman	M	Colchester	healing	doctor	1590	1,064
('one Creek'	M	Cobduck, Suffolk	'help'	—	1591	1,073)
'one Bryant'	M	Weleigh	healing	?surgeon	1591	1,080
John Carter	M	Weleigh	lost goods	—	1591	1,079
Anne Moore	F	Rayleigh	lost goods/soothsayer	—	1595	951
— Carter	M	Barking	lost goods	—	1595	953
Robert Browning	M	Aldham	lost goods	—	1598	417
Marcel Goodwin	M	Colchester	lost goods	physician	1598, 9	1,096, 1,173
(Anne Cryx	F	Newcastle	anti-witch	—	1599	1,173)
George Tailer	M	Thaxted	lost goods/anti-witch	—	1599, 1602	957, 1,121
†Thomas Maunde	M	Great Dunmow	'wizard'	—	1602	1,120
'one Brite'	M	—	—	—	1602	1,120
†William Duffield	M	Great Waltham	'using witchcraft'	—	1605	1,136
Richard Banckes	M	Earl's Colne	'sorcery'	—	1605	1,138
Edwin Hadesley	M	Willingale Doe	conjurer	—	1606	1,181, 488
('Gressam' (Edward)	M	London	lost goods	yeoman	1610	974)
Giles Payson	M	Nasinge	soothsaying	—	1612	977
Gilbert Wakering	M	Halstead	lost goods	astrologer	1620	553b
†(Dr. Francklin	M	Ratcliffe	anti-witch	surgeon	1621	1,183)
Alice Soles	F	Leigh	'sorcery'	'Dr'	1622	1,127
Edmund Rowlande	M	Stifford	healing	—	1631	1,126
†White family	M/F	(wandering)	fortune-tellers	physician	1639	(Q/SR 304/152)
— Barnard	M	Danbury	lost goods	—	1641	839
('one Hoveye'	F	Hadleigh, Suffolk	anti-witch	—	1645	Pamphlet, p. 1)
William Hills	M	Berden	lost goods	miller	1651	845–6
(Mr. Ladland	M	London	lost goods	—	1651	846)
John Lock	M	Colchester	lost goods	labourer	1653	847–8
Benjamin Brand and wife	M/F	Stebbing	lost goods	comber	1653	849
†Thomas White	M	—	conjuring	'gent'	1653–4	851, 854
Mr. Higgs	M	—	lost goods	—	1664	855

Key: ( ) is used when the cunning man lived outside Essex. † means that it is not absolutely certain that the person *was* a cunning man. M = Male, F = Female. The types of activity are explained in the text.

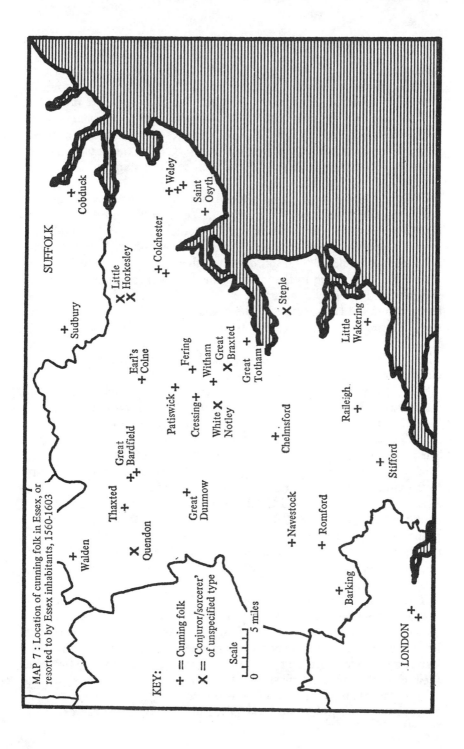

MAP 7 : Location of cunning folk in Essex, or resorted to by Essex inhabitants, 1560-1603

KEY:

+ = Cunning folk

X = 'Conjuror/sorcerer' of unspecified type

Scale

0   5 miles

LONDON

Barking

Romford

Navestock

Stifford

Raileigh.

Chelmsford

Little Wakering

Steple

Great Totham

Great Braxted

Witham

Fering

White Notley

Cressing

Patiswick

Earl's Colne

Colchester

Little Horkesley

Sudbury

SUFFOLK

Cobduck

Weley

Saint Osyth

Great Dunmow

Great Bardfield

Quendon

Thaxted

Walden

folk were mentioned as being consulted concerning possible witchcraft.[5]
Since it seems that it was primarily the magical activity associated with
trying to discover lost goods that was prosecuted, there is a bias towards
men in the table, and in the following calculations. There are other distortions also. As with prosecutions for black witchcraft, but even more so
in this instance, we are dealing with activities which have left only a
marginal trace in the surviving records. It is largely for this reason that the
following reconstruction depends heavily on contemporary opinions of the
activities of cunning folk.

Gifford described a cunning woman who had 'a great name' and to
whom there was 'great resort . . . dayly'.[6] Yet it is difficult to obtain any
quantitative estimate of how many people actually did go to cunning folk
or in what percentage of all cases of illness, suspected witchcraft, or theft
they were consulted. 'Out of question they be innumberable which
receive helpe by going to the cunning men' argued the same author. He
also provided the only quantitative estimate when he said that 'There be
thousands in the land deceived. The woman at R.H. by report hath some
weeke fourtie come unto her, and many of them not of the meaner sort.'[7]
It is also interesting that in all but one of the nine cases in which Gifford
described counter-action against suspected witchcraft in his *Dialogue* the
victim or near friend went to a cunning man.[8] If people consulted cunning
folk in only half the many hundreds of cases of suspected witchcraft, it
seems likely that such practitioners must have been more numerous and
important than Table 9 suggests. Cunning folk themselves infrequently
described their clients. When such descriptions survive they are vague.
For instance, an Essex cunning man admitted, in 1651, that, 'there have
come unto him div[er]s people in these three yearse last past to inquire
in the same kind for stollen goods, but how many he cannot tell'.[9] In the
Archdeaconries of Essex and Colchester thirty-seven cases of resorting to
cunning folk were presented, but it is impossible to tell how large a
proportion of the actual instances this was.[10] Thus we never hear of any of
the clients of either Thomas Maunde, to whom 'ignorant people resorte
. . . as a wysard', or those of Henry Gower, who had deceived 'many
people'.[11]

The location of known Essex cunning folk and the movement of their
clients are plotted in Maps 6 and 7. Although cunning folk continued to
be accused until the end of our period, Map 7 is limited to the period of
Elizabeth's reign; this is the best-documented period, since Church courts
were throughout active centres of the presentation of cunning folk and
their clients. This map illustrates that nowhere in Essex was there a
village more than ten miles from a known cunning man. The county was
covered by a network of magical practitioners, sometimes several in a

town, as at Colchester, Great Bardfield, or Weeley, but usually more scattered. Map 6, showing the distances people travelled to consult wise men and women during the whole period, reveals that people even travelled beyond the county boundaries in search of help. Suffolk, London, and even Newcastle were the homes of a number of experts consulted by Essex villagers.[12] Thus we know that people travelled over five miles on more than nineteen occasions, and more than twenty miles on eight of these nineteen journeys. Gifford seems to have been accurately reflecting the situation when he made a man wonder whether to go twenty miles to a cunning man or twenty-five to a cunning woman.[13] The distance travelled cannot be used to measure the availability of cunning folk; as at Navestock in 1570, sufferers seem to have travelled to further-off cunning folk in preference to local practitioners. Increased prestige through remoteness was possibly one of the attractions of London cunning folk. Bernard suggested that it was a common technique of cunning folk who had failed to advise clients to go to another, more powerful, practitioner.[14] Thus, when an Essex man in 1651 failed to receive help at near-by Berden, he went to London.[15]

Cunning folk were, according to the records, primarily consulted about health and lost property. It is quite possible, however, that people also brought to them other problems of a personal nature.[16] One of the rare known cases of this was the woman presented at the Archdeacon of Colchester's court for using magic 'to know whether a woman be w[ith] childe w[i]th a man childe or a woman Childe'.[17] As an Essex clergyman admitted:

> as the Ministers of God doe give resolution to the conscience, in matters doubtfull and difficult; so the Ministers of Satan, under the name of Wisemen, and Wise-women, are at hand, by his appointment, to resolve, direct and helpe ignorant and unsetled persons, in cases of distraction, losse, or other outward calamities.[18]

If this was true, it seems that a person might have gone to consult a cunning man in many situations of anguish or indecision. Unfortunately, however, it is only when the cunning folk clashed with the direct interests of other professional groups, particularly the clergy and doctors, that their activity has been recorded.

Cunning folk were only consulted about theft and illness in special circumstances. In several of the cases of theft where they were consulted it was the rumoured suspect who went to a wise man to clear himself. Thus one man said he had been to a wise man 'to clear himself of stealing the shirt, and . . . the cunning man gave him a note to clear himself'; another went to London to free himself from suspicion.[19] Gifford provided an excellent example of how, when normal legal methods were impossible because a theft was within a household, a cunning man was consulted.[20] Thomas Ady gives a further evidence that cunning folk helped people locate their enemies in intimate situations which prohibited open or immediate accusations. He remarked that 'Cunning Men, or good Witches . . . will undertake to shew the face of the Thief in the Glass, or of any other that hath done his Neighbour wrong privily'.[21] It was the secret wrongs of neighbours, relatives, or supposed friends which called for secret detection. This aspect is especially important when the cunning man was being consulted about possible witchcraft. As we will see, one of the main attractions of cunning folk was that they provided an outside, apparently objective and impartial, analysis of a person's relationships. A cunning man from a distant village with prestige and confidence-inducing techniques could provide a means of bringing suspicions out into the open, despite the pressures against open hostility between neighbours. /

/ Bernard suggested that three principal reasons for the popularity of cunning folk were that their clients could not get help from elsewhere and were in 'great torment'; that many had received successful treatment from them; and 'that they have helpe from these at a little or no cost at all, whereas Physicke is very chargeable'.[22] All three statements are supported by actual Essex cases.[23] One other incentive to go to cunning folk is omitted by Bernard. This was their ability to provide not only a remedy for the physical pain, but also an explanation of why the suffering had occurred: that is, they could confirm that the misfortune was the result of witchcraft. An excellent description of how someone received more satisfaction from visiting a cunning man than an ordinary doctor is given in 1582. A sailor, landing at Ipswich, found that his daughter was very ill and therefore took a sample of her urine to a local physician. The sailor asked the doctor 'if that his daughter were not bewitched', but the latter replied 'that hee woulde not deale so farre to tell him', so, 'not satisfied to his minde', the sick child's father went to a local cunning man, who confirmed that the child was bewitched.[24] The cunning man, we see in this case, dealt with both physical and mental needs, and translated, at his client's request, a physical misfortune into a symptom of spiritual malice.

The actual methods employed by cunning folk in Essex are only vaguely suggested in the records. Techniques clearly differed from practitioner to practitioner and depended on whether they were asked about theft, illness, or other problems. When the client first arrived, he was often warned that he was only just in time for help. Thus, in the description of the Ipswich affair referred to above, the sailor was told that 'if hee had not commen with some great haste to seeke helpe, hee had come too late'. This would arouse the interest of the client and provide a loophole if remedies failed.

Thus a cunning woman in 1582 said that 'she doubted she shoulde doe it [a sick child] any good, yet she ministered unto it'.[25] The next stage in the consultation was the vital one. The cunning man would inquire about the nature of the trouble and seek to find out about the social relationships of the victim, especially who he or she suspected of inflicting the misfortune. People usually seem to have visited cunning folk with some idea of what was wrong with them and of who was to blame; the cunning man's aim was to bring this out into the open and to give it confirmation. There are numerous examples of this process. A cunning woman confirmed that a sick man was bewitched, 'She saith he is forspoken indeede';[26] Gifford said explicitly that people 'run to Coniurers to know if they be not witches who they suspect'.[27] Scot noted that it was a normal practice of cunning folk to ask the client 'whether they mistrusted not some bad neighbour'.[28] This process of confirmation of pre-existing suspicions is vividly shown in an Essex examination in 1570. A woman 'suspecting that she was bewitched by the said Anne, went to one Cobham of Romford, who was thought to be cunning in such matters; and he declared to her that she was bewitched by the same woman, telling her the words which passed betwixt Anne Vicars and her'.[29] Sometimes, it seems, the client was not as consciously aware of the likely witch as in the above case. Ady suggested that cunning folk initiated suspicions, that they 'will undertake to tell them who hath bewitched them, who, and which of their Neighbours it was'.[30] This was probably true in the sense that the client was not aware, before questioning, that he already suspected someone. It was not until the cunning man had asked probing questions, making suggestions that were not open to discussion with neighbours and using his magical apparatus to give them authority, that the client's suspicions became focused.

Probably the cunning folk were unwilling actually to suggest the name of a likely witch, preferring to leave the final decision to the client. For instance, in Essex in 1645, a man deposed that, his wife being sick of a disease that he believed to be 'more than meerly naturall', he went to a cunning woman[2]

who told this Informant, that his wife was cursed by two women who were neere neighbours to this Informant, the one dwelling a little above his house, and the other beneath his house, this Informants house standing on the side of an Hill: Whereupon he beleeved his said wife was bewitched by one *Elizabeth Clarke*.[31]

Here we see three stages. The client made the original selection and chose to believe that the illness was supernaturally inspired; the cunning woman confirmed this and, probably through discreet questions, learnt that her client was particularly anxious about his near neighbours and directed the worried man into consciously examining which of these might be the guilty person; the client then made the final selection himself. He would do this by combining his own hostility with more general suspicions that a certain person was a witch. This gradual elimination and concentration is further illustrated by Gifford. A cunning woman told a client that:

> he was plagued by a witch, adding moreover, that there were three women witches in that towne, and one man witch: willing him to look whom he most suspected: he suspected one old woman, and caused her to be carried before a Justice of Peace.[32]

Cunning folk would have known, from gossip, rumour, and previous consultations, the names of local witches. They would convey this information to their clients, releasing them in this manner from individual anxiety and putting them in touch with suspicions circulating in their own village. In a sense they acted as information centres, entrepreneurs in the business of allocating blame and distributing antidotes. Many features of their activities—for example, their reluctance actually to name the culprit —are well shown in the most detailed Essex account of an interview between a client and a cunning man. When the client first arrived the expert 'made the matter straunge to him', but shortly after 'told this examinate he woulde doe the best he coulde for him'. This was the preparatory stage, in which the practitioner warned the client of the difficulties inherent in the situation. Then the client was told to go away for nine days while the cunning man decided whether he could help. This was possibly a general practice and would allow cunning folk time to make inquiries and to sound local gossip. The client, on his return, looked in a magic mirror and was instructed by the cunning man that 'as farr as he could gesse, he shulde see the face of him that had the said lynnen', but, when the client saw a face and pressed for absolute confirmation, the cunning man refused to say that the mirror image was definitely the culprit.[33] Again, the final decision was with the client; the cunning folk only provided the mechanisms for making a choice.

In their attempts to turn vague suspicions into concrete beliefs, the cunning folk were aided by various magical devices. Possibly they started off with a psychological advantage by wearing strange costumes and filling their consulting room with impressive pieces of equipment.[34] What is more certain is that they had at their command a host of spells, oracles, and other devices.[35] Two of these seem to have been especially favoured in Essex. The first was the oracle of the 'sieve and sheeres'. Gifford stated that some wisemen 'deal with the Sive and a paire of sheeres, using certain words';[36] among the Essex cases of their use was the detection of Alice Reade, who used them to find lost goods.[37] A contemporary description of how this oracle was to be worked suggests that, like any other method of divination, subtle questioning and sleight of hand could be used to influence an apparently external and objective test.[38] Hidden thoughts could be brought into the open and made to appear as if they were dictated by a power outside the consulter. The other most popular Essex oracle, the mirror, basin of water, or other reflecting surface, also reveals this process of projection of inner thoughts on to an external object. Scot realized that the state of mind of the client could be externalized by a reflector: 'you may have glasses so made, as what image of favour soever you print in your imagination, you shall thinke you see the same therein'.[39] Contemporaries stated that this was one of the most popular methods employed by cunning folk,[40] and Gifford described the use of reflecting devices on several occasions.[41] One Essex woman admitted that she went to a conjurer on London Bridge for lost money and he showed 'her in a glass a boye in a sherte gleninge Corne resemblinge the countenance of John Hayes that had her monye'.[42] An even better account is given in the 1578 interview already quoted. The cunning man took his client out into the hall, and:

> browghte with him a looking glasse, (about vii or viii inches square), and did hange the said glasse up over the benche in his said hawle, upon a nayle, and bad the said examinate look in yt, and said as farr as he could gesse, he shulde see the face of him that had the said lynnen.[43]

The guilty party was duly seen.

/ In locating stolen goods, the cunning man's activities ceased when he had helped his client to find the thief or the property, but in cases of illness, and especially where witchcraft was selected as the reason for the disease, further treatment was necessary. Cunning folk prescribed 'Charmes of words' to be used over the victim; herbs, bags of seeds, or holy writings were also recommended to be worn by the victim.[44] Sometimes they cured the witchcraft immediately. One cured a 'mouth drawne awrye' by taking a cloth and, covering his client's eyes, striking 'him on the same side with a stronge blowe'.[45] Others passed on traditional remedies—for instance, the red-hot spit stuck in cream, or the burning of the victim's hair.[46] /As purveyors of magical counter-activities, suggesting and circulating methods of keeping evil under control, they played an especially important part in both spreading and directing witchcraft beliefs./ There is no evidence in Essex, however, that they extracted 'nayles, needles, feathers' and other articles from the victim, persuading their clients that they would recover if the witchcraft 'poison' was extracted, though this remedy was current in Europe.[47] Nor is there Essex evidence for sympathetic suffering on the part of cunning men, though this is a phenomenon described by more general English authorities.[48] These omissions are probably due to the apparent absence of 'diabolic possession' in Essex; on only one occasion do we know of an Essex cunning man being employed to exorcise spirits in a possessed person.[49]

There was considerable contemporary argument as to the origins of the power of cunning folk. Since no Essex cunning folk have left a record of their opinion on this subject, we have to rely on contemporary writers, mostly hostile, for suggestions. Gifford wrote that cunning folk believed that 'the spirits which appeare unto them in the Christall, or in the glasse, or water, or that any way do speake, and shewe matters unto them' were 'holy Angels, or the soules of excellent men, as of Moses, Samuel, David, and others'.[50] Gaule likewise wrote that some cunning folk 'have imagined their Familiars to be no other than good Angles [sic]'.[51] Those who opposed the cunning folk, especially the clergy, preferred to see their power as derived from the Devil.[52] Yet all agreed that their power was supernatural, that they learnt to control spirits, or to say spells of great force. They were believed to use powers already at work in the universe, channelled by their special rituals. In this we can distinguish them from their enemy, the witch, whose power lay primarily within her, in an evil essence rather than in the acquisition of a set of magical techniques. Cunning folk worked 'by vertue of words',[53] often they used purely automatic devices which seem to have involved no animistic power. Unlike Essex witches, they did not employ small animals, 'familiars', to carry out their instructions. Yet, for those who sought to discredit them, they were still working, albeit at second hand, with the Devil.[54]

Just as their power differed from that of witches, so did their motives. To a certain extent they worked for money, though their fees were less than those of doctors.[55] Fees were related to the type of activity undertaken and the degree of success.[56] Some cunning folk refused payment. 'Some may not take any thing at all, as some have professed, that if they should take any thing they could doe no good.'[57] Others left fees to the discretion of their clients.[58] It is also clear that cunning folk sometimes put pressure on their clients, and also that extra payments or presents were made if success attended their efforts. For instance, an Essex cunning man who claimed that he did not exact fees, also admitted that in one consultation his clients 'did give him a shilling for his paines, and [he, i.e. the cunning man] told them that for ye p[re]sent it should suffice, but withall, if they had the goods againe he desired further satisfaction'.[59] This partly reflected the precarious legal position of cunning folk; they were less vulnerable to an action of fraud if they could show that their fees were voluntary. Otherwise they might suffer the fate of the Essex surgeon who, in 1620, was prosecuted at the Assizes because he had taken 5s. from a man to tell him who had stolen his cloth and had failed to name the culprit.[60] Usually the fees seem to have been less than this. In 1582 a cunning woman offered to cure a woman of lameness for 12*d*.,[61] and the Chelmsford cunning man was given 8*d*. and 10*d*. on separate occasions.[62] Though it may have been a lucrative profession when combined with astrology in a city,[63] the general impression from Essex material is that cunning folk were neither professional nor full-time practitioners. It was as much, or more, the desire for prestige rather than payment which attracted people. Scot said their motives were 'glorie, fame, or gaine', and it is the former that Bernard stressed when he said that they were 'fantastically proud', and boasted of 'their gift and power'.[64]

Further evidence that cunning folk acted only part-time comes from an analysis of their professions and status. Only the male practitioners have recorded occupations, and these are listed in Table 9. Seven out of twenty-three whose occupation we know were connected with the medical profession;[65] another three were probably clerics.[66] A further six, consisting of two schoolmasters, two astrologers,[67] a churchwarden,[68] and a 'gent' were in the upper professional group. Only one-third were artisans or agriculturists, consisting of two yeomen, two labourers, a miller, a comber, and a shoemaker. There is some evidence as to their degree of literacy. One gave a 'note' to a client;[69] another had been taught by the astrologer William Lilly and could 'cast a figure' with pen and paper;[70] a third maintained some impeccable churchwardens' accounts. Unfortunately, we have little information concerning their character and mentality, beyond the general criticism that they had 'a mind addicted unto curiosity and vaine estimation'.[71]

It has already been suggested that bias in the records distorts any impression of the proportion of male to female cunning folk. This even deceived contemporaries. Thus John Stearne wrote that black witches were nearly all women, while cunning folk 'almost generally they be men'.[72] On the other hand, Thomas Cooper assumed that cunning folk would be women.[73] From the Essex evidence it seems that while men were more likely to be presented at court, since they predominated in finding lost goods, and possibly as healers, women were often consulted in the attempt to counter witchcraft. We only hear of the latter indirectly,[74] or when their previous reputation as a cunning woman later led them to be accused of black witchcraft. Thus in 1582 Ursley Kempe, formerly a 'white' witch, was accused at the Assizes for 'black' witchcraft. Similarly, in 1572, Margery Skelton was prosecuted at the same court for evil witchcraft, whereas she had been summoned to the ecclesiastical court six years previously for 'white' witchcraft.[75] The same was true in the cases of Catherine Reve and Edwin Hadesley.[76] Yet, though there may have been other cases, those who were accused of both black and white witchcraft seem to have been few in Essex. Of forty-one definite Essex cunning folk, only four were later recorded as accused of 'black' witchcraft, while less than half a dozen of a total of over 400 persons accused of black witchcraft are known to have been cunning folk.

There can be little doubt that cunning folk were often successful. Though hostile, Gifford could not deny that 'out of question they be innumerable which receive helpe by going to the cunning men'.[77] On visiting wise-men 'the meanes are received, applied, and used, the sicke partie accordingly recovereth, and the conclusion of all is, the usual acclamation; Oh happie is the day, that ever I met with such a man or woman to helpe me!'[78] There are a number of examples in Essex records of successful cures. Gifford gave cases of the successful recovery of a Communion cup, the curing of a sick child, and the saving of bewitched cream on the advice of a cunning man.[79] Margery Skelton claimed that she had healed seven people.[80] A woman was healed by having a seed-bag strapped to her in 1582;[81] another recovered her health in 1570.[82] Lost property was recovered in 1578 and 1651.[83] Even their failures could be woven into the system and be made to support witchcraft suspicions. Bernard noted that:

> These Witches, to keepe their credit, often deliver the medicines with an *If*: If it doe no good, come againe. When they returne and finde that the Devill hath not removed the disease . . . the Wizards blame them, that they came not in time, or they applied not the meanes aright, or that they wanted faith to beleeve, or at least they acknowledged their power not great inough, and therefore they advise them to goe to a more cunning man or woman.[84]

Thus successes were noted and praised, while failures were explained within the context of witchcraft beliefs by attributing them to mistakes in performing rituals or to particular circumstances. The basic premises were meanwhile left unchallenged.[85]

One possible reason for failure, Bernard suggested, was that the client 'wanted faith to beleeve'. This faith-healing element was of considerable importance in a number of cures. Gifford stressed that when a charm was used a patient was told by the cunning man that 'you must beleeve it will helpe, or els it will doe you no good at all'.[86] As he said, 'Imagination is a strong thing to hurt, all men doe finde, and why should it not then be strong also to help, when the parties mind is cheered, by beleeving fully that he receiveth ease?'[87] If, as suggested earlier, cunning folk were principally consulted in cases of indecision, when an objective, outside, opinion was needed to clear away anxiety and doubt, their promise of hope when others had despaired, and their sympathetic probing of the mind of the patient, may have helped to a considerable extent. They foreshadowed modern psychiatrists in relating physical illness to disturbed social relationships. They interpreted the feelings aroused by disturbances in current, witchcraft, terms. Here they filled a vacuum and supplied a need.[88] They admitted that 'they cannot heale such as doe not beleeve in them',[89] and perceptive doctors realized that magical cures could work 'by reason of the confident perswasion which melancholike and passionate people may have in them'.[90] There is no evidence as to whether the cunning folk themselves believed in their cures and methods. Undoubtedly some of them used sleight of hand and other tricks,[91] yet this does not necessarily mean that either they or those who were aware of such tricks questioned the general efficacy of white witchcraft. Many people probably agreed with Joseph Glanvil when he argued that one true story of witchcraft 'is worth a thousand tales of forgery and imposture'.[92]

Contemporaries varied enormously in their attitude towards cunning folk. Even legal authorities wavered. Although cunning folk could be prosecuted at both ecclesiastical and secular courts, yet their accusation was a 'great presumption' in the case against a black witch.[93] Most vehement in their hostility were Puritan writers. William Perkins warned that Christians should 'abhorre the wizard, as the most pernicious enemie of our salvation . . . as the greatest enemie of Gods name, worship, and glorie, that is in the world, next to Satan himselfe'.[49] He believed that, like black witches, they should be executed.[95] Gaule argued that they were even worse than black witches, and that seeking to them constituted a tacit compact with the Devil.[96] This horror reflected their real threat to the monopoly and assumptions of Christianity. They used methods and provided explanations based on supernatural power, but power not derived directly from the Christian God. Their prescription for pain was neither ordinary physic nor prayer and soul-searching. They suggested that misfortune was not related to the guilt of the sufferer, but to that of another human being. In problems concerning the spirit and emotions of men, traditionally the preserve of the clergy, they competed with successful solutions. The clash is well demonstrated in the penance enjoined on one of their clients in Essex in 1585. He was ordered to stand up in church and to confess 'him self hartelie sorie for sekinge mans helpe and refusinge ye helpe of god'.[97] If God would not help, the Puritans argued that 'better it were to loose a thing finally, and by faith to expect till God make supplie another way; then in this [i.e. by recourse to judicial astrologers] to recover it againe'.[98] Essex villagers, however, often felt differently.

The Essex records show that people went long distances to consult cunning folk, despite the censure of the Church. The friendly attitude towards cunning folk on the part of the majority of the Essex population was reflected by Gifford when he made one of his country characters say of a wise-woman that 'she doeth more good in one yeare than all these scripture men will doe so long as they live'.[99] No wonder the 'scripture men' were apprehensive! Even when reprimanded, people clung to their views. Thus the man whom we saw ordered to confess himself sorry for 'sekinge mans helpe' had earlier admitted to going to a cunning man 'and saethe yt [that] for the helpe of his wief he went to him and if it weare againe he wold do the like to helpe his wief'.[100] It is possible that some of the country clergy more than tolerated them;[101] they may even have been seen as godly parishioners.[102] Churchwardens' behaviour may be taken as an example of the ambivalent attitude towards these practitioners. As officials they were expected to present cunning folk and their clients; as private individuals they often approved of them. One of them was himself a cunning man;[103] another went to a cunning man for news of his land-lord's lost horse.[104] Gifford tells that on one occasion 'the Communion cup was stollen: the Churchwardens rode to a wise man, he gave them direction . . . and certainly they had it again'.[105] One result of this was that they were slack in their presentments: on two occasions in Essex they were detected for not presenting 'witches'.[106] Likewise, village constables, as in 1651,[107] might patronize wise-men.

There can be little doubt concerning the popularity or versatility of Essex cunning folk. As in other parts of England, 'Charming is in as great request as Physicke, and Charmers more sought unto then Physicians in time of neede'.[108] What is less clear is when they originated. This problem lies outside the scope of this work and it can only be suggested that the pre-Reformation clergy undertook many of the activities later performed by cunning folk. They probably cursed for theft, helped people take decisions, and resolved quarrels between neighbours. They also prescribed charms and blessed against evil.[109] By our period such activities were looked on by the Anglican Church as popish and evil, yet they were still in demand. Consequently, cunning folk remained powerful in Essex until at least the nineteenth century: the most famous of them died in 1860! But it was especially in the century after 1560 that they played a major role in directing witchcraft suspicions.

NOTES

1. There were a number of interchangeable terms for these practitioners, 'white', 'good', or 'unbinding' witches, blessers, wizards, sorcerers; cunning folk or wise-men are used in this chapter, since they were the most frequent terms. See F. J. Pope, 'A Conjurer or Cunningman of the Seventeenth Century', *The British Archivist*, i, No. 18 (1914), pp. 145-7.
2. Kittredge, *Witchcraft*, pp. 211-12; Robert Burton, *Anatomy of Melancholy* (Oxford, 1621), p. 289. Scot, *Discovery*, p. 27, put the numbers even higher.

3. Stearne, *Confirmation*, p. 11.
4. Catherine Reve in Table 9, p. 117, above.
5. These cases are listed in Table 9, pp. 117–18, above.
6. Gifford, *Dialogue*, sig. B.
7. Ibid., sigs. G3, H.
8. For convenience 'cunning man' will be used as the singular of cunning folk, though the practitioners were often female. The cases in Gifford's *Dialogue* are on sigs. B, B, Bᵛ, B2ᵛ, C, D4ᵛ, E3ᵛ, E3ᵛ, I3ᵛ.
9. Case 846.
10. For example, cases 898, 942, 1,065.
11. Cases 1,120 and 1,115.
12. One Newcastle case (1,173) is listed in Table 9; the other (1,072) is omitted, since no cunning man was named. Both clients lived in estuary towns and there is no other 'New Castle' in East Anglia.
13. Gifford, *Dialogue*, sig. B.
14. Bernard, *Guide*, p. 147; Scot, *Discovery*, p. 33, made the same point.
15. Case 846.
16. This was certainly the case with their more sophisticated counterparts, the judicial astrologers, as can be seen in the notebooks of William Lilly and Richard Napier— for example, those cited in case 1,206. For cunning folk consulted on marital problems in Norfolk, see Kittredge, *Witchcraft*, p. 107.
17. Case 1,060.
18. Introduction to Perkins, *Damned Art*, p. 3.
19. Cases 855 and 846; case 839 seems similar.
20. Gifford, *Discourse*, sig. H2.
21. Ady, *Candle*, p. 40.
22. Bernard, *Guide*, pp. 151–3.
23. For fees of cunning men and their success see later in the chapter; the type of illness they were asked to cure is discussed on pp. 122-3, above.
24. 1582 Pamphlet, sigs. E–Eᵛ.
25. Ibid, sig. A3ᵛ.
26. Gifford, *Discourse*, sig. H.
27. Ibid., sig. I; there are other examples in Gifford, *Dialogue*, sigs. D4ᵛ, C.
28. Scot, *Discovery*, p. 221.
29. Case 1,204.
30. Ady, *Candle*, p. 159; Bernard, *Guide*, p. 154, suggested that white witches 'discover' black witches.
31. 1645 Pamphlet, p. 1.
32. Gifford, *Dialogue*, sig. C.
33. Case 809.
34. This was certainly so in nineteenth-century Essex (E. Maple, *Dark World of Witches* (Pan edn., 1965), p. 175).
35. For instance, John Gaule gave a list of over fifty methods of divination in his *Mag-Astro-Mancer* (1652), pp. 165–6.
36. Gifford, *Dialogue*, sig. F4ᵛ.
37. Case 1,130.
38. Scot, *Discovery*, p. 224.
39. Ibid., p. 265.
40. Among them Bernard, *Guide*, p. 137; Ady, *Candle*, p. 40.
41. *Dialogue*, sigs. B, E4, F3.

42. Case 886.
43. Case 809.
44. Examples and methods are described in Perkins, *Damned Art*, p. 175; Bernard, *Guide*, pp. 99–100, 133–5; 1582 Pamphlet, sigs. A7ᵛ, C2ᵛ; Gifford, *Dialogue*, sig. Bᵛ. A number of remedies were suggested by Richard Napier, the astrologer, in case, 1,207.
45. 1582 Pamphlet, sig. C7.
46. Gifford, *Dialogue*, sigs. B2ᵛ, E4.
47. E. Jorden, *Briefe Discourse of a Disease Called the Suffocation of the Mother* (1603), p. 24ᵛ.
48. For instance, in Bernard, *Guide*, pp. 138, 141.
49. Case 1,183.
50. Gifford, *Dialogue*, sig. Fᵛ; see also sig. E2ᵛ.
51. Gaule, *Select Cases*, p. 125.
52. This was argued, for example, by Bernard, *Guide*, p. 134, and Perkins, *Damned Art*, p. 175.
53. Ady, *Candle*, p. 63.
54. Supernatural power could only be derived from God or the Devil, Gifford argued, and since cunning folk were clearly not divinely inspired, they must be in league with the Devil (Gifford, *Dialogue*, sig. F4ᵛ, and *Discourse*, sig. B3ᵛ).
55. Doctors, echoing Bernard, *Guide*, p. 153, could argue that it was 'a miserable sparing, to spare the purse, and to damne the soule'.
56. Only a 'penny and a loaf' was claimed by cattle-curing cunning folk according to Scot, *Discovery*, p. 211.
57. Bernard, *Guide*, p. 131.
58. Ibid., p. 131; for an Essex example see case 809.
59. Case 846.
60. Case 553b.
61. 1582 Pamphlet, sig. A2ᵛ.
62. Case 846.
63. For example, the retired Cambridge cunning man referred to in Bernard, *Guide*, p. 138, claimed that he could have made 'two hundred pounds *per annum* of his skill'.
64. Scot, *Discovery*, p. 30; Bernard, *Guide*, p. 132.
65. Only two of these have been discovered in other records. Marcell Goodwin of Colchester's will survives at Chelmsford (see p. 76, above) and Gilbert Wakering of Halstead subscribed to the Oath of Supremacy in 1631, J. H. Bloom and R. R. James, *Medical Practitioners in the Diocese of London* (Cambridge, 1935), p. 72.
66. Mr. Fountayne, Mr. Hawes, and Henry Gower; none of them, however, appeared, in Newcourt or other sources, to have had livings in Essex.
67. John Thomas, who lived on London Bridge, may have been the John Thomas who published a *Prognostication rectified and composed for Bridgwater* in 1612. It seems more certain that the 'Gressam' of London was Edward Gresham who published almanacks in 1598, 1604–6, and who died in 1612 (Short Title Catalogue, No. 12,360, and Bodleian Library, Ashmole MS. 242, fol. 200).
68. Miles Blomfield was presented as a cunning man in 1578; he was churchwarden between 1582 and 1587 and owned a house bordering on the churchyard; his churchwardens' accounts are excellent; see Irvine Gray, 'Footnote to an Alchemist', *Cambridge Review*, lxviii, No. 1,658 (1946), p. 172.

69. Case 855.
70. Case 845.
71. Gifford, *Discourse*, sig. I2.
72. Stearne, *Confirmation*, p. 11.
73. Thomas Cooper, *Mystery of Witchcraft* (1617), p. 219.
74. Examples are given on p. 127, above.
75. For Margery Skelton see cases 46–8, 873.
76. Cases 1,007, 1,167 (Reve) and 488, 1,181 (Hadesley).
77. Gifford, *Dialogue*, sig. G3.
78. Perkins, *Damned Art*, p. 175; see also Gifford, *Discourse*, sig. H.
79. Gifford, *Dialogue*, sigs. B^v, B2^v, E3^v, G4, L3^v.
80. Case 873.
81. 1582 Pamphlet, sig. C2^v.
82. Case 1,204.
83. Cases 846 and 809.
84. Bernard, *Guide*, pp. 146–7.
85. Though, clearly, some people—for instance Scot and Ady—saw 'through' cunning folk.
86. Gifford, *Dialogue*, sig. G4^v.
87. Ibid., sig. G4.
88. The faith-healing element was normally missing in ordinary physic, said Bernard, *Guide*, p. 139.
89. Idem.
90. E. Jorden, *Briefe Discourse of a Disease Called the Suffocation of the Mother* (1603) p. 25.
91. For instance, the fraudulent methods in Essex described in Ady, *Candle*, p. 62.
92. J. Glanvil, *Philosophical Considerations Touching the Being of Witches* (1667), pp. 33–4. Like many of the hypotheses in this chapter, it cannot be fully proved, although it can be shown to be true in contemporary societies. Thus the above description is similar to the reaction to failure and fraud described in Evans-Pritchard (1937), pp. 183, 193, 248, 255.
93. Bernard, *Guide*, p. 212; Perkins, *Damned Art*, p. 209, also maintained an ambivalent attitude to the legality of evidence produced by cunning folk.
94. Perkins, *Damned Art*, pp. 177–8.
95. Ibid., p. 255.
96. Gaule, *Select Cases*, pp. 30–1.
97. Case 911; as Perkins wrote (*Damned Art*, p. 257), people depended on the white witch 'as their god'.
98. Perkins, *Damned Art*, p. 88.
99. Gifford, *Dialogue*, sig. M3^v.
100. Case 911.
101. Scot, *Discovery*, p. 27, implies this.
102. A Somersetshire white witch had the reputation of being a 'religious woman' (Meric Casaubon, *A Treatise Proving Spirits* (1672), p. 116).
103. Case 809.
104. Case 1,096.
105. Gifford, *Dialogue*, sig. E3^v; there are actual cases of churchwardens in Berkshire, and a whole congregation in Lincolnshire, sending to cunning folk in Kittredge, *Witchcraft*, pp. 197–8.
106. Cases 1,128, 1,063; the latter, however, may have been a 'black' witch.

107. Case 846.
108. Perkins, *Damned Art*, p. 153.
109. For an Essex case of the alleged prescription of charms by Roman Catholic clergy see Ady, *Candle*, pp. 58–9. As late as the nineteenth century, in Yorkshire, 'priests o' t'au'd church' were believed to have been powerful conjurers, according to J. C. Atkinson, *Forty Years in a Moorland Parish* (1891), p. 59; the same author, pp. 103–25, gives a superb account of Yorkshire cunning folk.

Chapter 9

The witch-finding movement of 1645 in Essex

At the Summer Assizes held at Chelmsford in 1645 there were fifty indictments against suspected witches. These were exceptional, in number, content, and in occurring after years of gradual decline in witchcraft prosecutions at the Assizes.[1] Since they have received more attention from subsequent writers than other aspects of Essex prosecutions, only a short analysis of them will be given here.[2] Some separate analysis is necessary, however, for various reasons. The 1645 trial was described in greater detail than any other Essex witchcraft inquisition.[3] It is therefore easier to reconstruct the pressures behind the accusations in 1645 than in earlier prosecutions. Secondly, many of the recent theories attempting to explain witchcraft prosecutions are based on evidence from this trial.[4] Thirdly, a comparison of events in 1645 with the descriptions of prosecutions in the Elizabethan period enables us to see in what ways beliefs concerning witches changed over time. Finally, the 1645 prosecutions are the only ones which can be definitely related to the presence of 'witch-hunters'— that is, people who seem to have specialized in accusing and finding witches. It seems to be correct that, as Gaule argued, 'such a Profession [i.e. witch-finding] or occupation has not beene heard of heretofore'.[5] While it is true that cunning folk, as we have seen, gave advice to those supposedly bewitched, they seem to have acted in a far less formal capacity. They did not travel from village to village searching for witches and being paid for this; nor did they play a major part in the actual trials of witches.[6]

Some thirty-six suspects, all women, were imprisoned or tried for witchcraft at the 1645 Essex Assizes. Of these, nineteen were almost certainly executed, nine died of gaol fever, six were still in prison in 1648, and only one, a woman from another part of Essex, was acquitted and escaped free. Another woman, Rebecca West, was also released after acting as the Crown's chief witness. Compared to other trials, the percentage of the accused who were executed was abnormally high. Another marked contrast to earlier trials (except that of 1582) was the geographical concentration of the prosecutions. Thirty-five of the suspects came from twelve villages, all within fifteen miles of Manningtree.[7] The witnesses

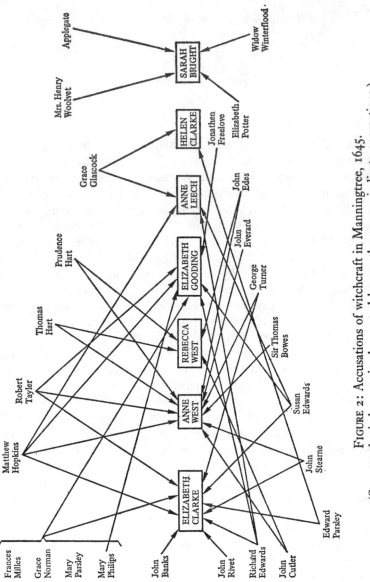

FIGURE 2: Accusations of witchcraft in Manningtree, 1645.
(Suspected witches are in the central boxes; the arrows indicate accusations.)

against the witches included men and women from all levels of society; in all, the indictments and pamphlet name some ninety-two such witnesses, fifty-eight male and thirty-four female. The two 'witch-finders', Matthew Hopkins and John Stearne, obviously found ready support for their accusations. Among the witnesses were three clergymen, John Edes, George Eatoney, and Joseph Longe.[8] They witnessed to the appearance of familiars and corroborated Hopkins and Stearne. One clergyman, however, helped to procure a reprieve for a suspect.[9] A special group were the women searchers, a panel of professed experts whose names appear with

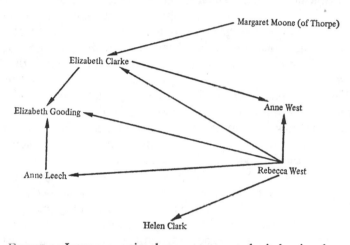

FIGURE 3: Inter-accusation between suspected witches in 1645.
(An arrow represents an accusation made by one suspected witch against another
All except Margaret Moone lived in Manningtree.)

regularity in different indictments and who witnessed, as the pamphlet shows, to the presence of suspicious lumps or other marks on witches.[10] Otherwise, as far as we can tell, the witnesses were normal citizens, many of whom can be traced in contemporary wills, Ship Money assessments, or lists of Presbyterian elders.[11] Different groups of individuals acted as witnesses in different villages. Hopkins and Stearne, for example, only appeared as witnesses against suspects from four of the twelve neighbouring villages involved: Langham, Mistley, Ramsey, and Manningtree. In other villages, other groups of inhabitants supported and formulated the accusations.

Even near Manningtree, the efforts of Hopkins and Stearne could not have succeeded without wider support; over twenty people, including these two, witnessed against the six most notorious witches. The direction

of accusations is shown in Fig. 2. Here we see the complicated overlapping
of accusations, centring on Elizabeth Clarke and Anne West. One Manningtree suspect, Sarah Bright, appears to have been independently accused.
The cumulative effect of such corroboration was further consolidated by
the inter-accusation between the suspects. This also can be best demonstrated in a similar way in Fig. 3. Here we see especially clearly the importance of the Crown's witness, Rebecca West.

If we concentrate our attention even more and select just one of the
witnesses in the first figure, Richard Edwards, we begin to see the way in
which suspicions reflected much wider tensions, not merely the malice of
two witch-finders. As can be seen from the figure, Edwards was one of the
three men who witnessed against more than two women. Further than this,
Edwards claimed that his son had been bewitched to death by Margaret
Moone of Thorpe and Elizabeth Clarke of Manningtree; both of them
confessed to this offence, as did a Mistley woman who also bewitched his
beer. His alleged misfortunes did not end here; Rebecca West corroborated
his own account of how his horse, crossing a bridge, had been frightened
by a strange shriek and had nearly thrown him: again the work of a witch.
Thus it was on Edwards that the Manningtree witches were supposed to
have focused their activities.[12] But he was a dangerous enemy to rouse.
From the assessment for the Ship Money in 1637, it appears that he
owned property in Ramsey, was the third largest property-holder in
Mistley and the second largest in Lawford. In Manningtree itself he was
styled 'gent' and was assessed to pay £3; the next highest assessment in
that village was 14s.[13] It is almost certain that he was Chief Constable of
Tendring Hundred in 1642.[14] He was thus not only one of the most
attacked, but also one of the most powerful men in the area.

While we can see that Hopkins and Stearne were only part of an influential group who wished to exterminate witches, there is also evidence of
counter-pressure. Again this illustrates the way in which witchcraft
accusations mobilized wider rivalries in the village. Stearne described how
more than forty people, among them himself, had been outlawed on a writ
of conspiracy for witch-hunting 'by the means of one who is reported to
have been one of the greatest agents in Colchester-businesse, within the
Towne'. He then went on to describe earlier opposition. This is worth full
quotation, since, largely overlooked by historians,[15] it is a unique example,
in Essex, of a faction struggle over the guilt of a supposed witch:

> This man [Stearne wrote] with another who is likewise reported to have been
> fellow-agent with him in that businesse, and the two chiefest in it, was the
> cause that some were not questioned in that Town: but for his part, I saw him
> labour and endeavour all he could to keep this woman, whom he so much held
> withal from her legal Trial, and likewise heard him threaten both me and all

that had given evidence against her . . . as I since have heard, she was condemned at that Assize, and by his procurement reprieved.[16]

Unfortunately, it is not possible to identify with certainty either the defenders or the women they reprieved.

There are a number of ways in which the 1645 trial seems to have been similar to those described in earlier pamphlets. The motive of the witch, the methods she was supposed to employ, the length of time she was believed to have been a witch before being accused, all these are similar. Likewise, comparison of the indictments and the other accounts show how much the former omit. Although only twenty-three of those accused at the Assizes were described in the pamphlet account, we learn of another forty-nine offences not mentioned in the indictments. Several witches mentioned in the pamphlet do not appear in surviving legal records; there is no record of Elizabeth Clarke's mother and kinsfolk, who were supposed to have been executed for witchcraft, nor of the previous accusation against Margaret Moone.[17] Neither Goodwife Hagtree, who had brought a woman her familiars some ten years before,[18] nor Judith Moone, on whom the witch's mark was found,[19] appear in other records. In certain ways, therefore, the trial of 1645 can be seen as a continuation of earlier tendencies.

In other ways, however, it was different. The difference has already been noticed in the abnormal proportion of executions, in the geographical concentration, and in the presence of witch-finders. Another unusual feature was the exceptionally high proportion of indictments for merely entertaining evil spirits: eighteen of the twenty-eight known indictments for this offence during the whole period in Essex came from this trial. The familiars also had become much more strange. Though plentiful in earlier pamphlets, none had been as bizarre as the legless dog, ox-headed greyhound and other monstrosities which visited one of the suspects as she was being watched by eight people. Nor were their names as fanciful, on the whole, as the *Vinegar Tom*, *Sacke and Sugar*, *Griezzell Greedigutt*, and others described in the 1645 pamphlet. Nor is there any trace in earlier evidence of the ritual marriage of the witch and Devil, of the appearance of the Devil as a man, or of sexual intercourse between the Devil and the witch.[20] Among other innovations were the idea of the weekly (Friday) meeting of witches, and the description of their activities at this meeting, including reading out of a book.[21] Here, it seems, we see the influence of Continental ideas, perhaps mediated through Matthew Hopkins.[22]

The evidence from the 1645 trial is further biased because special methods were used to induce confessions. Pricking the witch to see if she had any dead spots, thought to be a sure sign of guilt; searching the suspect for any strange excrescences; swimming her to see if she floated; keeping her awake for several nights and walking her back and forth until her feet were blistered—all these were methods used at the Chelmsford trial.[23] We have seen that people confessed and were found guilty in the Elizabethan period when all these methods, except the searching for a spot or lump, were absent. Therefore it is clear that we must not place too much stress on physical pressure as the cause of witchcraft beliefs. Likewise, it is wrong to think that such methods were highly illegal. They were done with the cognizance of the Essex justices, Sir Harbottle Grimston and Sir Thomas Bowes;[24] only later were some of these methods disallowed.[25] Nevertheless, as Ady pointed out, the combination of sleeplessness and isolation 'will tame any wilde Beast . . . how much more may it make men or women yeeld to confess Lyes, and impossibilities'.[26] Peculiar means resulted in a unique trial.

The usual explanation for the prosecutions is that they were stirred up by Hopkins and Stearne. The usual motive ascribed to them is greed. They were certainly paid for their witch-hunting activities in other counties, but the suggestion that they started looking for witches because they were impecunious, though often repeated, appears to have no factual basis.[27] The other suggested motive for their activity is religious fanaticism; again there is little evidence that Hopkins was moved by religious enthusiasm.[28] Among their victims were clergymen and ardent churchgoers, among their opponents Puritan extremists.[29] The real spur to their activity, at least in Essex, seems much more prosaic. It seems to have been a combination of curiosity, bewilderment, and anxiety, with a desire to exercise power and perform a useful public duty. Though Hopkins claims to have been, with Stearne, in personal danger,[30] the total impression is that this was in the background: more striking is the feeling of surprise, mingled with horror, at the conspiracy which they had unearthed. Such a conclusion can only remain an impression culled from the pamphlet and other accounts. A similar impression is that Hopkins and Stearne, like the justices, clergymen, and other notable inhabitants, really believed that they were performing a public service, dealing with a public menace. The witchfinders repeatedly asserted that they did not go around stirring up trouble, but only answered a public demand: as Hopkins said in a letter, he only went to towns where he was welcomed and given 'thankes and recompense'.[31] Stearne denied the allegation that they did this work 'for their owne private ends, for gaine and such like'.[32] He also stated that he was only called in after the Manningtree suspicions had already been voiced.[33] Of course, there is a danger in accepting the witch-finders *post facto* defence of their motives. But it would also be naïve to isolate these two as black-hearted villains leading on an innocent populace,[34] as some have done: examination of the 1645 trial in its historical and local setting does not support such a conclusion.

The pressures behind the trials could not have been exerted by a small group of witch-finders; they were distributed far more widely, and even the victims played a part. One example of an unexpected pressure is given by Hopkins when he was discussing water ordeals. He argued that the Devil:

> perswading many to come of their owne accord to be tryed, perswading them their marks are so close they shall not be found out, so as diverse have come 10 or 12 miles to be searched of their own accord, and hanged for their labour, (as one *Meggs*, a Baker did, who lived within 7 miles of *Norwich* and was hanged at Norwich Assizes for witchcraft), then when they find that the Devil tells them false, they reflect on him and he, (as 40 have confessed) adviseth them to be swome.[35]

This argument, that swimming was only used at the request of the victims, was repeated by Stearne, but it has been ignored by subsequent historians.[36] The simplest explanation of the voluntary ordeal would be that it performed a cathartic function. Villages were still intimate societies within which a suspected witch would feel increasingly isolated, surrounded by a wall of hostility. She might, therefore, welcome an ordeal as a deliverance from otherwise irrefutable suspicions, especially since she would naturally be convinced of her innocence.[37] This may have been connected with a possible millenarian tinge to the movement. Since witches were the cause of so much evil their extinction, it was argued, would make the world into a more prosperous and happy place. Thus Gifford had earlier scoffed at the simple countryman's belief that 'the country being rid of the witches and their spirits, mens bodies and their cattel should bee safe'.[38] Though there is no explicitly millenarian statement by the movement leaders in East Anglia in the 1640's, it seems that villagers, already imbued with millenarian concepts,[39] viewed the witch-finders with considerable excitement. As Gaule, one of Hopkins' opponents, complained, 'the Cuntrey People talke already, and that more frequently, more affectedly, of the infallible and wonderfull power of the Witchfinders; then they doe of God, or Christ, or the Gospell preached'.[40] Given the demand for their services, Hopkins and Stearne could well argue that they merely gave local authorities expert advice. No doubt they exacerbated the prosecutions by their reputation and energy, but all the time, as we have seen in Essex, they were building on pre-existing and localized tensions. Although not as free from the charge of using physical pressure, they may be compared to the leader of a contemporary witchfinding cult:

> The general impression I got of him was that he is very genuinely concerned with the growing incidence of man's wickedness. . . . His function is comparable with that of a father-confessor or a psychiatrist in our own society . . . he may be misguided, his sincerity seems striking.[41]

The idea of Matthew Hopkins as the instigator of prosecutions may have as little truth as the myth which reflected it, that Hopkins himself was swum as a witch.[42]

If we minimize the personal influence of Hopkins and Stearne in the Essex prosecutions, we are left with the central problem: Why were there savage prosecutions in 1645? The answer seems to lie in a combination of particular factors, especially the disruption of local government and justice by the Civil War and, possibly, the economic, spiritual, and other tensions which war created, with beliefs in witchcraft which, though usually kept just below the surface, were no less widespread and powerful than they had been in the sixteenth century. Wallace Notestein,[43] having dismissed the suggestion that Puritanism was to blame for the prosecutions, suggested the lack of government as a major factor. If he had been aware of the existence of Assize court records for 1645 he would not have stated that 'England was in a state of judicial anarchy' in that year. If this had ever been true, it was in 1643 when the Assizes do not appear to have been held. Thus lack of government, by itself, cannot explain the 1645 trial.

NOTES

1. See cases 599–648(g); Diagram 1, p. 26, above, shows how exceptional the trial was.

2. The best account of the Essex trial and of Hopkins's tour through Suffolk, Norfolk, Cambridgeshire, Northamptonshire, Huntingdonshire, and the Isle of Ely is still Notestein, *Witchcraft*, pp. 164–205. The Assize documents, unused by Notestein, are printed in Ewen, I, pp. 221–31; Ewen discusses and analyses these in his second book, Ewen, II, pp. 254–79. Other works on Hopkins are cited in the Bibliography, but none adds significantly to these accounts.

3. The main sources are the 1645 Pamphlet, the Assize records cited above, Hopkins, *Discovery*, and Stearne, *Confirmation*. For reasons outlined in the Bibliography, a very distorted pamphlet written in 1700 has not been used.

4. For instance, M. A. Murray, *Witch-cult in Western Europe* (Oxford paperback edn., 1962), used the depositions at this trial on over twenty occasions to prove the existence of covens and Sabbats in England.

5. Gaule, *Select Cases*, p. 88.

6. The only real comparison is with Brian Darcy in the 1582 trial; see p. 85. Gifford, however, suggested that 'divers well disposed men . . . have seriously taken the matter [i.e. witchcraft] in hande, and have hunted those puckrils out of their neastes' (Gifford, *Discourse*, sig. G3). For witch-finders in other parts of Britain see Ewen, I, pp. 69–70.

7. See Map 5, p. 71, above.

8. John Edes, who gave evidence against Rebecca West of Lawford (case 609 and 1645 Pamphlet, p. 11), was Rector of Lawford between 1615 and 1658. He was a minister in the Tendring Classis and signed the Presbyterian Testimony in 1648; Davids, *Annals*, p. 296; H. Smith, *Ecclesiastical History of Essex* (n.d.), p. 110;

Venn, *Alumni Cantabrigiensis*. George Eatoney appeared as 'clericus' as a witness in the indictments against three suspects (cases 605–6, 639, 640), but he is absent from both the 1645 Pamphlet and from the standard ecclesiastical histories of Essex, as well as Venn and Foster. Joseph Longe gave evidence in the 1645 Pamphlet, pp. 18–19, concerning the spirits of Anne Cooper of Clacton, and was a witness in the indictments of three Clacton women, cases 631–6, 629. Depositions had been taken against him the previous year as a pluralist and he had been deprived of Fingeringhoe, but he retained the Vicarage of Great Clacton until 1662. He was also accused of being 'cruel in exacting his tithes; an innovator; would not give the sacrament but to those who come up to the rails; a common alehouse haunter, obscene in his discourse, and a usual swearer by his faith', Davids, *Annals*, p. 396; Venn, *Alumni Cantabrigiensis*.

9. Mary Coppine, according to the gaol calendar, was reprieved 'uppon desire of Mr. Gray the minister'; she was still in prison three years later, however (case 624). Although there were parsons and rectors of that surname at Wickford, Wickham Bishops, and Mashbury in Essex at this time, no such named man is known to have been minister of Mary Coppine's town, Kirby.

10. See, for instance, the group of four women shown in Fig. 2.

11. All these sources could be used to reconstruct a detailed picture of the social and religious background of those involved. For instance, in the Ship-Money assessment in 1637, at least thirty of those later to be found as victims or witnesses appear; only one witch's husband was assessed, Edward Gooding of Manningtree at the low sum of 2s. 6d. (see cases 627 8). Among the twenty-two named elders of the Tendring Classis of the Essex Presbyterian movement were Sir Thomas Bowes and Sir Harbottle Grimston, the two magistrates who took most of the confessions, Robert Tayler, a principal witness in Manningtree (see Fig. 2), and George Francis, who believed his only son to have been bewitched (1645 Pamphlet, p. 12; Davids, *Annals*, pp. 296–9).

12. For Edwards' activities see cases 602–3, 611 and 1645 Pamphlet, pp. 3, 7–8, 12–13, 22.

13. E.R.O., T/A 42.

14. Assizes 35/83/T/42 at the P.R.O.

15. Notestein, *Witchcraft*, p. 192, merely notes the incident in passing, and Ewen does not refer to the episode.

16. Stearne, *Confirmation*, p. 58.

17. 1645 Pamphlet, pp. 1, 22; naturally it is impossible to be certain that Elizabeth Clarke's mother and kinsfolk do not appear elsewhere under a different surname.

18. Ibid., p. 29.

19. Ibid., p. 24. Sarah Barton, the sister of one of the accused, is also absent from the Assize records since she was dealt with by the Harwich borough authorities (case 1,219).

20. These activities are described in the 1645 Pamphlet (in the above order) on pp. 14–15, 32–3, 2.

21. Ibid., p. 12. There is very little evidence before 1645 that witches were believed to meet together or perform any joint rituals. Perhaps the nearest suggestion of this is a curious detail in a Colchester examination of 1599 (case 1,173) that a witch could not visit her victim's house until she had 'agreed w[i]th the villaynes', possibly meaning the other witches. See also the 'company of witches' in case 1,207.

22. Hopkins certainly knew King James I's *Daemonologie*, which contained such ideas as the use of the water ordeal (Hopkins, *Discovery*, p. 56).

23. They are all described in Hopkins, *Discovery*.

24. 'Upon command from the *Justice*', the witches were kept from sleep to see if their familiars came to them (Hopkins, *Discovery*, p. 50). Sir Harbottle Grimston was a moderate Puritan gentleman, later purged by Pride after earlier support of the Parliamentarians; he had a special interest in the trials, since he had been born at Bradfield Hall, near Manningtree, and held manors in Bradfield, Tendring, Mistley, Ramsey, Kirby, and Lawford, most of them inhabited by accused witches (*D.N.B.* and Morant, *Essex*, i, 464). Likewise, Sir Thomas Bowes, Justice of the Peace for Essex for fifty years, was intimately involved, since his home was in Great Bromley, a village some five miles south of Manningtree (Morant, *Essex*, i, 442).

25. For instance, keeping the witches awake was later 'not allowed of by the Judges and other Magistrates' (Hopkins, *Discovery*, p. 55). Nevertheless, confessions continued.

26. Ady, *Candle*, p. 99.

27. Ewen, II, p. 259, points out that no authority has been given for the constant assertion that Hopkins was an impecunious lawyer from Ipswich. For payments in other counties see the same page of Ewen.

28. As Montague Summers suggested in the introduction to Hopkins, *Discovery*, p. 23, Hopkins's defence is 'from a Puritan point of view' 'singularly lukewarm'. Stearne's work is fuller of references to the Devil and to biblical authorities.

29. Stearne commented on the fact that many proven witches were outwardly 'very religious people, and would constantly repair to all Sermons neer them'; he even suggested that sermons were used by the Devil to entice witches (Stearne, *Confirmation*, pp. 39, 59). For the execution of a clergyman in Suffolk, see C. L. Ewen, *The Trials of John Lowes, clerk* (n.p., 1937).

30. Hopkins, *Discovery*, p. 51; Stearne, *Confirmation*, p. 15.

31. Gaule, *Select Cases*, sig. A3^v.

32. Stearne, *Confirmation*, sig. A2^v.

33. Ibid., p. 14, which shows that he was not present at the first examination although he 'was one which caused her to be questioned'.

34. For one example of the extreme hostility to Hopkins see E. Maple, *The Dark World of Witches* (Pan edn., 1965), pp. 83–90.

35. Hopkins, *Discovery*, p. 56.

36. Neither Ewen nor Notestein mention this episode.

37. This is the interpretation given by Mary Douglas of a recent witch-finding movement in Africa (Middleton and Winter, (1963), pp. 133, 135, 140).

38. Gifford, *Dialogue*, sig. H2^v.

39. On millenarianism see C. Hill, *Puritanism and Revolution* (1958), ch. 12, and N. Cohn, *The Pursuit of the Millennium* (Mercury edn., 1962), pp. 321–78.

40. Gaule, *Select Cases*, p. 93.

41. M. G. Marwick, 'Another Modern Anti-witchcraft Movement in East Central Africa', *Africa*, xx, no. 2 (1950), p. 103.

42. For a refutation of the myth that Hopkins was himself swum as a witch, see Kittredge, *Witchcraft*, p. 595.

43. Notestein, *Witchcraft*, pp. 199–201.

Part 3
Witchcraft and the social background

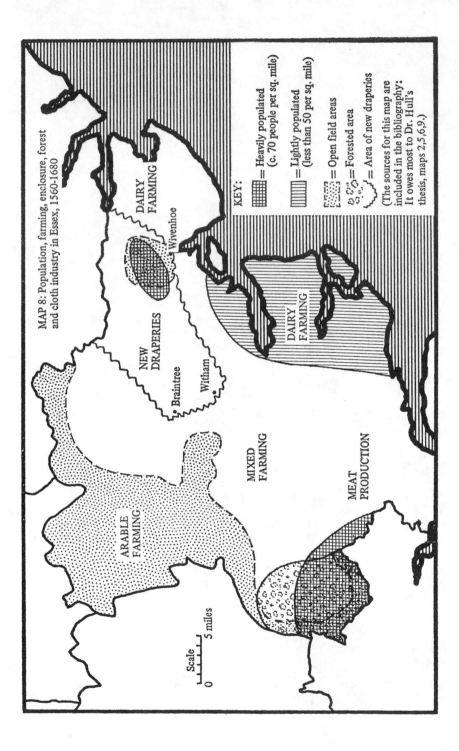

MAP 8: Population, farming, enclosure, forest and cloth industry in Essex, 1560-1680

KEY:

▦ = Heavily populated (c. 70 people per sq. mile)

▥ = Lightly populated (less than 50 per sq. mile)

⋮⋮ = Open field areas

🌿 = Forested area

〰 = Area of new draperies

(The sources for this map are included in the bibliography: It owes most to Dr. Hull's thesis, maps 2,5,6,9.)

DAIRY FARMING

• Wivenhoe

NEW DRAPERIES

• Braintree

Witham •

DAIRY FARMING

MIXED FARMING

ARABLE FARMING

MEAT PRODUCTION

Scale

0   5 miles

Chapter 10

Witchcraft prosecutions and economic problems

Previous chapters have described the sources for the study of witchcraft and analysed the general geographical and temporal distribution of prosecutions. In this and following chapters an analysis of prosecutions will be made in an attempt to correlate prosecutions with religious, economic, social, and other phenomena. Naturally, the boundaries chosen are unreal; the aged were a religious, economic, and social problem, though they are only treated under the last heading in the subsequent analysis.

It may be assumed that there was a considerable growth of population during the sixteenth and early seventeenth centuries, and that this levelled off after 1660.[1] At first sight this trend seems to mirror that of witchcraft prosecutions in Essex, and a causal connexion could well be suggested. Growing pressure on economic resources led to increasing tensions and hatred towards the old and the poor. Unfortunately, it is not possible to demonstrate any direct connexions. At the village level there was no obvious correlation between population growth and witchcraft accusations. An analysis of the parish registers of two of the sample villages, Little Baddow and Boreham, has failed to show any significant connexions between the fluctuations in deaths, births, or marriages and years of prosecution in those villages. Certainly there was, or would have been without migration, enormous growth. In both Little Baddow and Boreham the surplus of births over deaths between 1560 and 1600 would have nearly doubled the population by the latter date. There was an average surplus of six persons per year, rising as high as fifteen in 1577, in Boreham. The traditional social organization, the groups of neighbours and kin, must have come under considerable strain in the attempt to absorb the new children. In Little Baddow, a group of roughly sixty adult males in 1560 were working for an extra six mouths a year: without migration they would have been feeding an extra child each by 1566, for already births had exceeded deaths by sixty. However, there are no known witchcraft prosecutions in Little Baddow after 1570, despite continued population increase.

Nor does there seem to be any correlation at the county level between population density and witchcraft prosecutions. A comparison of a map of the distribution of prosecutions with tentative population figures based on the Essex Ship Money Assessment of 1638 shows no overlap with either the most densely or most sparsely populated parts of the county.[2] Prosecutions were most intense in the moderately populated central-northern belt of Essex. The dense area around Colchester and in the south-east and the lowly populated marshlands of the south-west were less often the areas of prosecution. The larger towns like Maldon, Colchester, and Harwich had their share of prosecutions, but there seems to have been no particular concentration varying with the size of the town or village. The outskirts of London appear to have been normal in the number of witchcraft indictments. Thus population factors, in themselves, cannot explain either the variation over time or area of Essex prosecutions.

Closely related to population growth was population movement, the patterns of migration. It has long been obvious that villages were not stable, unchanging units in the sixteenth century, but the social effects of rapid movement have received little attention.[3] One example from a village known to contain witches suggests the dimensions of the problem.

TABLE 10
Social mobility in Boreham from subsidy assessments, 1524–98[4]

	1524	1544	1566	1572	1598
Total of families assessed	42	36	30	23	10
Number of new families	—	24	15	2	4

This shows considerable change; between 1544 and 1566 the population changed to such an extent that only half those assessed at the latter date had been assessed twenty-two years earlier. By 1598 only three of the forty-two family names of 1524 were represented. Yet even this underrates the amount of movement: it only shows changes among the most propertied, and probably least mobile, elements in the village, and it only indicates that some member of the family stayed in the village. Those most likely to move were younger sons and daughters, leaving one member of the family on the land. Such extensive movement may have had far-reaching consequences. It may have affected people's feelings of security, whether people lived in groups of kin or neighbours, and the many personal problems of insurance, education, policing, and health in the village. Witchcraft prosecutions, also, may have been affected.

It is very difficult to generalize about whether accusations took place between long-established families in the village, or whether recently arrived individuals were thought of as witches. In the sample village of Hatfield Peverel it seems that the fiercest accusations took place between families who had been living in the village some forty years before. The four major families involved in witchcraft prosecutions, Duke, Frauncis, Osborne, and Waterhouse, had all been present in the village in 1524, as were a number of their victims' families, Wilmott, Hawkin, Higham, Augur, Wardoll.[5] In Boreham, only one family connected with witchcraft, the Pooles, had been assessed in 1524. But the other suspected witches were not newcomers; all of them are recorded in earlier local records. From this very small sample it would seem that accusations were not normally made against newcomers to the village as a veiled method of controlling or reacting to frequent movement. The only known case of a newcomer being prosecuted was that of Joan Cocke; this was almost certainly because she was already a known witch, suspected in the village in which she had previously lived.[6]

Another general economic change occurring during this period in Essex was the growth of a clothing industry in the region to the north and east of Colchester, producing both ordinary cloth and the new, lighter draperies.[7] Many of the centres of the cloth industry were also the centres of prosecutions: Bocking, Braintree, Coggeshall, Witham, Colchester, and Halstead were the main centres of the new draperies. All of them witnessed prosecutions. Manningtree, Dedham, Boxted, Langham, Wivenhoe, and Horkesley were the main cloth-making towns; all except Boxted suffered accusations. But any closer connexion is difficult to establish. Many villages and towns not concerned with the cloth industry were as severe in their indictments as the above; fluctuations in the cloth industry, particularly the crises of the 1620's and 1630's, were not reflected in sudden outbreaks of accusations; the actual individuals accused were not necessarily connected with cloth-making.[8] The relative importance of the cloth and other industries in Essex witchcraft prosecutions and the predominance of agricultural groups is shown in Table 11.

From the table it can be seen that only a very small proportion of individuals were connected in a full-time capacity, as tailors or weavers, to the cloth industry. On the other hand, a comparison of the occupations of the victims with those of the suspect's husbands suggests that small artificers and tradesmen were considerably more important in the former class. While nearly 80 per cent of the husbands of suspected witches were involved in agricultural work, only 60 per cent of the 'victims' were so engaged. While witchcraft accusations predominantly flowed between agriculturalists, sailors, bricklayers, and other non-agricultural workers were quite likely to be victims of witchcraft.

Another difference between suspected witches' husbands and their

TABLE 11

Occupation of the husbands and victims of those accused of witchcraft at the Essex Assizes, 1560–1680

	Husbands of accused witches	Victims of suspected witches (or their relatives)
Labourer	23	6
Husbandman	11	4
Yeoman	4	16
Gentleman	—	1
Beer brewer	1	—
Tailor	4	—
Weaver	1	1
Shoemaker	1	—
Sailor	2	5
Mason	2	1
Bricklayer	—	2
Carpenter	—	1
Fletcher	—	1
Basket-maker	—	1
Glover		2
Tanner	—	1
Smith	—	1
Butcher	—	1
Miller	—	1
	49	45

Note: The above occupations are given on the indictments; if the victim was a child or animal, the owner or father's occupation was often given. The occupations of male witches are analysed on p. 150, below.

victims, illustrated by Table 11, is in social class. While labourers predominate in the first list, yeomen are by far the largest single category in the second. Witches seem to have been poorer than their victims. The microscopic research necessary before it is possible to see whether there is any widespread connexion between a 'rising' yeoman class and the suspected witchcraft of their less successful neighbours has not been feasible. It is possible that those families seen to be declining in wealth would be feared as witches, for they would obviously feel envy, an emotion which easily led to witchcraft.[9] Evidence at the village level does suggest that victims were from more prosperous families than their bewitchers. This has already been shown in the case of the 1645 trial,[10] and it seems to have been the case in the three villages. A Hatfield Peverel witch gave her familiar to 'one mother Waterhouse her neybour (a pore woman)'.

Mother Waterhouse had been a widow for nine years, her husband, in all probability, had been assessed some twenty years earlier at 2*d*., the lowest assessment in the subsidy. In 1582 a woman was believed to have bewitched the collector for the poor because he would not give her 12*d*. for her sick husband,[11] and another woman, in 1589, became a witch when resident in the Almshouse.[12] Literary authorities agreed that witches often seemed poor,[13] and it was a characteristic feature of their behaviour to beg.[14] But it would be a mistake to assume that it was the poorest in the village who were automatically suspected. It was usually the moderately poor, like the woman who felt she ought to get poor relief, but was denied it, who were accused. The witch Margaret Poole of Boreham was married to a man who had been Constable of the village and who, in 1566, was one of the assessors of the lay subsidy and himself the sixteenth highest contributor. Elizabeth Frauncis, a notorious witch of Hatfield Peverel, was married to a man styled as a 'yeoman' in 1572, though she complained that he was 'not so rich' as the first man who promised to marry her.[15] Agnes Frauncis, of the same village, had a weaver as a husband. None of the ten people noted by the Boreham overseers of the poor as receivers of parish assistance during the later sixteenth century is recorded as a suspected witch.

The victims of the witches appear to have come from a slightly higher level. In Little Baddow they were described as 'husbandman' and 'yeoman' and belonged to influential village families, the Dagnetts and Bastwicks. In Boreham, one victim was a member of the Brett family, a group of considerable size and status, one of whose members, for example, was an overseer of the poor in 1590 and one of the thirteen taxpayers in the village in 1598. Another victim had as her father a weaver or coverlet-maker.[16] In Hatfield Peverel the victims included a miller, labourer, butcher, husbandman, the Constable of the village, and two yeomen. This does not include the Wilmott family, one of the leading yeoman families in the village, which was subjected to a mass attack by witches. A sample of the Hatfield Peverel Lay Subsidy for 1563 suggests the social level of some of the victims. Only twenty-eight people in this large village were listed, as compared to seventy in 1524, and they may therefore be taken to be the richest yeomen and above. Of these John Higham, assessed to pay 12*s*., Walter Wilmott (8*s*.) John Bird (5*s*.), Alexander Wilmott (16*d*.), John Some (30*s*.) and James Hawkins (15*s*.) are all known to have been involved, as victims, in witchcraft accusations. To take only one further example, the widow of James Hawkins, bewitched in 1589, held fifty-eight acres of land of the manor of Mugdon Hall according to a manorial survey taken the same year. On the whole it seems to have been among the middle and upper ranks of village society that witchcraft tensions arose.

There is other evidence that sheer destitution did not lead to witchcraft accusations. If this had been so, we would have expected there to be some reflection of high prices and bad harvests in the accusations. One example will show that this did not happen. It seems evident that the last five years of the sixteenth century saw a minor economic crisis in parts of Essex. For example, in Boreham, the poor overseers' accounts show a sudden increase, and so do their disbursements. In Hatfield Peverel there was a simultaneous worsening of conditions. In 1594 a villager of Hatfield was indicted at the Assizes for saying that 'Corne wilbe dere and ther is one in the tower that doth prophecye that wheate wilbe at Sixteene shillinges a Bushell shortely'.[17] Yet there were no witchcraft accusations after this date in any of the three villages; in Essex, generally, the accusations appear to have been lower, in the later 1590's.[18] Nor do English wheat prices show any significant correlation with witchcraft prosecutions in Essex. According to Professor Hoskins, the years of highest prices in England between 1560 and 1619 were 1562, 1565, 1573, 1586, 1594–7, 1608, 1613. These years do not coincide with Essex prosecutions, which were at their highest in the early 1580's and early 1590's, two periods of relatively plentiful harvest.[19] Two other indications that prosecutions were not directly related to localized famines are the widespread location of accusations in any one year, and the fact that such accusations occurred in different years in the three neighbouring villages selected for detailed study.

Nor do the seasonal variations in supposed bewitchings suggest agricultural fluctuations and shortages. Calculations based on the Assize indictments suggest that February to June were the times of most bewitchings, while August to October were freest from them, but the differences are hardly significant.[20] There does not seem to have been a significant increase of accusations in the early spring resulting from hunger.

Another way of measuring the extent to which accusations of witchcraft centred on agricultural problems is to examine the nature of injuries attributed to witches; to see whether their attacks were mainly on domestic livestock or on manufacturing processes. Table 12 gives the offences for which individuals were accused at the Assizes:

From the table it would seem that humans were the most likely victims of witchcraft, and that death, rather than illness, was most likely to be attributed to witches. The 'other property' listed in Table 12 was as follows: two barns burnt down, twenty brewings of beer spoilt, one windmill bewitched, cheese prevented from forming, and four gallons of cream prevented from becoming butter.[21] While these figures usefully indicate the type of offence forming indictments, comparison of indictments with pamphlet accounts of the trials show that only the more serious suspicions were selected for formal charges and that there were many other acts of witchcraft suggested by villagers, yet never recorded. This is shown in

TABLE 12
Victims of witchcraft in Essex assize indictments 1560–1680

	Number of cases
Humans	
illness	108
death	233
total	341
Animals	80
Other property	6

Table 13, where the offences of eighteen suspected witches who appear described in both Assize records and pamphlets are compared. /

TABLE 13
Nature of the injuries blamed on eighteen Essex witches, 1566–89

	In the indictments	*In the pamphlets*
Humans:		
death	21	32
sickness	4	17
Animals (usually death of)	3	14
Miscellaneous:		
burning a barn	1	1
spoiling beer	—	7
spoiling butter	—	3
preventing spinning	—	1
cattle give blood	—	1
familiars steal milk	—	1
knocking down tree	—	1
knocking down wood-pile	—	1
mysterious rocking of cradle	—	1
cart stuck fast	—	1

This table shows that the supposed activities of witches were far more diverse than the indictments would suggest. Causing the death of humans, though still the most important single category, only accounts for about 40 per cent of cases instead of roughly 70 per cent. Witches were blamed in an increased number of cases for agricultural misfortunes; the injury of

animals, the loss of butter and beer, mysterious accidents to carts and
piles of wood. In only one case, where spinning was prevented, did
witches attack 'industrial' activities. It was primarily for injuries to humans
that witches were blamed and secondly for loss of animals and farm
produce. The value of the animals supposedly bewitched provides some
indication of the current preoccupation with witchcraft. From Tables 12
and 13 it would seem that the eighty recorded indictments for bewitching
animals represent less than one-quarter of the actual suspected attacks.
Yet, analysis of the eighty cases alone suggests extensive damage to property.
Indictments record the number, kind, and suggested value of animal
victims. These are analysed in the following table:

TABLE 14
Animals recorded as bewitched in assize indictments, 1560–1680

	Number bewitched	Value of an animal (c. 1580)
Cows/calves	110	£1–2
Horses/colts	63	£2–4
Pigs/piglets	124	2–4s.
Sheep/ewes	123	2–3s.
Chickens/capons	11	4–6d.

One suspected witch might be accused of causing considerable damage. In
1593 a woman was accused of bewitching to death twenty-two sheep
valued at £5, one cow valued at 40s., one pig valued at 8s., and a calf
valued at 8s.[22] Even more expensive were the activities of a spinster of
Ingrave, who was accused of bewitching to death four geldings valued at
£12 and sixteen cows valued at £50.[23] There is no indication that it was
animals in the special care of women—for instance, poultry or young
animals—which were especially attacked, nor do certain animals seem to
have been more commonly bewitched than others.[24]

The agricultural background to Essex witchcraft prosecutions was
influenced by a number of factors, among them the extent of enclosure and
forest and the patterns of land inheritance. Most of Essex had been
enclosed before 1560, but there were one large and two small areas which
remained unenclosed until the late eighteenth century.[25] The large region
was the north-west corner, nearly one-fifth of the county, and the small
ones were round Colchester and along the south-west border of the county.
In the map of the distribution of witchcraft prosecutions there is a curious

ℭThe ende and last confes-
sion of mother Waterhouse at her
death, whiche was the
xxix. daye of July.
Anno. 1566.

Mother wa=
terhouse.

Fyrste (beinge redi prepared to receiue her death) she confessed earnestly that shee had bene a wytche and vsed suche execrable sorserye the space of. xv. yeres, and had don many abhominable dede, the which she repē- ted earnestely ꝗ vn- faynedly, and desy- red almyghty God forgeuenes in that she had abused hys most holy name by
A   her

7 *The ende and last confession of mother Waterhouse at her death, whiche was the xxix daye of July Anno 1566*
(Lambeth Palace Library)

The moſt wonderfull

and true ſtorie, of a certaine Witch
named *Alſe Gooderige of Stapen hill,*
who was arraigned and conuicted at Darbie
at the *Aſſiſes there.*

As alſo a true report of the ſtrange torments of Thomas
Darling, *a boy of thirteene yeres of age, that was pos-*
ſeſſed by the Deuill, with his horrible fittes and terri-
ble Apparitions by him vttered at Burton vpon
Trent *in the Countie of* Stafford, *and of his maruel-*
lous deliuerance.

Printed at London for I.O. 1597.

8 *The most wonderfull and true storie, of a certaine Witch named Alse*
Gooderige of Stapenhill, who was arraigned and convicted at Darbie at the
Assises there, 1597
(Lambeth Palace Library)

absence of witchcraft cases round Colchester, and prosecutions are generally sparsest in the north-west. Comparison with other counties will be needed before it is possible to see whether there were more prosecutions in the early-enclosed, enclosing, or open-field areas; if the Essex pattern is general, it may be that witchcraft was related to the problems of a growing population pressing on already enclosed land. On the other hand, there does not seem to have been any particular correlation between forested areas and areas of prosecution. There was little forest left in Essex by 1560; the bulk of what remained was on the outskirts of London, around Epping, and this was not peculiarly savage in its witchcraft prosecutions.[26] They were densest in the area of mixed farming, where wheat and hops were the main crops, in the centre and north of the county. Yet they also occurred in all the other regions.

While early enclosure may have prevented access to the land for a growing population, another factor which may have differentiated villages and caused more tensions in some than others were customs of inheritance, partible or impartible. Although the evidence is scanty, there does seem to have been some connexion between partible inheritance and witchcraft accusations. In all three manors upon which there is known to have been partible inheritance there were witchcraft accusations.[27] Nothing more than a tentative hypothesis can be advanced, however, until there has been further research to show whether some of the other villages where there were even higher numbers of accusations were also affected by partible inheritance.

Another possible connexion is between converted monastic property and the location of prosecutions. The first impression is that there was such a link. The concentration of witchcraft suspicions within the manor which had formerly been the Priory of Hatfield Peverel suggested that people might be reacting to increased severity on the part of lay landlords. The famous trials at the village where the Abbey of St. Osithes had been situated appeared to corroborate this view. Yet a wider comparison of maps of monastic property with maps of the distribution of witchcraft accusations does not bear out any such hypothesis. Prosecutions seem to have occurred with equal frequency on monastic and non-monastic land.[28]

The conclusions of this chapter have been largely negative; no single economic factor can explain the distribution of Essex witchcraft prosecutions. The major positive conclusion is that the suspects were, on the whole, of a slightly lower status than their accusers. Yet they were not necessarily the poorest in the village. No direct connexion can be drawn between poverty and accusations. Further evidence for this assertion is the absence of any correlation between areas of greatest poverty in the county and accusations for witchcraft. Small holdings, insufficient to

Witchcraft and the social background

support families, were most common in the north-west and north-east. The central region of Essex was, comparatively, the least troubled by poverty: this was the region of most accusation.[29] Thus the parish overseers' accounts of a north-western village, Heydon, show an acute problem of agrarian poverty, yet there were no known prosecutions in that village. In Boreham, however, the poor officers were always left with a surplus on their hands until 1594, yet there were a number of witchcraft prosecutions before that date.[30]

NOTES

1. As yet there has been no detailed analysis of population changes in Essex during this period; the general outline given above is that which has been suggested for the whole of England—for example, by Professor Habakkuk in *Population in History*, ed. D. V. Glass and D. E. C. Eversley (1965), pp. 147–8.
2. See Maps 1, 8, pp. 10 and 146, above. F. Hull, 'Agriculture and Rural Society in Essex, 1560–1640' (London Univ. Ph.D. thesis, 1950), pp. 552–7 and Map 6, form the basis for estimates of population density in 1638.
3. Massive movement in Elizabethan society has been emphasized in E. E. Rich, 'The Population of Elizabethan England' *Economic History Review*, 2nd series, ii (1949), 247–65; and in S. A. Peyton, 'The Village Population in the Tudor Lay Subsidy Rolls', *English Historical Review*, xxx (1915), 234–50.
4. This table is based on P.R.O., E. 179, 108/151, 108/241, 109/291, 110/422, 111/447, 111/501.
5. The sources used for the study of Hatfield Peverel, Boreham, and Little Baddow were described in ch. 6, p. 314 above, and are described in detail in the Bibliography, p. 94.
6. Cases 21 and 208–9. Local records prove that these cases referred to the same Joan Cocke.
7. A description and map of the cloth industry is provided by J. E. Pilgrim, 'The Rise of the "New Draperies" in Essex', *University of Birmingham Historical Journal*, VII, no. 1 (1958), pp. 36–59.
8. The most notorious Braintree witch, Alice Aylett, was the wife of a shoemaker, cases 301–5; on the other hand, a clothmaker was bewitched in 1582. Yet it was not a suspected witch, whom he employed as a spinner (Elizabeth Bennet), who attacked him, but rather another women, to whom he had refused poor relief as overseer of the poor (1582 Pamphlet, sigs. A4, A6ᵛ–A7, B4ᵛ, C6).
9. George Foster, 'Peasant Society and the Image of Limited Good', *American Anthropologist*, 67, no. 2 (1965), p. 302, points out that fear of the aggression of declining families is a characteristic of peasant societies.
10. Where the accusers, but not accused, had earlier been assessed for Ship Money, p. 143, n. 11, above.
11. 1582 Pamphlet, sig. A7.
12. 1589 Pamphlet, sig. B.
13. For example, Scot, *Discovery*, pp. 29, 30, 53, 374; Stearne, *Confirmation*, p. 33; Bernard, *Guide*, p. 155.
14. For example, Ady, *Candle*, p. 114.

15. Case 50 and 1566 Pamphlet, p. 318.
16. Edith Hawes' father was a weaver according to E.R.O., Q/SR. 126/24, 25.
17. P.R.O., Assizes 35/36/T, m. 39.
18. See Diagram 1.
19. W.G. Hoskins, 'Harvest Fluctuations and English Economic History, 1480–1619', *Agricultural History Review*, xii (1964), 39.
20. The indictments state when a bewitching began and ended, yet detailed analysis of the months of most bewitching showed no obvious patterns. For example, only eight people died of witchcraft in September and twenty-five in February, but bewitchings began almost as commonly in September as February.
21. In the order above, the cases were 166, 224, 171, 251, 293, 324.
22. Case 353.
23. Case 403.
24. There are detailed descriptions of the bewitching of cows, beer, and butter in case 1,207.
25. Essex enclosures are described in R. Coles, 'Enclosures: Essex Agriculture, 1500–1900', *Essex Naturalist*, xxvi (1937–40), 2–25.
26. R. Coles, 'The Past History of the Forest of Essex', *Essex Naturalist*, xxiv (1932–5), 115–33.
27. The manors were Hatfield Broad Oak, Waltham, and Thorpe le Soken. R. J. Faith, 'Peasant Families and Inheritance Customs in Medieval England', *Agricultural History Review*, xiv, part 2 (1966), 93–4
28. Felix Hull, 'Agriculture and Rural Society in Essex, 1560–1640' (London Univ. Ph.D. thesis, 1950), Map 9, shows the distribution of monastic property.
29. Ibid., p. 471.
30. The Heydon accounts and those of Boreham are described in F. G. Emmison, 'The Care of the Poor in Elizabethan Essex', *Essex Review*, lxii, No. 248 (1953), 7–28. Hull, on p. 479 of the thesis cited above, took a graver view than Emmison of the Heydon accounts, and stated that they showed 'an acute problem of agrarian poverty'.

Chapter 11

Witchcraft prosecutions and social phenomena (1): personality, sex, age, and marriage

Literary accounts of witches written in the sixteenth and seventeenth centuries often stress the suspect's ugliness. For instance, Gaule suggested that 'every old woman with a wrinkled face, a furr'd brow, a hairy lip, a gobber tooth, a squint eye, a squeaking voyce, or a scolding tongue' was 'pronounced for a witch'.[1] Other authorities described them as 'commonlie lame', 'foule', 'toothless', 'leane and deformed', 'of an horrid countenance'.[2] Although there were occasional references to lame witches in Essex, the descriptions of actual trials lay no particular emphasis on the physical stereotype of the witch.[3] Nor does Gifford's description of Essex witchcraft suggest that people were selected as potential witches because of their looks. The impression from Essex evidence is that actions and personality, rather than physical factors, were the determining criteria. It may, however, have been true, as Ady suggested, that someone began to look like the stereotype of the witch when she acted like one.[4] This sequence was reflected in the other physical characteristic of supposed witches, their mark. People were first suspected because they acted like witches; only later were they searched for some physical oddity, protuberance, or cavity, which would confirm or refute suspicions. Such a mark was usually in a secret place.[5]

Several writers outlined the personality types associated with witchcraft. Those who were boastful, illiterate, miserable, lustful, and leading a 'lewd and naughty kind of life', melancholy—all were likely to be witches.[6] Above all, they were thought to be the type of person who went round begging[7] and those who had vicious tongues. Witches were people of 'ill natures, of a wicked disposition, and spitefully malicious';[8] 'malicious people, full of revenge, having hearts swolne with rancour'.[9] They were scolds and peevish.[10] These generalizations about the cantankerous and anti-social witch can be tested against the actual cases in the Essex records; furthermore, we are able to see whether suspected witches were often accused of other types of offence—for example, incest or petty crime.

Presentments for witchcraft at the ecclesiastical courts in Essex occasionally gave details of other offences also alleged against the suspect. One suspected witch failed to live with her husband, another was suspected of incest with her son, another allowed her daughter to be incontinent and was herself incontinent.[11] More vaguely, another was 'a light woman of filthey behaviour and hathe played the bawde'.[12] Several women were also scolds, 'sowers of discord', or brawlers. The narrow border between tongue-lashing and witchcraft was suggested by some churchwardens, who said that a woman was 'crymed [accused] for a wytche w[i]ch we know not but by here saye but she ys develishe of her tonge'.[13] As well as being a rumoured witch, a man was 'a comon Brawler and sower of discorde between neighbours', and Margaret Saunders admitted that 'she is suspected of witchcraft and thought to be a skoulde'.[14] But it was not only the witches who were of suspect behaviour. Those who resorted to cunning folk[15] and who called other people witches[16] might be just as evil. This last point suggests that it would be an over-simplification to see a necessary connexion between witchcraft and other anti-social behaviour. The above instances represent only a very small proportion of the individuals presented for 'witchcraft and sorcery' at the ecclesiastical courts. Analysis of the witchcraft pamphlets, where the suspected witch is often described in considerable detail, further suggests that witches did not necessarily misbehave in other obvious ways. Some forty-three suspected witches were described in the Essex pamphlets. Of these, only nine had a wider reputation for misbehaviour. Four had had illegitimate children or became pregnant before marriage;[17] one was suspected of incest with her son;[18] one had quarrelled with her husband;[19] one said her prayers in Latin;[20] two others were called 'old whore' or 'a lewd woman'.[21] But one type of behaviour seems to have been common to all of them. This was begging, combined with grumbling or cursing when they were refused. For example, Mother Cunny asked a neighbour for some drink, but 'his wife being busie and abrewing, tolde her she had no leysure to give her any. Then Joane Cunnye went away discontented.' Next day her refuser was in terrible pain.[22]

Detailed analysis of offences in the three sample villages also suggests that people suspected of various anti-social activities—for instance, sexual misdemeanours or theft—were not necessarily believed to be witches and vice versa. In the table of offences for the three villages there was little overlapping between witchcraft and other crimes.[23] Of the twenty suspects in the three villages, only three are known to have been accused of other offences. Agnes Duke was probably accused of theft some twenty years before being accused of witchcraft;[24] Mary Belsted quarrelled with her husband;[25] Alice Bambrick was accused of theft, not attending church, and because she was 'a troublesome woman in her tonge amongeste her neighboures'.[26] Meanwhile, of the approximately 180 people who are known to have been suspected of sexual offences in the three villages, only Alice Bambrick was also suspected of witchcraft. Again, only one in five of those formally accused of scolding or quarrelling were also accused of witchcraft. This adds confirmation to the impression that when people suspected witchcraft they did not automatically select the most notorious prostitutes or criminals in the neighbourhood as likely witches; rather, as will be seen, they examined their relationship to others. These others might well be law-abiding citizens.

Comparison of witchcraft and other offences has shown that witches were not necessarily suspected of sexual offences.[27] Nor does a sexual element seem to have been important in Essex prosecutions generally. It is true, that as contemporaries observed,[28] witches were usually women. Only twenty-three of the 291 accused witches were men.[29] Even among these twenty-three, eleven were either married to an accused witch or appeared in a joint indictment with a woman. Seven of them were found guilty, a slightly lower proportion than among women; their occupations were diverse. There were twelve labourers, three yeomen, one gentleman, one beer-brewer, one clerk, one joiner, and two tailors and two glovers. Men were accused in every decade between 1560 and 1670, except for a gap between 1616 and 1647. Thus, there does not seem to have been any obvious objection to the idea of male witches. Yet women predominated. Any explanation of witchcraft prosecutions must account for this fact. Certain hypotheses do not find support in the Essex material. There is no evidence that hostility between the sexes lay behind the prosecutions. Essex pamphlets show women witnessing as often as men against other women, nor does the following table of the sex of those supposed to be bewitched show any particular attack on males:

TABLE 15

Sex of those recorded as bewitched in assize indictments, 1560–1680

Period	Death		Illness	
	Male	Female	Male	Female
1560–79	20	22	11	8
1580–99	41	58	18	21
1600–19	17	13	6	17
1620–39	7	7	3	5
1640–59	13	12	6	5
1660–79	5	4	1	1
	103	116	45	57

Total male: 148   Total female: 173

From this we see that females were slightly more likely to be bewitched, in most periods, than males. Analysis of the types of offences attributed to witches in Essex showed no sexual content. They did not attack virility in any form, either by blasting the crops or bewitching men's genitals. Essex witches, as described in the pamphlets and by Gifford, were not believed to attend sexual orgies, have sexual relations with their familiars, or fly. They were not searched, except by other women, and the phallic witch-pin or suggestive broomsticks, upon which they rode in myth in other countries, were absent. The only suggestions of a sexual motif in all the Essex evidence comes in the trial of 1645 in the demure accounts of two women's sexual relations with the Devil. This trial, it has been argued, was exceptional, and influenced by Continental ideas.[30]

Contemporary writers saw the explanation of the predominance of female witches in the temperament of women. They suggested that the female sex was both weak and vicious—weak towards Satan and vicious towards fellow human beings. Perkins observed that 'the woman being the weaker sexe, is sooner entangled by the devills illusions with this damnable art, then [*sic*] the man'.[31] Stearne suggested that it was because women were 'commonly impatient, and being displeased more malicious, and so more apt to revenge according to their power, and thereby more fit instruments for the Deville'.[32] This interpretation is roughly similar to that advanced later in this book. If, as is argued later, witchcraft reflected tensions between an ideal of neighbourliness and the necessities of economic and social change, women were commonly thought of as witches because they were more resistant to such change. It was their social position and power which led to mounting hatred against them. As wives and mothers and gossips, they tended to be more intimately connected with various village groups; they were the co-ordinating element in village society. People would feel most uneasy about them when society was segmenting. It was they who borrowed and lent most, and it was their curse which was most feared.

Related to the problem of the sex of witch and victim is that of their age. Contemporaries suggested that witches were, almost without exception, 'old'.[33] Just how old they were it is impossible to tell in the majority of cases, since indictments do not record ages. But from incidental information in the pamphlets and coroners' inquests on some of those imprisoned in 1645, we know the age of fifteen of those accused at the Essex Assizes.[34] Of these, two were between forty and forty-nine, three between fifty and fifty-nine, seven between sixty and sixty-nine and three between eighty and eighty-nine. Although some of the ages were stated to be approximate, it does seem reasonable to argue that, in Essex, the likeliest age for a witch was between fifty and seventy. The pamphlets suggest that people gradually became witches in their own and their neighbours' eyes, and that the longer a witch lived the greater her power was supposed to be. This was noted by John Gaule when he remarked that 'the longer Witches are suffered to live, the worse they are, not onely do they do more mischiefe to others, but grow more wicked within themselves'.[35] Children could not be powerful witches: thus Stearne told of a boy of nine in Northamptonshire who was accused of witchcraft 'when all know he could not be of much capacity'.[36] In one long description in 1564 both mother and daughter were believed to be witches, but the daughter claimed that her mother was 'the stronger witch'. She also suggested that a person of good reputation when young might gradually become hated and suspected; as she lamented to her daughters, 'I am bro[u]ght out of my good name to an yll'.[37] The way in which suspicions gradually built up in a village has already been outlined; this process was reflected in the confessions of suspected witches, who echoed their neighbours' fears. They all stated that they had 'acquired' witchcraft some years before, rather than being born with the power. In 1566 Elizabeth Francis claimed to have been initiated by her grandmother at the age of twelve, but she kept her familiar for fifteen or sixteen years before she handed it over to Agnes Waterhouse. Agnes said, in the same pamphlet, that she had been a witch for fifteen years. In the 1589 pamphlet all three confessions included the length of time the suspect believed themselves to have possessed diabolic power: Joan Cunny had received her witchcraft some twenty years before and claimed to have hurt many people during the last sixteen or twenty years; Joan Upney said she had been given her witchcraft some seven or eight years previously; the Devil had first appeared to Joan Prentice six years before the trial. Those who confessed in 1645 were divided between nine who stated that they had been witches for a considerable length of time, averaging some fifteen years, and five who said that they had become witches some six months before their examination. The latter group were possibly a product of the exceptional circumstances of 1645.

While suspected witches were characteristically middle-aged or old,[38] their victims appear to have been younger adults. The Assize indictments often stated, in the case of children, the age of the victim; in a number of instances the victim was said to be the 'son of' or 'daughter of' another person. It seems likely that this was only recorded when the victim was a child. The ages of children are given in Table 16.

As well as these cases, there were sixty in which the victim was described as the 'son' or 'daughter' of another. Comparing these ninety-two victims with the total of 341 victims altogether, it would seem that over two-thirds of those believed to be bewitched were adults: mortality at childbirth, as Table 16 shows, hardly ever seems to have been ascribed to witches.

TABLE 16

Number of children of various ages recorded in the assize
indictments as bewitched, 1560–1680

Age	Number
An unborn child[39]	1
Months:	
3	3
6	1
9	1
'Infant'	3
Years:	
1	4
2	2
3	3
4	4
5	3
6	1
7	1
8	2
9	1
10	1
11	1

This picture of predominantly adult victims of witchcraft becomes even
stronger when we remember that even where a child was bewitched it was
the parent who brought the accusation and felt the attack. As with attacks
on property, the 'victim' might be the person who was indirectly injured.
Unfortunately, it has been impossible to collect information on the exact
age of accusers; only indirect evidence, such as the presence of young
children in the family who were bewitched, remains. This gives an impression that they were quite often a generation younger than the accused.

One explanation of the fact that witches were usually old was suggested
by Reginald Scot. He argued that it was because old women were often
suffering delusions because of 'the stopping of their monethlie melancholike flux or issue of bloud'; such women were widely believed to have
the evil eye.[40] This explanation hardly seems helpful in explaining Essex
accusations, where the major problem is the reason for accusations rather
than confessions. The theory that will be advanced later concerning the
origin of witchcraft beliefs will attempt to account for an apparent tension
between generations, rather than the particular psychology of the old.
Pressure on economic resources and growing unease at the neighbourly
values of village society, it will be argued, naturally tended to cause

friction with the older inhabitants who, by their very presence, made demands on younger village families. The problem of the aged was likely to be particularly acute when methods and ideals of charity were changing, as they seem to have been in this period. Such a clash might lead to many situations of worry. When widow Susan Cock was refused relief at the age of about fifty and was told that 'shee was a young woman, and able to worke for her living', she was believed to have bewitched some livestock of her refuser.[41] Thus witchcraft prosecutions, to a certain extent, may be seen as a response to changes in the age-structure of the population, and the methods of dealing with the aging process. Age brought with it mystical power which could be used for good or, in the case of the witch's curse as employed in Essex, evil.

Just as suspected witches seem to have been old, so thay were almost always 'wives and widows' rather than unmarried women.[42] Unfortunately the Assize indictments often leave the marital position of the accused vague, describing her as 'spinister'. Thus of 277 accused women we only know that sixty-eight were married and forty-nine widowed; if there was no bias in recording married suspects, this would suggest that just over 40 per cent of the accused were widows. When a person was designated a 'spinster', this did not necessarily mean that she was unmarried; the witches Grevell, Newman, and Glascock in 1582, for example, were described as 'spinster' in the indictments, while two were specified as married and one as widowed in the pamphlet.[43] The marital state of the accused was particularly well recorded in the indictments for 1645, and from these we know that sixteen were married, thirteen were widows, and three 'spinsters'. Again, it seems as if married suspects were slightly more common than widows. The proportion is reversed in the sample three villages. Of the nineteen women who were accused of witchcraft in all three villages, we only know for certain that one was unmarried; that was Joan Waterhouse, aged eighteen, who was acquitted. We do not know the marital state of four of the accused, but all the rest were, or had been, married. Of the fourteen about whom we can be certain, eight were widows while six were married. Two of the six married suspects had far from satisfactory marriages.[44] This high proportion of witches who were widows does suggest that widowhood was a serious problem in Elizabethan villages.[45] But it also seems clear that widowhood, in itself, was not enough to bring suspicion of witchcraft. The parish register of Boreham recorded the names of twenty widows buried in the village between 1560 and 1599, none of whom are recorded witches. In Little Baddow, only one of the ten buried widows was a suspected witch. Nor, as we have seen, were married women, many of them with children, safe from suspicion.[46]

NOTES

1. Gaule, *Select Cases*, p. 5.
2. Scot, *Discovery*, pp. 29, 34, 190; Bernard, *Guide*, p. 138. Other literary caricatures of the witch are quoted in K. M. Briggs, *Pale Hecate's Team* (1962), pp. 83, 90.
3. Elizabeth Clark in the 1645 Pamphlet, p. 6, and Ursley Kempe in that of 1582, sig. A7, were both lame; both were key suspects.
4. Ady, *Candle*, p. 114.
5. Examples of the searching of Essex witches *after* they were suspected occur in the 1582 Pamphlet, sig. E5ᵛ and case 843.
6. Such adjectives were used by Bernard, *Guide*, p. 103: Gaule, *Select Cases*, pp. 51, 64, 80; Scot, *Discovery*, p. 29.
7. Ibid., p. 30.
8. Bernard, *Guide*, p. 156.
9. Stearne, *Confirmation*, p. 20.
10. Gaule, *Select Cases*, p. 85; Scot, *Discovery*, p. 50.
11. Cases 892, 910, 934.
12. Case 1,086.
13. Case 1,024.
14. Cases 1,017, 882; case 1,132 is even more extreme.
15. Case 1,088.
16. Cases 1,103, 1,106.
17. Elizabeth Frauncis in 1566, Ursley Kempe and Annis Herd in 1582, and Joan Cunny in 1589.
18. Joan Pechey in 1582 Pamphlet, sig. C6.
19. Alice Newman in 1582.
20. Agnes Waterhouse in 1566.
21. Elizabeth Bennet in 1582 and Elizabeth Gooding in 1645.
22. 1589 Pamphlet, sig. Aiv.
23. See p. 98, above, for the table.
24. Agnes was accused of witchcraft in 1584 (case 203); a woman of the same name and village was accused of theft in 1564, E.R.O., Q/SR., 16/17, 17/45.
25. The quarrel is described in considerable detail; E.R.O., D/AEA/9, fols. 32, 36, 63ᵛ, 87, 114ᵛ.
26. Ibid., Q/SR., 14/3; D/AEV/1 fol. 18; D/AEA/3 fols. 36ᵛ, 63ᵛ, 125.
27. Nor were sexual offenders necessarily suspected as witches; of the twenty-five cases of incest noted in the Essex archdeaconry records, 1570–1670, only one was definitely connected to witchcraft suspicions.
28. For instance, Gaule, *Select Cases*, p, 52, and Stearne, *Confirmation*, p. 10.
29. Cases 1, 6, 45–8, 125, 133–5, 210–11, 224–5, 272, 280–2, 391–2, 392(*b*), 403, 459, 488–9, 510–11, 518–20, 519–20, 532, 649, 659–61, 736, 753, 762.
30. See p. 139, above.
31. Perkins, *Damned Art*, p. 168.
32. Stearne, *Confirmation*, p. 11; see also Scot, *Discovery*, p. 236.
33. For instance, Perkins, *Damned Art*, pp. 186, 191; Scot, *Discovery*, pp. 25, 53. A discussion of old age and witchcraft, suggesting psychological reasons for the connexion, is given by S. R. Burstein, 'Aspects of the Psychopathology of Old Age Revealed in Witchcraft Cases of the Sixteenth and Seventeenth Centuries', *British Medical Bulletin*, Vol. 6, No. 1–2 (1949), pp. 63–9, a reference I owe to the

kindness of Professor Norman Cohn. The evidence is almost entirely Continental, however.

34. Only between 1645 and 1647 were the ages of suspected witches recorded in coroners' inquests: four examples are cases 648(c)–(f).
35. Gaule, *Select Cases*, p. 175.
36. Stearne, *Confirmation*, p. 19; the only recorded young suspect in Essex (Joan Waterhouse, 1566 Pamphlet, p. 320) was aged eighteen; perhaps this was the reason for her acquittal, despite her confession, case 19.
37. Case 861.
38. Further evidence of their age, albeit impressionistic, comes from the pamphlet descriptions of 'old women' who were witches. As was shown in Table 7, p. 95, above, a number of women remained suspected for many years; when they were buried they might be recorded, as was the witch Mary Belsted or Middleton of Boreham as 'an old woman'.
39. Case 145.
40. Scot, *Discovery*, pp. 65, 399.
41. 1645 Pamphlet, p. 32.
42. Ady, *Candle*, p. 110.
43. Cases 158, 160, 155.
44. Elizabeth Fraunces bewitched her husband after constant friction with him, 1566 Pamphlet, p. 318.
45. Little is known concerning the percentage of women over the age of forty who were widows; the fact that 15.3 per cent of Clayworth households in 1676 were headed by widows, suggests, however, that the number might be large (*An Introduction to English Historical Demography*, ed. E. A. Wrigley (1966), p. 203). A connexion between widows and witches, as well as some illustrations of the number of solitary widows in various villages, is suggested in P. Laslett, *The World We have Lost* (University paperback edn., 1965), pp. 95–6.
46. There seems to have been no connexion between childlessness and witchcraft; a number of the suspects were accused by their children or were believed to have given their witchcraft to them.

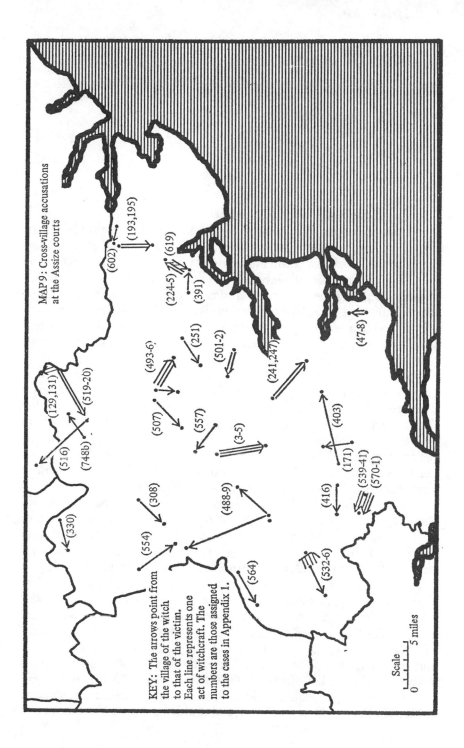

MAP 9: Cross-village accusations at the Assize courts

KEY: The arrows point from the village of the witch to that of the victim. Each line represents one act of witchcraft. The numbers are those assigned to the cases in Appendix 1.

Scale
0   5 miles

Chapter 12

Witchcraft prosecutions and social phenomena (2): kin and neighbours

There is no doubt that witchcraft prosecutions were made between people who knew each other intimately. Very few accusations were made against people who lived far away. As shown in Map 9, only fifty out of 460 indictments at the Assizes for bewitching property or persons placed victim and witch in different villages. Only five accusations occurred over a distance of more than five miles. Thus accusations seem to have been limited to the area of intense relationships between individuals. The power of the witch was limited to a few miles. As Reginald Scot argued, their power reached as far as their social contacts, which was not far: 'for their furthest fetches that I can comprehend, are but to fetch a pot of milke, &c.: from their neighbors house, halfe a mile distant from them'.[1] The Essex pamphlets give abundant evidence that witch and victim were linked in many ways. They even, occasionally, show that suspect and accuser were living next-door to each other. For instance, a man in 1645 was told that his sick wife 'was cursed by two women who were neere neighbours to this Informant, the one dwelling a little above his house, and the other beneath his house', the house being on a hill.[2] A contemporary map of Stock Common in 1575 shows the house of the notorious witch Widow Sawel, and next-door that of her victim's father, Roger Veale.[3] Only very detailed research will show exactly how close were the houses of victim and witch and whether they tended to be in the village or outlying farms. Preliminary research on the village of Hatfield Peverel suggests that those involved in prosecutions not only lived in the same village, but came from the same part of the village.

Hatfield Peverel contained two large and three small manors in the sixteenth century, of which the two largest have surviving court records. The contrast between the number of persons connected with witchcraft prosecutions holding land in these two manors is considerable. The manor of Mugdon Hall in the southern part of the parish was surveyed in 1589, and this survey, combined with a list of those who took homage in the 1550's, provides a list of twenty tenants. Of these, three possibly had connexions with prosecutions.[4] Two, however, also had land in the manor of Hatfield Peverel, once the Priory, and it may have been by virtue of this that they came into contact with suspected witches, for the situation on this second manor was quite different. A simple analysis of those who paid homage at the manor court in June 1566, the first witchcraft trial year, shows that, of fifteen resident families, eight were directly connected with witchcraft prosecutions.[5] Those involved in prosecutions were thus related not only through the village church, through co-residence, and through the bonds of neighbourhood, but also through the manorial organization and economic ties.

Another possible link between witch and accuser is that of kinship. The tensions between kin have been stressed by anthropologists as one of the major factors in African witchcraft suspicions.[6] There is little evidence that relationship by blood or by marriage was important in Essex witchcraft prosecutions. The surnames of victims in indictments were hardly ever the same as those of witches; this eliminates certain family relationships—for instance, that between husband and wife—from obvious importance in the accusations. No contemporary writers noted any particular likelihood of bewitching occurring between blood relatives. Nor has detailed analysis of the kinship structure of the village of Boreham, where there were known witches, shown any connexion by blood between the accused and accusers.[7] For instance, there is no evidence that the suspected witches Agnes Haven or Margaret Poole were related to any other families in the village. Nor do the pamphlet accounts, which often go into great detail, suggest that those involved were anything but neighbours. There is, however, a certain amount of evidence that witchcraft accusations sometimes reflected tensions between affines—that is, between relations by marriage. Two cases from the Essex pamphlets are those of John Chaundler, whose wife having been executed as a witch, demanded money from his wife's daughter, upon which she supposedly bewitched him;[8] and that of a woman who believed that she had been bewitched by her sister-in-law.[9] Most common of all was the bewitching of the husband by the wife. Perhaps because it was difficult to prove, no indictments for this offence are known for Essex. Yet the pamphlets describe a few instances, and other instances occasionally emerge by chance. In 1564 a man blamed his lameness on his wife,[10] and two years later both Agnes Waterhouse and Elizabeth Fraunces confessed to bewitching their respective husbands.[11] In 1582 both Alice Newman and Margaret Grevell were supposed to have bewitched their own husbands to death.[12] Close to this was the case of the man who went round trying to presuade his sick neighbours that they were bewitched by his wife.[13] When placed against the hundreds of other bewitchings in Essex, these few cases do not seem of great importance. Yet they show that it was believed possible for a witch to attack her husband, just as it was possible for her to attack her child.

As Gifford pointed out,[14] children quite frequently gave evidence against their parents in cases of witchcraft. For instance, the son of a witch gave evidence against his mother in 1579 in Essex,[15] and two bastard boys gave 'great evidence' against their mother and grandmother in 1589.[16] Nevertheless, it would be mistaken to see child–parent hostility as an important contributing factor in witchcraft prosecutions. Not only do the pamphlets, and witnesses' names on the indictments, show that the majority of cases were tried without child witnesses, but it also seems apparent that such witnesses were only brought in to give added proof. They did not start suspicions, but were persuaded to give testimony. 'Many go so farre, that if they can intice children to accuse their parents, they thinke it a good worke.'[17] Often children must have supported their parents, as in 1564.[18] It is possible that an added pressure on children was the knowledge that if they refused to support charges against their parents they, in turn, might be accused of being witches. It is clear that there was a strong popular belief that witchcraft was hereditary. 'Suspected Ancestors' were to be used as evidence that a person was a witch.[19] Witches, said the Essex witch-hunter Stearne, 'leave' witchcraft to 'Children, servants, or to some others': people born of 'bad and wicked parents' were deemed likely to be witches.[20] If we turn to the actual Essex cases, there are a considerable number of examples of daughters, and even granddaughters, of accused witches being suspected of the same crime. In 1566 several of the witches were related by blood,[21] and three generations of suspected witches are illustrated in the Harwich Borough records and two in those of Maldon.[22] Other cases can be found in the 1582, 1589 and 1645 pamphlets.[23] Possibly this was a feature in nearly one in ten of the Essex cases.

While it has been demonstrated that witch and victim lived close to each other, no important ties of kinship seem to have linked them. Much more important were the bonds of neighbourliness. That witches were supposed to bewitch their neighbours is clear from the Essex evidence. Widow Tibboulde was 'a slaunderer of hir neighbours, And because some of hir neighbours after she hathe fallen out w[i]th them have had evell successe w[i]th the Cattell therfore they have conceived an opinion that she ys a witche'.[24] In Hatfield Peverel this link of neighbourliness is clearly implied. One witch gave her familiar to 'mother Waterhouse her neighbor' and she, in turn, 'falling out wyth another of her neybours' killed three geese and 'falling out with another of her neybours and his wife' killed the husband. Mother Waterhouse's daughter employed witchcraft after being refused bread and cheese at the house of 'a girl a neybours chylde'. The same Mother Waterhouse admitted that she was unable to bewitch 'one Wardol, a neighbour of hers'.[25] In 1579 Elizabeth Frauncis explained how 'she came to one Pooles wife her neighbour' and later bewitched her.[26] In

9 Frontispiece from Matthew Hopkins *The Discovery of Witches*, 1647
(British Museum)

A Detection
of damnable driftes, practized by three VVitches arraigned at
Chelmiffozde in Effex, at the
laste Affifes there holden, whiche
were executed in Apzill.
1 5 7 9.

Set fozthe to difcouer the Ambufhementes of
Sathan, whereby he would furpzife vs
lulled in feruritie, and hardened
with contempte of Gods
vengeance thzeatened
foz our offences.

Imprinted at London for Edward White,
at the little North-dore of Paules.

10 Title-page of a contemporary tract on the second major trial
of witches at Chelmsford, 1579
(British Museum)

the same village, an analysis of those who witnessed the wills of one of the most witch-attacked families, the Wilmotts, shows that the three major witch families in the village, the Fraunces, Duke, and Osborne families, were all linked to the Wilmotts by friendship as well as by witchcraft. Other victims of witchcraft were also interlinked in this way.[27]

The methods supposedly employed by witches, and the counter-actions used by their victims, provide further evidence that strains and tensions between neighbours were linked to witchcraft accusations. Essex suspects

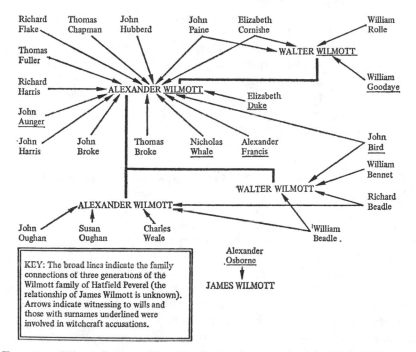

FIGURE 4: Witnessing to wills and witchcraft accusations in Hatfield Peverel, 1540–1599.

do not seem to have employed complicated methods of bewitching. They did not stick pins in images of their victim, or make poisons out of human fat. Their two principal techniques, if such simple activities can be given such a title, were sending their familiars to bite or frighten their victim, or making some remark which might be interpreted as vicious. In fact, these two were not sharply divided; often a familiar would first appear when a woman cursed a neighbour.[28] Often their words to a neighbour were spiteful. 'Witches', Perkins wrote, 'are wont to practise their mischevous facts by cursing and banning.'[29] There are a number of Essex examples, ranging from an unusual rhyming curse and ritual cursing on the knees[30] to hardly audible mumbling in discontent which was interpreted by the future victim as evil.[31] What seems clear is that it was not the content of the remark which mattered, but rather the context in which it was spoken and the interpretation put on it. Thus even outwardly friendly overtures might be interpreted as malicious. For instance, three women in 1582 admired and fondled a child, saying 'here is a iolie and likely childe God blesse it';[32] it promptly sickened and died of witchcraft. The same fate befell some pigs praised by a Colchester suspect.[33] Similarly, actions were carefully interpreted, and the most innocent neighbourly gesture might be shunned as likely to lead to a bewitching. One Essex suspect, in 1645, was especially notorious for giving children gifts, an apple, or bread and butter, and also complimenting them or kissing them, all of which led to subsequent disaster.[34] Another was described as bewitching people through gifts of food, a drink, and an apple cake.[35] An exceptional case was the drawing of a circle outside a neighbour's door; even here the activity was interpreted differently by the witch, who claimed she was making a 'shityng house', and the victim, who subsequently became ill on the spot.[36]

One way of explaining these supposed methods of witches is to link them to the relations ideally obtaining between neighbours. Whereas neighbours normally lent each other small objects and showed concern and interest in each others' business, witches were, in a sense, either too good as neighbours or impossible. Either they cursed and banned and became intolerable, or, perhaps worse than this, they were too solicitous, too eager to lend and borrow. This belief has already been seen at work in the counter-actions against witches, many of them involving the severing of all connexions with the suspect.[37] It can also be illustrated from the occasions when witchcraft was most feared. Illness was a time when neighbours co-operated and showed mutual concern in village society, but it was also the occasion when witches were most active. Diligent inquiry after a sick person, though an action to be commended when it occurred between rea friends, was prime evidence that the inquirer was a witch if relations were felt to be strained.[38] One of the best methods of detecting, or proving, a witch was to burn some object belonging to either witch or victim, and then to see whether the suspect hurried round to inquire how the sick person fared.[39] An extreme example of this occurred when the witch Elizabeth Bennet visited a neighbour and, seeing the neighbour sick, said 'how thou art loden, and then clasped her in her armes, and kissed her: Whereupon presently after her upper Lippe swelled and was very bigge, and her eyes much sunked into her head.'[40] Illness was the time when people would draw closer together, when past quarrels would be forgiven, the occasion when people brought 'some small thing to curry favour againe'.[41] It was also a time when relationships were finally severed, and decisions about whether a person was really a witch were made.

The clearest evidence, however, that witchcraft accusations occurred in the context of quarrels between neighbours are the supposed motives of witches. Witches did not act without some provocation, and commentators noted that their common emotion was discontent and a desire for revenge.[42] They acted, Ady suggested, after being refused by a neighbour.[43] Anger at being denied the benefits of neighbourly help was the dominant emotion

TABLE 17

Alleged motives of witches tried at the assizes in 1582

Name of accused	Alleged motive	Sig. ref.
Ursley Kemp	was refused nursing of a child	Av
	was refused a promised payment	A2v
	was refused a loan of 'scouring sand'	A3
	had been called 'whore' and other names	B2
	was physically attacked	E5
Joan Pechey	a food dole given to her not of sufficient quality	A4
Alice Newman	was refused 12d. for her sick husband	A7
Elizabeth	was cursed, maligned, and her cattle cursed,	B6v,
Bennet	her swine beaten and pitchforked	B7
Elizabeth	her daughter, a servant, threatened	C7
Ewstace	her geese driven off a neighbour's land and hurt	E4
Cicely Celles	was denied 'mault' at the price she wanted	C8v
	her cattle hunted off a neighbour's land	C8v
	was refused the nursing of a child	D8v
Alice Hunt	was denied a piece of pork	D5
Alice Manfield	a thatcher refused to work for her	C6v
	was refused a 'mess of milk'	E2v
	was denied 'curdes'	D6v
	a 'green place' in front of her house made muddy	D7
Margaret	was denied 'Godesgood'	E2v
Grevell	was denied mutton	E3
Anne Herd	was not offered sufficient support at church court	E6v
	bough she placed over muddy patch removed	E7
	it was implied that she would keep a borrowed dish	E8
	money she had borrowed demanded back	F
	a promised pig given to another by victim	F2
	was accused of stealing ducklings	F2v
Joan Robinson	was denied a 'hayer'	F6
	was denied the hire of a pasture	F6
	was denied the use of another 'hayer'	F6v
	was refused the sale of a pig	F7
	was refused a cheese	F7v
	was refused a pig	F8
	was refused payment for goods 'at her own reckoning'	F8

leading to witchcraft acts, suggested Gifford.[44] Commenting on the confessions of Essex and other suspects, Stearne remarked that 'you may observe in most of their Confessions, they did it because they had not such things as they desired, or used to have'.[45] These general comments are amply substantiated in the Essex records of prosecutions whenever details are given. Table 17 gives the motives suggested by confessing suspects or their accusers as reported in the 1582 pamphlet.

The motives ascribed to witches, listed above, immediately suggest that it was tension between neighbours which led to acts of witchcraft. A person was refused some small object and in her anger retaliated by bewitching her refuser. The sphere of neighbourly conduct was not merely limited to gifts; it included all the ways in which people were linked. For example, as we see in the case of Anne Herd above, even an action like removing a piece of wood from a muddy patch might be construed as unneighbourly and lead to tension. Another feature common to all the motives is that it was the victim who had made an open breach in neighbourly conducts, rather than the witch. It was the victim who had reason to feel guilty and anxious at having turned away a neighbour, while the suspect might become hated as the agent who caused such a feeling. The 1582 pamphlet also makes it clear that there was often a relationship between the type of motive and the type of injury. Thus when a cart which was fetching dung made a mess in front of a suspected witch's door it was the cart that was later bewitched.[46] When a woman refused a neighbour some milk on the excuse that she had not got enough to suckle her own calf, the calf was soon destroyed by witchcraft.[47]

The pamphlet of 1582 is in no way exceptional in showing that witchcraft occurred after neighbours had fallen out over their mutual obligations. In 1570, also, acts of witchcraft were believed to be repaying lack of charity on the part of the future victim. One woman was bewitched after refusing to bring home some sprats from the London market for her neighbour; another suffered after turning an old woman off a piece of common where she used to collect wood. A classic instance of the neglected neighbour at neighbourly celebrations also occurred on this occasion. A man 'having a sheep-shearing about that time, and not inviting her [i.e. the witch] thereto, being his neighbour, she, as he supposed, bewitched two of his sheep'.[48] The pamphlet of 1645 suggests similar tensions. In seven cases the motive for an act of witchcraft was alleged to be the refusal of a loan or a gift of food or money: in one instance the victim refused to pay back a 2*d*. loan; in another the victim slandered the suspect; once the witch was refused credit at a shop and went away mumbling; another time a woman's daughter refused to fetch wood for her mother and was bewitched. There were two cases of the beating of the children of supposed witches by a neighbour leading to witchcraft in retaliation. One woman was angry at the impressment of her husband as a soldier. On two occasions a person was filled with rage at being evicted from her house. Detailed ecclesiastical depositions in 1564 give further examples of the type of quarrel that led to accusations. After a squabble over the right to work, a woman openly accused another of lying and being a witch; the accuser subsequently

TABLE 18
Types of dispute leading to witchcraft prosecutions in Essex, 1564–89

Kinship relationships:

Husband-wife	4	Unspecified quarrels (2)
		Sexual jealousy (1)
		Broken marriage contract (1)
Stepfather-stepchild	1	Over inheritance
Grandmother-grandchild	1	Obligation to collect wood
		TOTAL 6

Neighbourly relationships

Object of dispute:

Food/drink	12	
Animals	4	
Money	8	
Implements	4	
Unspecified loans	3	
Boundaries/land	4	
Children	3	
Obligations:		
to speak to	1	
support at law	1	
not to attack by word or deed	6	
Privilege of:		
spinning	1	
nursing child	1	TOTAL 48

suffered. On another occasion a victim lost two pigs mysteriously, soon after demanding back a loan of 6s. 8d. Most curious of all, a witch was suspected of killing a lamb by witchcraft; on visiting a neighbour, she had found the lamb being fed with white bread and milk and had yelled 'must yt be fed w[i]th the mete of childrene': the lamb died the next day. In the first case it was the victim who called the other a liar and witch; in the second it was the victim who broke off a relationship by demanding her loan back; in the third it was the victim who was offending against the ethics of a subsistence economy by feeding animals on food suitable for children.[49]

The relative importance of disputes between neighbours and between kin is of such crucial interest in an analysis of Essex prosecutions that one more table is included to demonstrate the area and objects of disputes. This is based on the pamphlets of 1566, 1579, 1582, and 1589 and the depositions of 1564.

Thus we see that, in the limited evidence available, quarrels over gifts and loans of food, and to a lesser extent, money and implements, precipitated the majority of the witchcraft attacks. The actual object of the dispute, the loan of an implement or the demand that money should be returned, was merely the final stage in the severing of a relationship. Much more was at stake than the particular article or privilege; in effect, it was the total relationship between two neighbours. Viewed in this way, the enormous emotion generated by an apparently simple act like asking for a few pennies to be returned becomes understandable.

NOTES

1. Scot, *Discovery*, p. 374.
2. 1645 Pamphlet, p. 1.
3. Case 108; the map is in the E.R.O.
4. These were William Bastwick, John Fraunces, and James Hawkins.
5. Those probably connected were Robert Waterhouse, Walter Wilmott, Henry Jenyn, James Hawkyn, Alexander Fraunces, William Higham, John Burde, and Thomas Carsey, e.g. William Higham was bewitched in 1566.
6. See pp. 234-6, below, for witchcraft and kinship.
7. The results are too detailed to include here; the major families in the village, and especially all those related to prosecutions, were reconstituted, on the basis of the parish register and wills, for the period 1560-1600.
8. 1579 Pamphlet, sig. Av^v.
9. 1582 Pamphlet, sig. E5.
10. Case 861.
11. 1566 Pamphlet, pp. 318-19.
12. 1582 Pamphlet, sig. F8^v.
13. Case 981.
14. Gifford, *Discourse*, sig. G4^v.
15. 1579 Pamphlet, sig. Avi^v.
16. 1589 Pamphlet, sig. Aiv.
17. Gifford, *Dialogue*, sig. L.
18. Case 981.
19. Gaule, *Select Cases*, p. 46.
20. Stearne, *Confirmation*, pp. 12, 29, 33; among those who made the same point were Bernard, *Guide*, pp. 211-12, and Perkins, *Damned Art*, pp. 202-3.
21. Elizabeth Fraunces claimed that she had been given her familiar by her grandmother. Agnes Waterhouse was the mother of Joan Waterhouse and sister to Mother Osborne; all three were suspected witches.

22. At Maldon, Ellen Smith was the daughter of Alice Chaundler (1579 Pamphlet, sig. Av^v) and, at Harwich, Elizabeth Hanby, executed in 1601, was the mother of Jane Prentice or Hanby, tried in 1634 and again in 1638, with her daughter Susan (cases 1,146, 580, 586, 588, 589).
23. 1582 Pamphlet, sig. C4; 1589 Pamphlet, sig. B; 1645 Pamphlet, pp. 1, 12. Four cases of mother and daughter being suspected witches are listed in case 1,207.
24. Case, 1,046.
25. 1566 Pamphlet, *passim*.
26. 1579 Pamphlet, sig. Aiv.
27. See Fig. 4.
28. For instance, in the 1579 Pamphlet, sig. Aiv.
29. Perkins, *Damned Art*, p. 202.
30. Both occur in case 861; such methods are discussed in Thomas Cooper, *Mystery of Witchcraft* (1617), pp. 208–9, but they seem rare in Essex.
31. Examples are numerous—for instance, 1582 Pamphlet, sig. A3. Vague threats, also, might be interpreted as dangerous—for example, in the 1582 Pamphlet, sig. C7^v, or Gifford, *Discourse*, sig. G3.
32. 1582 Pamphlet, sig. D3; see case 843 also.
33. Case 1,173. Foster suggests why compliments are rare in peasant societies and why 'the person who compliments is, in fact, guilty of aggression' (George Foster, 'Peasant Society and the Image of Limited Good', *American Anthropologist*, 67, No. 2 (1965), p. 304).
34. 1645 Pamphlet, pp. 17, 20.
35. 1579 Pamphlet, sigs. Aiv^v–Av.
36. Ibid., sig. Aviii^v.
37. See p. 104, above.
38. Michael Dalton, *The Countrey Justice* (1630), p. 273.
39. 1579 Pamphlet, sig. Avi, is an example where it was the supposed familiar of the witch that was burnt.
40. 1582 Pamphlet, sigs. B5^v–B6; another example is given in the same pamphlet, sig. E5.
41. Bernard, *Guide*, p. 207.
42. Among those who suggested such motives were Thomas Cooper, *Mystery of Witchcraft* (1617), p. 57; Gaule, *Select Cases*, p. 51.
43. Ady, *Candle*, pp. 114, 129.
44. Gifford, *Discourse*, sigs. G3–G4, I2,
45. Stearne, *Confirmation*, p. 36.
46. 1582 Pamphlet, sig. D7.
47. Ibid., sig. E2^v. Other examples in the same pamphlet are on sigs. F^v, F6^v, F7^v.
48. Case, 1,204; a Continental parallel, of a woman neglected at a wedding, is described in Henry More, *An Antidote Against Atheism* (1655), p. 173.
49. Case 861.

Chapter 13

*Witchcraft prosecutions
and illness*

It has frequently been suggested that witchcraft prosecutions merely reflected the high incidence of illness and the lack of medical knowledge in sixteenth- and seventeenth-century England.[1] This explanation cannot, by itself, account for the growth of accusations in Essex after 1560 or their decline after 1650. To do so it would have to show either that illness became worse in some way after 1560 and declined rapidly in the early seventeenth century, or that medical ignorance grew in the early sixteenth century, while knowledge of the cause of various diseases grew rapidly 100 years later. Finally, it might be argued that a combination of these two factors made the period between 1560 and 1650 peculiar. All that can be said is that such changes in illness or in remedies have not been demonstrated at the village level.[2] Until they are, such an explanation seems unhelpful. Without denying that frequent and incurable illness may have been an essential background to witchcraft beliefs, it does not seem that changes in beliefs can be explained merely by reference to the medical conditions and changes of the period. An examination of the actual types of illness which were blamed on witches in Essex provides further evidence on this problem.

There is little doubt that much illness and many deaths were explained without reference to witches in sixteenth-century Essex. This can be demonstrated by comparing known cases of witchcraft suspicions with all the illness and death in the three sample villages. Even allowing for the fact that the known suspicions only represent a quarter or less of actual fears, there is a huge gap between the total number of accidents and the number of witchcraft explanations. The two witches in Little Baddow were believed to have killed three people and injured another two. As a proportion of all death and illness in the village during forty years, this was very small. Between 1560 and 1599, the parish register records the deaths of 175 people. In Boreham witches were accused of killing one child, making another man languish, destroying a horse worth £3 and four hogs valued at 26s. 8d. There is no record of animal illness in parish sources, but the one death they were blamed for can be compared to the 351 recorded in the parish register for the period 1560–99.

Lack of parish registers makes such a comparison impossible for Hatfield Peverel. Yet a useful comparison can be made for that village by using the information, recorded by the coroners, on sudden deaths. In 1562 a labourer fell down and broke his leg and subsequently died; the verdict was 'death by misfortune'.[3] The same verdict was returned in 1570, a year sandwiched between two series of witchcraft prosecutions, when a servant of William Higham, another of whose servants was bewitched nine years later,[4] fell from the pear tree in which he was climbing and immediately died.[5] Another explanation was given for the death of Richard Duke, possibly a relation of the witch Agnes Duke. He was judged to have died '*ex visitacione divina*'—in other words, of plague.[6] These inquisitions were held before leading villagers, most, if not all, of whom must have been aware that witchcraft was a possible explanation of an accident. Yet there is no suggestion that they believed witchcraft to have been involved. The same was true in Boreham. Verdicts of death 'by misfortune' were returned on the bodies of two young men who were squashed to death by a landslide, and in 1581 on the body of another inhabitant who fell into a stream and drowned.[7] Analysis of the Essex coroner's inquests for the sample years 1580–9 gives the impression that, concurrently with the years of fiercest prosecution, many people died sudden deaths which were not blamed on witches. Some forty-three people in all are named, their cause of death varying from drowning to being squashed by collapsing buildings or trees. None of them have been traced as supposed victims of witches.[8] It is possible, of course, that those most intimately connected with the deceased always attributed the death to the malice of witches. In this case a suspicion would remain dormant unless it was shared by a large enough group of villagers. It is more likely, however, that there were certain types of misfortune which were hardly ever blamed on witches. It will also be argued that the explanation suggested for illness and death depended on the social relationships of the injured individual.

One type of illness which does not seem to have borne any necessary relationship to witchcraft prosecutions was 'plague', using that word to cover the variety of epidemic diseases prevalent in the period. This negative conclusion can be seen at both the county and village level. The worst years for plague in Essex during our period were 1597–9; these were not exceptional for the number of prosecutions.[9] Nor do individual villages show a coincidence. At Great Clacton there was high mortality in 1561–2, 1570–1, 1587–9, and 1602; the only known witchcraft prosecution occurred in 1593.[10] The only prosecution recorded for the town of Saffron Walden occurred in 1594. At first sight, the two indictments against one person in that year might be seen as connected to the plague of the previous year. In fact, they illustrate clearly how it was *not* plague deaths which were blamed on witches. Although ninety-seven deaths had occurred during the previous year, almost twice the yearly average, Agnes Bett was accused of bewitching a man in 1591 and a *calf* in 1593.[11] There are no reasons for believing that the 1580's, the worst years for Essex witchcraft prosecutions, were particularly plague-ridden, or that 1645, the year of exceptional prosecutions in the seventeenth century, was an epidemic year. The three sample villages show the same absence of connexion between years of high mortality and accusations: for instance, in Little Baddow the actual year in which prosecutions took place, 1570, saw a high number of deaths, twelve in all, but there were equally high numbers in 1566, 1567, and 1602 and no prosecutions. The actual deaths blamed on those prosecuted in 1570 were supposed to have occurred in 1568 and 1569, neither of them noted for particularly high death-rates.

Infant mortality was another phenomenon which does not seem to have been directly related to prosecutions. Analysis of the age of victims of witchcraft has already shown that only nine of the 341 victims recorded in Assize indictments were children of under a year old.[12] Nor do midwives seem to have been important in Essex prosecutions, except as searchers for the mark of the witch. No suspected witches in Essex are known to have been midwives, nor is there any counterpart to Continental fears that midwives killed the delivered babies with long pins.[13]

Some indication of the types of suffering caused to human beings can be gained from the Assize indictments, where the date of both the beginning and end of a supposed act of witchcraft were recorded. The length of time in this source is analysed below.

TABLE 19

Duration of illness ascribed to witches in Essex assize indictments, 1560–1680

Length of time	Illness	Illness leading to death
Immediate	—	17
1–7 days	5	38
8–30 days	7	43
1–3 months	10	70
4–11 months	4	33
1–3 years	6	13
over 3 years	1	—
'languished'	50	—
'lamed'	10	—

It is apparent that it was not immediate, sudden, deaths which were most commonly attributed to witchcraft. Rather it was a death in which the deceased had lingered in illness for between a week and three months. The same lingering nature of illness attributed to witches is apparent in the large number who 'languished' and were 'lamed' without a specific term being set to their misfortune. They were probably often still suffering when the suspect was tried; for instance, a man was stated to be 'lamed in his body and yet is' in 1572.[14] These lingering illnesses are often described in the contemporary accounts. Such descriptions enable us to see whether it was not only prolonged, but also particularly painful or violent types of illness which were ascribed to witchcraft.

The symptoms of illnesses ascribed to the power of witchcraft were so diverse that it is clear that no particular types of disease were always explained in this manner. In the seven cases where details are given in the Assize indictments the injuries were as following: a girl was 'made decrepid in her right leg and in her right arm'; another woman 'became decrepit and so remained'; one man totally lost the sight of an eye; a boy became lame, 'both his feet remaining crooked and useless'; a woman 'lost the use of the upper part of her body'; a person's right thigh 'did rot off'; and a man languished 'troubled in his left leg'.[15] The symptoms were further elaborated in the pamphlets. One child's hands were 'turned where the backes shoulde bee, and the backe in the place of the palmes', another 'appeared to bee in most pitious sort consumed and the privie and hinder partes thereof, to be in a most strange and wonderfull case'.[16] One man was hurt in the back 'whereof hee languisheth and is greatly payned'; a woman, having been kissed by a witch, 'her upper Lippe swelled and was very bigge, and her eyes much sunked into her head'; another woman 'by many yeares past . . . was much troubled with straung aches in her bones, and otherwise: wherof she consumed by the space of two or three yeares'. Among other victims were a man with his 'mouth drawne awrye, well neere uppe to the upper parte of his cheeke'; a girl who was 'stroke . . . at the hart, in such sort as shee could not stand, goe nor speake', and a man who was likewise 'cast amongest Bushes, and was in that case that hee coulde neyther see, heare, nor speake'. Sometimes, however, the manner of death was not strange; it was merely the unexpectedness that caused wonder. A witch being asked 'what she thought of the sodaine death of Johnson the Collector, saith, he was a very honest man, and dyed very sodainly'. A child aged four 'being in good liking and well, went but out of the doores into the yarde, who presently feel downe dead, and after by helpe being brought to life, the saide childe was in a pitious case, and so died presently'. The other pamphlets and depositions show a similar variety of symptoms: loss of the use of limbs, inability to keep down food, swelling of the body.[17] Thus the malice of a witch might be used to explain a wide range of illnesses afflicting all parts of the body. It is difficult to show that it was particularly associated with any major type of disease.

The assertion that witchcraft accusations were not connected with any specific diseases contradicts the opinion of a number of writers of the sixteenth and seventeenth centuries. Matthew Hopkins suggested that witches were blamed for 'sudden disease, (as by experience I have found) as *Plurisie, Imposthume,* &c.',[18] while Gifford argued that it was lingering sickness that provoked suspicions.[19] Both kinds have been shown in the Essex evidence. Even more emphasis was laid on the strange and inexplicable nature of the disease. Perkins argued that enchanters procured 'strange passions and torments in mens bodies',[20] and children who were 'visited with diseases that vex them strangelie: as apoplexies, epilepsies, convulsions, hot fevers, wormes, &c.' were suspected to be bewitched, Scot remarked.[21] The strangeness was indeed stressed in some Essex cases: for example, a little child 'fell so straungely sicke as for the space of a Weeke, as no bodie thought it would live'.[22] On the other hand, the illness—for example, in the case where a woman was believed to have caused a 'bludye fluxe'—were not always unusual.[23] Nor were all cases of strange illness attributed to the power of witches: when a woman suffered from a 'disease called the mother' for six years in Boreham, she did not blame witches. Nor did Hugo Gill of Little Baddow, who explained his absence from church by saying that 'by reason he hathe bene visited by the hande of god w[i]th greate paine in one of his knees' he was unable to 'sturre for the space of viii of ix weekes'.[24] Thus Gaule was going too far when he stated that 'every disease whereof they neither understand the Cause, nor are acquainted with the Symptoms must bee suspected for witch-craft'.[25] As Reginald Scot pointed out,[26] witchcraft was only suspected if the victim had previously quarrelled with someone. It was the social relationship of the victim, rather than the painful or inexplicable nature of the illness, that determined a person's reaction to misfortune. This interpretation explains why witches were blamed for such a variety of evils, from burning barns and knocking down trees, to making legs crooked and causing heart-attacks. In accounting for the growth and decline of witchcraft fears, therefore, the problem is not to prove that there was more sickness in the late sixteenth century than earlier, and that both conditions and knowledge of the scientific basis of illness improved, suddenly, in the middle of the seventeenth century. Rather, it is to show that the social relationships which determine the way in which people react to misfortune changed.

A final illustration that witchcraft prosecutions did not merely arise out of a combination of violent illness and lack of medical knowledge is the reaction to hysterical outbreaks, the 'apoplexies, epilepsies, convulsions, hot fevers' listed by Reginald Scot. Essex records describe over twenty cases of insanity: for instance, a man was noted in the Great Coggeshall parish register as dying 'sodainlye uppo[n] an apoplexie'.[27] Yet none of these have been related to witchcraft prosecutions. On the other hand, as we have seen, the vast majority of the injuries blamed on witches were either to animals, dairy products, or physical illness to humans. There is only a very slight connexion, in Essex, between mental derangement and witchcraft beliefs. The only reference in the pamphlets to such an injury was in 1579 when a woman 'fell distraught of her wittes' after seeing a witch's familiar.[28] George Gifford, a sensitive observer, made little connexion between mental breakdown and witchcraft.[29] There are, it is true, three cases where the victim suffered convulsive fits,[30] and there is a particularly extraordinary case where a man 'crowed like a Cock, barked like a Dogge, sung tunes, and groaned'.[31] Yet these were a very small proportion of all the injuries. Nor does the Essex evidence suggest that diabolic possession—that is, the belief that the contortions of the victim were caused by the Devil being inside the afficted person—was at all common in Essex. The only prosecution recorded in the legal records was discovered to be a fraud,[32] although there may have been one or more cases of a more serious nature around the year 1600 to which there are several literary references.[33] Neither these, nor a description of another fraudulent case in the 1650's at Braintree,[34] have survived as prosecutions. In fact, the only detailed description of a case of possession in Essex is of one that occurred in 1700.[35] Only in this case, and in the fraudulent possession of 1621, do we know of attempts to exorcize the Devil. Thus Essex witchcraft prosecutions continued without, as far as we can tell, the presence of a band of exorcists or a series of sensational cases of possession.

A final problem which is of considerable importance is the extent to which illness supposedly caused by witchcraft was psychosomatic. It has already been suggested that one reason for the success of cunning folk was their ability to relate physical illness to mental strains, their provision of an explanation, not only of the physical pain, but also of the feelings of hostility and indecision associated with the witch. Their clients were often cured 'when the parties mind is cheered', and this implies that some, at least, of the illness arose out of mental instability. Although there are several well-documented cases where this process of worry leading to illness seem to be illustrated,[36] it is impossible to give anything approaching a statistical answer to the problem. Perhaps the most conscious connexion between anxiety and bewitching was given in an ecclesiastical presentment where the churchwardens stated that 'Barbara Pond falling out with one of her neighbors she sayd it had byn better for her she had delt so w[i]th her wherupon the woman fell lame & p[er]swaded her self she was bewiched by her the same Barbara Pond'.[37] Yet even in this case it is impossible to prove that the illness was psychosomatic; it may have merely been an instance of the interpretation of future misfortunes being influenced by fear of witchcraft. The many injuries to the animals, children, and other property of the person who had quarrelled with a witch suggest that illness of a psychosomatic nature only played a small part in witchcraft prosecutions.

The reaction of physicians to witchcraft prosecutions seems to have been ambivalent. This is illustrated by Thomas Ady. Probably a licensed physician himself and very sceptical about the power of witches,[38] he harshly castigated his fellow practitioners, many of whom confirmed that their patients were bewitched.[39] In theory, physicians were to be consulted before witchcraft prosecutions took place;[40] but it seems likely that in many cases no doctor was available. Perhaps the best evidence that medical practitioners were unlikely to provide a bulwark against witchcraft prosecutions is the fact that nearly a third of the twenty-three cunning men whose professions are known were either surgeons or physicians.[41] It seems hardly surprising that, if a doctor as eminent as Sir Thomas Browne endorsed current witchcraft beliefs, there should be no Essex evidence that country practitioners opposed prosecutions.[42]

NOTES

1. For instance, by Kittredge, *Witchcraft*, p. 5, among modern writers, and Ady, *Candle*, pp. 103–4, among contemporaries.
2. It could plausibly be argued, indeed, that overcrowding worsened health in the later seventeenth century, as suggested in W. G. Hoskins, *Provincial England* (1964), p. 148. E. A. Wrigley, 'Family Limitation in Pre-industrial England', *Economic Hist. Rev.*, 2nd ser., xix, No. 1 (1966), p. 101, gives figures to show increased infant mortality in the late seventeenth century in Colyton, Devon. He also refers to forthcoming evidence which will show increased mortality at all ages.
3. P.R.O., K.B. 9, 605, m. 69.
4. 1579 Pamphlet, sig. Av.
5. P.R.O., K.B.9, 628, m. 234.
6. Ibid., 662, m. 172.
7. Ibid., 608, m. 129 and 656, m. 155.
8. Ibid., files 650–74; only deaths 'by misfortune' are counted here.
9. See Diagram 1, p. 25, above. I am indebted to Mr. Paul Slack of Balliol College, Oxford, for the following details concerning plague in Essex taken from his forthcoming Oxford, D.Phil. thesis, 'Plague in England, 1538–1640'.
10. Case 367.
11. Cases 387–8.

12. See p. 163, above, for a more detailed analysis of victims' ages.
13. Until an authoritative list of Essex midwives is available, the lack of connexion between midwife and witch must remain tentative.
14. Case 56.
15. Cases 19, 559, 285, 108, 346, 299, 286, in that order.
16. These two instances, and the following, are all taken from the 1582 Pamphlet as follows, sigs. Av, B, B4v, B6, C2, C7, D4v, EVv, C6, D8v.
17. All three instances come from the 1579 Pamphlet, sigs. Bii, Avv, Aviiiv. Other symptoms are described in detail in case 1,207. They varied from menstrual disorders to toothache.
18. Hopkins, *Discovery*, p. 60.
19. Gifford, *Discourse*, sig. H.
20. Perkins, *Damned Art*, p. 128.
21. Scot, *Discovery*, p. 30.
22. 1579 Pamphlet, sig. Aviii.
23. 1566 Pamphlet, p. 319.
24. E.R.O., D/AED/1, fol. 26v, and D/AEA/13, fol. 161.
25. Gaule, *Select Cases*, p. 85.
26. Scot, *Discovery*, p. 30.
27. E.R.O., D/P, 36/1/1. Most of the other cases occur in court records—for example, a coroner's inquest returned a verdict of 'misfortune' on a victim of 'falling sickness' or epilepsy (P.R.O., K.B.9, 658, m. 402).
28. 1579 Pamphlet, sig. Aviv.
29. He briefly discussed exorcism and diabolic possession in his *Dialogue*, sig. I2v.
30. 1579 Pamphlet, sig. Aviii; case 861; case 1,162.
31. 1645 Pamphlet, p. 31.
32. Case 1,183.
33. Case 1,205; E. Jorden, *A Briefe Discourse of a Disease Called the Suffocation of the Mother* (1603), p. 17; John Swan, *A True and Briefe Report of Mary Glovers Vexation* (1603), p. 70.
34. Ady, *Candle*, p. 79.
35. William Clark, *True Relation of one Mrs. Jane Farrer's of Stebbin in Essex, being possess'd with the Devil* (1710).
36. Especially in the 1582 Pamphlet, sigs. F2v–F3v, E4v; also Gifford, *Dialogue*, sig. L3.
37. Case 1,125.
38. A Thomas Ady of Wethersfield was a doctor (J. H. Raach, *A Directory of English Country Physicians, 1603–1643* (1962), p. 21).
39. Ady, *Candle*, p. 115.
40. Bernard, *Guide*, p. 24.
41. They are described on pp. 117–18, above. A number of them were, however, unlicensed.
42. Browne's views are suggested in *Religio Medici* (Everyman edn., 1962) pp. 34–5.

Chapter 14

Witchcraft prosecutions and religion

Essex during our period was renowned for its radical religious tradition. It may, therefore, be wondered how far Essex witchcraft prosecutions reflected religious tensions, whether, as some have argued,[1] witch-hunting was encouraged by Puritanism, and whether Roman Catholics were often the victims of witchcraft prosecutions. At this level a direct connexion between religious affiliations and those involved in witchcraft prosecutions is sought. In a subsequent chapter the broader links between religious change and witchcraft beliefs will be examined. The distinction is between the sociological analysis of those known to be involved, and a more philosophical analysis of the assumptions upon which witchcraft accusations were based.

Superficially, there seems to be much evidence in Essex for the argument that Puritanism was a major factor in causing withcraft prosecutions. The two periods of most marked Puritan activity, the 1580's and 1640's, were also those of the greatest number of prosecutions. Villages such as Hatfield Peverel were the centres of both Puritanism and prosecutions. The very fact that witchcraft prosecutions were so common in a strongly Puritan county, suggests furthermore a connexion.[2] Closer examination, however, destroys any such simple correlation. Of the literary commentators on Essex witchcraft, or those born in that county, the majority were both Puritan and either uninterested in or sceptical of witchcraft. The Puritan preacher Richard Rogers did not mention it in his diary. Arthur Wilson, Protestant steward to the Earl of Warwick, showed unusual scepticism when describing a witch trial. George Gifford, Puritan preacher at Maldon, showed both compassion and scepticism in his works on witchcraft.[3] On the other hand, the witch-finder Matthew Hopkins, the most vehement man in Essex in his denunciation of witches, cannot be shown to have been a Puritan, or particularly interested in religion at all.

If we compare the temporal and geographical distribution of witchcraft prosecutions with what we know about Puritanism in Essex, we find that there is little overlapping. References in the 1566 pamphlet to learning witchcraft long before, and to sending for the 'priest', suggest that witchcraft beliefs were prevalent well before 1558 and the return of the Marian exiles.[4] There were a number of witchcraft trials in the early 1560's and 1570's, before Puritan teaching could have spread widely. Nor did prosecutions end in 1586 after the crushing of the Puritan Classical movement by Bishop Aylmer; they continued in full force well into the 1590's. Finally, when the Puritans were in power between 1641 and 1660 prosecutions did not continue. After 1646 there were no more executions for witchcraft. Likewise, a comparison of the villages in which prosecutions took place and those known to have been the residence of a Puritan cleric shows no more than chance overlapping. Of the seventy-six towns and villages listed by Dr. Collinson as, at one time or another during the 1570's and 1580's, the residence of Puritan ministers, only twenty-five also produced witchcraft cases.[5] Less than a dozen Essex clergy are known to have been involved in witchcraft prosecutions, and, of these, only five were witnesses against suspected witches. Not only is this a minute fraction of the hundreds of witnesses named in the pamphlet accounts and indictments, but there is nothing to suggest that these five were on average more Puritan than their colleagues.[6] Combined with the mild punishments inflicted by the Church courts, this fact rules out the possibility that witchcraft prosecutions were primarily the work of a persecuting clergy. This lack of influence on the part of the clergy can further be illustrated from the three sample villages.

As with the whole of Essex, a first glance at the three villages seems to bear out a direct correlation between Puritanism and witchcraft prosecutions—an impression subsequently destroyed by closer analysis. While Hatfield Peverel was well known as the meeting-place of a possible conventicle and the home of one of the most adamant and persecuted of Elizabethan Puritans, Thomas Carew, it was also notorious as the centre of witchcraft prosecutions.[7] The other two villages had unpreaching ministers in 1586, and far fewer witchcraft cases.[8] Yet detailed examination has revealed that neither Carew nor the members of his conventicle were directly connected with prosecutions in Hatfield, whereas the unpreaching Gilbert Annand of Boreham was, in his village.[9] Yet it was not Annand who introduced accusations into the village. His predecessor, Edmund Blackbourne, one-time Roman Catholic priest, and Vicar until 1567, was present during the first Borcham cases.[10] Similarly, in Hatfield Peverel prosecutions occurred despite constant changes of Vicar.[11] In fact, it may possibly be that prosecutions occurred partly *because* of the constant changes, which in turn were caused by friction between two of the leading village families over the right of presentation. The background to three witchcraft prosecutions in 1584 was a town where 'the abuses . . . grew to be so great' that 'the people could neither meete to serve God, nor to take Order for Towne Matters, the poore crying out for lack of food, and people became Strangers one to another'.[12] This gives a hint of the situation out of which prosecutions might emerge. Yet in the neighbouring village of Boreham there were accusations without similar recorded confusion. At all events, the actual personality of the Vicar seems to have been of secondary importance: prosecutions were made regardless.

Just as there seems to be no particular connexion between Puritan ministers and the witchcraft accusations, so there is no evidence that lay Puritans were especially interested in prosecuting witches. Very little direct information can be obtained on the religious position of those involved in witchcraft trials; one of the few feasible methods is to use the pious formula at the beginning of wills.[13] Judging from those who invoked the 'precious merits and death' of Christ in Hatfield Peverel and Boreham, there seems to be no more than a random correlation between those who prefaced their wills in this manner and the victims and accusers in witchcraft cases. None of the ten men in Hatfield Peverel who made particularly devout wills between 1580 and 1600 are known to have been connected with witchcraft, nor are any of the ten in Boreham who commenced their wills in the same manner between 1570 and 1600. Nor is there any evidence that those who were accused were either Roman Catholics, or heretics, or ungodly. None of the several hundred accused witches in Essex is known to have been a Roman Catholic. Neither the ecclesiastical court presentments, which often gave other offences of the accused, nor the pamphlet accounts, which frequently described the character of the accused, suggest a connexion with Roman Catholicism. Although papists were sometimes generally termed 'witches' and even reading the psalms was termed 'conjuration', there is no convincing evidence that witchcraft prosecutions were linked to an attack on Roman Catholics.[14] The pamphlets show that the accused were often church-goers, and John Stearne explicitly stated that they often seemed 'by their carriage' 'to be very religious people, and would constantly repair to all Sermons neer them'.[15] Of the twenty accused witches in the three sample villages, only one was among the 104 people presented at the Church courts for non-attendance at church: the other nineteen were, presumably, church-goers.[16]

People did not accuse their neighbours of witchcraft out of religious fervour. As Gifford remarked 'it is no godly zeale but furious rage' which led to the punishment of witches.[17] The atmosphere of fear and hostility within which accusations were nurtured has already been described; it had little to do in a direct way with particular religious creeds. Nor was the assumed motive of the witch—anger at being treated in an unneighbourly manner—directly related to religion, even if it was of ethical concern. Witchcraft was treated by the authorities as a breach of Christianity; the guilty witch was exhorted to confess her sin and ask the forgiveness of God and the congregation, whether at the ecclesiastical court or the gallows.[18] Yet the impression from the Essex evidence is that those who brought the accusations were mostly uninterested in the supposed compact with the Devil, the loss of the accused person's soul, or any presumed attack on Christianity. The Devil never appeared as a man in Essex before the exceptional trial of 1645; when he did appear before then it was usually as a small animal—a cat or a ferret.[19] This was far from the awful conception of Satan harboured by the Puritans. As one of Gifford's characters asked scornfully after a description of a tree-dwelling devil, 'doe you thinke Satan lodgeth in an hollow tree? Is hee become so lazy, and idle? hath he left off to be as a roaring lion?'[20] In the majority of the descriptions of Essex witchcraft there was no mention of the Devil at all, or of a supposed compact by the witch, who thereby exchanged her soul for diabolic power.[21] The problem of where the power of witchcraft originated does not seem to have particularly interested Essex villagers. Their concern was to show the link between anger and accident. Nor were they curious as to the method used in bewitching. Few accounts described the use of elaborate magical devices, and there is no suggestion that witches perverted normal Christian rituals to gain power, or used Roman Catholic practices.[22] Both these might have been expected if the fear of witchcraft had been linked to religious tensions. Likewise, it seems probable that the ecclesiastical authorities would have examined those presented as witches at some length if they had suspected witchcraft to be a brand of heresy. There is little evidence that they did so.[23] Indeed, as we have seen, the Church authorities were far less severe towards witchcraft than the officers of the State.

Witchcraft prosecutions in Essex cannot be directly related to religious tensions through the study of particular individuals. Yet, as a method of explaining misfortune and evil, witchcraft beliefs to some extent over-lapped with religious explanations. Thus changes in religious thought during the sixteenth and seventeenth centuries are of immense importance in understanding the rise and decline of prosecutions. An approach to the immense problems involved in tracing intellectual changes affecting witchcraft prosecutions will be made in the next chapter.

NOTES

1. For example, R. Trevor Davies, *Four Centuries of Witch-Beliefs* (1947), *passim.* Kittredge, *Witchcraft*, ch. xviii, argues against a connexion.
2. Thus it has been argued that 'the history of the persecution of witches in England

... directly parallels the career of the Puritans', M. Walzer, 'Puritanism as a Revolutionary Ideology', *History and Theory*, iii, No. 1 (1963), p. 77.

3. These writers are discussed in ch. 5, p. 86 above.

4. 1566 Pamphlet, pp. 317, 322. Among those present at the 1566 trial was Dr. Thomas Cole, himself a Marian exile (Newcourt, *Repertorium*, i, 73). Yet the general impression from the pamphlet is that the pressures were from below and that the judges were curious spectators.

5. P. Collinson, 'The Puritan Classical Movement in the Reign of Elizabeth I' (London Univ. Ph.D. thesis, 1957), pp. 1,255–8. Only witchcraft prosecutions occurring in the years 1570–90, that is, when a Puritan minister was possibly present, have been counted. The proportion is roughly equivalent to that for the whole of Essex.

6. George Eatoney, John Edes, and Joseph Longe, witnesses in the 1645 trial, are described on p. 137, above; Edes was a Puritan, Longe a pluralist and alehouse-haunter. Richard Harrison is described on p. 107, above; there is no evidence that either he or William Denman, witness in case 1,173 and Rector of Greenstead from 1598, according to Newcourt, *Repertorium*, ii, 287, were Puritans. It is significant that none of the more extreme Puritans who met as the Dedham Classis between 1582 and 1589 is known to be directly connected with a witchcraft prosecution (R. G. Usher (ed.), *Presbyterian Movement in the Reign of Queen Elizabeth* (1905), pp. xxxv–xlviii), although they discussed the subject on one occasion (p. 70).

7. On Puritanism in Hatfield Peverel see Davids, *Annals*, pp. 118–19.

8. Gilbert Annand was described as 'an alehouse haunter and gamester' and Henry Steare of Little Baddow as 'a gamester, sometime a tailor' in a Puritan survey of ministers made in 1586 (Davids, *Annals*, p. 98).

9. It is almost certain that the 'Mr. Gilbert' mentioned in case 892 was Gilbert Annand.

10. Newcourt, *Repertorium*, ii, 75.

11. It has been impossible to find the names of any Vicars before 1584. In the twelve years following 1584 there were six different Vicars; Newcourt, *Repertorium*, ii, 318, gives four of them.

12. MS. transcript of *The Seconde Parte of a Register*, p. 653, in the Dr. Williams's Library, London.

13. The majority of the wills commenced, 'I commend my soul into the Hands of Almighty God and my body to be buried in the churchyard of . . .' But some 33 per cent of the thirty Boreham wills for the period 1560–99 and 18 per cent of those from Hatfield Peverel for the same period had a more extreme introduction. This usually spoke at some length of being 'saved' by the 'precious merits and death' of Christ. For example, that of William Bretton of Boreham commences: 'I commend my soul to the Almighty God, my maker and to his son my Redeemer and to the Holy Ghost my comforter in whom and by whose death and passion I do verily trust to be saved and my sins to be forgiven, in this is my very and true faith and belief' (E.R.O., D/AER 14/282).

14. Ady, *Candle*, p. 56, called Roman Catholic clergy 'the Witches of these latter times' and Scot, *Discovery*, p. 29, was among others who connected the two in a general way. Case 1,135 illustrates the tendency to call all High Church activity 'witchcraft'. None of the recusants listed in M. O'Dwyer, 'Catholic Recusants in Essex, *c.* 1580–1600' (London Univ. M.A. thesis, 1960), are known to have been accused witches. The only connexion in the Essex evidence is the witch who was asked why she failed to say her prayers in English, 1566 Pamphlet, p. 324.

15. Stearne, *Confirmation*, p. 39. In case 1,173 a man told how his wife was bewitched after thrusting past Parnell Abbott, who was already seated in church. Scot, *Discovery*, p. 29, however, argued that witches were often irreligious.
16. For the cases per village see Table 8, p. 98, above.
17. Gifford, *Discourse*, sig. H4.
18. Confession at the gallows is described in the 1566 Pamphlet, p. 324.
19. Elizabeth Fraunces was told to give her blood to Sathan, who was 'delyvered her in the lykenesse of a whyte spotted Catte' (1566 Pamphlet, p. 317). The Devil appeared to Joan Prentice 'in the shape and proportion of a dunnish colloured ferrit' (1589 Pamphlet, sig. B).
20. Gifford, *Dialogue*, sig. K.
21. Among the few exceptions was the testimony of a girl of eighteen that her mother's familiar asked her 'what she wolde geve hym, and she saide a red kocke, then sayde hee no, but thou shalt geve me thy body and sowle' (1566 Pamphlet, p. 320).
22. In this, as in other ways, Essex witchcraft differed from that described by Continental demonologists.
23. The only detailed examination before ecclesiastical authorities is case 861 in 1564. The references to a kneeling invocation to Christ to come and kill her enemies makes the examination of Elizabeth Lowys very close to a heresy trial.

Chapter 15

Witchcraft beliefs as an explanation of suffering and a means of resolving conflict

Those who stormed against the folly of believing in witchcraft stated that nearly every strange or painful event was blamed on witches. Ady complained that—

> seldom hath a man the hand of God against him in his estate, or health of body, or any way, but presently he cryeth out of some poor innocent Neighbour, that he, or she hath bewitched him.[1]

Reginald Scot also remonstrated:

> that fewe or none can (nowadaies) with patience indure the hand and correction of God. For if any adversitie, greefe, sicknesse, losse of children, corne, cattell, or libertie happen unto them; by & by they exclaime uppon witches.[2]

Analysis of the Essex prosecutions, however, and particularly comparison of death and sickness in the sample villages with known cases of witchcraft, has shown that witchcraft was suggested as a cause of misfortune in only a small proportion of the accidents occurring during our period. This poses the problem of why people blamed certain misfortunes and not others on witches. Several possibilities have already been ruled out. Although there was sometimes an emphasis on the strangeness of an event, for instance, when a woman was suddenly covered by lice which 'were long, and lean, and not like other Lice',[3] strangeness, in itself, was not enough to produce a suspicion of witchcraft. Likewise, witches were not merely sought when there was a gap in contemporary medical knowledge or when a death was particularly sudden, painful, or unexpected. It is true that individual witchcraft only explained particular, as opposed to general, misfortunes. While witches, in theory, were believed 'to raise winds and tempests' and cause 'thunder and lightning', the actual court prosecutions show that they were only blamed for specific damage.[4] But the variety of the damage blamed on witches, and the many misfortunes which were not attributed to their power, suggests that there was another, determining, factor. This factor, it will be argued, was the relationship between witch and victim.

When witchcraft was used as an 'explanation' of a misfortune, this did not necessarily preclude other explanations. For analytic purposes, there-fore, we need to distinguish between natural and supernatural explanation: thus witchcraft was a supernatural cause of an illness, while syphilis, for example, was a 'natural' cause. Since the interpreters of an accident might be seeking to 'explain' a variety of things, the supernatural and natural might coexist. Thus a villager might recognize quite clearly the series of events leading up, on the physical side, to an accident. He might see that a child died 'because' it fell from a chair and broke its neck. 'Because' here meant 'how' it died, the outward, observable, reasons. Explanation was also needed as to 'why' it died. Why *this* child, on *this* day, died.[5] This would explain to an anxious parent why her child, rather than that of a neighbour, had died. Thus witchcraft could be the 'cause' in the sense that it explained the purpose, motive, or will behind an injury, while the 'cause', in another sense, was a perfectly well understood disease or accident. This distinction meant that the same symptoms might be interpreted in very different ways, depending on the attitude of the sufferer. The two levels of causation were recognized by the Essex witch-finder Matthew Hopkins, who distinguished between a natural illness and super-natural malice:

> God suffers the Devill many times to doe much hurt, and the devill doth play many times the deluder and imposter with these Witches, in perswading them that they are the cause of such and such a murder wrought by him with their consents, when and indeed neither he nor they had any hand in it, as thus: We must needs argue, he is of a long standing . . . and so have the best skill in *Physicke*, judgment in *Physiognomie*, and knowledge of what disease is reigning or predominant in this or that man's body (and so for cattcl too) . . . as *Plurisie*, *Imposthume*, &c.

The Devil waits until a person is nearly dead, then offers to kill him for his enemy, a witch. He dies, and everyone believes that the witch has done it 'when and indeed the disease kills the party, not the witch, nor the Devill'.[6]

Hopkins implied that the disaster would have happened in any case. Here he was probably more sceptical than the majority of the Essex population, as well as many other writers. While they would have agreed that the misfortune might occur, on occasions, without being sent by a witch, yet they stressed that it happened more often and more horribly because of the will of evil people. This was the opinion of Sir Thomas Browne when asked for his advice at a witchcraft trial in 1664. He stated that the witches and Satan only worked on natural causes, but such natural causes were exacerbated by supernatural methods.[7] This view was echoed by William Perkins. The Devil, he wrote, was the principal agent of evil, but the witch was rightly punished, 'because if the devill were not stirred up, and provoked by the Witch, he would never do so much hurt as he doth'.[8] A similar view seems to have been held by Essex villagers. They were convinced that many accidents would never have happened if there had been no witch. Gifford expressed this popular attitude with clarity:

> men looke no further then unto ye witch: they fret and rage against her: they never looke so high as unto God: they looke not to the cause why ye devil hath powers over them: they seeke not to appease Gods wrath. But they fly upon ye witch: they think if shee were not, they should doo well enough: shee is made the cause of all plagues & mischiefes.[9]

Thus witchcraft was an explanation which involved the idea that pain was not random, but caused by the motive or will of a person. An event which could, from one angle, be seen as the culmination of a series of uncontrollable physical circumstances would, from another, be examined for origins in human or divine planning.

It is very difficult to estimate what percentage of accidents in our period demanded an interpretation in terms of personal will. It has been suggested that in a small-scale, 'face-to-face' society where there are few specialized relationships and where close personal bonds serve most men's interests, 'all events tend to be explained by what occurs in those relationships'.[10] The many deaths by 'misfortune' listed in the Essex coroner's inquisitions suggest that English society may have already passed beyond this stage and people may have accepted that illness and death often occurred without purpose.[11] Yet the comments of Puritan writers show clearly that a connexion between sin and disease, or between suffering and human failure, was often drawn. The difference between the Puritans and those they castigated was merely in the details of the connexion. Once a person sought to relate an injury to personal motivation there were three alternatives from which to choose. He could either blame himself, his neighbours, or God. While those who advocated the punishment of witches chose the middle solution, Puritans laid stress on the first and last of the three alternatives. George Gifford's complaint was that people would not face up to the responsibility of admitting that misfortune was their own fault. 'They can by no means see, that God is provoked by their sinnes to give the devill such instruments to work withall, but rage against the witch.'[12] Persons thinking themselves bewitched will find on self-examination, William Perkins declared, 'that their owne sinnes are the true and proper causes of these evills'.[13] Ady commented that 'no Inchantment can hurt us, but the only thing that can hurt any man is sinning against God'.[14] If such an interpretation had been widely accepted it would have led to an enormous weight of guilt for the individual, since all natural misfortunes would have had to be related back to personal failure. Others would have been in the position of Ralph Josselin, who blamed his own unseasonable chess-playing for the death of his infant son.[15] The alternative offered by the Puritans was based on the story of Job and stressed patience in the face of the testing hand of God. This might, however, face the individual with a contradiction between a benign and loving Father, and the idea of a torturing and cruel task-master.[16] Moreover, this interpretation lacked one great advantage of the other alternatives, the possibility of counter-action, of taking active steps to avoid future suffering and end present misery.

It is arguable that the Catholic Church in England before the Reformation provided a more satisfactory answer to the problem of explaining suffering. Catholic ritual, with its dramatization of the expulsion of evil and communal propitiation of God, may have offered a solution to the misfortunes of daily life which did not involve the blame being centred on either the individual or his neighbours. Prayers and activities offered people satisfactory counter-action in times of distress and also the hope that their environment might be controlled. At the Reformation, it might be suggested, the misfortunes and worries continued, but the whole ritual framework designed to deal with them was destroyed. This huge topic cannot be dealt with satisfactorily in a sociological analysis of prosecutions in one county starting in 1560;[17] but Essex material does suggest that witchcraft beliefs were one method of dealing with problems of human suffering, and hence they pose the question: How were such problems solved in previous centuries?

In the classic instance of witchcraft being used as an explanation of *why* a misfortune happens, people suffer an injury first and then look round to see who might have bewitched them.[18] Individuals are not permanently thought of as witches and the incident is soon forgotten. In Essex prosecutions the process seems to have been different; once a suspicion had arisen about a certain person future injuries were blamed on her. Someone first offended a neighbour, and subsequently suffered. In fact, the links were more complicated than this. Often, it seems, a person would not remember that he had denied a neighbour until some tragedy happened. Yet there is little doubt that the stress was on the motive for the bewitching, not on the strangeness of the injury. What was being explained, in fact, was the feeling between two people rather than a physical injury. When a person felt that he had angered someone, he himself felt angry and worried. The subsequent hostility could be interpreted in the ideology of witchcraft. The victim would feel justified in hating someone because she was an evil witch and had injured him physically: her rage was felt to be the rage of a wicked woman. This interpretation also accords with the conclusion that only certain injuries were blamed on witches and that these misfortunes

were not necessarily exceptional in any way. It was the social context
which determined the interpretation. A man who knew he had deeply
offended a neighbour and that she had reason to curse him would interpret subsequent events differently from the man who felt no particular
malice towards, or from, his co-villagers. Furthermore, it has been argued
that it was often the victim who felt the hostility and guilt and projected
this on to the witch. It was only when hatred was known to be prevalent
that people would feel precarious enough, angry enough, and anxious
enough to press a charge of witchcraft. Thus witchcraft was not just an
automatic explanation of all, or specific, types of misfortune. Rather, it was
a combined solution of why a certain painful event had happened, and why
a person felt a certain painful emotion. To both types of uncertainty it
promised relief.

Witchcraft prosecutions, we have seen, were usually between people
who knew each other intimately—that is, between village neighbours.
They almost always arose from quarrels over gifts and loans in which the
victim refused the witch some small gift, heard her muttering under her
breath or threatening him, and subsequently suffered some misfortune. It
was usually the person who had done the first wrong under the old ideals of
charity who felt himself bewitched. The weight of these traditional ideals,
as well as the belief that a moral offence would be afflicted by physical
punishment, is excellently illustrated by Thomas Ady:

> God hath given it as a strict Command to all men to relieve the poor, *Levit.*
> 25.35. and in the next Chapter it followeth, vers. 14, 15. *Whosoever hearkneth*
> *not to all the Commandements of the Lord to do them*, (whereof relieving the poor
> is one) *the Lord will send several crosses and afflictions, and diseases upon them*,
> as followeth in the Chapter, and therefore men should look into the Scriptures,
> and search what sins bring afflictions from God's hands, and not say presently,
> what old man or woman was last at my door, that I may hand him or her for a
> Witche; yea we should rather say, Because I did not relieve such a poor body
> that was lately at my door, but gave him harsh and bitter words, therefore
> God hath laid this Affliction upon me, for God saith, *Exod.* 22.23, 24. *If thou*
> *any way afflict widows, and fatherless, and they at all cry unto me, I will surely*
> *hear their cry, and my wrath shall wax hot against thee.*[19]

Physical afflictions were the punishment for social deviation and men
might well tremble when they heard a widow's curse, backed, as it was
said to be in the Bible, by God's power. But by suggesting that the widow
was a witch the power of the old sanctions to neighbourly behaviour,
especially cursing, was broken. As Ady recognized, an accusation of
witchcraft was a clever way of reversing the guilt, of transferring it from
the person who had failed in his social obligation under the old standard
to the person who had made him fail. Through the mechanism of the law,

and the informal methods of gossip and village opinion, society was permitted to support the accuser.

From a certain viewpoint, therefore, witchcraft prosecutions may be seen as a means of effecting a deep social change; a change from a 'neighbourly', highly integrated and mutually interdependent village society, to a more individualistic one. Both the necessity and dangers of such a change are illustrated by Thomas Cooper when he warned the godly in 1617 to forgo indiscriminate charity and to be especially hard on suspected witches, 'to bee straight-handed towards them, not to entertaine them in our houses, not to relieve them with our morsels': not to fear the spiritual consequences, to 'use a *Christian courage* in all our *Actions*, not to *feare their curses*, nor seeke for their blessings'.[20] Among the counter-actions against witches a number have already been noted that would have the effect of severing relationships between neighbours. The danger was again emphasized by an Elizabethan preacher who told his congregation that 'we may see how experience, and the very confessions of witches, agree that the merciful lenders and givers are preserved of God, and unmerciful usurers and covetous Nabals are vexed and troubled of Satan'.[21] Thus witchcraft beliefs provided both the justification for severing contact, and an explanation of the guilt and fear still felt by the individual when he did so: he might expect to be repaid on the spiritual plane for his lack of charity, but could be satisfied that this was witchcraft, and thus evil, rather than punishment for his own shortcomings. In one sense, witchcraft beliefs can be seen as a form of reciprocal relationship. One neighbour injures another, both on the physical level, by refusing a gift, but also, more generally, by denying the existence of a mutual relationship. The witch reciprocates on two levels also, through a physical attack which is accompanied by a malice equivalent to that of the victim. All this occurred within the context of village life where there were immense difficulties facing those who wished to deny the existence of a neighbourly bond. Christianity, as we have seen from Ady's quotation from the Bible, still upheld communal values. There was no code to which a person who felt the need to cut down or re-direct his relationships could appeal. Yet, through the idiom of witchcraft prosecutions, the older values were undermined or changed, while, on the surface, they were maintained. Witchcraft prosecutions, therefore, may have been principally important as a radical force which broke down the communal pattern inherited from the medieval period. Anthropologists, perhaps because they tend to make static studies, usually stress the conservative effects of witchcraft beliefs. They argue that such beliefs maintain and reinforce social relationships.[22] A historical study suggests that prosecutions may just as well be a means of destroying old relationships and ideals.

Yet this explanation leaves many unanswered problems. Some villages were free of witchcraft accusations in Essex. Clearly witchcraft accusations were not the necessary or only mechanism for dealing with a conflict between an ideal of neighbourliness and the practical consequences of social and economic change. Nor does it seem probable that disputes between neighbours were absent before 1560, or that they ended abruptly in the middle of the seventeenth century. This leads us directly to the problems surrounding the rise and decline of witchcraft accusations.

NOTES

1. Ady, *Candle*, p. 114.
2. Scot, *Discovery*, p. 25. See also Gaule, *Select Cases*, p. 85.
3. 1645 Pamphlet, p. 23.
4. Gifford, *Discourse*, sig. H4^v; Ady, *Candle*, p. 113. Thus there seems to have been a direct relationship between the dimensions of the misfortune and the size of the enemy blamed; Ady, *Candle*, p. 104, noted that general misfortunes (tempests, plagues) were blamed on the large company of dead witches, rather than on specific, living ones.
5. This classic distinction is discussed on pp. 241–3, below.
6. Hopkins, *Discovery*, pp. 59–61. This is an almost exact paraphrase of Bernard, *Guide*, pp. 202–3, and was therefore presumably well known to the jury-men for whom Bernard wrote and who tried witchcraft cases.
7. *A Tryal of Witches at Bury St. Edmunds on the Tenth Day of March 1664* contained in *A Collection of Rare and Curious Tracts relating to Witchcraft* (1838), p. 16.
8. Perkins, *Damned Art*, p. 253.
9. Gifford, *Discourse*, sig. H3.
10. Gluckman (1963), p. 95. This topic is further discussed on p. 241, below. There is a statistical analysis of the proportion of injuries attributed to witches in Marwick (1965), pp. 15, 37, 73.
11. This probably constitutes one of the major differences between English and Zande society, and hence their systems of witchcraft. The Azande say, 'Death has always a cause, and no man dies without a reason', according to Evans-Pritchard (1937), p. 111.
12. Gifford, *Dialogue*, sig. D3^v.
13. Perkins, *Damned Art*, p. 230.
14. Ady, *Candle*, p. 53.
15. This point in Josselin's diary is cited in W. Notestein, *English People on the Eve of Colonization* (Harper Torchbook edn., New York, 1962), p. 152.
16. This problem is discussed further on pp. 242–3, below.
17. The forthcoming book of Mr. Keith Thomas will deal comprehensively with this problem.
18. 'A Zande is interested in witchcraft only as an agent on definite occasions and in relation to his own interests, and not as a permanent condition of individuals,' writes Evans-Pritchard (1937), p. 26.
19. Ady, *Candle*, p. 130.
20. Thomas Cooper, *The Mystery of Witchcraft* (1617), p. 288.

21. J. O. W. Haweis, *Sketches of the Reformation and Elizabethan Age* (1844), p. 224.
22. For example, Marwick (1965), p. 221, argues that 'sorcery and witchcraft emerge as conservative social forces; and their conservative character is brought into sharp relief when they operate under conditions of social change'.

Chapter 16

Reasons for the rise and decline of witchcraft prosecutions

Even after extensive research, the factual outlines of witchcraft prosecutions are still blurred. It is particularly difficult to assess the number of witchcraft prosecutions before 1560. In Essex, for example, only one case has been discovered before that date. Even this was 'white witchcraft', blessing a plough.[1] Yet it is hardly surprising that no cases have been found in Assize, Quarter Sessions, or ecclesiastical records, the main sources for prosecutions in the later period, since these only survive from 1560 onwards in Essex.[2] The problem is in many ways similar for the whole of England. Although scattered cases of witchcraft can be discovered in medieval literature or court records,[3] it is doubtful whether statistical comparison will ever be possible between the Elizabethan and earlier periods. Printed ecclesiastical records show a considerable number of sorcery cases in the fifteenth and early sixteenth centuries, possibly on a level with those for the period we are studying.[4] There are also references in early Privy Council records and earlier Assize rolls.[5] Nevertheless, the general impression, based on a brief examination of printed medieval court records, is that prosecutions for witchcraft were not widespread.

The picture is clearer after 1560. In Essex the worst years for suspected witches were from 1570 to 1600. The severity of the courts was definitely lessening after about 1620. Apart from 1645, there were no executions at the Assizes for this county after 1626. Bills of presentment were increasingly often rejected by the grand jury from 1650 onwards. The last known ecclesiastical court case appeared in 1638, the last at the Quarter Sessions in 1664, the last at the Assizes in 1675. In some other parts of England the prosecutions continued in force until the beginning of the eighteenth century.[6] In Essex, as elsewhere in England, there were informal attacks on suspected witches after prosecutions had ceased at the courts. Old women were thrown into ponds by angry mobs, and people burnt their animals to prevent them being bewitched.[7] But the formal prosecutions ended over fifty years before the Witchcraft Act was repealed in 1736.

To attempt an explanation of changes in the intensity of witchcraft beliefs is really beyond the scope of this work, since we need to know far more about earlier beliefs and about accusations in other counties before any reasonable account can be given. The following hypotheses, therefore, are at a much more speculative and general level than the conclusions in earlier chapters. They are merely suggestions as to the way in which one might approach an explanation. They look forward to work that needs to be undertaken rather than back over facts established by the Essex material. Nevertheless, although they cannot all be fully documented as yet, all the arguments to be presented seem to fit the Essex situation.

One possible reason for variations over the years was the legal treatment of witchcraft, both the laws and court procedure. Although it could be forcefully argued that without the law against witches in 1563 there would have been few witchcraft prosecutions, a law by itself cannot generate beliefs. It may be that there were many witchcraft tensions before 1560 which lay hidden for lack of a secular law. We do not know. But the situation at the end of the period shows that people need not avail themselves of a law; it provides the possibility of action, but not the impulse. Witchcraft accusations, we have seen, declined some fifty years before the law was repealed, at least in Essex. Nor can any change in legal procedure explain this decline. The law against witches may have provided the indispensable framework for accusations, and the court cases may have spread and strengthened witchcraft beliefs. In this sense the institutionalization of the punishment of witches can be seen as a 'necessary' cause of witchcraft prosecutions, but it is not a 'sufficient' one.

Another reason for changes was the intellectual framework upon which witchcraft beliefs were based. Previous chapters have tended to concentrate, in their sociological analysis, on the groups involved in accusations rather than on the ideas behind prosecutions. Yet, as a belief, it is clear that witchcraft charges need to be understood, partially at least, as one type of idea and not merely as a tension or emotion. At the very simplest, there cannot be a belief in witchcraft if it is thought impossible for one human being to harm another physically through non-physical means. If, as today, there is no general belief in the possibility of one person damaging another at a distance merely by wishing him evil, then witchcraft beliefs are without foundation. Witchcraft beliefs, in fact, presuppose a world in which the thoughts and words of one person are believed to have the power to damage another. The power of cursing and prayer in the Middle Ages is the best illustration that people lived in such a world before our period.[8] It has been argued that the power of curses was still felt as a sanction during the sixteenth century in Essex. It could be further argued that, among certain groups at least, changes occurring during the century after the Reformation undermined both the intellectual and emotional foundation of such an assumption. As the gentry became more educated, as their close and multiple personal ties with villagers became weakened, the idea of interdependence not only on the physical but also on the spiritual level suffered attrition. The assumption that a neighbour's malice will cause another person physical harm may indeed be founded on experience in a subsistence-level village where people are intimately connected in everyday life and where co-operation and unanimity is vitally necessary.[9] But during the sixteenth and seventeenth centuries the combination of a less collectivist religion, a market economy, greater social mobility, and a growing separation of people through the formation of institutional rather than personal ties would have serious effects on such beliefs. The gentry, who formed the juries in Essex which first rejected witchcraft indictments in the 1650's, may not have felt so involved with their neighbours that they feared them, nor have believed that evil will alone could lead to physical harm. In some strange way the particular interrelationship of moral and physical spheres had become split. Hostility and anger could be permitted without leading to disruption. A person could feel bitterly about his neighbour without either being accused of being a witch or feeling it necessary to project the bitterness on to another who he believed to be bewitching him. People were far enough apart, so to speak, to be able to hate each other without repercussions on the mystical plane. The way in which this actually happened can only be established after extensive studies of attitudes to prayer, cursing, hostility, and similar topics.

Another obvious factor is the amount of physical suffering in a society and the methods prescribed by that society to deal with it. It has already been argued that the actual amount of physical pain is not, in itself, a direct cause of changes in witchcraft beliefs. Firstly, it would be difficult to show that disease and loss increased in mid-sixteenth century Essex or declined in that county after about 1650. Secondly, we have seen that witchcraft suspicions only occurred in certain cases of death and illness— that, for instance, very few witches were blamed for the death of infants. Nor do changes in medical knowledge provide a complete explanation of changes in beliefs. There is little evidence, of course, that there was a deterioration in medical knowledge in the early sixteenth-century, nor is there evidence that juries and justices knew more about the majority of human or animal illnesses in 1660 than they had done in 1600. Decline in witchcraft beliefs predated the revolution in medical knowledge and techniques, which only occurred in the nineteenth century.

Another reason why it seems improbable that changes in medical knowledge could have had much effect on witchcraft beliefs has already been suggested. This is the fact that a witchcraft 'explanation' could coexist beside a perfectly adequate 'explanation' of how the illness occurred.[10] When a person died after a long illness his relatives might be aware that he had died of a known disease, but might also seek an explanation of why he, rather than another person, had caught this disease. In this sense death can never be 'explained' by medical science. The painful emotions it arouses need an 'emotional explanation'—that is, a series of counter-actions and beliefs which bring relief as well as intellectual knowledge. A death is treated like a murder. It is not enough to know the weapon, the time and manner of death: one must also know the motive behind the killing and the identity of the murderer. What really needs to be explained, therefore, is why a proportion of deaths in Essex villages ceased to be treated as murders. Part of the answer may lie in the nature of suffering and loss. Changes in the structure of society during our period may have meant that economic loss, the loss of children, death, all became more bearable. This might have happened in a number of ways. Future studies of insurance against the many losses by fire and other accidents, both through economic aid, through religious assurance and through social relationships, may show how this occurred. Yet anyone who reads contemporary diaries—for instance, the mid-seventeenth-century Essex diary of Ralph Josselin,[11] will be aware that people continued to live in a constant state of personal anxiety about possible threats of illness and accident throughout the seventeenth century. It could be argued, however, that anxiety lessened.

Another part of the solution lies in the ideas about causation current during our period. To blame a witch was to explain misfortune in personal terms. As such it competed with other explanations. For analytic purposes it could be argued that a person seeking to explain misfortune could seek a solution either in terms of personal will—that is, in the design or scheme of a living creature—or in impersonal forces which moved either randomly or according to scientific, mechanistic, laws. The 'personal' explanation could again be subdivided into three, as we saw in the previous chapter. The misfortune could be ascribed to God, to another person, or to the individual himself. The idea that God was punishing a person was sometimes an indirect way of saying that an individual's suffering was his own fault, but he might also be punished for the sins of the community. These explanations can best be distinguished by looking at the counter-actions which they enjoin. God requires prayer, propitiation, and sacrifice. He may be placated either by the whole community or the individual. Explanations in such terms have the advantage of providing a set of counter-rituals which may alleviate pain and prevent future misfortune. It seems probable however, that this type of explanation became less convincing after the Reformation. It might explain general misfortunes to the whole village, but when a specific person was injured God may have seemed too distant and impersonal an explanation. The effectiveness of a communal propitiation may have seemed less. This would lay more stress on the other two interpretations.

Where a personalized agent was sought, the third solution, self-blame, may have been the most attractive in certain circumstances. For instance, to blame misfortunes on one's own sins gives control over accident and suffering. Avoidance of sin will lead to a happy life. Both explanations interlink sin and misfortune in such a way as to provide an automatic set of sanctions in which moral rules are supported by natural events. Individuals conform, since any pain they suffer is interpreted both by them and their neighbours as punishment for their nonconformity. This interlocking system is appropriate for a society where moral rules are unchanging.

The especial advantage of the middle explanation, in which another person is blamed, is that, by breaking automatic sanctions against nonconformity, it allows considerable changes to occur. If a neighbour is blamed for one's misfortunes there is a double effect. On the one hand, the sufferer is allowed to escape from the circular, automatic controls of a collective society. Although still holding the belief that pain is not random and beyond human control, he does not need to examine and modify his own behaviour, but can blame another. On the other hand, he may cut off relations with his supposed attacker. Instead of being drawn closer to his fellows through acknowledging his break with communal values, or by partaking in a communal ritual to a universal God, he can put himself at a distance.

While witchcraft accusations were founded on an implicit acceptance of the mystical link between individuals in which one person's well-being was dependent on the attitude of others, they also helped to differentiate and distance people by giving them a reason for turning from their neighbours. As has already been stressed, a witchcraft accusation was a mechanism whereby a person who broke with communal values, and who was expecting retaliation for this, could reverse the guilt. Instead of accepting ensuing suffering as deserved punishment, he could project the blame on to the person who had ostensibly been upholding such values. Thus the woman who went round making demands on neighbours in Essex, and who used traditional sanctions, such as cursing, to enforce them, was the witch. Witchcraft accusations occurred when there was an overlap between an old idea that misfortunes were the result of personal will and a new social and economic atmosphere in which people wished to adopt new values and modes of behaviour.

The overlap ended when the explanation of misfortune ceased to be sought in personal will. It was a change from a view of causation that is personalized to one where it is accepted that death and suffering may be the result of 'abstract' forces. Sometimes these abstract forces can be analysed as scientific 'laws'. On other occasions they seem to work at random, by 'luck' and 'chance'. In this sense the crucial change in the seventeenth century was not the growth of scientific knowledge, but the decline of the area where personalized explanations in terms of human will were sought. It was the growth in the area of 'chance' that was important. The history of this growth is clearly beyond the scope of this book. Its effect, however, may well be traced by future research into the attitude of the gentry and yeomen towards personal misfortune. It is likely that the decline in witchcraft beliefs occurred at the same time as a decline in the belief that suffering was the result of personal sin or God's punishing hand.[12]

One final factor needs consideration. This is the considerable social and economic change occurring during our period. Witchcraft prosecutions in Essex centred on the relationship between middling to rich villagers and their slightly less prosperous and older neighbours. These neighbours were usually women, and often widows. It seems, therefore, that, as well as that of suffering, two other problems were of particular importance in witchcraft accusations: the first was that of poverty, the second was that of the old. Neither of these was narrowly confined in a sixteenth-century village. The problem of 'poverty', viewed broadly, included the relative wealth of villagers, their interdependent labour co-operation, their mutual insurance and help in periodic economic crises. Within the problem of 'old age' was included that of the relations between the old and young in matters of authority, as well as the burden of old people and the methods of inheritance of possessions.

It could be argued that the significant changes during our period were twofold. Firstly, it seems that population growth and changes in land-ownership created a group of poorer villagers whose ties to their slightly wealthier neighbours became more tenuous.[13] People increasingly had to decide whether to invest their wealth in maintaining the old at a decent standard of living or in improvements which would keep them abreast of their yeomen neighbours. Secondly, it seems that there were two stages in the response to such changes. During the period between 1560 and about 1650 the informal institutions which had dealt with the old and poor, Church relief, the manorial organization, and neighbourly and kinship ties were strained.[14] This was the period of witchcraft accusations. People still felt enjoined to help and support each other, while also feeling the necessity to invest their capital in buying land and providing for their children. The very poor were not the problem. They could be whipped and sent on their way, or hired as labourers. It was the slightly less affluent neighbours or kin who only demanded a little help who became an increasing source of anxiety. To refuse them was to break a whole web of long-held values.

The situation may have changed in two ways in Essex during the seventeenth century. The problems of old age and poverty may have lessened with changes in population and price trends. But what seems likely to prove more important were alterations in the attitudes and institutions for dealing with these problems. Once workhouses had been established, when it had become a Christian's duty to abstain from indiscriminate charity,[15] as soon as there had been a change from the informal, day-to-day, treatment of the poor and old to a more conscious and formal situation, the anxieties may have lessened. Rules were laid down and each individual did not need to take exceedingly painful choices about his priorities. The conflict between ideals and behaviour which, it has been argued, lay behind the witchcraft accusations died away. There is little doubt that villagers still believed in witchcraft long after indictments ceased coming to the courts. But such beliefs ceased to be felt by a large enough proportion of the influential villagers to be made into formal charges. One of the facts demonstrated in this book has been that witchcraft accusations were not merely the result of tensions between two individuals, but rather between a group of villagers and an individual suspect. In a situation where witchcraft continued to be an explanation of personal misfortune, but had ceased to represent a wider feeling of loathing on the part of a number of families who felt guilty at having denied neighbourly help to someone, witchcraft accusations lost something of their energy.

In this chapter the microscope has been abandoned and the telescope employed. The resulting attempt to provide a very general framework of problems for future discussion has necessitated many generalizations and much guesswork. The hypotheses are obviously at a very tentative stage. Every assertion needs qualification and documentation. It is believed, however, that only by looking at the witchcraft prosecutions in Essex in the total intellectual and social background of sixteenth-and seventeenth-century England will a solution be found to the problem of why they arose and declined.

NOTES

1. Two women were accused, at a Colchester Law Hundred in 1532, of blessing a plough (*Essex Review*, 47 (1938), p. 167).
2. In fact, the Quarter Sessions Rolls commence in 1556.
3. For example, there are miscellaneous cases cited in Kittredge, *Witchcraft*, ch. 2; Notestein, *Witchcraft*, ch. 1; Ewen, I, pp. 1–12.

4. For some examples see *Depositions and Other Ecclesiastical Proceedings from the Courts of Durham*, ed. James Raine (Surtees Soc., xxi, 1845), pp. 27, 29, 33; William Hale, *Series of Precedents and Proceedings in Criminal Causes, 1475–1640* (1847), pp. 3, 7, 10, 11, 16, 17, 20, 32–3, 36–7, 61, 63, 77, 102, 107–8, 139; *Visitations in the Diocese of Lincoln, 1517–1531*, ed. A. H. Thompson (Lincs. Rec. Soc., xxxiii, 1940), i, xlix; *Tudor Studies, presented to A. F. Pollard*, ed. R. W. Seton-Watson (1924), pp. 72–4.

5. See, for example, *Select Cases before the King's Council, 1243–1482*, ed. I. S. Leadam (Selden Soc., xxxv, 1918), pp. xxxiv-xxxv. A witchcraft case in a Northumberland Assize roll of 1279 is described in Kittredge, *Witchcraft*, p. 47. The general impression is that witchcraft was infrequently prosecuted at the medieval Assizes; thus there are no cases in the Assize rolls published by the Selden Society (vols. xxx, liii, lvi, lix), or by the Lincolnshire Record Society (vols. 22, 36).

6. Late cases in the Home Circuit are printed in Ewen, I, pp. 261–5, and Notestein, *Witchcraft*, ch. 13, discusses trials elsewhere in England.

7. A number of instances are cited in R. Trevor Davies, *Four Centuries of Witch-Beliefs* (1947), pp. 188–200.

8. Fines for cursing are instanced in G. G. Coulton, *Medieval Village, Manor, and Monastery* (Harper Torchbook edn., 1960), p. 91. The biblical justification for cursing is set out by George Herbert in *A Priest to the Temple* (Everyman edn., 1908), p. 288.

9. This idea is based on the discussion in M. Gluckman, *Politics, Law and Ritual in Tribal Society* (Oxford, 1965), pp. 243–4.

10. As an anthropologist has written, 'The decline in belief in witchcraft and sorcery is not purely a matter of extending scientific knowledge—our answer must cover the astute Pondo teacher who said to me: "It may be quite true that typhus is carried by lice, but who sent the infected louse? Why did it bite one man and not another?"' (M. Wilson (1951), p. 313).

11. The edited version of Josselin's diary in the *Camden Society* (3rd ser., xv (1908)) omits much of the detailed account of daily fears and anxieties of the original. I hope to give a fuller account of this background of sickness and death in a forthcoming study of the *Family Life of Ralph Josselin* (Cambridge, 1970).

12. The interpretation of misfortune in personal terms has been extensively studied by anthropologists. In Ceylon 'villagers tend to attribute all misfortune and illness to sin', writes E. R. Leach, *Pul Eliya* (Cambridge, 1961), p. 36. See also V. W. Turner, *Schism and Continuity in an African Society* (Manchester, 1964), pp. 142–3. As R. H. Tawney put it in *Religion and the Rise of Capitalism* (Penguin edn., 1961), p. 41: 'Much that is now mechanical was then personal, intimate, and direct'.

13. This process has been described for the Leicestershire village of Wigston Magna (W. G. Hoskins, *The Midland Peasant* (1957), chs. 5–7) and a Cambridge village (M. Spufford, *A Cambridgeshire Community* (Leicester Univ. Press, 1965), pp. 31–52). Unfortunately, there are as yet no detailed studies of Essex villages from this aspect. It is therefore impossible to be certain whether there were growing class distinctions.

14. These broad generalizations are purely speculative and cannot be substantiated until detailed studies of the treatment of the poor and old, of kinship and neighbourly values, and of many other subjects have been undertaken.

15. A change discussed in C. Hill, *Puritanism and Revolution* (Mercury edn., 1962), ch. 7, on 'William Perkins and the Poor'.

Part four

A comparative framework: Anthropological studies

The anthropological approach to the study of witchcraft (1): beliefs and counter-actions

In the first section of this book the historical sources for the study of witchcraft were described. In the next two sections a number of questions were put to these sources and various hypotheses concerning the relationship of witchcraft to other phenomena were tested. In this fourth section the English conclusions will be placed in the context of modern investigations of witchcraft by anthropologists.[1] Anthropological studies, based on actual experience of witchcraft beliefs and accusations, provide an invaluable list of questions for the historian. They also provide some alternative theories to those suggested above. It is hoped that a survey of the type of problems discussed by anthropologists will also provide a 'model' for future historical investigation. The work of social scientists may be arbitrarily divided into four parts: a study of witchcraft beliefs, of counter-actions against witches, of the 'sociology' of witchcraft—that is, 'who bewitches who', and the interpretations suggested by anthropologists to account for the phenomena. We commence, therefore, with the beliefs concerning witches.

1. THE IDEOLOGY OF WITCHCRAFT[2]

When and where witches meet

Among the Navaho, witches are active primarily at night.[3] This is also so among the Tale,[4] the Azande[5] and the Amba,[6] but there is little trace of night meetings in Essex. Navaho witches are believed to meet most frequently in a cave, and there is general agreement that all types of witch activity must be carried on away from home.[7] Likewise, witches among the Kaguru meet in unfrequented places—mountain-tops and deserted villages, for example.[8] All Mbugwe witches 'ride hyenas to a prearranged place in the forest for their saturnalian gathering'.[9] Again, there is little evidence that Essex witches were believed to retire to deserted spots.

The distance witchcraft can cover

The Azande believe that the farther removed a man's homestead is from his neighbours the safer he is from witchcraft. A sick man can elude witchcraft by hiding in the bush.[10] Likewise, homesteads among the Mandari are widely separated, partly because, in their words, 'A witch cannot throw his eyes over miles of bush'.[11] On the other hand, the range of witchcraft among the Pondo is not limited; it may now even be sent by post, it is said.[12] This, however, seems to be exceptional. We have seen that Essex witches were believed to operate over only short distances.

Organization of witches

Witches are sometimes believed to act alone; sometimes they are part of an organization. 'Night-witches [among the Lovedu] form a sort of fraternity; they all know one another and meet at night to drum and dance for amusement.'[13] Witches among the Gusii do not operate alone but in a group.[14] In other societies witches can operate alone *or* in company. Thus witches among the Nyakusa attack either singly or in covens.[15] While some witches practise alone, others share in their necrophagous feasts among the Kaguru and are organized locally.[16] Finally, there are societies where witches are lone individuals. Among the Gisu 'Witchcraft is performed by individuals against other individuals, not by a group against an individual nor by an individual against a group'.[17] Witchcraft is similarly the activity of individuals working alone among the Dinka.[18] If witches do co-operate there is often some kind of hierarchy amongst them. The Azande believe that there is 'status and leadership among witches' and that 'experience must be obtained under the tuition of elder witches before a man is qualified to kill his neighbours'.[19] Proceedings at night witch meetings, the Navaho say, are directed by a chief witch who, with his leading helpers, is thought of as rich, but they are assisted by a class of menial 'helpers' and these are said to be poor.[20] Essex witchcraft, with the exception of the 1645 cases, appears to be closer to the individual, solitary witch pattern.

How the power of witchcraft is acquired

The three principal ways of acquiring witchcraft are by birth, by purchase, and by training. Usually at least two of these methods are combined—thus, among the Mbugwe, witches must both be instructed in the secret art of harming people and given a special constitutional trait by committing incest with a witch relative,[21] and among the Lovedu witchcraft is said to be imbibed with the mother's milk, but also involves a strenuous course of learning.[22] The most usual way of combining the hereditary and teaching principles is by saying, as do the Gusii,[23] that witchcraft is an acquired **art** which is usually handed down from parent to child. Thus witches among the Mandari teach their children how to dance at night.[24] Essex witches, it seems, usually acquired their witchcraft later in life, though there was a strong contemporary belief that witchcraft was also hereditary, and up to 10 per cent. of the accusations may have been against daughters of known witches.[25]

Methods witches use to injure victims

Witches are often cannibals, feeding either on the living souls and bodies, or necrophagous, as they are among the Mandari.[26] They kill people by eating their souls among the Tallensi.[27] Another method favoured by witches is some unclean act—defecating or urinating into a person's house or food, for instance. A witch may thus secretly defecate or urinate into a victim's water, beer, or food among the Kaguru;[28] a certain type of witch among the Lugbara vomits blood or defecates near doorways,[29] and the same is said of Dinka witches.[30]

Daytime witches favour pointing gestures and staring. Among the Lovedu, to point at a man in a menacing way, or to say the words, 'You will see', suffices, should evil befall him, as ground for an accusation of witchcraft,[31] and among the Gisu the evil eye is supposed to harm by excessive admiration or staring.[32] Essex witches, we have seen, tended either to use the spoken word—cursing or praising—or sent their familiars to harm their victims.

Types of injury caused by witches

Though, in theory, any kind of misfortune is likely to be ascribed to witchcraft among certain peoples,[33] in fact this explanation is invoked only in certain situations. For instance, general disasters are not usually believed to be caused by witchcraft. Crop failure over a wide area or epidemics are said to result from the anger of the ancestors among the Gisu.[34] Local drought among the Mandari is blamed on witches—universal misfortunes are acts of God, to be met by sacrifice and prayers;[35] widespread misfortunes among the Kaguru are likewise thought to be caused by the anger of ancestors owing to some person's having broken a clan rule, while the misfortunes of *individuals* are thought to be owing to witches.[36] Witchcraft and religious rituals therefore serve different purposes as responses to individual and collective disaster.

Witches usually attack human beings, but they do not attack all classes of humanity, nor do they bring certain kinds of death or illness. Often very young children are excepted from their attack: thus among the Azande[37] the 'deaths of babies from certain diseases are attributed vaguely to the Supreme Being', while among the Lele the deaths of women in childbirth and deaths of infants are not considered to be caused by sorcery.[38] This is related to Evans-Pritchard's observation that 'it is the social situation' which indicates the relevant cause of misfortune:[39] to ascribe the very frequent deaths of children in a primitive society to witchcraft would be to overload the concept. Sometimes the determining factor is the type of disease; thus sudden sickness is attributed to sorcery and magic, not to witchcraft, among the Azande,[40] for it is slow, wasting disease that is caused by witchcraft. On the other hand, among the Nupe, accusations were formed around some unexplained *sudden* death or rapid deadly illness—not always mysterious, but always sudden.[41]

Witches wither and stunt crops, dry up milking cows, cause women to be barren and miscarry and in other ways hinder essential fertility among the Mandari.[42] Physical beauty, outstanding gardens or cattle, are the most likely to be attacked among the Dinka,[43] where they also set light to the thatch of byres and huts. Misfortune in hunting is attributed to witchcraft among the Mbugwe,[44] and witches make love potions among the Kaguru as among other peoples.[45] In Essex, we we have seen, they principally attacked human beings, but also farm stock and equipment.

Other activities of witches

The witch is the archetype of evil, and horror is piled on horror in the creation of this mysterious mythical figure: 'he embodies those appetites and passions in every man which, if ungoverned, would destroy any moral law'.[46] His behaviour 'is inverted, physically, socially and morally',[47] and if we are careful we can learn much about the values he is supposed pervertedly to reflect.

Witches travel in curious ways. Firstly, they defy the laws of gravity—a concept necessary to explain how they strike so secretly at a distance. Sometimes they just run very fast, with the help of human flesh, among the Gusii.[48] Usually, however, they fly as among the Cewa,[49] the Tallensi,[50] and Nyakusa.[51] When they walk or stand around they often do this in a peculiar fashion; among the Kaguru they walk around upside-down on their hands,[52] and Amba witches pass leisure moments in their hectic lives standing on their heads or resting hanging upside-down from limbs of trees.[53] Both in their journeys and their meetings they are often naked. Among the Navaho they are naked at their nightly meetings, except for masks and jewellery.[54] Witches among the Amba,[55] and the Gusii,[56] to mention only two cases, travel around naked.

They indulge in various forbidden and revolting activities at their meetings. They eat human flesh—preferably the corpses of victims—among the Gisu,[57] the Cewa,[58] and Nyakusa.[59] This seems to be a very general feature. They are often extremely greedy, stealing milk from their neighbours' cows, as they do among the Nyakusa,[60] or sitting in a circle surrounded by piles or baskets of corpse flesh among the Navaho.[61] Their eating habits are generally eccentric: for instance, they eat salt to quench their thirst among the Amba.[62] Another common feature of the witch-meetings is sexual obscenity. Witches meet at night to have intercourse with dead women among the Navaho;[63] they perform obscene rites at their saturnalia among the Mbugwe.[64] They are often said to commit incest, fornication, and adultery among the Lugbara,[65] while among the Pondo they indulge in sexual relations with their hairy familiars.[66]

Essex witches, in comparison with their African counterparts, lived an austere and blameless life, neither flying, dancing, feasting on human flesh, nor indulging in sexual perversions.

The supposed motives of witches

Witches among the Lovedu try to harm people from motives of jealousy, revenge, frustration, or anger.[67] Similarly, a Zande witch attacks a man when motivated by hatred, envy, jealousy, and greed.[68] All witchcraft and sorcery comes from jealousy, anger, and spite, the Gisu say,[69] and jealousy is believed to be the foundation of the witch's character among the Mandari.[70] There seems to be an important distinction between witches, whose acts are prompted by unappeasable motives—lust for food or sex, hatred of all the normal human values—and sorcerers, who act because of a specific grievance which they have really suffered. The idea that the witch's heart can be softened by kindness and an appeal to mercy, or by reparation for an injury received, which is held by the Amba[71] and the Lugbara,[72] seems likely to lead to the conclusion that a man who is bewitched or 'ensorcelled' is partly to blame for it—a concept which the Lugbara do indeed have.[73] The Cewa also sometimes imply that the witches' victim often gets his deserts. The twin concepts could be stated differently. On the one hand, it is usually believed that 'even a witch does not injure or kill someone unknown to him and from whose sickness and death he will not derive some benefit', as the Gisu point out.[74] If one is going to pin witchcraft on to certain individuals they must have had some reason for acting; therefore, when witchcraft is suspected among this tribe both victim and diviner look for some motive of witchcraft: someone injured or insulted, an obligation unfulfilled or some favour refused. This places the responsibility of conflict on both accuser and accused, though this may not be openly recognized. Witches among the Nyakusa select as victims those against whom they have a grudge; 'they act illegally and immorally but not without cause'.[75] There has to be a motive and a will of evil before latent witchcraft takes effect among the Azande.[76] But in other instances the motive may not be connected with the activities of the victim. The Pondo seem to conceive of witches as acting without a particular cause, thus breaking the link between misfortune and morality.[77] The activities of Amba witches are ultimately inexplicable to their country-men, for they are motivated by an abnormal desire for human flesh.[78] As we have seen with the Pondo, this leads to a state of hopelessness, since one cannot take logical action against illogical activity. The motives of Essex witches, we have seen, were clearly understood. They sought revenge for unneighbourly acts done against them.

The relationship of witches to other evil agents

Witches are often one of a number of supernatural agents which bring misfortune on a people. Others are ancestors, sorcerers, ghosts, and spirits. Which agent is blamed usually depends on the amount of injury done and whether the attack is considered to be justified. It has been said that 'witchcraft attacks the virtuous, ancestors attack the wicked',[79] and this is certainly true among the Gusii.[80] But some societies do not make this division, and believe that ancestors can act wrongly, and on these occasions show anger against them.[81] Kin, prophets, sacred chiefs, and others may all cause injury similar to witchcraft among the Dinka, but in their case it is believed to be justified.[82] As far as can be seen, Essex witches do not appear to have competed with so many other agents of misfortune. Ghosts, ancestors, evil fairies appear to have played little part as bringers of affliction.

The personality and physical characteristics of the witch

Usually those actually accused are not as ugly, antisocial, or perverted as might be expected from the witch 'legends'. The stereotype of the witch is often far from the reality. But the stereotype is, nevertheless, important. Witches are often thought of as old—the older the witch among the Azande 'the more potent his witchcraft and the more unscrupulous his use of it'.[83] Another feature which is often given in the myth is the sex of the witch; thus men and women are equally witches among the Azande.[84] Night-witches among the Mandari are invariably male[85] and, though both men and women may become witches among the Navaho, male witches are thought to be considerably more numerous.[86] On the other hand, the Lovedu[87] and Gusii[88] agree that, though a witch can be of either sex, the great majority are female.

Beliefs vary as to the outward and inward physical attributes of witchcraft. Some people believe that though there are no outward signs, witchcraft is a substance, discoverable by autopsy, in the body of witches.[89] Night-witches are said to be white or grey in colour among the Lugbara,[90] and similarly to smear themselves white with ashes among the Kaguru.[91] But, like the small tail which they are supposed to have among the Dinka,[92] these outward signs are kept so secret that they are no help in actually finding who is bewitching one. On the whole, it seems to be believed that witches do not have any special stigmata or outward signs which mark them off from other people. When there is an ideal type, this is in keeping with the antisocial motives we have noted earlier. Thus the Kaguru describe a witch 'as an ugly person with dark skin and red eyes,'[93] but, like the Mandari, whose witches are ideally ugly, deformed, and dirty,[94] observation shows that those accused are often the very opposite. It is true that a person with an unpleasant face is often thought of as a witch among the Lovedu, even though nothing has definitely been attributed to him,[95] but it is ultimately on his behaviour that a witch is detected—behaviour arising from the motives we have studied earlier. The same appears to be true of Essex. Though the witch's 'mark' might be important in proving a person a witch, it was her behaviour that led to the suspicions and accusations.

2. COUNTER-ACTION AGAINST WITCHCRAFT

Wide variations in beliefs concerning witches and their activities have been discovered by anthropologists, even within one region of Africa. It seems likely that similar variations occurred, both within Europe and within England, in the sixteenth and seventeenth centuries. Essex beliefs are similar to modern African beliefs in a number of ways; they also differ in some features. Likewise, similarities and differences appear if we analyse the counter-actions taken against witches. Wherever witchcraft beliefs are prevalent there are also a complex of charms, spells, rituals, and officials whose function it is to find the witch and protect the victim, either by curing or by preventing the work of witches. This activity can be observed by the anthropologist, and thus provides concrete evidence about the 'ideology of witchcraft'. We learn which of the beliefs are powerful enough to influence daily behaviour. We can test whether witchcraft, by giving stereotyped reactions to certain anxieties, really does function as a beneficial, problem-solving, belief. This counter-activity is intimately linked with the witchcraft configuration in each society and therefore differs from place to place. It is possible, however, to extract some common factors—for instance, the use of ordeals and the presence of a class of 'diviners', and to say generally that there are three main branches of counter-witchcraft action: finding out if one is bewitched and who is the witch, curing witchcraft once it has been used (which includes the punishment of supposed witches), and preventing witchcraft before it has become active.

Finding the witch

Witchcraft suspicions begin in the home and are based on the types of injury described above. The first stage in locating the witch is usually divination. This can either be done by the victim/accuser (or his family and friends) or by a professional diviner. The questions asked are 'Am I bewitched?' and if so 'By whom?' and often counter-measures are discussed. We are told that a Cewa diviner is able to arrive at an acceptable answer by: '(a) being a keen student of local friendships, animosities, and kinship ties; (b) insisting on an interval between the opening of the case and the actual consultation or seance; (c) requiring that the client should be accompanied by a relative or close acquaintance; and (d) skilfully drawing the client into arguments he has with his divining apparatus during the seance'.[96] The same author points out that 'any diviner worth his fee gives an answer that his client finds acceptable'.[97] Like Azande consultation of oracles, where the names of *suspects* are placed first before the poisoned chicken or rubbing-board, this means that this stage in the mechanism is largely confirmatory. Diviners among the Bunyoro indicate the identity of the sorcerer, 'not directly but rather by confirming the suspicion voiced by his client'.[98] This reluctance actually to name the suspect, but the provision of clues which will guide the victim, seems a general feature; thus the diviner among the Kaguru does not name a suspect, but provides general indications.[99] The actual oracles and source of power of the diviners are varied. Kaguru diviners 'gaze into a container of oil or water, listen for sounds in a pot, cast beans'.[100] Lovedu use dice.[101]

As with the witch, the diviner is of different sex in different societies. Men alone discover and battle with witches according to the Nupe [102] and sorcery-removers and diviners are invariably men among the Gisu,[103] but Gusii diviners, like their witches, are women.[104] The financial arrangements also vary. Gisu diviners diagnose the cause of trouble for a fee,[105] and it is alleged that sorcery doctors sometimes deliberately introduce horns into rich people's houses that they may be profitably employed to remove them.[106] But in the 1947 witch-finding movement in east central Africa the 'witch-doctors' did not receive any payment for their work,[107] and Nandi witch-finding, a part-time and low-paid occupation, is not a lucrative business.[108]

The next major stage is the ordeal. In this the witch is tested—usually publicly. Often, as happens among the Gusii,[109] this involves the suspect touching something very hot and if he does not scald he is innocent. Often poison is given to the suspect, or to some person or animal representing him, and his guilt is judged on the behaviour that follows. These ordeals are often the most decisive forms of proof, and as such they are sometimes sought out by people who consider themselves to be suspected and wish to establish their innocence. Thus a person accused of witchcraft by a diviner among the Tallensi would insist on undergoing the arrow ordeal (or his/her family would insist on this) to clear the earlier suspicion.[110] It has been pointed out that the anti-witchcraft movement of 1947 had a cathartic value in cleansing the air of otherwise permanent suspicions: many 'went to gain proof of their own innocence with which to silence their accusers at home'.[111]

The emphasis on obtaining a confession from a witch is immense. Among the Navaho if a suspected witch, on being questioned, proves recalcitrant, 'he is tied down and not allowed to eat, drink, or relieve himself until he confesses';[112] placing hot coals on the feet of accused witches to make them confess was a former practice of this tribe. The confession and retraction of a spell by a witch are often thought to be the only cure for the victim. This emphasis is at least partly explained by the unofficial, even shaky, methods used to detect witches. The witch's confession will justify individual suspicions and provide final proof of his or her guilt. Many of the features both in the detection and trying of the witch, it will be obvious, were paralleled in Essex.

Preventing witchcraft

Counter-action against witchcraft begins long before an actual person is suspected. There are two major forms of this preventive activity, the one mystical and the other practical. One involves the use of medicines and charms, the performance of dances or the presence of anti-witchcraft cult organizations; the other dictates behaviour towards others in an attempt to avoid giving witches a motive for bewitching one.

The charms, medicines, and amulets used against witches are numerous and varied; each society and each specialized form of witchcraft and sorcery within that society has its specific antidotes. Gall medicine is the most frequently mentioned protection against witchcraft named by the Navaho, and it is carried by them when travelling or mixing in crowds;[113] the same tribe use small sand or pollen paintings as further protection. The Nupe use *cigbe*, or medicine, against witchcraft,[114] and protective charms are used widely by the Mbugwe—though there is little confidence in them.[115]

Depending on the supposed motive of witches, people try to avoid provoking witchcraft attacks. The only sanction against cruelty to dogs (and not a very strong one at that) among the Navaho is said to be the fear that animals will bewitch their owners in revenge.[116] The Navaho also take great care in disposing of waste body materials—hair, urine, nail-parings—in case they should be used by witches.[117] Since the old are often especially feared, certain peoples—for instance, the Dinka,[118] the Navaho,[119] and the Azande[120]—are studiously kind to old people for fear of arousing their hostility. A jealous man among the Azande will curb his jealousy lest he annoy people into bewitching him,[121] and children among the Nyakusa are warned not to be quarrelsome or boastful lest they arouse the anger of witches.[122] The Azande are also careful not to anger their wives gratuitously,[123] and the Nyakusa believe that a man who keeps on friendly terms with his neighbours has little to fear from witchcraft.[124] Since envy is often a basic motive of witches, people fear to be conspicuously successful among this same tribe.[125] Closely related to this in effect, if opposite in cause, is the fear of being thought a witch: thus with the Lele the danger of being accused of sorcery is said to encourage 'a modest placatory demeanour in older men'[126] and fear of accusations leads to kindness to sick siblings among the Navaho.[127] When witches are supposed to be motivated by lust for food, this will lead to certain counter-measures. For instance, the Amba give feasts to the whole village in the hope of satisfying the hunger of a witch,[128] and the Nyakusa make a direct connexion between feeding potential witches on beef and protecting oneself.[129] In cases of witchcraft administered through food, divining for a witch is seldom successful, according to the Mbugwe, and they therefore eat privately to prevent this catstrophe.[130] Preventives, both magical and natural, were widespread in Essex, and very similar to those described above.

Curing witchcraft: magical and supernatural methods

As with the prevention of witchcraft, there are, roughly, two major types of action one can take if bewitched. Firstly, one can perform rituals, use medicines, invoke the aid of gods or curers, and send back vengeance magic; secondly, one can take action against the witch himself, scratch him, force him to leave the village, wound or kill him, make him confess to his crime and withdraw his evil. The second set of actions are clearly thought of as associated with the former; making the witch confess or burning him has repercussions in the supernatural field.

One method of curing witchcraft is by sacrifice to god, who, for example, the Mandari believe,[131] 'may free the good man from the evil intention.'

Another is to join in the annual 'cleansing' ritual which embraces the whole of the community among the Gwari.[132] These public performances, often including dancing and singing, are often conducted by organized, sometimes itinerant, anti-witchcraft societies—as among the Nupe[133] where the secret anti-witchcraft society tours and 'cleanses' villages. Various plants are used as medicines, as are certain short prayers, chants, and prayer ceremonials or 'big prays'.[134]

Curing witchcraft: accusations and attacks on witches

The Navaho believe that if a witch confesses, the victim will at once begin to improve, and the witch will die within the year from the victim's symptoms.[135] The idea that to attack, claw, wound, kill, or force the witch to withdraw her evil will alleviate the suffering of the victim overlaps with the idea of vengeance. Together they motivate the often startlingly harsh attacks on witches. Punishment of witches is not just sadism and vengeance. It is justified, in theory, by the belief that it may contribute to the well-being of the individual bewitched, and certainly to that of the community. The sorcerer who pronounces a spell is the only one who can take it off among the Nandi,[136] and the Mbugwe believe that a witch *must* confess his crime if the sickness is to disappear.[137] The ways of obtaining such a retraction vary. If a man among the Gisu suspects a particular person of bewitching him, 'he may go and threaten him with violence or even attack him',[138] but often a person will go and ask quite civilly that the witch withdraw his evil, as among the Azande[139] and Lugbara.[140]

There are many other considerations dictating one's attitude to a suspected witch, one of the most important being the necessity for social co-operation and inter-family links. It is often in the interest of both victim and accused that they should not be estranged, as Evans-Pritchard has pointed out, for 'they have to live together as neighbours and co-operate in the life of the community'.[141] Among the Azande if a person accused of witchcraft keeps to the expression of traditional formulas and promises that he will withdraw his witchcraft the incident closes without bitterness.[142] Here witchcraft genuinely seems to function as an explanation of misfortune, in contrast to those societies where, it has been argued, witchcraft provides an outlet for aggression or a means of severing strained but otherwise unbreakable links. In the former type of society, confirmed witches are often 'respected fathers and husbands', welcome visitors, and influential councillors at court.[143] Among the Mandari there is a compromise: there is careful avoidance of a witch, but never direct ostracism; courtesy without intimacy is the usual policy.[144] The Amba, like the Kaguru,[145] believe that since witchcraft only acts over a short distance, it is best to flee or expel the witch when bewitched.[146] If one cannot place distance between oneself and the witch, or force him to retract his power, there is one other solution—his death.

Until recent times witches are said to have been punished in various ways, but the common factor seems to have been the harshness of the punishment—either death or expulsion—and the fact that death was often administered at night by a group of men acting for the 'general will' of the community. When a person was found guilty among the Gusii he or she was clubbed at night,[147] and similarly among the Gisu the witch was killed communally.[148] This is explained in these two cases, by the anthropologist concerned, as an attempt to prevent vengeance by the witch's family. The death punishment is said to have been widespread; for instance, sorcerers among the Bunyoro were burnt to death,[149] witches among the Kaguru were clubbed to death.[150] The alternative, expulsion, has the same effect, eliminating the supposed cause of misfortunes and tensions. Since witchcraft is a deadly power and, in a sense, often inexorable, outside the control of the witch, there is no point in using punishment as correction or even deterrent. Furthermore, the harshness of the punishment arises from the nature of the crime. The witch has not only caused death and suffering; he has done so traitorously, from within the group.[151] As it has been said, the witch is an outlaw who may be killed because 'he has forfeited his value as a human person by acting as an enemy of the community'.[152] The harsh, informal attacks on English witches, and savage punishments at the courts, reflect similar fears.

Do people ever practise, or believe themselves to have practised, witchcraft?

It does not need physical pressure to force a person to confess to witchcraft. There are many possible motives for such a confession: spite towards another whom one can implicate, various mental states which lead to compulsive confessions, and, not least, the pressure of others in the society. The process of confession has been investigated among the Azande. Witchcraft, we are shown, is so taken for granted and its working so little understood that an individual may easily believe himself a witch when accused—'some think, for a short time at any rate, that perhaps, after all they are witches'.[153] A man has accused others; he believes in witchcraft; when the finger points at him he is bewildered. Perhaps he has been bewitching someone unconsciously (though he knows everyone else bewitches consciously)? The pressures to conform to the opinions of neighbours and superiors are complex and powerful.

Anthropologists have, among other topics, investigated anti-witchcraft movements. The motives of the leaders, the popular appeal of their techniques, the millenarian flavour of the outbursts have all been studied.[154] Another aspect of witchcraft accusations which has also received considerable attention has been the question of whether the 'cures' for witchcraft are ever effective. It has been suggested that counter-action against witches at least provides the sufferer with some sort of comfort. Misfortune is turned into something partially controllable.[155] Both in the witch-finding movement of 1645 in Essex and in the popularity of counter-witchcraft activities there is a close enough parallel between the historical and anthropological material for a fruitful exchange of ideas.

NOTES

1. With the exception of the American Navaho tribe all the examples of modern witchcraft beliefs are drawn from Africa and from the works of British social anthropologists. The full titles of works cited by author and date only are given on pp. 323–4 of the Bibliography.
2. Many of the following references and examples will be taken from *Witchcraft and Sorcery in East Africa* eds. John Middleton and E. H. Winter, which will be referred to by the abbreviated title of Middleton (1963). This is a collection of essays on the following peoples, by the following anthropologists: Nyoro (John Beattie), Kaguru (T. O. Beidelman), Mandari (Jean Buxton), Lele (Mary Douglas), Mbugwe (Robert F. Gray), Nandi (G. W. B. Huntingford), Gisu (Jean La Fontaine), Gusii (Robert A. Levine), Lugbara (John Middleton), Amba (E. H. Winter).
3. Kluckhohn (1944), p. 15.
4. Fortes (1949), p. 33.
5. Evans-Pritchard (1937), p. 33.
6. Middleton (1963), p. 292.
7. Kluckhohn (1944), p. 16.
8. Middleton (1963), p. 64.
9. Ibid., p. 166.
10. Evans-Pritchard (1937), pp. 36–7.
11. Middleton (1963), p. 109.
12. Wilson (1951), p. 309.
13. Krige (1943), p. 251.
14. Middleton (1963), p. 226.
15. Wilson (1951), p. 308.
16. Middleton (1963), p. 64.
17. Ibid., p. 213.
18. Lienhardt (1951), p. 309.
19. Evans-Pritchard (1937), p. 39.
20. Kluckhohn (1944), p. 16.
21. Middleton (1963), p. 169.
22. Krige (1943), p. 250.
23. Middleton (1963), p. 228.
24. Ibid., p. 100.
25. See p. 170, above.
26. Middleton (1963), p. 113.
27. Fortes (1949), p. 33.
28. Middleton (1963), p. 66.
29. Ibid., p. 262.
30. Lienhardt (1951), p. 307.
31. Krige (1943), p. 254.
32. Middleton (1963), p. 194.
33. Evans-Pritchard (1937), p. 63.
34. Middleton (1963), p. 191.
35. Ibid., p. 102.
36. Ibid., p. 63.
37. Evans-Pritchard (1937), p. 77.
38. Middleton (1963), p. 128.
39. Evans-Pritchard (1937), p. 74.
40. Ibid., p. 38.
41. Nadel (1954), p. 187.
42. Middleton (1963), p. 103.
43. Lienhardt (1951), p. 316.
44. Middleton (1963), p. 167.
45. Ibid., p. 66.
46. Lienhardt (1951), p. 317.
47. Middleton (1963), p. 67.
48. Ibid., p. 226.

49. Marwick (1965), p. 76.
50. Fortes (1949), p. 33.
51. Wilson (1951), p. 308.
52. Middleton (1963), p. 65.
53. Ibid., p. 292.
54. Kluckhohn (1944), p. 16.
55. Middleton (1963), p. 292.
56. Ibid., p. 225.
57. Ibid., p. 197.
58. Marwick (1952), p. 215.
59. Wilson (1951), p. 308.
60. Ibid., p. 308.
61. Kluckhohn (1944), p. 16.
62. Middleton (1963), p. 280.
63. Kluckhohn (1944), p. 16.
64. Middleton (1963), p. 166.
65. Ibid., p. 263.
66. Wilson (1951), p. 309.
67. Krige (1943), p. 250.
68. Evans-Pritchard (1937), p. 100.
69. Middleton (1963), p. 192.
70. Ibid., p. 280.
71. Ibid., p. 290.
72. Ibid., p. 265.
73. Ibid., p. 272.
74. Ibid., p. 202.
75. Wilson (1951), p. 308.
76. Evans-Pritchard (1951), p. 100.
77. Wilson (1951), p. 309.
78. Middleton (1963), p. 281.
79. Gluckman (1963), p. 93.
80. Mayer (1954), p. 9.
81. Ibid., p. 9.
82. Lienhardt (1951), p. 305.
83. Evans-Pritchard (1937), p. 30.
84. Ibid., p. 31.
85. Middleton (1963), p. 100.
86. Kluckhohn (1944), p. 15.
87. Krige (1943), p. 252.
88. Middleton (1963), p. 225.
89. Evans-Pritchard (1937), p. 21.
90. Middleton (1963), p. 262.
91. Ibid., p. 65.
92. Lienhardt (1951), p. 306.
93. Middleton (1963), p. 68.
94. Ibid., p. 105.
95. Krige (1943), p. 269.
96. Marwick (1952), p. 216.
97. Ibid., p. 216.
98. Middleton (1963), p. 42.
99. Ibid., p. 70.
100. Ibid., p. 70.
101. Krige (1943), p. 259.
102. Nadel (1954), p. 177.
103. Middleton (1963), p. 191.
104. Ibid., p. 232.
105. Ibid., p. 199.
106. Ibid., p. 46.
107. Marwick (1950), p. 112.
108. Middleton (1963), p. 186.
109. Ibid., p. 231.
110. Fortes (1949), p. 33.
111. Middleton (1963), p. 124.
112. Kluckhohn (1944), p. 28.
113. Ibid., p. 27.
114. Nadel (1954), p. 189.
115. Middleton (1963), p. 171.
116. Kluckhohn (1944), p. 32.
117. Ibid., p. 31.
118. Lienhardt (1951), p. 316.
119. Kluckhohn (1944), p. 31.
120. Evans-Pritchard (1937), p. 115.
121. Ibid., p. 117.
122. Wilson (1951), p. 308.
123. Evans-Pritchard (1937), p. 117.
124. Wilson (1951), p. 308.
125. Ibid., p. 308.
126. Middleton (1963), p. 131.
127. Kluckhohn (1944), p. 64.
128. Middleton (1963), p. 290.
129. Wilson (1951), p. 308.
130. Middleton (1963), p. 163.
131. Ibid., p. 121.
132. Nadel (1952), p. 20.
133. Ibid., pp. 189, 196–7.
134. Kluckhohn (1944), p. 29.
135. Ibid., p. 28.
136. Middleton (1963), p. 178.
137. Ibid., p. 154.
138. Ibid., p. 198.
139. Evans-Pritchard (1937), p. 84.
140. Middleton (1963), p. 265.
141. Evans-Pritchard (1937), p. 97.
142. Ibid., p. 87.
143. Ibid., p. 114.
144. Middleton (1963), p. 119.
145. Ibid., p. 73.
146. Ibid., p. 290.
147. Ibid., p. 231.
148. Ibid., p. 199.

149. Ibid., p. 46.
150. Ibid., p. 72.
151. Mayer (1954), pp. 17–18.
152. Lienhardt (1951), p. 307.
153. Evans-Pritchard (1937), p. 124.
154. Two good examples are Marwick (1950) and A. I. Richards, 'A Modern Movement of Witch-finders', *Africa*, viii, No. 4 (1935), 448–61.
155. This point is made, for example, in Kluckhohn (1944), p. 61, and Middleton (1963), p. 50.

Chapter 18

The anthropological approach to the study of witchcraft (2): the sociology of accusations.[1]

Specific people are accused of being witches, other people are named as their victims. These are observed facts and can be analysed sociologically, unlike the 'ideology of witchcraft' which can only be interpreted. The two basic facts we may discover are the position, sex, age, and other details of witch and victim, and their relationship to each other. The study of the relationship between witch and victim has especially attracted anthropologists, for it illuminates not only the tensions which precipitate witchcraft accusations, but, more generally, indicates the major stresses in the interpersonal relationships of a society. We will start by describing separately the characteristics of the witch and victim, but it should throughout be remembered that each detail about the victim (age, sex, personality) must be related to that of the witch and vice versa. Thus it is not enough to learn that Nupe witches are old women; we must also remember that their victims are usually young men under their influence.[2]

THE PHYSICAL AND MENTAL ATTRIBUTES OF THE WITCH

In myth, witches are ugly, deformed, and dirty; in reality looks appear to be a very vague indication of a witch. Those who suffer from some physical deformity or who have been mutilated among the Azande are suspected of witchcraft, since they are likely to be harbouring a grievance.[3] Cripples may be suspected of witchcraft among the Lugbara, but this is not universal.[4] 'Men with clubfeet or hunchbacks are not thought to be witches among the same people unless they are also bad-tempered.'[5] Personal appearance is of little help in identifying a witch among the Kaguru.[6] It seems to be generally true that physical appearance, by itself, is not an important sign of a witch.

It has been suggested that there is a link between witchcraft and insanity. In fact, the connexion seems tenuous. An insane person is more likely to be a victim than a practitioner of witchcraft. It is true that the highly neurotic are especially thought to be witches among the Kaguru,[7] and it is likely that slight mental 'oddness', eccentricity, and various perversions, such as transvesticism and homosexual behaviour, are indications of a witch. But, Nadel points out,[8] it is not physical abnormality, ugliness caused by ill-luck, or mental abnormality, lunacy and various kinds of mental breakdown, but 'abnormality of social or moral deviants' which is attacked in witchcraft accusations; in other words, *wilful* deviation. In Essex the physical and mental attributes of the witch appear similar. Although there was a stereotype of the ugly witch, and suspects may sometimes have been slightly mentally unbalanced, neither of these features were fundamental in the selection of likely witches.

THE CHARACTER AND BEHAVIOUR OF THE WITCH

'Witches tend to be those whose behaviour is least in accordance with social demands' we are told.[9] These demands vary with the society, and it is therefore only possible to show what types of character and behaviour certain societies condemn; we have already indicated some of these earlier when discussing the 'supposed motives' of witches.

Generally speaking, as we have seen, the absence of the accepted mores —for instance, the lack of friendliness or any other 'atypical' or abnormal behaviour among the Nupe[10]—attracts attention. In the Gisu tribe, likewise, the eccentric is branded as a witch, and this, as is frequently pointed out, makes witchcraft function as a sanction to conformity.[11] Nonconformists—the very outspoken, eccentrics of various kinds—are believed to be witches among the Mandari.[12] Father Berard has said of the Navaho that 'to disregard anything to be feared or tabooed is to expose one's self deliberately either to danger and death, or to be branded as a witch'.[13] The notion of 'recklessness' is attached to all forms of witchcraft among this same tribe: the witch is one who foolishly transgresses taboos, especially supernatural sanctions.[14]

Among the Azande a spiteful disposition arouses suspicions of witchcraft; those who make a nuisance of themselves to their neighbours, those who are glum and ill-tempered, those who speak in a roundabout manner, those who threaten others with misfortune, those who are unmannerly and enter without knocking, who make offensive and insulting remarks and cannot conceal their greed, whose habits are dirty—urinating in public, eating without washing their hands, eating bad food—are all suspected of witchcraft. Men fear to refuse requests lest a sponger bewitches them, and they say 'a man who is always asking for gifts is a witch'.[15]

'Witchcraft is seen in the eyes' in dourness, absence of smiles, of pleasant speech, of laughter and playfulness among the Nupe.[16] Case-histories show that women accused have usually shown unusual independence: they are ambitious patrons, 'berate their husband's younger brother for contributing too little to the household budget', lord it over their sick husband, run away to a mission, are unfaithful to their husband, neglect their children.[17]

It was similar in Essex, where any type of behaviour might be interpreted as evidence that a person was a witch. Often suspected people appear to have exhibited the same morose and bitter temper as their African counterparts: but even when they acted in a friendly manner they might be regarded with hostility and suspicion.

THE WEALTH, STATUS, AND OCCUPATION OF WITCHES

There has been little investigation of this topic. Sometimes witches are the rich; economically successful people, those with a large number of wives and property, shop-owners and affluent cultivators among the Kaguru, at least in myth[18]—sometimes the very poor, who are forced by their poverty to become helpers to witches according to Navaho beliefs.[19] Of the 222 cases Kluckhohn analysed, seventeen were described as poor or very poor, 115 as 'rich' or 'well-off'. Women 'traders' are believed to be bad and indulge in witchcraft among the Nupe,[20] and this, like other accusations against exceptionally rich people, is usually ascribed by anthropologists to jealousy.[21] Economic factors are part of the broader question of the status or occupation of the witch.

In some societies certain classes or positions are thought to be 'above' witchcraft. This is nearly always said about whites, and often, as among the Azande,[22] of members of the princely class, governors of provinces, men of the court, and other men of wealth and influence. This fact is sometimes explained by the argument that it would be very foolish and dangerous for a commoner to accuse such a person, and anyhow the social frictions are missing. On the other hand, this is not a uniform rule. Powerful chiefs, headmen, and Church leaders are especially suspected of being witches among the Kaguru,[23] and twenty-one out of 184 men accused among the Navaho were 'headmen' or 'chiefs'—a *very* high proportion of these officials, according to Kluckhohn.[24]

Another group which is sometimes involved as men of power and position are spiritual leaders; we have already seen Church leaders included above. Among the Nupe, diviners are believed to give advice and medicine to witches,[25] while 140 out of 184 men accused are described as ceremonial practitioners of some sort among the Navaho.[26] Other professions associated with witchcraft are returned war veterans among the Kaguru;[27] thieves among the Mandari,[28] and clients (usually kinless) among the Lugbara.[29]

Clients often come from outside the society, and it is aliens and immigrants who are often first suspected of witchcraft. Destitute and fugitive persons and migrating groups are suspected of witchcraft among the Mandari and a distinction is made between owners and mere settlers. The latter, not without some reason, are thought of as usurpers, destructive and a threat—in fact, witches.[30] Men who wander about the country, if they move rapidly, are more likely to be accused of sorcery than witchcraft, for they are not a perennial, secret, inside challenge to a group, but just passing threats; in this way petty traders, hawkers, local government and mission employees, and labour migrants are thought to employ an indiscriminate type of sorcery among the Lugbara.[31] The Kaguru have a similar suspicion of foreigners—for instance, tribal leaders who have settled in Ukaguru are especially thought to be witches,[32] while a Kaguru arriving from another locale about whom little is known will also be suspect.[33] Outsiders, travelling conjurers, and treasure-hunters, were also suspected in Essex. As in Africa, the higher social classes do not appear to have been accused by villagers and the majority of accusations occurred between people of roughly the same status.

THE AGE OF WITCHES

It is generally agreed that children do not have the force to use witchcraft, a belief we find, for instance, among the Gisu.[34] All 222 of the accused persons Kluckhohn studied were adults.[35] In general they seem to be old people. This is so in myth, as we have seen—another example being the beliefs of the Lovedu that a very old person, 'bartering the lives of young persons for his own', is a witch:[36] a witch is often middle-aged or old in practice among the Nupe.[37]

The most detailed study of the question of age has been made by Kluckhohn.[38] All women in the Navaho tribe accused of witchcraft were definitely old, and 131 out of 184 of the men likewise. The old are more feared after their hair has turned white or grey.[39] Kluckhohn proceeds to make a number of suggestions why this should be. Perhaps the old are resented as an economic liability; possibly Navahos unconsciously place witchcraft as a substitute for the power which the old have lost in the world; perhaps much-prized old age and nearness to death gives them an awe and fearsomeness which easily turns into spiritual evil; possibly (as was suggested above) old people are thought to be witches because they suck the vitality of others to keep themselves alive; conceivably witchcraft reflects Navaho dislike of extremes the *very* rich, the *very* powerful, and the *very* old.[40] It is also suggested that the old become witches because they are dissatisfied with the cessation of sexual activity—as we will see,

women are usually past the menopause—and the Navahos themselves say
that the very old will die very soon anyhow and are thus prepared to take
all sorts of chances with the culturally prohibited—in other words,
witchcraft.[41] A similar type of interpretation is given for the Lele image of
the sorcerer, which is said partly to reflect the precarious privilege of age,
for on arriving at this much-desired state people are disappointed and
thus embittered.[42] The person accused among the Luvale is 'almost
invariably an old woman'.[43] This is explained by reference to the tensions
arising out of the kinship and age system. Essex witches, likewise, were
usually elderly. It was considered almost impossible for a young person to
be a witch.

THE SEX OF WITCHES

In some societies a witch may be of either sex—for instance, among the
Amba[44] and the Cewa.[45] In others, women alone are witches, or at least
really evil ones. Thus women alone are *evil* witches among the Nupe,[46]
and in all the ten known cases of witchcraft accusations among the Tallensi
the accused was a woman.[47] While most of the celebrated professional
sorcerers are usually men among the Bunyoro; most sorcery accusations in
domestic conflicts are against women.[48] Men are also witches, however.
The Gisu say that women, weaker in personality, are not such strong
witches as men,[49] and the Lugbara night-witches are always men.[50] Of the
222 people accused and studied by Kluckhohn in the Navaho tribe 184
were men.[51] The accused was a woman in twenty-six out of thirty-five
cases from the Luvale.[52]

If the witch is a woman it often makes a difference whether she is
married or single. Witches are always married women among the Nupe,[53]
while among the Navaho they are usually either childless or past the
menopause.[54] Apparently there is a connexion between willed female
sterility and witchcraft among the Nupe, and this, it is suggested, is
owing to a combination of guilt projection by women and the anger of men
at such unnatural activities.[55] Kluckhohn suggests that the Navaho
unwillingness to attribute witchcraft to those who are bearing and rearing
children is due to the fact that they are 'the focus of the sentiment system'.[56]
Again Essex resembles some of the African examples. The majority of
witches were women, but it was not conceived impossible for a man to be
a witch also.

An analysis similar to that above can be made of the victims of witchcraft. The most detailed study appears to be that of Navaho victims. As
regards sex, ninety-seven out of 164 victims of witchcraft were men,
sixty-seven women. Of these 164 victims, six were of 'medium' wealth,

twelve 'poor', and 133 rich. As for age, the distribution seems to be random, except for the fact that 123 out of 164 were adult.[57] It is likely that societies vary in the proportion of child victims; for instance, children are thought to be particularly vulnerable to witchcraft, since they have weak personalities, among the Gisu.[58] It is worth noting that witch and victim often act alike Thus the kind of person likely to be attacked by Nyauksa witches is very like the attacker, having the same anti-social tendencies—moroseness, lack of sympathy, ambition.[59]

THE RELATIONSHIP OF WITCH AND VICTIM ACCUSER

Though victim and accuser are often technically different people—for instance, a child may be bewitched and her mother be the accuser—for the sake of simplicity 'accuser' and 'victim' will be treated as interchangeable terms in this analysis. Thus, for example, if a person's child is killed and he accuses a neighbour, he will be treated as the victim, as he indeed probably feels himself to be.

As long ago as 1937 it was pointed out that 'oracle consultations [therefore] express histories of personal relationships'.[60] Since then there has been a growing emphasis on the importance of studying the age, status, sex, and, above all, family relationship between witch and victim. Such an approach attempts to show both what types of tension generate witchcraft accusations and, using witchcraft friction as an index, which are the conflict-filled relationships in a given society. Roughly, there are two stages in the formation of an accusation: firstly, the presence of some tension or anxiety or unexplained phenomenon; secondly, the directing of this energy into certain channels. But accusations are not a straight reflection of tensions: not only must we study the tensions in a society, but also the other mechanisms for blocking or relieving tensions—legal, political, or otherwise.[61] Witchcraft accusations must be related to the whole social structure, not studied as isolated indications of friction. Only between certain people does 'society' allow witchcraft accusations.[62]

AGE RELATIONSHIP

We have seen that witchcraft power is usually thought to increase with age and that, though there are exceptions, witches are usually middle-aged or old. The age-relationship varies. Among the Gusii, in virtually all cases of witchcraft accusations, relationships are between persons of the same generation.[63] On the other hand, the Mesakin believe that older relatives always attack younger ones,[64] and Nupe accusations are similarly made by younger men against older women.[65] Though this pattern is perhaps the most general,[66] it is not followed among the Cewa and Yao, where witch-

craft accusations are mostly made against the young, and tend, it has
suggestively been pointed out, to have a conservative effect.[67] It might be
argued that witchcraft accusations vary in their disruptive or conservative effect, depending on this age-relationship. Thus those made by the
young against the old tend to be provoked by desire for change, while
those made by the old downwards have the conservative effect suggested
above. Mesakin accusations by the young against the old are related to the
structure of their society which forces tension between social and physical
age.[68] Not until more accused persons have been traced in village records
will it be possible to prove the hypothesis that in Essex, also, there was a
tension between age-groups—between the middle-aged and the elderly.

THE SEX RELATIONSHIP

In many societies there is no sex polarity between witches and victims.
Both men and women are equally liable to harm, either men or women
among the Lovedu,[69] and Gwari witchcraft beliefs involve no sexual
antagonism—witches and their victims are indiscriminately male or
female.[70] Azande men may be bewitched only by members of their own
sex; a sick man usually asks the oracles about his male neighbours, while,
if he is consulting them about a sick wife or kinswoman, he normally asks
about other women; this, we are told, is because ill feeling is more likely
to arise between man and man and between woman and woman. Never is a
man bewitched by a kinswoman or a woman bewitched by a kinsman.[71]
But in some societies there does seem to be a polarity. For instance, only
in one out of nine cases did a witch attack another woman among the
Nupe,[72] and the Kaguru make frequent accusations against their wives.[73]
    When there is polarity and antagonism, various theories are put forward
to explain it. Likewise theories have been suggested why women appear
less frequently as witches in some societies than men. For instance,
Navaho male witchcraft is explained partly by the fact that few singers or
ceremonial practitioners (of whom people express jealousy in witchcraft
accusations) are women, but more importantly by the fact that the solidarity of this society, still predominantly matrilineal and matrilocal as
it is, centres in women.[74] This explanation in terms of family organization
has been suggested to explain the pre-eminent part of women in certain
witchcraft complexes, both as accusers and accused. It is Kluckhohn's
impression 'that women, as a group, characteristically manifest more
anxiety about witchcraft than do men as a group',[75] and he suggests that
this is because women are less able to escape from the inbred emotionalism
of the home through travel and business and are thus more likely to need
witchcraft as an outlet.[76] He deduces from this that, tension being greater,

witchcraft will be more rife among patrilocal groups where women are more constricted in their contacts.[77] His theory has been echoed with regard to Bunyoro sorcery, where the fact that women are more often accused of interpersonal domestic sorcery is said to reflect their inferior and frustratingly confined position.[78] It is important to distinguish here the factors which make women more anxious and insecure and afraid of witchcraft (and also those which allow them to express their feelings more easily) and the factors which lead men to attack them as competitors or rivals. Under the former division we find, for instance, that the patriarchal hierarchy of the Gusii allows women to vent their hostility more easily. Women, not responsible for maintaining order in the family, are freer to make accusations and pass on malicious gossip, while the men prefer to ignore this, since it is a threat to social cohesion.[79] Sometimes, as with the Mbugwe,[80] women are just more aware than men of the hostilities between different lineages and hence more conscious of witchcraft. Under the second division it has been suggested that women are accused of witchcraft in patrilineal families because they really are outsiders, whose loyalty, it is suspected, is often withheld, especially in inter-marriage between hostile tribes.[81]

The Nupe appear to show sex-antagonism in their witchcraft beliefs, and Nadel has made a number of suggestions why this should be. In comparing two tribes, the Nupe and Gwari, he explains the absence of sex-antagonism in the latter and its presence in the former mainly in terms of the economic independence of women and the consequent jealousy of their position by men among the Nupe. Nupe marriage is full of stress and mutual hostility, and the woman's power is greater in fact than it should be according to the ethical system.[82] The Nupe seem in a similar position to the Kaguru, where the men are extremely insecure—afraid of adultery and insubordination—and where their wives' dreaded independence, or even hostility, are expressed in songs and proverbs as unquenchable sexual voracity. Here there is also sex-antagonism in witchcraft accusations.[83] These theories and others were outlined more fully by Nadel in 1954.[84] Looking at the problem more broadly, the Pondo emphasis on sexual activities in witchcraft is not due to the individual frustrations, caused, for instance, by rigid pre-marital control, but to the kinship system, which forbids sexual relationships with large numbers of neighbours.[85] Sexual antagonism appears to have played little part in Essex witchcraft: accusations were as often between women as between persons of the opposite sex and there appears to have been little sexual content to the beliefs about witches. The situation was very different from that of the Nupe.

STATUS/OCCUPATION RELATIONSHIP

There appears to have been relatively little analysis of the actual occupations of witches and their victims, but there have been some suggestions as to the effect of the competition for status. This competition will be further discussed when we come to examine the effect of Westernization on African witchcraft.

The Cewa recognize an exception to the usual inter-matrikin witchcraft —that between persons in strong competition for an object, status, or person. An early analysis of twenty cases shows us the importance of status as a cause of witchcraft tension.[86] The Mandari are not continually apprehensive about neighbours; since witchcraft is a role tied to status, only certain of their neighbours can be witches.[87] Naturally, status is not the only source of friction between neighbours, for among the Gisu there are tensions over straying animals, boundary disputes, tools borrowed and forgotten, or fights between children, none of which, if within a lineage, can find outlet in either open hostility or litigation.[88] Nor is it exclusively between neighbours that dispute over status occurs; for instance, there is ambiguity of rank among wives and sons in a Gusii family and there is inevitably competition and witchcraft-accusation.[89] But on the whole, it is in those societies where witchcraft relations are often between unrelated or distantly related persons, age-mates, and neighbours, that this kind of friction is most important—for instance, among the Nyakusa, where village neighbours (more than one-third of all the witches) are the most important category of witches.[90]

We are told that among the Azande a man quarrels with, and is jealous of, his social equals and so accuses only them, and that a wealthy commoner will be patron to a poorer commoner and there will seldom be malice between them.[91] But this is not a general rule. For instance, patronage arouses envy and feelings of inferiority, it is believed by Mandari landowners, and consequently they accuse their dependants of witchcraft, projecting fear for their own position on to the supposed hostility of their workers.[92] Essex accusations also show traces of slightly asymmetrical status relations. Accused witches, to judge from the occupations of their husbands, were of slightly lower status than their accusers.

KINSHIP RELATIONSHIPS

Professor Evans-Pritchard early pointed out that 'the operation of witchcraft beliefs in the social life are also closely connected with the kinship system, particularly through the custom of vengeance'.[93] Since then, anthropologists have concentrated on the relationship of witchcraft accusations to the structure of the family. They ask which relationships produce the tensions and which allow their release in witchcraft accusations and why this should be so.

In certain societies witches hardly ever attack their kinsmen; thus only very rarely is an accusation of witchcraft lodged against a kinsman among the Nyakusa, probably because they live in age-villages.[94] In other societies, as we have seen, there are intra-lineage accusations, although this is not recognized openly in myth or conversation. For instance, it is said among the Kaguru that persons within a clan are less apt to bewitch each other than outsiders, while actual cases reveal that accusations occur with some frequency within the same matrilineage.[95] In yet others, nearly all suspicion and accusation is between relatives: in 90 per cent of the 101 Cewa cases analysed, the witch was believed to have attacked a relative.[96] Of fifty Lovedu court cases 70 per cent involved close relatives.[97]

Certain family relationships are expected to cause witchcraft, in others accusations never occur. Thus the Dinka single out the relationship between a woman and her brother's wife, the relationship between half-brothers, and the relationship between co-wives as likely, and the mother-in-law–daughter-in-law relationship as unlikely, to be situations of witchcraft.[98] Likewise with the Lovedu, where cattle-linked brothers or sisters, fathers, father's brothers, and grandparents never bewitch.[99]

In polygynous societies, such as the Nyakusa and Pondo[100] and the Kaguru,[101] there is frequently friction between co-wives, resulting in witchcraft accusations. This is the most prolific single source of witchcraft accusations among the Lovedu (some 24 per cent).[102] Various explanations have been given, the most frequent being that exogamy makes a woman a stranger in her husband's home and polygamy produces many tensions between wives who are rivals for their husband's favour.[103] These suspicions are often carried into the next generation by the sons of the various co-wives, also competitors for their father's favour.[104]

Very few societies allow witchcraft accusations between parent and child. The Lovedu believe that a woman never bewitches her own children,[105] and whatever difficulties a Zulu woman may have with her son she would be considered crazy if she accused him of bewitching her.[106] References to children bewitching their parents and vice versa are almost non-existent among the Navaho.[107] Even among the Nupe, where there are three cases of witches attacking children, only one was her own child— the other two being her husband's brother's and a co-wife's.[108] Like the absence of the child-grandparent relationship, this is usually explained partly by the fact that it would disrupt the central emotional bond of society, partly by the fact that the normal motives for witchcraft—jealousy and envy—are absent in this relationship, even if hostility is present.

Witchcraft accusations are more frequent against affines than against

agnates. The most obvious affinal relationship is that between husband
and wife. While certain societies hardly ever allow accusations between
spouses—this is true of the Navaho, for instance—[109] others do. Among the
Lovedu, spouses frequently bewitch each other, but, as we will find with
nearly all societies, wives kill or injure their husbands much more often
than the other way round.[110] In fifty Lovedu legal cases 20 per cent of the
total were wives bewitching husbands or in-laws, 16 per cent vice versa.[111]
The bulk of accusations between Kaguru spouses are probably by husbands
against their wives.[112] There is no known case among the Azande in which
a man has been accused of bewitching his wife (though men frequently
consult oracles about their own wives), since no one, the Azande say,
wishes to kill his wife, and anyhow a woman cannot consult oracles and has
to entrust this duty to her husband.[113] Husbands are less likely to accuse
wives who have borne them children, for various reasons, including the
dangers to his children of doing so where witchcraft is hereditary.[114]

Conflicts between wife and husband are part of the larger problem of
affinal relationships. Nupe witches often bewitch their affinal relatives,[115]
and women accuse their affines of attacking them, particularly in the early,
insecure, years of marriage, among the Gisu.[116] Tension among in-laws
sometimes has other outlets: for instance, among the Lovedu where there
is not much witchcraft accusation in this relationship.[117] In other instances,
such as the Navaho, where, of 103 cases in which a relative was accused,
eighty-one involved affinal relatives,[118] this is the predominant kind of
intra-family accusation. Societies vary as to which affinal relationships are
most likely to be characterized by witchcraft accusations. Thus the typical
accusation of witchcraft in Pondoland is between a mother and daughter-
in-law who live in the same homestead,[119] while Zulu men accuse
daughters-in-law and sisters-in-law of witchcraft.[120] Sorcery seldom occurs
between a man and his mother's people, according to the Bunyoro,[121] but
fourteen out of 103 of the cases in which Navahos accused relatives were
against a maternal uncle.[122] The extensive discussion of witchcraft and
tensions between kin has little to offer in the case of Essex, but other
counties, when studied, may show a closer correspondence. The typical
Essex accusation appears to have been between unrelated village neighbours.

THE FUNCTION AND CAUSE OF KINSHIP WITCHCRAFT

Anthropologists have found several 'functions' for witchcraft in the kinship sphere, principally in the processes of 'fission' and 'fusion'—in other
words, in integrating or splitting lineages. On the one hand, witchcraft
may promote solidarity within a lineage group.[123] Thus we have seen how

counter-action to supposed witchcraft may draw a family together, and this consolidating effect may be increased in other ways. For instance, among the Mbugwe witchcraft beliefs promote the integration of the group by 'prohibiting witchcraft, and aggressive behaviour in general, between members of the same matrilineage', and, further, 'the belief that women are specially prone to bewitch members of sister lineages in the same clan tends clearly to separate these groups, which otherwise are not very sharply demarcated from one another'.[124] More attention, however, has been paid to witchcraft's disruptive effects. Cewa witch beliefs 'afford a means of rupturing social relations when these become too cramping or too pervasive',[125] a process which has been excellently illustrated with reference to the Kaguru[126] and the Lugbara.[127] Thus witchcraft within a lineage may be 'the mechanism by which a perfectly normal social process which preserves the form of the society is effected'.[128] But we are also warned that witchcraft accusations are a neutral weapon; they may also be used to prevent necessary fission as a reactionary and conservative force.[129] As we saw with age, the effects of accusations depend on the relative status, sex and age of the people involved.

One of the problems of interpreting the relationship between kinship tensions and witchcraft accusations is that tension in one relationship may be projected into another. For instance, witchcraft is said to be trans-formed or projected from the tension generated in the relations between agnates among the Gisu, and made a 'quasi-legitimate sanction for the rights and duties between neighbours and age-mates',[130] and Kluckhohn seeks to show that in general the Navaho relieve the tensions arising out of everyday contacts by displacing them on to distant 'witches'. Most African tribes differ from the Navaho pattern: for instance, the Gusii blame persons with whom they are in close contact, and thus witchcraft is not explicable as a 'displacement of aggression' on to foreigners.[131]

Sociological analyses by anthropologists are immensely valuable to the historian of witchcraft, for they suggest a number of questions which may be asked of the evidence. The historian can then expand the sociological approach. With a larger number of cases and, often, more detailed infor-mation on each case than the anthropologist can obtain, he can draw the maps and graphs of accusations which allow him to compare distribution of accusations both in time and space with other social phenomena.

NOTES

1. Some use has been made of the work of M. G. Marwick, especially of his earlier articles, but his comprehensive treatment of Cewa sorcery (Marwick, 1965) unfortunately became available after the text of this chapter was completed. Many

of the problems dealt with below—for instance, the age/sex/kin relationship of witch and victim—are given detailed statistical treatment on pp. 103–7 of his work.

2. Nadel (1954), p. 187.
3. Evans-Pritchard (1937), p. 112.
4. Middleton (1963), p. 263.
5. Ibid., p. 263.
6. Ibid., p. 68.
7. Ibid., p. 74.
8. Nadel (1954), p. 171.
9. Evans-Pritchard (1937), p. 112.
10. Nadel (1954), p. 171.
11. Middleton (1963), p. 217.
12. Ibid., p. 104.
13. Kluckhohn (1944), p. 35.
14. Ibid., p. 35.
15. Evans-Pritchard (1937), pp. 111–12.
16. Nadel (1954), p. 170.
17. Ibid., p. 187.
18. Middleton (1963), pp. 74, 93.
19. Kluckhohn (1944), pp. 16, 34.
20. Nadel (1954), p. 175.
21. Kluckhohn (1944), p. 59.
22. Evans-Pritchard (1939), pp. 32–3.
23. Middleton (1963), p. 74.
24. Kluckhohn (1944), p. 34.
25. Nadel (1954), p. 170.
26. Kluckhohn (1944), p. 34.
27. Middleton (1963), p. 74.
28. Ibid., p. 104.
29. Ibid., p. 263.
30. Ibid., pp. 107–8.
31. Ibid., p. 270.
32. Ibid., p. 74.
33. Ibid., p. 84.
34. Ibid., p. 202.
35. Kluckhohn (1944), p. 34.
36. Krige (1943), p. 269.
37. Nadel (1954), p. 173.
38. Kluckhohn (1944), p. 34.
39. Ibid., p. 34.
40. Ibid., pp. 59–60.
41. Ibid., pp. 39 and 59–60.
42. Middleton (1963), p. 130.
43. White (1961), p. 66.
44. Middleton (1963), p. 280.
45. Marwick (1965), p. 103.
46. Nadel (1954), p. 169.
47. Fortes (1949), p. 33.
48. Middleton (1963), p. 32.
49. Ibid., p. 215.
50. Ibid., p. 262.
51. Kluckhohn (1944), p. 34.
52. White (1961), p. 66.
53. Nadel (1954), p. 173.
54. Kluckhohn (1944), p. 60.
55. Nadel (1954), p. 177.
56. Kluckhohn (1944), p. 60.
57. Ibid., p. 34.
58. Middleton (1963), p. 215.
59. Wilson (1951), p. 308.
60. Evans-Pritchard (1937), p. 102.
61. Krige (1943), p. 264.
62. Evans-Pritchard (1951), p. 101.
63. Middleton (1963), p. 241.
64. Nadel (1952), p. 23.
65. Ibid., p. 173.
66. White (1961), p. 66.
67. Middleton (1963), p. 126.
68. Nadel (1952), pp. 22–6.
69. Krige (1943), p. 263.
70. Nadel (1952), p. 20.
71. Evans-Pritchard (1937), pp. 31–2.
72. Nadel (1954), p. 187.
73. Middleton (1963), p. 87.
74. Kluckhohn (1944), p. 60.
75. Ibid., p. 34.
76. Ibid., p. 57.
77. Ibid., p. 57.
78. Middleton (1963), p. 32.
79. Ibid., p. 247.
80. Ibid., p. 159.
81. Mayer (1954), p. 19.
82. Nadel (1952), p. 21.
83. Middleton (1963), pp. 86–7.
84. Nadel (1954), pp. 172–81.
85. Wilson (1951), p. 312.
86. Marwick (1952), p. 217.
87. Middleton (1963), p. 120.
88. Ibid., p. 204.
89. Ibid., p. 253.
90. Wilson (1951), p. 309.
91. Evans-Pritchard (1937), p. 104.
92. Middleton (1963), pp. 107–8.
93. Evans-Pritchard (1951), p. 102.
94. Wilson (1951), p. 309.
95. Middleton (1963), p. 74.

96. Marwick (1965), p. 99.
97. Krige (1943), p. 263.
98. Lienhardt (1951), p. 315.
99. Krige (1943), p. 264.
100. Wilson (1951), p. 312.
101. Middleton (1963), p. 88.
102. Krige (1943), p. 263.
103. E.g. Middleton (1963), p. 207.
104. Ibid., pp. 241–4.
105. Krige (1943), p. 263.
106. Gluckman (1963), p. 92.
107. Kluckhohn (1944), p. 60.
108. Nadel (1954), p. 187.
109. Kluckhohn (1944), p. 15.
110. Krige (1943), p. 263.
111. Ibid., p. 264.
112. Middleton (1963), p. 86.
113. Evans-Pritchard (1937), pp. 31–2.
114. Middleton (1963), p. 86.
115. Nadel (1954), p. 174.
116. Middleton (1963), p. 207.
117. Krige (1943), p. 264.
118. Kluckhohn (1944), p. 34.
119. Wilson (1951), p. 310.
120. Gluckman (1963), p. 98.
121. Middleton (1963), p. 51.
122. Kluckhohn (1944), p. 34.
123. Middleton (1963), p. 80.
124. Ibid., p. 160.
125. Marwick (1952), p. 232.
126. Middleton (1963), p. 83.
127. Ibid., p. 269.
128. Ibid., p. 19.
129. Ibid., p. 125.
130. Ibid., p. 205.
131. Ibid., p. 252.

Chapter 19

Some anthropological interpretations of witchcraft

Very broadly we may distinguish three major anthropological interpretations of witchcraft beliefs suggested in recent years. Although no investigator limits himself to any one type of analysis, we may for convenience group each approach round one book. Firstly, there was the pioneering work of Professor E. E. Evans-Pritchard, *Witchcraft, Oracles and Magic among the Azande* (1937), upon which most subsequent study has been based. This represents the 'explanation' approach. It asks how witchcraft beliefs are related to a people's system of thought, how far they form a logical and coherent structure, explaining to members of the society various unusual or unpleasant phenomena. In 1944 Clyde Kluckhohn's *Navaho Witchcraft* presented what may be termed the 'functional' approach. The investigator working on these lines asks how witchcraft is related to the personal tensions and anxieties of the individual, how such beliefs and accusations function as a release for otherwise unbearable emotions and as a form of social control. Such a set of questions naturally includes a discussion of the nature of inter-personal conflicts, and here they merge into the third type of analysis, the 'structural one'. The recent study of *Witchcraft and Sorcery in East Africa* (1963), containing essays by a number of distinguished anthropologists, represents an approach in which the primary concern is to see how witchcraft accusations mirror tensions between different groups within a society. Such approaches are complementary rather than opposed. Each has its value for the historian of witchcraft faced with the strange evidence contained in Tudor and Stuart court records.

It is necessary to stress that, because it has been shown that witchcraft beliefs serve certain functions, relieving certain tensions and explaining personal misfortune, they are not therefore necessarily either to be protected or commended. It may be that in some societies 'the euphoric effects of the witchcraft pattern . . . perhaps even outweigh the dysphoric effects at the present moment',[1] while in others such beliefs are an uneconomic solution to a man's problems, generating more tension and worry than they channel.[2] Understanding a phenomenon like witchcraft will necessarily involve the abandonment of the simpler, black-and-white, response which condemns the whole phenomenon as evil lunacy, the fabrication of diseased minds. The studies of Professor Evans-Pritchard and others have successfully shown that 'what at first sight seems no more than an absurd superstition' is 'the integrative principle of a system of thought and morals' in certain societies and has 'an important role in the social structure'.[3] But to understand all is not *necessarily* to forgive all.

I. WITCHCRAFT AS EXPLANATION

The Azande say that 'Death has always a cause, and no man dies without a reason',[4] but death is not the only misfortune which needs an explanation. Of every misfortune the Azande ask, '*Why* did it happen to a certain person at a certain time?' For instance, when an elephant and a man meet it is obvious that the natural cause of death, the 'how' of the death if one likes, was the elephant, but the Azande also seek the metaphysical cause, the 'why' or purpose of the death. Thus witchcraft as a metaphysical explanation does not exclude rational observation of the natural world. Nor does it exclude human responsibility. It is only when human skill and goodness have been utilized to the uttermost that witchcraft can be invoked as an explanation of misfortune. If one tells a lie, commits adultery, steals, deceives a prince, one cannot blame witchcraft for subsequent misfortune. The mistakes of children are blamed on their carelessness and ignorance; they cannot plead witchcraft. Witchcraft, like scientific explanations in a Western court of law, may not be invoked when it clashes with personal responsibility.[5]

Since the analysis of Azande witchcraft, this approach has been corroborated for other societies. Among the Navaho, witchcraft is able to give reasons which are satisfying in such problems as stubborn illness without medical explanation and death without visible cause.[6] Gisu beliefs in witchcraft provide an acceptable excuse for failure.[7] The Kaguru explain the difficult fact that crime often pays by ascribing the immoral persons' success to witchcraft.[8] But we may wonder why 'witchcraft' is used as an explanation in some societies and not in others.

Various suggestions have been made in answer to this problem. One reason is that witchcraft, involving a human agent, provides not only a stereotyped method of reacting to anxiety, but also allows practical activity. Action against a buffalo or a ghost is difficult, but if the buffalo is thought to have been sent by a neighbouring witch a person can seek revenge.[9] Other suggestions have been made as to why all evil events should be personified; for the typical Zande believes that 'almost every happening which is harmful to him is due to the evil disposition of someone else'.[10] One hypothesis is that chance and evil are personified by adults because in their youth 'practically everything that happens is mediated by human agents'—parents and others.[11] Another thesis is that it is in the very nature of a small primitive society to interrelate sectors of activity which we normally split; thus linking the moral (social) and physical phenomena of the world. 'Bad feeling,' we are told, 'is charged with mystical danger; virtue in itself produces order throughout the universe'; nothing happens by chance in such a society: 'natural events and the morality of social relations are involved in one another'. Professor Gluckman concludes that in small-scale, 'face-to-face' societies where 'there are few specialized relationships and these are not linked together in large-scale institutional arrangements', 'close personal relationships serve most of men's interests' and thus 'all events tend to be explained by what occurs in those relationships'.[12] Suggestive as this hypothesis is, it does not help us to see why certain small-scale societies have witchcraft beliefs and others do not.

Certain societies link misfortune and sin, while others do not: Monica Wilson asks why this should be so.[13] Each culture gives a different answer to the problem of the causation of evil. In some societies it is ascribed to the unfathomable workings of God, testing his servants as he tested Job; in others it is caused by the wrath of ancestors, kindled by the breaking of some taboo. In yet others it is the result of the working of Providence, Chance, Fate—in other words, of forces which are either random or beyond human comprehension. Finally, in Western society, scientific rationalism, the mechanistic 'laws of nature', are often cited.[14] Often there are a mixture of causes and the one selected on any occasion depends on whether the misfortune is considered deserved or not. 'Troubles' among the Gusii are caused by ancestors or witches, according to whether they are deemed just or not. Naturally, a victim is likely to consider the injury as unfair more often than an observer. It has been suggested that two sets of ideas are unlikely to be compatible with witchcraft beliefs: the idea of 'Job', that a man can suffer misfortune though righteous, and 'scientific rationalism', which teaches that everything may be interpreted as the outcome of natural, non-human, causes.[15] If we accept this, we are driven to asking why a particular society has a particular set of religious beliefs. The Azande have no powerful supreme being or ghosts to appeal to as arbiters of morals and sanctions of conduct, so they have witches.[16] But why, we may ask, do they choose to believe in witches rather than a supreme being?

This problem was studied with some care in the case of Nupe religion. Here witchcraft was first seen as a necessary concomitant of belief in a divinely, beneficently, ordered universe. The conflict between a loving, guiding God and personal misfortune, Nadel suggested, might be resolved by a belief in the Devil and witches which 'saves' belief in the general order by explaining the exceptions. Though this may be true in some societies, Nadel soon found that the hypothesis would not work for the Nupe, since they do not have such a deity; their god is unconcerned, vague. Undismayed, Nadel turned his theory on its head and suggested that precisely *because* the world around them was uncertain, lacking the emotional security which all men crave, therefore the Nupe conjure up an arch-enemy whom they may blame and witches with whom they may grapple. Malevolence is clearly defined even if beneficence is not, thus equally providing people with reactions to misfortune.[17]

We may wonder whether the 'witchcraft as explanation' approach is entirely sufficient. It has been suggested that certain peoples do not primarily see witchcraft as an explanation of misfortune. Thus, although the Lovedu do interpret misfortune in these terms, the value of witchcraft as an explanation is not great.[18] It has also been argued that a tribe like the Lubgara are not concerned with *why* things happened to a certain person —why he was struck by lightning or killed by a buffalo, for instance—but rather witchcraft is 'almost always associated with social relations of authority and power'.[19] This view represents the approach which sees the social structure, rather than belief system, as the crucial variable. Probably the two approaches can be combined. We could distinguish those societies —for instance, the Azande—who are only interested in witchcraft 'as an agent on definite occasions . . . and not as a permanent condition of individuals',[20] from those which regard certain categories of people as likely witches and pin on to them any misfortune that happens. There seems an important difference beween looking round for a witch after some disaster has happened and looking round for some disaster (not necessarily consciously) after one has discovered some witch. In the Azande-type society the major questions concern the metaphysical ideas of the people. In the second situation the major problems for the investigator are why, psychologically, people 'need' witches, and why, sociologically, some groups and some relationships are more 'witch-prone' than others. Before we move to these later approaches, however, it is worth stressing how much the analysis of witchcraft beliefs in England owes to the 'explanatory' theory. Instead of being forced, as earlier historians were, to dismiss the whole phenomenon as illogical and nonsensical, or to posit, as Margaret Murray did, the existence of an elaborate witch cult, we are able to take a middle position. We can see witchcraft beliefs as one among a set of possible theories of causation, logically consistent once the premises were accepted.

2. THE FUNCTION OF WITCHCRAFT AS A RELEASE OF TENSION

It will perhaps be simplest to discuss this complex interpretation by outlining the theories of its earliest and most thorough exponent, Clyde Kluckhohn. Work by subsequent writers will then be sketched in very briefly. If we oversimplify drastically, there are three stages in witchcraft suspicions as Kluckhohn described them for the American Navaho tribe. First, there are certain instincts and energies in mankind which seek an outlet. Secondly, there are certain checks and channels for these in each society. Thirdly, one of the most effective of these channels is a witchcraft accusation. Stated in this bald fashion, the analogies with a cork, which, kept down in one place, will bob up elsewhere, are obvious. The really crucial part of the argument as far as we are concerned is the transference from stage two to three: Why should witchcraft be chosen rather than other outlets? The Navaho are a very insecure people, subject to all the difficulties of pre-industrial living: constant, painful sickness and high mortality rates, economic insecurity, the tensions of very intimate relationships. As with all societies, Kluckhohn argues, socialization brings frustration and unconscious hostility. Such conflicts must find an outlet in conscious thought and actions, since 'free-floating' anxiety is intolerable to human beings.[21] So the internal conflicts are projected on to the outside world; such projection is defined as 'escape from repressed conflict by attributing one's own emotional drives to the external world'.[22] Those insecure and hostile in themselves believe others to be hostile towards them. But the necessity for co-operation in a pre-industrial society makes the expression of aggressive tendencies difficult. The individual finds it hard to withdraw or to find substitutes in warfare or alcohol. In this situation witchcraft beliefs occur. 'A person who unconsciously hates his fellow-men has every reason to dread them, or their possible revenge.'[23] By attributing to others the aggressive impulses which the individual himself feels, some release is obtained from guilty feelings. There are other advantages about witches. By processes of identification and projection, witchcraft beliefs provide a 'socially recognized channel for the culturally disallowed'. For instance, impulses towards incest and necrophilia are incorporated into the myth.[24] Witches are potentially, at least, controllable by the society, while the caprices of the environment are not. It is a particularly adjustive response, since it justifies the individuals' anxiety without placing any blame on him: the witch victim is guiltless.[25] The difficulties in this argument, particularly its inability to show why frustrations and anxieties common to mankind should in some societies lead to witchcraft beliefs and in others not, will be investigated shortly.

S. F. Nadel was among those to be influenced by Kluckhohn. He also, postulated that 'witchcraft beliefs are causally related to frustrations, anxieties, or other mental stresses.[26] In two early articles, M. G. Marwick further refined Kluckhohn's connexion between anxiety and witchcraft.[27] Anxiety arises from conflict, he argued, and such conflicts vary in intensity in various societies. Childrearing methods, the uncertainties of the physical environment, and the gap between ideals and practice are three of the most potent causes of anxiety. Such anxiety may also be much higher in societies in which status is 'achieved' by personal effort than in those in which it is automatically 'ascribed' on the basis of blood or wealth. Such anxiety, as Kluckhohn argued, is projected on to the external environment so that the individual really feels that he has a justifiable cause for worry.

The above approach helps us to understand why witchcraft becomes *more* intense in certain societies and at certain periods, and why certain relationships are particularly prone to such suspicions. But it cannot be used to answer the basic problem of why certain societies and not others have witchcraft beliefs. As Marwick himself points out, modern Western society has a very high 'anxiety-load' and yet witchcraft beliefs are absent. A further stage in the argument is suggested in Marwick's recent work, *Sorcery in Its Social Setting*, a book which develops and refines the earlier hypotheses. It is argued that witchcraft accusations are not merely the product of conflict, but of conflict within a tight-knit, highly personal, and 'face-to-face' society. Such a situation exists in many tribal and peasant societies today, as it did in Tudor and Stuart England. But the 'emergence of a large-scale society in which many relationships are impersonal and segmental' (presumably at some point in the seventeenth and eighteenth centuries) eliminated one of the necessary pre-conditions of such beliefs.[28] This is obviously a most suggestive hypothesis when applied to the English material.

The crucial element of 'projection' suggested in the 'function of witchcraft' hypothesis is often explicitly recognized by African tribesmen. For instance, the Azande know that those accusing others are often the haters and the real witches themselves.[29] It is also often recognized by those involved that there is a connexion between mutual suspicions of witchcraft and strained relations between people.[30] The Gisu are one people who recognize that certain relationships where there should be harmony, produce friction and hence witchcraft.[31] This is one aspect of the general problem of witchcraft and conflict. 'Witches and their accusers are individuals who ought to like each other, but in fact do not', we are told.[32] Often this is because two ideals of behaviour are in conflict—for instance, the religious system may dictate love and friendship, the economic or family situation may promote competition.

3. WITCHCRAFT AND THE SOCIAL STRUCTURE

Recent studies of witchcraft have concentrated on how witchcraft accusations are related to the whole social structure rather than individual tensions. Instead of seeing witchcraft as the result of the conflict between the individual and society, the phenomenon is analysed in terms of the relationship between various groups in society. Instead of isolating an individual witch or victim to see why he is either particularly distressed or in what ways he has offended against social norms, this approach studies the witch-victim relationship and attempts to correlate this with faults in the whole social structure. As has been shown, 'witchcraft is not just hatred, it is hatred working in some social relationships and not in others'.[33] Furthermore it has been argued that the witchcraft relationship is not a 'functional' one, in Radcliffe-Brown's use of that word, for it does not necessarily 'exist in order to meet a need of the system of social interaction'. Rather it is a 'structural' relationship: 'there is a formal congruence between the set of ideas and the social structure'.[34]

An excellent example of this structural approach is the study of Pondo and Nyakusa witchcraft beliefs by Monica Wilson.[35] She demonstrates that the differences between Pondo and Nyakusa ideas of witchcraft are directly connected with differences in their social structure. Among the Pondo, kinship-based villages lead to wide incest taboos and hence an emphasis on the sexual element in witchcraft. The Nyakusa, on the other hand, live in age-villages, where the chief problem is scrounging neighbours; Nyakusa witches are obsessive about food rather than sex. In the kinship-dominated situation tension is between mother-in-law and daughter-in-law, and witchcraft centres on this relationship, while in the age-based Nyakusa villages witchcraft occurs between village neighbours, as in Essex. Another example of this 'structural' analysis is an essay by Nadel on 'Witchcraft in Four African Societies'.[36] He relates the sex antagonism of Nupe witchcraft to the presence of economic and moral conflict. This conflict is absent among the Gwari, and so is witchcraft. The profusion of witchcraft beliefs held by the Mesakin he relates to the tension caused by a large gap between physical and social age in this tribe. Such a disparity is absent in Korongo society: so are witchcraft beliefs.

There are almost always tensions between individuals, groups, and ideals in any society. To show the presence of such tensions and to show witchcraft acting within such a context still leaves open the problem of why witchcraft accusations rather than another form of activity were chosen. A partial answer to this problem is suggested by the relationship between witchcraft and litigation. It is apparent that witchcraft accusations do not necessarily seek the same end as litigation. As we have seen, such attacks are often a means of breaking off relations, whereas litigation, ideally at least, is usually an attempt to settle a dispute. But witchcraft may also replace, or rather provide a substitute for, the law. For instance, it has been argued that Cewa quarrels within the matrilineage are not susceptible to the legal arbitration that is possible between unrelated persons. Such quarrels are therefore expressed in witchcraft accusations, which are, in a sense, an appeal to an outside arbitrator, even if this only takes the form of an amorphous public opinion.[37] In this society Marwick notes 'a dearth of witchcraft accusations in which the persons implicated could have settled their quarrel by resort to ordinary judicial proceedings'.[38] We will return to this point shortly when we discuss witchcraft as a form of social control.

Since this final chapter is not intended as a comprehensive survey of all anthropological theories of witchcraft, but merely as an introduction to some of the more notable contributions, we can end by suggesting briefly the work of three other recent writers on the subject.[39] The first is Professor Gluckman, whose two chapters devoted to witchcraft in recent general books provide a clear synthesis and elaboration of the work of Evans-Pritchard.[40] Especially interesting are the discussions, already alluded to, of the way in which evil thoughts and evil events are interlinked in small-scale societies, and the argument that witchcraft accusations are common where there are no other institutionalized outlets for conflict. Another recent approach to the problem of witchcraft has been suggested by Dr. Mary Douglas.[41] She argues that witchcraft beliefs work in the 'unstructured areas of society', and, developing this argument, that beliefs will differ in intensity, depending on the authority systems of various peoples. Another interesting suggestion on future areas for research, as well as a critique of previous theories of witchcraft and the definitional distinction between 'witchcraft' and 'sorcery', is provided by V. W. Turner.[42] He points out that witchcraft accusations cannot be understood without further analysis of the conditions of illness and death in pre-industrial societies.

Both the 'functional' and the 'structural' approaches have something to offer to the historian of English witchcraft, and he may modify them to suit his material. Examination of the historical material soon made it clear that witchcraft prosecutions could not be fully accounted for merely by seeing them as a form of explanation, competing with other explanatory systems, although this provided an invaluable start for investigations. At this point the hypotheses discussed in the two sections above became extremely helpful. They suggested the idea that witchcraft beliefs acted in areas where people were anxious, in situations where ideal and practice came into conflict. The ideas of anthropologists provided the framework within which it became possible to see accusations as being made by people who were guilty of breaking with the traditional morality and who were appealing to village opinion for support. The similarities and differences between the historical and contemporary situations are further illustrated when we turn to look at witchcraft as a mechanism of social control and as a reaction to social change.

4. WITCHCRAFT AND SOCIAL CONTROL

We can distinguish two major ways in which accusations of witchcraft may act as a form of social control: firstly, through the fear of being bewitched; secondly, through the fear of being thought a witch. A number of writers have suggested how witchcraft beliefs may act as a conservative force. Gisu children are indoctrinated that conformity is best,[43] old men are warned that their age does not permit any licence, through such beliefs. The threat of an accusation of witchcraft among the Navaho 'acts as a brake on the power and influence of ceremonial practitioners';[44] it leads to economic levelling among the Kaguru;[45] a Zande man knows that he will be hated and envied if he has any special eminence or wealth and will be either bewitched or thought a witch.[46] The fact that witchcraft can be used to preserve a group's or a society's equilibrium by keeping all disruptive elements in control,[47] and by encouraging such virtues as 'good neighbourliness' and charity, has frequently been emphasized.[48]

We are told that it is in the idiom of witchcraft that the Azande 'express moral rules which lie mostly outside criminal and civil law';[49] that witchcraft is a sanction upholding the rights of age-mates among the Gisu;[50] that the Mesakin witch is a person who cannot live up to the social values of the society, yet cannot openly rebel against them.[51] 'No man is an island' in a pre-industrial society and witchcraft accusations, combined with joint rituals, 'dramatize the destructive force of interpersonal strife'.[52] In such a society exceptional achievement, like exceptional behaviour, is a threat to all. The behaviour of the individual is necessarily the concern of the whole group. Each man's activity and status is severely demarcated and impinges on that of others. It has even been suggestively argued that the amount of wealth, health, and other 'good' in the environment is seen as 'limited'. If one individual gains a disproportionate amount it is believed to be at the expense of others. He must be using witchcraft against them.[53]

In the Essex situation, it has been suggested, witchcraft beliefs and accusations were a neutral weapon, not necessarily only at the command of conservative forces. They might not only be used to 'express moral rules . . . outside the criminal and civil law', but also to generate the energy for the creation of *new* 'moral laws'. The witch epitomized the older social sanctions, the collectivist tradition in which every man was responsible for his neighbours. While such conservative sanctions were still recognized by the very belief in witchcraft, the flow of accusations from slightly richer to slightly poorer, from slightly younger to slightly older, from men and women to preponderantly women, suggests that the effects were radical rather than conservative. The English accusations occurred during a period of great change, social, enomonic, religious, and political. We may therefore wonder what the effects of changes in these areas has been on contemporary African witchcraft beliefs.

5. 'WESTERNIZATION' AND WITCHCRAFT

It is recognized, both by anthropologists and their informants, that periods of stress are likely to increase witchcraft suspicions. For instance, the Kaguru claim that there is an increase of witchcraft at the commencement of cultivation when work is at its peak. Drought, like famine, may well lead to the hunt for a witch in the same tribe.[54] When traditional ways are violently disturbed by contact with Western ideas and techniques we may well wonder whether witchcraft beliefs will rise, both as an outlet for anxiety and as a means of controlling the disruptive new pressures. How typical, we may ask, was the Navaho case where the society was believed to be especially prone to witchcraft accusations in the period after the Fort Sumner episode when Navaho morale had been destroyed by war and captivity?[55]

Some anthropologists have argued that there has been an increase in witchcraft fears with the introduction of Western industry, education, and religion. It is in densely populated areas, conglomerations created by Western bureaucracy and industry, that accusations are most rife, and witch-smellers flourish among the Gusii.[56] The Kaguru, likewise, consider certain areas to be more witch-ridden than others, and these tend to be where rather large settlements exist *not* for common defence or co-operation, but for employment, trade, or education.[57] The Cewa, finally, are apparently unanimous in saying that the advent of Westernization has led to an increase in witchcraft fears, and they point out that those who have been most influenced by the West are often those who are most apprehensive of witchcraft.[58] Some writers, however, dispute the necessary correlation between social change and witchcraft fears. We are told that Luvale beliefs offer no evidence of such a correlation, and the author agrees with Goody that 'there is no sound means of measuring whether euphoria or malaise was greater or lesser at the beginning of the century than it is today'.[59] Until we have some detailed studies of witchcraft beliefs in

African towns we will not know for certain what are the effects of urbanization on traditional beliefs.

Despite the absence of an agreed framework, however, the speculations
of anthropologists on how social change *may* have affected witchcraft
beliefs are of crucial interest to the historian, who is concerned with just
this problem: How far do changes in the economic, religious, political, and
social structure affect beliefs? A number of conjectures have been made.
We may make a preliminary and somewhat arbitrary distinction between
new factors which may add to the 'anxiety-load', and factors which destroy
the traditional methods of dealing with such anxiety. An example of the
distinction would be a society where, on the one hand, competition for new
types of labour and frustration at the inability to attain higher standards of
living added to anxiety; on the other hand, the traditional religion is
undermined and methods of dealing with anxiety are weakened. Anxiety,
arising out of conflict between the old and the new, may arise in many
ways. One of the most common is the introduction of a cash economy, as
among the Bunyoro, which increases the power of the individual at the
expense of the group.[60] This pressure combines with the egalitarian
teaching of schools and missions to bring new stresses into marital
relationships. Thus Western ideas had early undermined the power of the
royal class and the authority of men over women in Azande society.[61] The
economic aspect of such changes among the Gisu is described as follows:
'There is greater movement and the former parochial loyalties are breaking
down. Economic improvements have caused a great differential of wealth
and the introduction of cash-crops together with increasing land-shortage
has brought fiercer competition for this vitally important source of wealth.'[62]
The description could well be fitted to sixteenth-century England.

The other major aspect of change, the undermining of traditional ritual
and religion, could also be paralleled in the English case by the Protestant
attack on the magical elements in Roman Catholicism.[63] In Africa,
Christianity undermines the old ancestor and spirit cults with their ritual
and explanatory value and does not seem always to provide an adequate
compensation.[64] Furthermore, the traditional counter-actions for dealing
with the powers of evil have been abolished. The Cewa say that witchcraft
has increased because the Europeans have forbidden the *mwabi* poison
ordeal.[65] Instead of the occasional brutal and unanimous punishment
which focused suspicion on to one person, each person now suspects his
own witch. Each man is now his own witch-finder, just as each man was
his own priest in Protestant Europe.

From speculations about modern Africa we may return for one last look
at the historical evidence. A close examination of the records for one
English county has shown that witchcraft beliefs were an important part

of village life. As William Perkins put it, 'witchcraft is a rife and common sinne in these our daies, and very many are intangled in it'.[66] Likewise Gaule attacked the multitude who 'conclude peremptorily . . . that witches not only are, but are in every place, and Parish with them'.[67] These general impressions were echoed in Essex by Samuel's remark in Gifford's *Dialogue*, that 'there is scarce any towne or village in all this shire, but there is one or two witches at the least in it'.[68] A detailed study of all offences prosecuted in the three sample villages showed that witchcraft was one of the most common offences. Some 496 Assize indictments for black witchcraft from this county, estimated to be less than a third of all the suspected acts of witchcraft, further support Gifford's testimony. Of the 426 villages in Essex, some 229 are known to have been connected with witchcraft prosecutions in one way or another. At the peak period of accusations, 13 per cent of all types of cases occurring at the Essex Assize court concerned this offence. All this was merely the surface. The occasional glimpses afforded by the witchcraft pamphlets suggest a background of complex and widely distributed beliefs about witchcraft behind the formal accusations. Cunning folk and magical counter-action against witches seem to have absorbed much of the interest and time of villagers. It may well be asked whether Essex was exceptional in this, whether the majority of the English population during this period were living in a world of witchcraft and magic, an atmosphere which has only escaped the notice of the historian because of his lack of interest. If Yorkshire in the later nineteenth century was saturated in witchcraft beliefs to such an extent that it was 'difficult to exaggerate the dimensions of that element of folklore',[69] we may wonder how far this was true in the earlier period. Some comparisons of Essex and English evidence have been made in earlier chapters. These give the impression that although Essex cases were more frequent than those from other counties, most counties suffered accusations. Fortunately, a more comprehensive assessment of evidence from all over England will shortly be available in a masterly new study.[70] When it appears, the contribution that historical research may make to the social sciences will become clearer, at least in the field of witchcraft and magic.

Witchcraft prosecutions, it has been argued, were intimately linked to every other feature of society. A sociological analysis of some of these links has been made in order to demonstrate that it is more fruitful to investigate how such an apparently strange and monstrous set of beliefs fitted into the society, rather than to isolate it and thereby make it even more extraordinary. Attempts directly to correlate prosecutions, either in time, area, or personnel, with economic, religious, medical, or social factors have only been partially successful. But the attempt has suggested, it is hoped, some new areas of inquiry for the historian, and shown that the society of the sixteenth and seventeenth centuries is as susceptible to sociological and anthropological analysis as any modern housing estate or African tribe. Certainly it has borne out Hutchinson's warning that 'As the very Nature of the Subject carries both Horror and Difficulty, polite Men and great Lovers of Ease, will turn away their Thoughts from it with Disdain'.[71]

NOTES

1. Kluckhohn (1944), p. 40.
2. Nadel (1954), pp. 205–6.
3. Evans-Pritchard (1951), p. 102.
4. Ibid., p. 111.
5. Ibid., p. 75.
6. Kluckhohn (1944), p. 48.
7. Middleton (1963), p. 216.
8. Ibid., p. 85.
9. Evans-Pritchard (1937), p. 73.
10. Ibid., p. 113.
11. Kluckhohn (1944), p. 61.
12. Gluckman (1963), pp. 93–5.
13. Wilson (1951), p. 313.
14. Gluckman (1963), p. 84.
15. For an excellent discussion of this problem see Mayer (1954), pp. 9–11.
16. Evans-Pritchard (1937), p. 110.
17. Nadel (1954), pp. 203–5.
18. Krige (1943), p. 270.
19. Middleton (1963), p. 272.
20. Evans-Pritchard (1937), p. 26.
21. Kluckhohn (1944), p. 60.
22. Ibid., p. 57.
23. Fenichel, quoted in Kluckhohn (1944), p. 57.
24. Kluckhohn (1944), pp. 56–61.
25. Ibid., p. 61.
26. Nadel (1952), p. 18.
27. Marwick (1948) and (1952).
28. Marwick (1965), pp. 295–6.
29. Evans-Pritchard (1951), p. 100.
30. Marwick (1952), p. 216.
31. Middleton (1963), pp. 202–3.
32. Mayer (1954), p. 12.
33. Gluckman (1963), p. 91.
34. Middleton (1963), p. 299.
35. Wilson (1951), *passim*.
36. Nadel (1952), *passim*.
37. Marwick (1952), p. 217.
38. Ibid., p. 133.

39. L. P. Mair, *Witchcraft* (1969,) provides a more detailed survey of current anthropological research on witchcraft.
40. Gluckman (1963), ch. 4; M. Gluckman, *Politics, Law and Ritual in Tribal Society* (Oxford, 1965), ch. 6.
41. Douglas (1966) and (1967).
42. Turner (1964), p. 315 and *passim*.
43. Middleton (1963), p. 217.
44. Kluckhohn (1944), p. 63.
45. Middleton (1963), p. 93.
46. Evans-Pritchard (1937), p. 100.
47. Kluckhohn (1944), pp. 63–4,
48. Middleton (1963), p. 52.
49. Evans-Pritchard (1937), p. 110, also p. 107.
50. Middleton (1963), p. 204.
51. Nadel (1952), p. 28.
52. Middleton (1963), p. 214.
53. George M. Foster, 'Peasant Society and the Image of Limited Good', *American Anthropologist*, 67, No. 2 (1965), 293–315.
54. Middleton (1963), pp. 90–1.
55. Kluckhohn (1944), p. 64.
56. Middleton (1963), p. 255.
57. Ibid., p. 84.
58. Marwick (1965), ch. 9 *passim*.
59. White (1961), p. 65.
60. Middleton (1963), p. 53.
61. Evans-Pritchard (1937), p. 18.
62. Middleton (1963), p. 219.
63. This subject will be dealt with in considerable detail in Mr. Keith Thomas' forthcoming work.
64. Middleton (1963), p. 219.
65. Marwick (1965), p. 92.
66. Perkins, *Damned Art*, p. 1.
67. Gaule, *Select Cases*, p. 4.
68. Gifford, *Dialogue*, sig. A4^v.
69. J. C. Atkinson, *Forty Years in a Moorland Parish* (1891), p. 74.
70. In the work of Mr. Keith Thomas, as yet unpublished.
71. Francis Hutchinson, *Historical Essay Concerning Witchcraft* (1718), p. vii.

Appendix 1

Abstracts of Essex witchcraft cases, 1560–1680

ASSIZE PROSECUTIONS

Abstracts from Assize indictments have already been printed in C. L. Ewen, *Witch Hunting and Witch Trials* (hereafter referred to as Ewen, I). To include full abstracts of the Essex Assize cases would add some 20,000 words—and provide little material that is not already available in printed form. This Appendix, therefore, merely summarizes the cases printed by Ewen; giving the date, name, and place in the original indictment. Ewen's numbering is adopted and, since he included cases from four other counties in the Home Circuit omitted here, this will explain the gaps in the numbers. Any additional material, as well as slight corrections to Ewen's transcripts (which corrections are in italics) are given in the right-hand column. The corrections are not extensive and only ten new suspected witches are added to Ewen's list. Such added cases are given sub-numbers.

The indictments come from the records of the Clerks of Assize for the South-Eastern Circuit, which are deposited at the Public Record Office (Assizes 35). In order to economize on space, references have only been given by date. Thus, for example, a new indictment, number 403*b*, is merely given the reference of the date 1595T. 'T' indicates Trinity Assize, 'H' the Hilary or Lent Sessions. To order this document, therefore, the files for the thirty-seventh year of Elizabeth (i.e. 1595) would have to be ordered at the Public Record Office. The boxes are numbered by regnal years, so this would be box 37. Within the box would be the file for the Essex Trinity Assizes. Thus the full location would be Assizes 35, box 37, file 2.

References to imprisoned witches in the gaol calendars or gaol delivery rolls (abbreviated as g.c. or g.d.r.) have been given in the right-hand column only when they add something new and previously unknown. Deaths by 'divine visitation', termed 'plague' in the Appendix, as recorded in the coroners' inquests, are included with their full P.R.O. reference. Also, a petition for the pardon of nine of those found guilty at the Assizes in 1645, made to the House of Lords in March 1646 (House of Lords *Main Papers*, 10 March 1645/6, fol. 136) is noted in the appendix as 'Lords pardon, March 1646'. Throughout the Appendix 'f.' is used for folio, 'm.' for membrane.

Names of the accused have been left in the original spelling, with Christian names modernized or abbreviated; for example, Jn. is employed for John and Eliz. for Elizabeth. The names of villages have been modernized. 'Samon/Smythe' or 'Salmon, also Smythe' denotes a pseudonym.

For the overlapping of cases between different courts, and between different years at the same court, see Map 1 and the Place Name Index. In that map all prosecutions, from whatever source, are grouped under villages. Prosecutions against a single individual are linked. Thus, if one wished to discover whether any further accusations had been made against a person listed in this Appendix, it would be best to look under the village name in Map 1 and the Place Name Index. This would give all other cases concerning that individual. In the few cases where the village of the accused is unknown this is denoted by a '—' sign. If the indictment does not state the village, but it can be added from other sources, this is shown by bracketing the name of the village.

CASES

No.	Date	Name of accused	Village	Additions/corrections to Ewen, I
1	1560T	Jn. Samond/Smythe	Danbury	
2	„	Joan Haddon	Witham	
2b	1561H	Jn. Samon/Smythe	Danbury	cf. Ewen, II, p. 46 (also a a writ.)
3	1564T	Eliz. Lowys	Great Waltham	John Wodley, *aged three months*
4	„	„	Great Waltham	
5	„	„	„	for yeoman read labourer
6	1564T	Wm. Rande	Great Totham	cow *languished until 17 January* died of plague, 30 Oct. 1564; K.B. 9 610 m. 244
8	1565H	Anne Vale	White Roding	Jn. Berde, *husbandman;* pigs died 28 Oct.
16	1566T	Lora Wynchester	Hatfield Peverel	
17	„	Eliz. Fraunces	Hatfield Peverel	remanded in g.c., H and T 1567
18	„	Agnes Waterhowse	„	
19	„	Joan Waterhouse	„	
20	1567H	Alice Prestmarye	Great Dunmow	died of plague, 7 May 1567; K.B. 9 619 m.102
21	„	Joan Cocke	Kelvedon	
22	„	Joan Osborne	Hatfield Peverel	
23	1567T	Alice Atrum	Great Coggeshall	
29	1570H	Alice Swallow	Little Baddow	Ewen, I, 29–33, wrongly dated
30	„	„	„	
31	„	„	„	
32	„	„	„	
33	1570H	Alice Bambricke	Little Baddow	
42	1571H	Eliz. Egles	Fifield	

No.	Date	Name of accused	Village	Additions/corrections to Ewen, I
45	1572H	Wm. Skelton	Little Wakering	
46	,,	Margery Skelton	,,	
47	,,	Wm. and Margery Skelton	,,	
48	,,	,,	,,	
49	,,	Katherine Pullen	Tollesbury	
50	,,	Eliz. Francis	Hatfield Peverel	remanded in g.c., H and T 1573
55	1572T	Jn. Smythe/Salmon	Danbury	'guilty' added above 'not guilty'
56	,,	,, and Joan	,,	
57	,,	Joan Smyth	,,	
58	,,	Agnes Francys	Hatfield Peverel	remanded in g.c., 1573H and T; died of plague, 10 Dec. 1573; K.B. 9 636 m.239
59	,,	,,	,,	
60	,,	,,	,,	
61	,,	,,	,,	
62	,,	Agnes Steadman	Halstead	remanded in g.c., H and T 1573
63	,,	,,	,,	
64	,,	,,	,,	
64*b*	1573T	Robt. Wallys a tailor	Chishall	on 20 June, at Rochford and elsewhere, falsely pretended that he could obtain treasure by invocation of evil spirits; not guilty, but guilty of vagabondage
67	1574H	Alice Chaundeler	Maldon	
68	,,	,,	,,	
69	,,	,,	,,	
70	,,	Joan Stubbinge	Ridgewell	
71	,,	,,	,,	
75	1574T	Cecilia Glasenbery (also Arnold/Whitcote)	Barking	
76	,,	,,	,,	
77	,,	,,	,,	
78	,,	,,	,,	
79	,,	,,	,,	
80	,,	Eliz. Taylor	Thaxted	
81	,,	,,	,,	
82	1574T	Alice Hynckson	Thaxted	remanded in g.c., 1575H; died of plague, 4 May 1575; K.B. 9 640 m.305
83	1574T	Agnes Dix	Belchamp Walter	

No.	Date	Name of accused	Village	Additions/corrections to Ewen, I
84	1574T	Agnes Dix	Belchamp Walter	
95	1576H	Margery Pavett	High Roothing	
96	,,	,,	,,	
97	,,	Agnes Bromley	Hatfield Peverel	remanded in g.c., 1576T
98	,,	,,	,,	
99	,,	,,	,,	
100	,,	Margt. Saunder	Rainham	
101	1576T	Margery Spencer	Halstead	
102	,,	,,	,,	
103	,,	Joan Baker/Johnson	Brentwood	
104	,,	,, and Eliz. Aylett	,,	
105	,,	,, ,,	,,	
106	,,	Agnes Berden	Elsenham	
107	1577H	Robert Chambers	West Ham	Robert Chambers, *yeoman*
108	,,	Agnes Sawen	Stock	
108*b*	,,	,,	,,	Inquisition, same as indictment, 25 jurors.
108*c*	1578H	Cecily Turner (spinster)	Roydon	On 1 July at Roydon bewitched Robt. Hill, whereby he languished until 4 Feb. 1578, when he died; true bill; not guilty
108*d*	,,	Thos. Barker	Hockley	On 1 July 1577 invoked an evil spirit at Hockley with the intention of gaining large sums of money, and Jn. Foxe of the same was present; true bill; not guilty; labourers
108*e*	,,	,,	,,	memorandum: that Thos. Barker of Gestingthorpe, surgeon, should appear at next court; meanwhile to conjure no spirits
108*f*	,,	Margt. Ganzey or Harvey	(Borley)	recognizance that Thos. Shave, husbandman, Jn. Taps, wheelright, and Joan his wife and John Semer, labourer, all of Elsenham, give evidence against aforesaid Margt. a witch
114	1578T	Joan Prestmary	Great Dunmow	
115	1578T	Jane Buxtone	Stratford Langthorne	
115*b*	,,	,,	,,	recognizance printed in E 1, pp. 56–7

No.	Date	Name of accused	Village	Additions/corrections to Ewen, I
115c	1578T	Joan Norfolk	Borley	recognizance that Jn. Bragge, Wm. Fyrmyn, Wm. Blackewell, Nicholas Norfocke of Borley, husbandmen, and Alice Fyrmyn and Alice Byrde of same, widows, give evidence *re* witchcraft of said Joan
115d	,,	Joan Prestmary	Great Dunmow	recognizance that Nicholas Whale, husbandman, and Wm. Long, yeoman, of Great Dunmow, see to appearance of said Joan, imprisoned in Colchester Gaol for suspicion of witchcraft
118	1579H	Margt. Rogers	Stratford Langthorne	
119	,,	Ellen Smythe	Maldon	
120	1579H	Alice Nokes	Lamborne	
121	,,	Margt. Ganne/Welles and Joan Norfolke	Borley	
122	,,	Margery Stanton	Wimbish	
123	,,	Eliz. Fraunces	Hatfield Peverel	
125	1579T	Richard and Joan Prestmary	Great Dunmow	
126	,,	Eliz. Hardinge	Barking	
127	,,	,,	,,	on 1 Nov., 20 Eliz.
128	,,	,,	,,	
129	,,	Joan Norfolke	Borley	
130	,,	,,	,,	
131	,,	Margt. Welles/Gan	,,	
133	1580H	Jn. Symonde	Shenfield	
134	,,	,,	,,	
135	,,	,,		
136	,,	Agnes Mylles	Dedham	for Perpoyne read Perpoynt
137	1580H	Eliz. Hardynge	Barking	still in prison
141	1580T	Rose Pye	Canewdon	Richard Snow, *tailor*
142	,,	Joan Dowtie	Brightlingsea	
143	1581H	Joan Turner	Stisted	
144	,,	,,	,,	
145	,,	,,	,,	
146	1581T	Alice Mylles	Brightlingsea (cf. Dedham)	
147	,,	,,	,,	on 8 March 23 Eliz.
148	,,	,,	,,	

No.	Date	Name of accused	Village	Additions/corrections to Ewen, I
149	1581T	Margt. Rogers	Stratford Langthorne	
150	,,	Benneta Buxton	,,	
155	1582H	Agnes Glascock	St. Osyth	
156	,,	,,	,,	
157	,,	,,	,,	
158	,,	Margt. Grevell	Thorpe-le-Soken	
159	,,	Cecilia Celles	Little Clacton	remanded in g.c., 1582T
160	,,	Ursula Kemp/Grey and Alice Newman	St. Osyth	Alice Newman remanded in gaol; 1582T, 1584T, 1585T, 1586H, 1586T, 1587H, 1587T, 1588H.
161	,,	,,	,,	
162	,,	,,	,,	
163	,,	Alice Hunt	,,	in g.c., 1582T
164	,,	,,	,,	
165	,,	Eliz. Bennett	,,	wife of John, *husbandman*
166	,,	Cecilia Celles and Alice Manfield	Clacton Thorpe-le-Soken	
167	,,	Agnes Heard	Little Okely	
168	,,	Eliz. Ewstace		
169	,,	Joan Pechye		in g.c., 1582T
171	1582T	Agnes Bryant	Great Burstead	
172	1582T	,,	,,	
173	,,	,,	,,	
174	,,	Anne Swallowc or Eswell	St. Osyth	
189	1583T	Margt. Hogden	Stebbing	
190	,,	,,	,,	
191	,,	,,	,,	
192	,,	Anne Smythe	—	in g.c. 1584 H and T; pardoned in g.d.r. 1585H
193	1584H	Joan Thatcher/Dyxe	Lawford	died of plague, 11 June 1584; K.B. 9 660 m.267
194	,,	,,	,,	
195	,,	,,	,,	
196	1584H	Margery Barnes	St. Osyth	
197	,,	Agnes Byllynge	North Ockendon	
198	,,	,,	,,	
199	,,	,,	,,	
200	,,	Eliz. Brooke	Great Leighs	
201	,,	,,	,,	
202	,,	Joan Dale and Margery Barnes	St. Osyth	

No.	Date	Name of accused	Village	Additions/corrections to Ewen, I
203	1584H	Agnes Duke	Hatfield Peverel	died of plague, 12 Jan. 1590; K.B. 9 676 m.232; in g.c., 1590H. died on 23 Feb.
204	,,	Lucy Fyssher	Feering	
205	,,	,,	,,	
206	,,	,,	,,	
207	,,	,,	,,	
208	,,	Joan Cocke	Hatfield Peverel (cf. Kelvedon)	
209	,,	,,	,,	
210	,,	Thos. Kynge	South Hanningfield	
211	,,	,,	,,	
212	1584T	Joan Colson	East Mersea	on 12 Jan., 23 Eliz.; remanded in g.c., 1585T
213	,,	,,	,,	
214	,,	Joan Thorock	Burnham	
215–19	,,	,,	,,	
220	,,	Margt. Lyttelberie	Bradwell-on-sea	remanded in g.c., 1585 H and T
221	,,	,,	,,	languished until 7 June
222	,,	Eliz. Morrisbee or Morsby	Great Chesterford	
223	,,	,,	,,	
224	,,	Edmund Mansell	Fingeringhoe and Feering	
225	,,	,,		
226	,,	Alice Bolton and Eliz. Lumney	St. Osyth	remanded in g.c., 1585H, delivered 1585T; Lumney not guilty
227	,,	,,	,,	
228	1585H	Lettice Tybbold	Maplestead	
229	1585H	,,	,,	
230	,,	,,	,,	
231	,,	Alice Dragge	Finchingfield	
232	,,	Agnes Thurrock	Burnham	
233	,,	,,	,,	
233b	1585T	Anne Bonner	—	g.d., 1585T: guilty of witchcraft and judged according to form of Statute; died of plague, 27 Aug. 1585; K.B. 9 665 m.223
237	1586H	Anne Joyce	Stanford Rivers	discharged in g.c., 1586T
238	,,	,,	,,	
239	,,	,,	,,	

No.	Date	Name of accused	Village	Additions/corrections to Ewen, I
239*b*	1586H	Elizabeth Barwick	—	cf. case 815: remanded in g.c., 1583T to 1587H, when she is noted as dead; died of plague, 12 Jan. 1587; K.B. 9 668 m.272
241	1587H	Jn. Smythe/Salmon	Danbury	
242	”	Joan & Frances Preston	Little Sampford	remanded in g.c., 1587T (Frances)
243	1587H	Joan Preston	”	remanded in g.c., 1587T
244	”	”	”	
245	1587H	Rose Clarens	Great Sampford	remanded in g.c., 1587T
246	”	”	”	
247	”	Jn. Smythe/Salmon	Danbury	8 cows worth £21, 6 calves worth 40s, 3 pigs worth 30s, 7 ewes worth 40s.
250	1587T	Jn. Smythe/Salmon	”	
251	”	Joan Gibson	Messing	
252	”	Alice Bust	Alphamstone	
253	1587T	Jn. Smythe	Danbury	
253*b*	”	”	”	inquisition, for same offence as 253
261	1588H	Eliz. Harris	Witham	
262	”	”	”	
263	”	Margt. Harrison	Hawkwell	
264–6	”	”	”	
267	1588H	Wm. Bennet and Edward Mason	Finchingfield Bardfield	both Bennet and Mason were acquitted in g.c., 1588T
268	”	” (Bennet)	Finchingfield	
269	1588T	Joan Pakeman	Great Oakley	
270	”	Katherine Harrys & Agnes Smythe/Lawsell	Sible Hedingham	
271	”	”	”	
272	1589H	John Heare/Jenny and Agnes Duke	Hatfield Peverel	
279	1589T	Joan Prentice	Sible Hedingham	
280	”	Richard and Agnes	Waltham Holy Cross	
281	”	Dunne	”	bewitched Henry Ladd
282	”	”	”	
283	”	Ellen Bett	Great Waltham	Margery *Baulderson;* remanded in g.c., from 1590H to 1591H
284	”	”	”	
285	”	Margt. Cony	Stisted	lost the sight in *one* eye; remanded in g.c., 1590T

No.	Date	Name of accused	Village	Additions/correctionss to Ewen, I
286	1589T	Margt. Cony and Avice	Stisted	Avice remanded in g.c., 1590T and 1590H
287	„	Avice „	„	
288	„	Joan „	„	
289–91	„	„ „	„	
292	„	Joan Dering	Theydon Garnon	
293–4	„	„	„	
295	„	Margt. Newman	Great Bentley	
296	„	Joan Uptney	Dagenham	
297	„	„	„	
299	1590H	Anne Crabbe	Colne Engaine	remanded in g.c., 1590T, 1591H and 1594H
300	„	Joan and Agnes Mose	Loughton	Agnes died of plague,19 Feb., 1590; K.B. 9 67 6 m.229
301	„	Alice Aylett	Braintree	remanded in g.c., 1590T and 1591H
302–5	„	„	„	
306	1590H	Agnes Whitland	Dagenham	remanded in g.c., 1592T
307	„	Alice Adcock	—	remanded in g.c., 1590T
308	1590T	Margt. Snell	Thaxted	
320	1591T	Ellen Graye	Dagenham	
321–4	„	„	„	
325	„	Margt. Rooman	Bocking	reprieved in g.c., 1592H. Thos. Olmesteede
326	„	Alice Crake	Finchingfield	
327	„	Agnes Whitland	Dagenham	
328–9	„	„	„	
330	„	Juliana Cocke	Ashdon	in g.c., 1592T; died of plague, 13 Apr. 1592; K.B. 9 683 m.154
335	1592H	Agnes Hales	Stebbing	in g.c., 1592T: died of plague, 19 June 1592; K.B. 9 683 m.153
336	„	„	„	
337	„	Margery Dickes	Bradfield	
338–9	„	also Thatcher	„	
340	„	Margt. Hogden	Witham	
341	„	Elizabeth Boxer	Aveley	
342–3	„	„	„	
344	1592T	Anne Scott	Great Dunmow	
345	„	Audrea Mathewe	„	remanded in g.c., 1593T
346	„	Agnes Draper	„	remanded in g.c., 1593T; Alice *Handley*, who lost the use of the *upper part of her body*

No.	Date	Name of accused	Village	Additions/corrections to Ewen, I
347	1592T	Jane Wallys	Stebbing	
348	„	„	„	
353	1593H	Alice Alberte	Felsted	remanded in g.c., 1593T and 1594H (dead)
354	„	Eliz. Esterford	Sible Hedingham	remanded in g.c., 1593T and 1594H
357	1593T	Agnes Haven	Boreham	
358	„	„	„	on 1 Dec., 30 Eliz.
359	„	Eliz. Easterford	Sible Hedingham	
360–1	„	„	„	
362	„	Margt. Saunder	„	
363	„	Margt. Mynnet	Woodham Ferrers	
364–6	„	„	„	
367	„	Eliz. Packman	Great Clacton	
387	1594H	Agnes Bett	Saffron Walden	
388	„	„	„	
389	1594H	Eliz. and Joan Garrett	Gosfield „	Joan remanded in g.c., 1595H
390	„	„	„	
391	„	Stephen Hugrave	Abberton	
392	„	„ and Alice	„	
392b	„	„ „	„	On 1 Apr. 1593 at Abberton bewitched four hogs worth 26s. 8d. and eight pigs worth 20s., belonging to Thos. Clarke senior, so that they died; true bill; not guilty.
393	„	Mary Belsted or Muldleton	Boreham	remanded in g.c., 1595H
394	„	Anne Harrison	Thorpe-le-Soken	remanded in g.c., 1595H (dead)
395	„	„	„	
396	1594T	Audrea Mathewe	Great Dunmow	
397	„	„	„	
398	„	Bridget Hayle	Thorpe-le-Soken	remanded in g.c., 1595H
399	„	„ and Eliz	„	
400	„	Anne Hervey	Manningtree	
401–2	„	„	„	
403	1595H	Jn. and Grace Trower	Ingrave	
403b	1595T	Rose More wife of James	Coggeshall	On 30 Nov. 1594, at Coggeshall, bewitched Jeremy W[arner] aged three

No.	Date	Name of accused	Village	Additions/correctionss to Ewen, I
				months, who languished until 3 March, following when he died; true bill; not guilty
403*c*	1595T	Margt. Childe	Great Horkesley	(badly torn) . . . a witch . . . oxen worth 30*s*.; true bill; guilty; judged
403*d*	,,	,,	,,	(badly torn) . . . June, Eliz. . . .; true bill; guilty; judged
410	1596T	Agnes Smithe	Stebbing	
416	1597H	Alice Warren	Brentwood	died of plague, 7 Aug. 1598; K.B. 9 696 m.7
416*b*	1597H	Joan Fysher spinster, wife of Christopher Fysher, labourer	Halstead	On 23 Sept. 1595 bewitched Joan Lewes, who languished until 14 Oct. following when she died; true bill; guilty; to be hanged
417	1598H	Robt. Browning	Aldham	died of plague, 20 Feb. 1599; K.B. 9 698 m.335
421	1600H	Isabella Whyte	Purleigh	
422	,,	,,	,,	
424	1600T	Rose Chapman	Belchamp Walter	in g.c., 1602H
424*b*	,,	,,	,,	recognizance of Wm. Payne of Belchamp, labourer, to give evidence against Chapman
424*c*	,,	,,	,,	recognizance of Edward Coe, of Belchamp, gent., to give evidence against Chapman, charged by Ellen, wife of Peter Cranfield of the same, with having caused the death of John Payne
424*d*	,,	,,	,,	recognizance of same Edward Coe against the same Chapman, charged by Maryan, wife of the same Edward, with causing death of Payne
429	1601T	Ursula Harvy	Ramsey	
430	,,	,,	,,	
431	,,	Anne Harris	Feeringe	
432	,,	,,	,,	until 10 July
433	,,	,,	,,	
434	,,	Helen Alyer/Ayleard	Black Notley	
435	,,	,,	,,	

No.	Date	Name of accused	Village	Additions/corrections to Ewen, I
436	1601T	Clemence Vale/Fall	Feering	
437	,,	Lucy Eltheridge	Thorpe-le-Soken	
438–9	,,	,,	,,	
440	,,	Magdalen Purcas	Panfield	
445	1602H	Anne Hyble	Shalford	
446	,,	Anne Wyrght	Hatfield Broad Oak	
447	1602T	Eliz. Pegge	Braintree	died of plague, 12 Aug. 1603; K.B. 9 712 m.178
448–9	,,	,,	,,	
450	1602T	Audrey Pond	Old Saling	
451	,,	,,	,,	
456	1603T	Margery Wilson	Black Notley	
457–8	,,	,,	,,	
459	,,	Jn. Banckes	Newport (Pond)	until 17 Feb.
460	,,	Joan Roath/Worth	Great Bentley	
461	,,	,,	,,	
462	,,	Anne Horne	Halstead	
481	1607H	Blanche Worman	Moulsham	
482–6	,,	,,	,,	
487	,,	Anne Harvye	Coggeshall	
488	1607T	Edwin Haddesley	Willingale Doe	
489	,,	,,	,,	
492	1609T	Anne Feilde	—	
493	,,	Mary Wade	Pattiswick	remanded in g.c., 1610H
494	,,	,,	,,	
495–6	,,	,,	,,	
497	,,	Alice Buske/Bust	Alphamstone	
498	1610H	Anne Prentice	Bocking	
499	,,	Katherine Lawrett	Wakes Colne	
500	,,	,,	,,	
501–2	,,	Anne Pennyfather	Little Totham	
503	,,	Lucy Buttler	Halstead	wife of *Thos. Buttler*
504	,,	,,	,,	
505	,,	Winifred Stowers	Halstead	
507	1610T	Alice Pitches	Stisted	
510	1612H	Richard and Ann	North Ockendon	
511	,,	John	,,	
514	1612T	Alice Batty	Toppesfield	
515–16	,,	,,	,,	
518	1613H	Robt. Parker	,,	
519	,,	,, and Jn. Cornell	,, Borley	
520	,,	,, ,, (both)	,,	

No.	Date	Name of accused	Village	*Additions/corrections to* Ewen, I
525	1615H	Grace Tabour	Stow Maries	
528	1616H	Blanche Prisley	Navestock	
529	"	Anne "	"	
530	"	Katherine "	"	
532	1616T	Jn Godfrie	Lambourne	
533	"	Sarah Godfrie	"	
534–6	"	"	"	
537	"	Margt. Lambe	South Ockendon	
538	"	Susan Barker	Upminster	
539–41	"	"	"	
545	1618H	Mary Holt	Little Leighs	
546	"	"	"	
552	1619H	Anne Byford	—	
553	1620H	Margt. Greene	Foulness	
553*b*	"	Gilbert Wakering surgeon	Halstead	on 3 Feb. and other days persuaded people that he could tell them who had stolen goods from them. On 3 Feb. he took 5s. from Richard Billingham of Bocking, fuller, to tell him name of the person who had stolen 20 yards of bays, worth 40s., from him, but Gilbert never told him the name. Witnesses: Richard Billingham, Francis Cornishe, Wm. Dodd; true bill; acquitted.
554	1621H	Eliz. Parnsbye	Rickling	
555	"	Anne Hewghes	Great Leighs	
556	"	"	"	
557–8	"	"	"	
559	1626H	Helen Pedder	South Halstead	
560–1	"	"	"	
561*b*	"	Anne Wilson	—	in g.c., committed by Richard Franck for witchcraft; prisoner dies in gaol
563	1626T	Dennis Nash	Springfield	
564	"	Joan Freeman	Harlow	
565	"	Dorothy Hills	Wethersfield	until 10 May following
566	"	"	"	
567	"	Katherine Kinge and Anne West	Shalford	
568	"	" "	"	2 Charles I

No.	Date	Name of accused	Village	Additions/corrections to Ewen, I
569	1627T	Barbara Augur or Bright	Upminster	
570–1	,,	,,	,,	
572	1628H	Anne Freeman	—	
573	1630T	Dionisia Josselyn	Great Canfield	
576	1631H	,,	,,	
576b	1631H	Parnell Smyth	—	in g.c., committed by Tho. Barrington for suspicion of witchcraft
580	1634H	Jane Prentice or Hanby	Harwich	
580b	,,	Anne Poulter	,,	sent from Harwich by a writ directed to the High Sheriff upon suspicion of witchcraft
580c	,,	Jane Wiggins	,,	,, ,, ,, ,,
580d	1634T	Jane Seabrooke	—	in g.c. and g.d.r.; committed by John Wakering for witchcraft, delivered by proclamation
585	1636T	Parnella Boutwood	Braintree	on 11 Jan., 11 Charles I
586	1638T	Susan Prentice	Harwich	
587	,,	Elinor Witherill	—	
588	,,	Jane Prentice	Harwich	
589	,,	,,	,,	
590	,,	Anne Cade	Great Holland	
593	1639T	Anne Lamperill	—	
594	,,	Robt. Garnett	—	
595	1641H	Anne West	Lawford	in g.c., 1642T, delivered by proclamation.
597	1642H	Anne Wace	—	
598	1642T	Mary Webb	Hatfield Broad Oak	
598b	1644T	Dorothy Ilford	—	printed in Ewen, II, p. 430; committed to Colchester Gaol suspected of witchcraft
599	1645T	Helen Bretton	Kirby-le-Soken	
600	,,	Margery Grew	Walton-le-Soken	John Munt, *husbandman*
601	,,	,,	,,	
602	,,	Anne Leach	Mistley	
603	,,	Eliz. Clarke	Manningtree	
604	,,	,,	,,	
605	,,	Rebecca Jonas	St. Osyth	
606	,,	,,	,,	
607	,,	Rebecca West	Lawford	
608	,,	Anne West	,,	

No.	Date	Name of accused	Village	Additions/corrections to Ewen, I
609	1645T	Anne West	Lawford	
610	"	Margt. Moone	Thorpe-le-Soken	
611–12	"	"	"	
613	"	Mary Sterling	Langham	Lords' pardon, March 1646; in g.c., 1647T and 1648H—to remain in gaol
614	"	"	"	Robert Potter, yeoman, *junior*
615	"	Anne Cate/Cade	Great Holland	
616	"	or Maidenhead	"	
617	"	Alice Dixon	Wivenhoe	
618	"	Mary Johnson	"	Lords' pardon, March 1646; in g.c., 1647T and 1648H—to remain in gaol
619	"	"	"	
620	"	"	"	Daniel Occlam, *seaman*
621	"	Joan Rowle	Leigh	
622–3	"	"	"	
624	"	Mary Coppin	Kirby-le-Soken	Lords' pardon, March 1646; in g.c., 1647T and 1648H—to remain in gaol
625	"	Ellen Clarke	Manningtree	
626	"	Sarah Bright	"	
627	"	Eliz. Goodwyn	"	
628	"	"	"	
629	"	Dorothy Waters	Great Clacton	Lords' pardon, March 1646; died of plague (aged forty), 24 Feb. 1646; K.B. 9 838 m.380
630	"	Eliz. Heare	"	
631	1645T	Mary Wiles	Great Clacton	
632–3	"	"	"	
634	"	Anne Cooper	"	
635–6	"	"	"	
637	"	Anne Therston	Great Holland	Lords' pardon, March 1646; in g.c., 1647T and 1648H—to remain in gaol
638	"	"	"	
639	"	Susan Cocke	St. Osyth	Lords' pardon, March 1646; died of plague (aged about fifty), 18 Oct. 1646; K.B. 9 838 m.376
640	"	Joyce Boones	"	
641	"	Margt. Landish	St. Osyth	
642	"	Sarah Hatyn/Hating	Ramsey	
643–4	"	"	"	

No.	Date	Name of accused	Village	Additions/corrections to Ewen, I
645	1645T	Eliz. Harvy	Ramsey	Lords' pardon, March 1646; died of plague (aged seventy) 30 Aug. 1645; K.B. 9 838 m.382
646	„	Mary Hockett	„	
647	„	Bridget Mayers	Great Holland	Lords' pardon, March 1646; in g.c., 1647T and 1648H—to remain in gaol
648	„	Susanna Went	Langham	Lords' pardon, March 1646; died of plague (aged seventy) 4 Apr. 1646; K.B. 9 838 m.381
648*b*	„	Mary Greencliffe	(Alresford)	Ewen, I, p. 222 and Appendix 1; died of plague (widow—aged about 84), 15 Aug. 1645; K.B. 9 838 m.377
648*c*	„	Rose Hallybread	St. Osyth	Ewen, I, p. 222
648*d*	„	Eliz. Gibson	Thorpe-le-Soken	Ewen, I, p. 222
648*e*	„	Joan Cooper	Great Clacton	Ewen, I, pp. 222–3
648*f*	„	Mary Cooke	Langham	Ewen, I, pp. 222–3
648*g*	„	Dorothy Brooke	—	Ewen, I, p. 222 and Appendix I; in g.c., 1647T and 1648H—to remain in gaol
649	1647H	Nicholas Leech	Manningtree	
650	„	Helen Disse	Ridgewell	
657	1647T	Jane Lavender	Navestock	
658	„	„	„	
659	1647T	Francis Lavender	Navestock	
660–1	„	„	„	
661*b*	1647T	Anne Clarke wife of Stephen, labourer	Waltham Cross	On 1 March 1647 there bewitched Philip Blott, whereby he was wasted and consumed. Witnesses: Thos Foreman, Henry Blott, Francis Burges, Edith Legge, Susan Killhogge, Anne Sherborne; true bill; not guilty. g.d.r., 1647T—to be delivered on payment of her fees
667	1649T	Ruth Stephens	—	
674	1650T	Eliz. Balden	Knebsworth	
675	„	Mary Welby	Newport (Pond)	
676	1650T	Eliz. Whitelocke	Great Chesterford	

No.	Date	Name of accused	Village	Additions/corrections to Ewen, I
677	1650T	Deborah Naylor	Elsenham	
679	1651H	Joan Wayte	Barnston	
680	"	"	"	
683	1652T	Eliz. Hynes	Thorpe-le-Soken	
702	1653H	Susan Haveringe	West Tilbury	
703	"	"	"	
704	"	Eliz. Wyndell	"	
711	1653T	Benjamyn Brand	(Stebbing)	
712	"	Mary Hurst	Nevendon	
712b	1653T	Mary Aylett wife of Richard, labourer	Bocking	On 10 Feb. 1653 bewitched Rich. Balls so that his body wasted away. Witnesses: Richard and Eliz. Balls. no true bill
713	1654T	Anne Clark	Waltham Holy Cross	
714	"	"	"	
721	1655H	"	"	
722	"	"	"	
726	1657H	Mary Symons	Great Totham	
736	1659T	Wm. Bones and Abraham Bones and Mary Warner	Finchingfield	
737	1659T	Alice Warner	—	
738	"	Anne Woolward	Chelmsford	
742	1660T	Eliz. Huntsman	—	
743	"	Bridget Weaver	Harwich	
745	1662H	Anne Silvester	Orsett	
746	"	"	"	
747	1663H	......lley	—	
748	1663H	Sarah Houghton	—	
748b	1663H	" spinster	Stambourne	On 19 Dec. .... (torn) and 14th at Ridgewell bewitched ... 30th year and by these 'consumed and made infirme' John Smyth who pined from 29th Dec. 1662; true bill. (*in another hand*, 'jury': Robt. Smyth, Mathew Butcher, Jn. Levett, Daniel Poulter, (*blank*) Nelson; guilty; to be hanged; reprieved after judgement
753	1664T	Robt. Copping	Woodham Ferrers	

No.	Date	Name of accused	Village	Additions/corrections to Ewen, I
754	1666H	Martha Driver/Chalk	Barking	
754*b*	1666H	Anne Betts spinster	Stapleford Tawney	Being a person of ill-fame, on 25 Jan. 1666, on pretence of telling the fortune of Mary Prescott, fraudulently obtained from her two silk scarves worth 20s. and 8s. in money. Witness: Mary Prescott. In Colchester Gaol
759	1670T	Margt. Leech	Bradfield	in g.d.r., 1670T—to be sent to the House of Correction for three months
760	,,	Sarah Ladbrooke	,,	,, ,, ,, ,,
761	,,	,, and John Wood	,,	,, ,, ,, ,,
762	,,	,,	,,	,, ,, ,, ,,
763	,,	Joan Crumpe	Weley	,, ,, ,, ,,
767	1675H	Eliz. Gynn	Great Dunmow	

QUARTER SESSIONS PRESENTMENTS

The records of the Essex Quarter Sessions are deposited in the Essex Record Office at Chelmsford; their nature is described in the bibliography. The abbreviations used in the following abstracts of cases are similar to those used and explained in the previous section. When the name of a village is not given in the records, yet we know the location of the case from other sources (as in the first case, number 791) brackets are employed. The date under 'Date/Source' is that of the meeting of the court, *not* that of the prosecution. Only three of the seventy-four cases have been discovered printed elsewhere. The *Hist. MSS. Commission 10th Report*, Appendix, Part IV (1885), pp. 473, 476, 511, printed extracts from cases 795, 809, 845.

No.	Date/Source	Name	Village	Offence
791	March 1565 Q/SR 13/15	Eliz. Lowes	(Great Waltham)	cf. case 3; tried and found not pregnant; indicted
792	March 1566 Q/SR 18/41	Agnes Duke	(Hatfield Peverel)	cf. case 203; guilty; no goods; pregnant
	,,	Robt. Wallys		cf. case 799; guilty, no goods, claims benefit of clergy
793	July 1566 Q/SR 19/5	Eliz. Fraunces	all taken at	suspected of witchcraft
		Joan and Agnes Waterhouse	Hatfield Peverel	,, ,, ,,

No.	Date/Source	Name	Village	Offence
		Emma Crosse	taken at Manningtree	suspected of witchcraft
794	July 1566 Q/SR 19/36	—	Boreham	„ jury present that there was a witch in Boreham 'and upon her confessyon before Mr. Archdeacon Cole she fled and went her way'
795	July 1567 Q/SR 21/19	Joan Cocke	Kelvedon	lamed Richard Sherman by touching his knee
796	„	wife of Noble	„	(daughter of Joan Cocke above), being refused butter, she bewitched three cows, one of which died, the others gave 'milke of all colors'; they were property of 'Belffilde's wyfe of Infforde' (Inworth)
797	July 1567 Q/SR 21/19	wife of Ram	Cressing	suspected by Jn. Wafforde to have bewitched his cattle
798	Jan. 1574 Q/SR 47/43	Joan Stubbyng	Ridgewell	a witch, to be apprehended by constables
799	Apr. 1574 Q/SR 48/61	Robt. Wallys	—	a wandering vagabond and 'soth-sayer'
800	May 1576 Q/SR 57/27	wife of Nicholas Baker (a painter)	Brentwood	suspected witch
801	May 1576 Q/SR 57/36	Agnes Berden (widow)	Elsenham	to answer to suspicion of witch-craft
802	May 1576 Q/SR 57/40	„	„	presentment as in case 106; victim languished for three days, his body vexed and troubled with a strange disease
803	May 1576 Q/SR 57/81	„	„	Agnes handed in bail to Jn. Stock and Jn. Waylett
804	Oct. 1576 Q/SR 59/9	Agnes Sawen	Stock	for bewitching Christopher Veale 'so that his feet were and now remain curved . . .'
805	Jan. 1577 Q/SR 60/2, 48, 49, 62 Q/SR 62/9, 56	„	„	writs for appearance of Agnes Sawen and Jn. Woode of West Hanningfield bound over to keep the peace towards Agnes
806	July 1577 Q/SR 63/16	Agnes Sawen Thos. Foster Richard Bale	„ — —	prisoners in Colchester Gaol; not guilty. Foster and Bale presented with the enchantress Sawen
807	Jan. 1578 Q/SR 65/2, 3	Thos. Barker (surgeon)	Gestingthorpe	handed in bail; not to conjure or invoke false spirits

No.	Date/Source	Name	Village	Offence
808	Jan. 1578 Q/SR 65/6	Thos. Barker (surgeon)	Gestingthorpe	for appearance of Barker
809	July 1578 Q/SR 67/2, 44–6	Miles Blomfield	Chelmsford	depositions of Sybell Browne, Thos Lynforde, and George Freeman concerning the activities of the cunning man Miles Blomfield, who discovered lost goods
810	Oct. 1578 Q/SR 68/35	Margery Stanton	Wimbish	inquisition as in case 122; jurors find her guilty
811	Oct. 1578 Q/SR 68/34	Margt. Ganne Joan Norfolk	Borley	for bewitching Jn. Furmyn to death as in case 121
812	Jan. 1579 Q/SR 69/47	Eliz. Fraunces	Hatfield Peverel	for bewitching woman to death, as in case 123
813	Apr. 1583 Q/SR 84/19, 35	Margt. Hogdine (w/Thos.)	Stebbing	for bewitching woman to death, as in case 191
814	Apr. 1584 Q/SR 88/86	Note of prisoners (properly an Assize document): Joan Colshall, a witch (deleted), Guilty. Eliz. Morsbye . . . Chester . . . a witch, for murder; Margt. Littleberrye of Bradwell, a witch; Joan Thurrock, a witch, for three murders; Joan Colson, a witch, for murder; Edmund Mansell, clerk, a witch; Alice Bolton and Eliz. Lumney of St. Osyth, for witches, not guilty (cf. cases 212–13, 214–19, 222–5, 227)		
815	Apr. 1586 Q/SR 96a/8	List of felons (properly part of an Assize roll): Eliz. Barwick, Alice Newman, and Anne Joyce for witchcraft (cf. cases 160–2, 237–9)		
816	March 1587 Q/SR 99/1	Gaol delivery roll (properly part of an Assize roll): Alice Newman—respited; Eliz. Barwick—dead; Jn. Smyth alias Salmon, a witch, not guilty; Rose Colyne; Rose Clarevence, guilty; Lettice Hayward. (cf. cases 160–2, 245–6, 250)		
817	July 1587 Q/SR 101/50	John Smyth/ Samond	Danbury	for bewitching cow, as in case 253
818	Oct. 1589 Q/SR 110/70	Agnes Whitland	Dagenham	for bewitching child to death, as in case 306
819	Oct. 1589 Q/SR 110/75–9	Alice Aylett	Braintree	for bewitching three people to death, as in cases 302, 304, 305
820	Jan 1589 Q/SR 148/171–2 (in fact part of roll 111)	Agnes Whitland	Dagenham	Richard Foster, Wm. Willis, Richard Burdhead, Henry Woodborne, all yeomen of Dagenham, to give evidence against the witch Agnes Whitland
821	Apr. 1590 Q/SR 112/42	,,	,,	a witch
822	July 1591 Q/SR 117/38	Mother Saunder	'Muche Bardwell'	being called a witch, she fled

No.	Date/Source	Name	Village	Offence
823	Apr. 1592 Q/SR 120/27, 28	Jane Wallis	Stebbing	for bewitching a cow and a man to death, as in cases 347, 348
824	July 1593 Q/SR 125/2, 43	Eliz. Pakeman (w/Ralph)	Great Clacton	Elizabeth to appear at next sessions to answer Thos. Crosse and Wm. Tiall, labourers of Great Clacton, concerning the breaking of the peace (cf. case 367)
825	Jan. 1596 Q/SR 132/77	Faith Somer	Wigborough	Thos. Wiseman to keep the peace towards Faith, wife of Thos. Somer of the same, husbandman
826	Oct. 1596 Q/SR 135/72	Faith Somer	,,	Thos. Wiseman and his servant Jn. Vickers to give evidence against Faith, committed for witchcraft
827	Jan. 1597 Q/SR 136/112	Joan Fisher (w/Chris- topher, labourer)	Halstead	for bewitching woman to death, as in case 416*b*
828	Jan. 1599 Q/SR 144/98, 106 (cf. Q/SR 145/2)	Christian Hunt (w/Jn.)	Tollesbury	Jn. Courtman and Jn. Marchant to ensure the appearance of Christian on a charge of witchcraft; Wm. Greene, yeoman, Richard Bampton and his wife, Henry Peroure and his wife, Wm. Wallis and Thos. Alleyn all of Tollesbury, to witness against her
829	Jan. 1600 Q/SR 148/37, 43	Isabel White	Purleigh	constables to ensure appearance of Jn. Hitch and his wife, Thos. Shettlewood, Jn. Purdye and their wives, and Margery Savory; all to give evidence against Isabel for bewitching cattle of Thos. Warde
830	Jan. 1600 Q/SR 148/141, 2	,,	,,	bewitched animals as in cases 421, 422
831	Jan. 1600 Q/SR 148/147	Alice Aylett (w/Thos)	Braintree	Mark Moote of Braintree, yeoman, Wm. Skinner, clothier, Wm. Huckabye, butcher, Thos. Egles, clothier, all of Braintree, to give evidence against Alice concerning her witchcraft; cf. cases 301–5 cases 301–5
832	Jan. 1601 Q/SR 152/172	Margt. Ellis (spinster)	Sible Hedingham	for bewitching two cows worth £4, one gelding worth 40*s*. (deleted), and one colt worth 10*s*. belonging to Thos. Hibbs, at the same, so that they died; not guilty. Witnesses Thos. Hibbs and Anthony Ellis

No.	Date/Source	Name	Village	Offence
833	Jan. 1603 Q/SR 160/217	Joan Thorndon	—	Names of prisoners in Colchester Gaol: J.T., by warrant of the Lord Suffragan of Colchester and William Ayloffe, esquire, for witchcraft; to the Assizes.
834	Oct. 1605 Q/SR 173/114	Nicholas Slater	Roydon	for calling a neighbour's wife 'pockye whoare and old witch'
835	Apr. 1609 Q/SR 187/54	Edmund Munt	Great Bentley	in anger, called wife of Jn. Haris 'old whore and witch'
836	May 1614 Q/SR 206/19 Q/SBa 1/16 Q/SPa 1/1	Alice Batty (widow)	Toppesfield	on 17 Sept. 1613 bewitched Thos. Perrie, son of Jn. Perrie, aged three years, who died on 30 Oct. Witnesses John Perrye, Olive Perrye, Jn. Drewrye. True bill; 'transmitted to the Assizes and there she was acquitted'
837	Apr. 1616 Q/SR 213/85	John Scates	Billericay	Rich. Tarling, husbandman, to give evidence against Scates, a weaver, for his 'conjuration and practising with the devill for money'
838	Oct. 1624 Q/SR 246/119	George Burre	Brentwood	to answer for suspicion of witch- craft
839	1641 Q/SBa 2/44	Thos. Fuller	Layer Marney	examination of Thos. Fuller who went to 'a supposed cunning man' named Barnard at Danbury, while his master, Henry Clitherowe, went to a cunning man at Ipswich. They went about lost plate and other goods stolen while Fuller was coachman to Clitherowe
840	1645 Q/SR 324/118– 119	various of Stisted		depositions of Martha Hurrell and Eliz. Gallant concerning magical rites, sexual promiscuity and feasting at various gentlemen's houses, including John Alston of Stisted, in 1643 (for a further description, see p. 306)
841	Apr. 1646 Q/SBa 2/60	Debora Nailer	Elsenham	information of Tewer Wade of Henham and Jn. Crabbe of Elsen- ham, who stated that George and Jn. Pakeman were convinced in their illness that Deborah Nayler had bewitched them. Information of Debora Nailer, daughter of above Debora, that there was a quarrel and her mother entreated Mr. Willson, Minister of the parish, to help her. Examination of Debora Nailer

No.	Date/Source	Name	Village	Offence
842	Apr. 1646 Q/SR 328/94	Debora Nailer (senior, widow)	Elsenham	to give evidence concerning the death by witchcraft of Jn. and George Pakeman to Henry Robson
843	1650 Q/SBa 2/74	,,	,,	information of 7 women appointed to search Nayler for suspicious witches' marks; also of Martha Cannon of Henham that she became sick after Deborah prayed for her health
844	1650 Q/SBa 2/74	Debora Nayler	Elsenham	information of Jn. Crabbe of Elsenham that Jn. Pakeman quarrelled with Debora and then fell sick, proclaiming himself bewitched; examination of Tewar Wade of Henham against Debora, concerning Jn. and George Pakeman's illness
845	July 1651 Q/SR 349/92, 125, 128	William Hills	Berden	Wm. Hills, James Winstanley, and his mother Eliz., Edward Stephen, all to give evidence in a case in which Hills was suspected of falsely pretending to help Eliz. to find some stolen goods
846	July 1651 Q/SBa 2/76	,,	,, (Ricking also)	long informations of Stephens, Hills, Eliz. and James Winstanley, and Thos. Law of how James Winstanley went to consult Hills, a cunning man, about some stolen property and also went to consult a 'Mr. Ladland att Puddledocke' in London, who was also a reputed cunning man. Hills was a pupil of William Lilly and gave detailed instructions on how to find the thief
847	Epiphany 1653 Q/SR 355/104, 105	John Lock	(Great Bentley)	calendar of prisoners in Colchester Gaol: committed for trying to find lost goods by magic; acquitted
848	Epiphany 1653 Q/SR 355/119	,, (labourer)	,,	indictment for trying 'by witchcrafts, inchantments, charmes and sorceries' to discover lost goods. Witness: Edmund Drury, gent. *Ignoramus*
849	Apr. 1653 Q/SR 356/18, 50, 89	Benjamin Brand and his wife Joan (Benjamin	Stebbing	indictment and recognizances for appearance of witnesses against, of Brand and his wife who used sorcery to tell where lost goods and cattle were. Witnesses: Wm.

No.	Date/Source	Name	Village	Offence
		= a comber)		Playle, Josias Stanes, Wm. Marriage. True bill; acknowledged and was committed to gaol for one year.
850	Michaelmas 1653 Q/SR 358/82, 87, 88	Helen Dishe (w/Jn. labourer)	Takeley	Thos. Bowier, haberdasher, and Reuben his son, both of Wickanbrook, Suffolk, to indict Helen Dishe. Helen was committed for a strong suspicion of bewitching Reuben Bowier whom she had formerly threatened and who had since then suffered from 'strong and painful fits'; to be tried at Assizes.
851	Michaelmas 1653 Q/SR 358/87–8	Thos. White	Great Braxted	calendar of prisoners: in gaol for using 'conjurations'
852	Oct. 1653 Q/SR 358/106–8	Helen Dishe	Takeley	inquisition, indictment, and recognizance for appearance of: on 3 Sept. she bewitched Reuben Bowier so that he languished until this day (4 Oct.). Witness: Thos. Bowier. Endorsed 'a true bill'
853	Oct. 1653 Q/SBa 2/85	,,	,,	information of Rewben Bowier, bewitched by Helen Dishe between Elsenham and Takeley: detailed.
854	Epiphany 1654 Q/SR 359/60	Thos. White	Great Braxted	Recognizance for appearance of Thos. White, gent., to answer an indictment for 'conjuration'
855	1664 Q/SR 402/128–9	John Webb	Woodham Mortimer	examination of Webb, blacksmith, who tried to clear himself of suspicion of stealing a shirt by going to a cunning man, Mr. Higgs. Information of Mary Tyler of the same concerning Webb.

ECCLESIASTICAL COURT PRESENTMENTS

Cases 861 to 1,138 are abstracted from the records of various ecclesiastical courts with jurisdiction in Essex. The majority of the cases come from the records of the Archdeacons of Essex and Colchester, but there are also a number of cases from the Bishop of London's Consistory and Commissary court archives. All these records are fully described in the Bibliography. Only seventeen of the 230 people accused in connexion with witchcraft at these courts have already appeared in print. Cases 863, 873, 885, 893, 911, 957, 984 were printed in William Hale, *Series of Precedents and Proceedings in Criminal Causes, 1475–1640* (1847), pp. 147, 148, 157, 163, 185–6, 219, 254. Cases 940–7, 953, appeared in *Lincoln Diocese Documents, 1450–1544* ed. Andrew Clark (Early English Text Soc., 1914), pp. 108–10. Three of these cases (940, 944, 947) and case

1,007, wrongly dated, were included in W. J. Pressey, 'Records of the Archdeaconries of Essex and Colchester', *Transactions of Essex Arch. Soc.*, n.s. xix (1927–30), pp. 18–20. Cases 1,133 and 1,135 were noted by F. W. X. Fincham, 'Notes from the Ecclesiastical Court Records at Somerset House', *Transactions of Royal Historical Society*, 4th Ser. iv (1921), p. 120.

The abstracts are only summaries of the accusations and procedure against suspects. For example, 'a witch' in the abstract might be 'that she used witchcraft charms and sorceries' in the original document. Under the heading 'Name' are the names of those accused at the courts for an offence related to witchcraft, though, as can be seen, they may not themselves be suspected witches. If the place of residence, or proceedings against the accused, are not given this is denoted by a '—' sign. The procedure at the ecclesiastical courts is outlined in Chapter 4, p. 66 above; the meaning of the terms 'contumacious', 'purgation', 'penance' and others are found there. When an accused person was married this is recorded as w/Jn. (wife of John). Seven of the cases, 863, 864, 867, 868, 869, 872, 877, were crossed out in the original. Since this seems merely to have denoted that the case was closed, they have been included in the abstracts.

Certain other abbreviations have been employed to prevent the abstracts from becoming intolerably long. They are:

next court/to appear	= to appear at the next court to undergo further process of law.
to P/4, or P fails/succeeds	= to purge herself with four people, or purgation fails/succeeds.
ex., or stands ex.	= excommunicated, or remains excommunicated.
penance/to confess	= to undergo a public penance in the church, including confession and promise of amendment of life.

Archdeaconry of Essex

No.	Date/Source	Name	Village	Offence/Process
861	June 1564 AEA/2 f.61	Eliz. Lowys (w/Jn.)	Great Waltham	questioned 'who it is that can unwyche that [whi]ch a nother wyche dothe bewyche a nother or who was she that Wodlands Karcher that dyed of wychecraft'. Her replies and other examinations are written at the end of the Act Book. For these, see p. 307; examined
862	July 1566 AEA/3 f.37	Widow Middleton	Boreham	a witch; denied, dismissed
863	July 1566 AEA/3 f.37ᵛ	Alice Gardiner	„	'she gave counsell to one Masons wief [sic] of boram who was a witche that she shulde confesse nothinge for yff thow dust thow

No.	Date/Source	Name	Village	Offence/Process
				wilt dyve for hit and thow wilt turne thcy neighbours to troble'; denied to P/4
864	July 1566 AEA/3 f.37ᵛ	Widow Stokes	Danbury	a witch; appeared
865	July 1566 AEA/3 f.40ᵛ	—— Lone	Creeksea (Rector of)	to witness concerning Mr. Hawes of Steeple and prove 'That the said Hawes did saie of him self that he was a forediviner or a southsaier'; next court
866	Sept. 1566 AEA/3 f.66	William Harris	,,	he said 'that Mr. Hawes sholld be a divinar or elles he had a Famyliar'; Richmond, another diviner, was quoted to the same effect, warning against Hawes as 'a naughtie man'; to be judged
867	Sept. 1566 AEA/3 f.79ᵛ	Mother Stookes	Danbury	a witch; denied to P/4
868	Sept. 1566 AEA/3 f.82ᵛ	—— Gyles	Springfield	a witch; denied to P/4
869	Sept. 1566 AEA/3 f.82ᵛ	Mother Wheatley	,,	a witch; denied to P/4
870	Sept. 1566 AEA/3 f.85ᵛ	wife of Nethersall	Maldon (St. Peter)	a witch; denied to P/8 is a pauper
871	Sept. 1566 AEA/3 f.95	Margery Skelton	Little Wakering	a witch; dcnied, to be examined
872	Sept. 1566 AEA/3 f.95	Eliz. Fullar	Rayleigh	a witch; denied fact to P/5
873	Sept. 1566 AEA/3 f.95ᵛ	Margery Skelton	Little Wakering	a sorceress; asked whether she ever healed women or children she said 'she hath w[i]th prayinge of her prayers' healed seven persons (named), cures included nut tree leaves and sage leaves; examined
874	Dec. 1566 AEA/3 f.106ᵛ	Mother Lewin	Bulphan	a witch; next court
875	Dec. 1566 AEA/3 f.124ᵛ	wife of Clarke	—	sent to a cunning man at Witham about her sick child; next court
876	Dec. 1566 AEA/3 f.125ᵛ	Mother Stockes	Danbury	a witch; her P/4 succeeded
877	Dec. 1566 AEA/3 f.126	—— Giles	Springfield	a witch; her P/4 succeeded
878	Dec. 1566 AEA/3 f.126	Mother Wheatley	Springfield	a witch; to P/4
879	— 1566 AEA/3 f.145ᵛ	Joan Knowlar	West Tilbury	a witch; denied to P/6
880	July 1570 AEA/5 f.72ᵛ	Agnes Coples	Romford	called Gentrie's wife a witch in anger; admitted penance

No.	Date/Source	Name	Village	Offence/Process
881	Dec. 1572 AEA/7 f.169ᵛ	—— Miller (w/Thos)	Haveringe	a witch, among those suspecting her were Mr. Willis, Curate of Haveringe; denied to P/6
882	Apr. 1574 AEA/8 f.14	Margt. Sanders	Rainham	a witch and scold; denied to P/6
883	Oct. 1574 AEA/8 f.97ᵛ	Anne Brewer (w/Robt)	Dunton	a witch; denied to P/4
884	Oct. 1574 AEA/8 f.98	Katherine Slowman	Horndon	a witch; denied to P/4
885	Oct. 1574 AEA/8 f.99aᵛ	Joan Allen	Leigh	went to a cunning woman, widow Jackson; she admitted that she had said this, but it was a lie; to confess her fault
886	Feb. 1575 AEA/8 f.136ᵛ	Juliana Woodward	Brentwood	she admitted 'that she went to one John Thomas a coninge man dwellinge uppon London bridge for vs of monie she loste and the same Coninge man did shewe her in a glass a boye in a sherte a gleninge Corne resemblinge the countenance of John Hayes that had her monye'; penance
887	Sept. 1575 AEA/8 f.230	Joan Turner	Romford	for going 'to a wise woman who told her yt [that] Stodies wiffe had bewitched her'; dismissed
888	— 1575 AEA/9 f.1ᵛ	Joan Litelberie	Bradwell-iuxta-Mare	a witch; dismissed
889	Jan. 1576 AEA/9 f.32	Margt. Poole (w/Roger)	Boreham	a witch; contumacious next court
890	Jan. 1576 AEA/9 f.32	Mary Belsted (w/Thos)	Boreham	a witch; denied to P/4
891	June 1576 AEA/9 f.63	Widow Sawell	Stock	a witch; denied to P/4
892	June 1576 AEA/9 f.63ᵛ	Margt. Belsted (w/Thos)	Boreham	a witch and not living with her husband; suspected a witch on the 'conference . . . of Mr. Gilbert'; penance
893	June 1576 AEA/9 f.72ᵛ	James Hopkinne	Hornchurch	for going to 'mother P(er)sorne at Navestocke Coninge Woman to knowe by what me[a]ns his masters Cattell was bewitched'; next court
894	Dec. 1576 AEA/8 f.247ᵛ	Joan Pynder (w/Geo.)	Barking	a curser and witch; denied to P/6
895	Jan. 1577 AEA/8 f.251ᵛ	„	„	a curser and witch (names of purgators); to P/6, P succeeds

No.	Date/Source	Name	Village	Offence/Process
896	Apr. 1577 AEA/8 f.285ᵛ	Margery Sowman	Bradwell-iuxta-Mare	a witch; to confess
897	Apr. 1577 AEA/8 f.285ᵛ	Joan Litelberie	„	a witch; to confess
898	June 1578 AEA/10 f.52	Ralph Grange	Chipping Ongar	went to cunning man about lost goods, paying 2s. fee; to confess
899	July 1578 AEA/10 f.61	Wm. Leonard and wife	Hornchurch	witches; deny, to P/6
900	Sept. 1578 AEA/10 f.141ᵛ	Wm. Leonard and his wife Brigit	Hornchurch	witches; P fails penance
901	March 1579 AEA/11 f.6	Wm. Elkin and wife	North Weald	went to a cunning man, 'one of Chelmsford', who told him which way his lost cattle had gone; to confess
902	May 1579 AEA/11 f.20	Joan Burton	Great Stambridge	a witch; denied to P/4
903	June 1579 AEA/11 f.35ᵛ	Thos. Longe	Lamborne	going to cunning folk 'for help'; contumacious ex.
904	Jan. 1580 AEA/11 f.109ᵛ	Joyce Duckerell (married)	South Ockendon	a witch; denied to P/4
905	March 1580 AEA/11 f.127ᵛ	Eliz. Boxworthe (w/Thos)	Stock	a witch; denied to P/3
906	Sept. 1583 AEA/12 f.14	Richard Barker and wife	Romford	'for usinge of theire talke some-thynge savoringe false doctryne. And she somthinge suspecte of wycherie'; next court
907	Sept. 1583 AEA/12 f.14ᵛ	Joan Barker (w/Rich.)	„	a witch (see above); denied to P/5
908	Dec. 1583 AEA/12 f.51ᵛ	Agnes Billinge	South Ockendon	a witch; to P/10
909	Jan. 1584 AEA/12 f.57	Joan Burton	Great Stambridge	a witch
910	Jan. 1584 AEA/12 f.62ᵛ	Agnes Billinge	South Ockendon	a witch, and also to confess for giving suspicion of 'incestuous lieff w[i]th hir sonne', lying in bed with him, he being aged seventeen or eighteen; P fails, to confess
911	Apr. 1585 AEA/12 f.255ᵛ	Jn. Shounke (senior)	Romford	went to a cunning man, 'father Parfoothe', for help for his wife; admits and says he would do the same again, to confess himself

No.	Date/Source	Name	Village	Offence/Process
				'hartelie sorie for sekinge mans helpe and refusinge ye helpe of god'; admits, penance
912	May 1585 AEA/12 f.271ᵛ	Cicily Makyn (w/Jn.)	Canewdon	a witch; denied to P/5—fails, to confess
913	Jan. 1586 AEA/12 f.361ᵛ	Agnes Welles	High Ongar	a witch; denied to P/6
914	Feb. 1586 AEA/12 f.371	Widow Joyce	Stanford Rivers	a witch; in prison
915	Nov. 1586 AEA/13 f.34ᵛ	Joan Foster	Broomfield	a witch; denied to P/5
916	June 1587 AEA/13 f.107	Margt. Harrison	Hawkwell	a witch; denied to P/4
917	July 1587 AEA/13 f.123	(Joan) Foster	(Broomfield)	a witch; P succeeded, dismissed
918	Oct. 1587 AEA/13 f.139ᵛ	Jane Cotsall	Upminster	called goodwife Locksmith a witch in anger; to admit guilt
919	Jan. 1588 AEA/13 f.177	Ellinor Bett	Great Waltham	a witch, on accusation of Margerie Dawson; presentation insufficient
920	Jan. 1588 AEA/13 f.183	Henry Barbor	Barking	'to be a Witche by his own confession'; next court
921	Feb. 1588 AEA/13 f.191ᵛ	Helen Bedwell	—	a witch and blasphemer
922	Jan. 1588 AEA/14 f.46	Ellena Bett	Great Waltham	a witch; next court
923	Jan. 1589 AEA/14 f.46ᵛ	Thos. Corde	Langdon Hills	went to cunning man for lost goods; to confess
924	May 1589 AEA/14 f.86	—— Upney (w/Wm.)	Dagenham	a witch; imprisoned at Colchester on relation of Mr. Lambert, Vicar of Hornchurch
925	May 1589 AEA/14 f.105	Margt. Johnson	Asheldham	a witch; denied, to bring six testimonials
926	May 1589 AEA/14 f.107	—— Hinckson	Rochford	a witch; next court
927	May 1589 AEA/14 f.107ᵛ	—— Hamond	Hadleigh	a witch 'and therefore our min[is]ter would not receive her to the Communion'; next court
928	June 1589 AEA/14 f.116ᵛ	Joan Hinckson	Rochford	a witch; Mr. John Frith, Rector of Hawkwell brought a certificate of her blamelessness and stated her virtue; dismissed
929	June 1589 AEA/14 f.124ᵛ	—— Sloughter (w/Thos)	Horndon	a witch, on suspicion of Wm. Coxall and Richard Hamon; ex.
930	Sept/1589 AEA/14 f.148ᵛ	Margt. Wright/ Willet	Havering	a witch; denied to P/3

No.	Date/Source	Name	Village	Offence/Process
931	Jan. 1590 AEA/14 f.193	Joan Burton	Great Stambridge	a witch; contumacious ex.
932	Jan. 1590 AEA/14 f.194	Agnes Hamon	Hadleigh	a witch; denied to P/4
933	Feb. 1590 AEA/14 f.210	—— Makins (w/Jn.)	Canewdon	a witch; stands ex.
934	May 1590 AEA/14 f.250	Agnes Berry (widow)	Great Burstead	a witch; her daughter accused of incontinency
935	June 1590 AEA/14 f.265ᵛ	Alice Bateman	East Hanningfield	a witch; denied to P/6
936	July 1590 AEA/14 f.287ᵛ	,,	,,	a witch, and also failed to receive Communion at Easter last; to P/6
937	July 1590 AEA/14 f.290ᵛ	Francisca Pashall	South Hanningfield	'sent to sorcerers for comforte'; stands ex.
938	Feb. 1591 AEA/15 f.72	wife of Thos. Sare	Barking	a witch, on suspicion of goodman Harwood, Shelton, and their wives because of this Sare and his wife fail to attend Communion; to receive Communion
939	March 1591 AEA/15 f.92	,,	,,	Harwood and Shelton say that the matter had long since been settled before a J.P., but Sare's wife 'hath nowe of late rene[we]d the said matter' and been 'a very Skoulding and disquiet woman among her neighbours'; to confess
940	July 1591 AEA/15 f.148	Widow May	Woodford	a witch, on suspicion of Wm. Foxe; stands ex.
941	July 1591 AEA/15 f.148	Widow Coppres	Woodford	a witch, suspected a long time and lately by Jn. Poole
942	Feb. 1592 AEA/16 f.17ᵛ	Jn. Monday	Loughton	went to cunning man for lost goods, denied, dismissed
943	May 1592 AEA/16 f.56	Alice Foster	Barking	a witch, but churchwardens say she is not thus suspected so; dismissed
944	May 1592 AEA/16 f.56	John Crave	Romford	for going to cunning folk; admits that his wife went to 'father Perfoche' for medicine for sick cattle; cautioned and dismissed
945	May 1592 AEA/16 f.56	Wm. Moushowe	,,	as in above; as above
946	May 1592 AEA/16 f.61	Joan Bell	Fobbing	for not receiving Communion; she alleges that 'one Whaple' made complaint of her as a witch; to bring certificate signed by four honest neighbours; to bring certificate

No.	Date/Source	Name	Village	Offence/Process
947	May 1592 AEA/16 f.64	Margt. Wiseman	Maldon	a witch (seven purgators named); P/7 succeeds, dismissed
948	July 1592 AEA/16 f.91ᵛ	Joan Playle	Great Waltham	a witch; stands ex.
949	July 1592 AEA/16 f.94	Margt. Wiseman (w/Jn.)	Maldon	a witch; to P/7 [*sic*]
950	March 1595 AEA/17 f.1ᵛ	Joan Foster	Broomfield	a witch; next court
951	March 1595 AEA/17 f.7	Anne Moore	Rayleigh	a soothsaier and sorceress, telling where lost goods were
952	July 1595 AEA/17 f.55	Joan Foster	Broomfield	a witch; denied to P/4
953	July 1595 AEA/17 f.64	—— Carter	Barking	a cunning man, telling where lost property was, e.g. two cloaks and a ring
954	Oct. 1595 AEA/17 f.80	Thos. Forby	Asheldham	for going to cunning folk for lost goods; next court
955	July 1596 AEA/17 f.164	—— Jones (w/Maurice)	Barking	on request of 'Robgent's wife' for medicine she fell on her knees and cursed her, since when Robgent's wife suffered; stands ex.
956	Jan. 1598 AEA/18 f.151	Thos. Morice	Beauchamp Roothing	went to 'worker w[i]th familiar spirites for certein fishes' that were lost and seldom attended church; denied, dismissed
957	Apr. 1599 AEA/19 f.198	Thos. Ward	Purleigh	'having lost certein cattell and suspecting that they were bewitched' went to 'one Tailer in Thaxted a wysard'; to confess
958	July 1599 AEA/19 f.272ᵛ	Eliz. Batcheler	Stifford	unable to receive Communion because called a witch by John Grene; to receive Communion
959	Sept. 1599 AEA/19 f.342	John Watson and wife	South Benfleet	for living disorderly together and she accuses him of incontinency with Snow's wife, 'calling honeste women witches'; cautioned, dismissed
960	Jan. 1600 AEA/20 f.37ᵛ	Stephen Vincent	Hockley	in anger suggested that Mary Hollinton had 'by her evill tonge' bewitched a horse, sheep and cattle; said he was sorry; cautioned, dismissed
961	Apr. 1600 AEA/20 f.74ᵛ	—— Lavander (w/Wm)	Doddinghurst	a witch; cited
962	Oct. 1600 AEA/20 f.217	James Hamon	East Tilbury	going to a conjurer or sorcerer; dismissed

No.	Date/Source	Name	Village	Offence/Process
963	Dec. 1600 AEA/20 f.237	Thos. Saye	Buttsbury	went to a wizard for help for his child, admitted he went to a man for medicine; cautioned, dismissed
964	Sept. 1601 AEA/21 f.193ᵛ	John Arwaker	Great Waltham	suspected charming with sieve and shears in his house; denied, dismissed
965	Feb. 1602 AEA/21 f.229ᵛ	Margery Murfield (widow)	Hockley	a witch and for incontinency
966	Apr. 1602 AEA/22 f.3ᵛ	Thos. Veare	Horndon-on-the-Hill	he said that goodman Clarke the carpenter had been to London 'at the banckes side' consulting a cunning woman about a stolen petticoat
967	May 1602 AEA/22 f.6ᵛ	Agnes Wilkine (w/Jn.)	North Weald	for going to cunning folk; next court
968	May 1602 AEA/22 f.7	Robt. Frend	Great Warley	for going to a cunning man about a lost purse
969	Oct. 1602 AEA/22 f.95	Agnes Gyll	Grays Thurrock	she and Jane Curtis, quarrelling, called each other whore and witch
970	Apr. 1604 AEA/23 f.12ᵛ	Katherine Weaver	Blackmore	a witch, but says that only one churchwarden presented her, and and he did it out of malice; cautioned, dismissed
971	June 1605 AEA/23 f.169	Grace Browne	Hadleigh	a witch; denied, to P/3
972	June 1608 AEA/25 f.41ᵛ	Various (see across)	East Hanningfield	Henry Pechie, his wife, and daughter Joan; Wm. Mawr and wife Suzanne, for witchcraft; dismissed
973	June 1608 AEA/25 f.41ᵛ	wife of Adam Seley	East Hanningfield	as in above case; dismissed
974	Jan. 1610 AEA/25 f.235	John Skafe	Great Burstead	for going 'to one Gressam a soth-sayer in London' about a lost horse and man
975	May 1610 AEA/25 f.278ᵛ	Anne Roberts	Little Thurrock	a witch; *egrotat*
976	Aug. 1610 AEA/25 f.322	——— Lunne	Mucking	burning a lamb alive 'supposing his shepe had bin bewicht'
977	May 1612 AEA/26 f.138	Giles Payson	Nazeing	offending against the article concerning 'soothsayinge Charmes &c' and other offences; next court
978	May 1612 AEA/26 f.138	Mary Clarke	,,	as above; next court
979	May 1612 AEA/26 f.138	Thos. Campe	,,	as above; next court

No.	Date/Source	Name	Village	Offence/Process
980	July 1612 AEA/26 f.217ᵛ	Agnes Rawlins (widow)	Hockley	a witch; next court
981	May 1619 AEA/31 f.69	Wm. Walford	Cold Norton	for living scandalously with his wife, calling her 'Jade queane witch etc' and persuading his neighbours that she had bewitched them; admits, fined, dismissed
982	Dec. 1620 AEA/32 f.76	Alice Trittle (w/Jn.)	Rettendon	a witch, suspected for many years and an 'evill tongued woman'; denied to P/4
983	July 1624 AEA/34 f.79ᵛ	John Crushe	Hawkwell	burnt a lamb alive during Sunday service, believing it to be bewitched and set the common alight so that service was disturbed; apologise
984	Aug. 1632 AEA/39 f.29	Mary Cutford (w/Hen.)	Rainham	'she did most wickedlie wishe herselfe to be a witch for a tyme that she might be revenged of her adversarie', Anne Dawdrie; admitted, to confess
985	Feb. 1638 AEA/41 f.220	Catherine Hooke/ Allison	Stanford-le-Hope	a witch; denied, dismissed
986	Nov. 1591 AED/3 f.113ᵛ–14 f.124–5	Sara Kempe	Stondon	Wm. Ingold, Wm. Tyng, Wm. Warner and Thos. Regnold, all of Stondon, depose that they heard the late Mr. Lawrence Hollingworth say that Sara Kempe had been driven out of White-chapel, London, for witchcraft

Archdeaconry of Colchester

No.	Date/Source	Name	Village	Offence/Process
991	Feb. 1573 ACA/5 f.121ᵛ	Helen Wedon	Colchester (St. James)	present at a magical ceremony ('*quod veneficia adiit*'); denied to P/5
992	Feb. 1573 ACA/5 f.122	Benjamin Fairstead	„	confessed that he had sent to 'mother Humfrey' for his hogs, which he thought were bewitched; admitted, penance
993	Oct. 1576 ACA/7 f.64	Various (see across)	Great Totham	Jn. Plummer, Joan Tomson, and Mary Tomson; Plummer admitted that they used the 'sieve and shears'; penance
994	March 1578 ACA/7 f.273ᵛ	Thomasina Wood (w/Rich.)	Fingringhoe	a witch; denied to P/6

No.	Date/Source	Name	Village	Offence/Process
995	July 1579 ACA/8 f.148	Joan Michell	Saffron Walden	medical sorcery; to confess offence to neighbours and five medical practitioners; to confess
996	Oct. 1579 ACA/8 f.205ᵛ	Robt. Crake	Boxted	for using sieve and shears; admitted, penance
997	Nov. 1579 ACA/8 f.233	Agnes Taster	Weeley	a witch and not receiving Communion; denied to P/4
998	Nov. 1579 ACA/8 f.238ᵛ	Eliz. Moresby	Great Chesterford	a witch; denied to P/5
999	Jan. 1580 ACA/8 f.251ᵛ	Agnes Taster	Weeley	a witch; penance
1,000	Jan. 1580 ACA/8 f.269	Jane Moresby	Great Chesterford	a witch; denied to P/5
1,001	March 1580 ACA/8 f.315ᵛ	Eliz. Moresby	,,	a witch; P/5 failed, penance
1,002	Jan. 1581 ACA/9 f.99	Mary Greane	Earls Colne	sorcery and witchcraft; denied to P/4
1,003	Apr.1582 ACA/10 f.45	Catherine Reve	Colchester (St. James)	a witch; denied to P/4
1,004	Apr. 1582 ACA/10 f.45	Henry Driver	Colchester (St. Leonard)	a witch; denied to P/5
1,005	Apr. 1582 ACA/10 f.45	Margt. Hobigge	Colchester (St. Leonard)	a witch; denied to P/5
1,006	Apr. 1582 ACA/10 f.45	Sara Hobigge	Colchester (St. Leonard)	a witch; denied to P/5
1,007	Apr. 1582 ACA/10 f.47	Catherine Reve	Colchester (St. James)	a witch, denied, but admitted that she had learnt a counter-witchcraft spell from goodwife George of Abberton and had used it on a cow and herself
1,008	Apr. 1582 ACA/10 f.50ᵛ	,,	,,	a witch; fails P/5 penance
1,009	Apr. 1582 ACA/10 f.50ᵛ	Henry Dryver	Colchester (St. Leonard)	a witch; fails P/5 penance
1,010	Apr. 1582 ACA/10 f.50ᵛ	Sara Hobig	Colchester (St. Leonard)	a witch; fails P/5 penance
1,011	July 1582 ACA/10 f.65ᵛ	Eliz. Newman	Wormingford	a witch; denied to P/4
1,012	Nov. 1582 ACA/10 f.102	Michael Smythe and Joyce his wife	Ramsey	witches; denied each to P/4
1,013	Feb. 1583 ACA/11 f.11	Wm. Curswell and wife (Joan)	Layer-de-la- Haye	witches
1,014	March 1584 ACA/11 f.23ᵛ	as above	,,	witches; denied each to P/5

No.	Date/Source	Name	Village	Offence/Process
1,015	March 1584 ACA/12 f.103ᵛ	Eliz. Moresby and daughter Jane	Great Chesterford	witches, on long suspicion; stand ex.
1,016	March 1584 ACA/12 f.107ᵛ	,,	,,	witches; denied to P/5
1,017	Nov. 1584 ACA/11 f.119	Stephan Hugrave	Abberton	a witch and 'comon Brawler and sower of discorde between neigh-bours'; denied to P/5
1,018	Nov. 1584 ACA/11 f.119	Alice Hugrave (w/Steph)	Abberton	a witch; denied to P/7
1,019	Feb. 1585 ACA/13 f.35ᵛ	Wm. Asplin	Great Bardfield	'we p[re]sent Wm Asplin o[u]r scolemaster to take upon him to tell fortunes' and to give out charms for agues; next court
1,020	June 1585 ACA/13 f. 78ᵛ	Agnes Lea	Great Tey	a witch: next court
1,021	Oct. 1585 ACA/13 f.110	Edward Mason	Great Bardfield	for using characters (a charm) for the ague; admitted passing on such a charm to 'one Asplin', but not to using it; cautioned, dismissed
1,022	Oct. 1585 ACA/13 f.116	—— Davye (widow)	Great Braxted	a witch; next court
1,023	Nov. 1585 ACA/13 f.123ᵛ	,,	,,	a witch; denied to P/5
1,024	Jan. 1586 ACA/13 f.142	Joan Page	Great Chesterford	a witch and 'develishe of her tonge'; stands ex.
1,025	May 1586 ACA/13 f.188ᵛ	Richard Cole	Hempstead	for using loving powder on a woman, but he says she made it up and he has not 'used any sorsery' or been adulterous; denied
1,026	Apr. 1587 ACA/14 f.145ᵛ	Joan Abbott	Mount Bures	a witch; next court
1,027	May 1587 ACA/14 f.155	Joan Abbott	Mount Bures	a witch; very sick, dismissed for poverty
1,028	Sept. 1587 ACA/14 f.198ᵛ	Alan Moore	Lexden	a witch and not receiving Com-munion; fails to appear
1,029	Oct. 1587 ACA/15 f.15ᵛ	Edward Mason	Great Bardfield	a sorcerer; next court
1,030	Sept. 1587 ACA/16 f.5	Eliz. Pillgram	Hatfield Peverel	a witch; to P/5
1,031	Sept. 1587 ACA/16 f.5ᵛ	Joan Osborne	,,	a witch; to P/5
1,032	Sept. 1587 ACA/16 f.5ᵛ	Mary Godfrey	,,	a witch; P succeeds, dismissed

No.	Date/Source	Name	Village	Offence/Process
1,033	Sept. 1587 ACA/16 f.5ᵛ	John Gosse and wife	,,	witches; next court
1,034	Oct. 1587 ACA/16 f.15ᵛ	Eliz. Pilgrim (widow)	,,	a witch; P/5 fails, penance
1,035	Oct. 1587 ACA/16 f.15ᵛ	Joan Osborne	,,	a witch; P/5 fails, penance
1,036	Oct. 1587 ACA/16 f.16	Jn. Gosse and wife	,,	witches; P/5 fails, penance
1,037	Oct. 1587 ACA/16 f.20ᵛ	Thos. Smithe	Earls Colne	a sorcerer; next court
1,038	Oct. 1587 ACA/16 f.23	Thos. Wayland	Witham	for going to cunning folk for help; ex.
1,039	Oct. 1587 ACA/16 f.23	Robt. Armon	,,	,, ,, ,, ,, ,,
1,040	Nov. 1587 ACA/15 f.23	Edward Mason	Great Bardfield	a sorcerer, denies and says that he is bound to appear at assizes for this; next court
1,041	March 1588 ACA/16 f.68	Margt. Ellys (w/Anthony)	Pattiswick	a witch; denied to P/5
1,042	March 1588 ACA/16 f.68	Margt. Murdett	Great Braxted	she said that 'Mr. Fountayne did cast a figure'
1,043	March 1588 ACA/16 f.78	(Margt.) Ellis	Pattiswick	a witch
1,044	Apr. 1588 ACA/16 f.88ᵛ	George Haven	Coggeshall	a witch 'or one that ys addicted to sutche develishe practizes'; next court
1,045	Apr. 1588 ACA/16 f.90	Margt. Ellis	Pattiswick	a witch (three compurgators named); P/5 succeeds, dismissed
1,046	Apr. 1588 ACA/14 f.291ᵛ	Widow Tibboulde	Langham	a witch, an unquiet and slanderous woman, and people falling out with her subsequently have 'evell successe' with their cattle; contumacious, hence ex.
1,047	June 1588 ACA/17 f.22	Katherine Hayr (widow)	Thorrington	a witch, on suspicion of neighbours and 'one Brian of St Osythes', a cunning man; to P/6
1,048	July 1588 ACA/17 f.33ᵛ	Widow Dawson	Salcott	a witch; to appear
1,049	July 1588 ACA/17 f.41ᵛ	Joan Pakeman (w/Thos.)	Great Oakley	a witch; next court
1,050	Nov. 1588 ACA/17 f.87	Widow Heard	Thorrington	a witch, next court
1,051	Nov. 1588 ACA/17 f.89	,,	,,	,, ,, ,,

No.	Date/Source	Name	Village	Offence/Process
1,052	Feb. 1589 ACA/16 f.184ᵛ	Thos. Harding and wife	Witham	witches (using 'Caricters'); brought testimonial, dismissed
1,053	Feb. 1589 ACA/15 f.147	Henry Perrye	Great Sampford	going to a cunning man for stolen money; next court
1,054	Apr. 1589 ACA/17 f.159	Margt. Newman	Great Bentley	a witch; next court
1,055	Apr. 1589 ACA/17 f.159	John Warman (*sic.*)	„	a witch; next court
1,056	Apr. 1589 ACA/17 f.159	Joan Warman (w/Jn.)	„	a witch; next court
1,057	May 1589 ACA/17 f.177	Widow Hare	Thorrington	a witch; denied to P/6
1,058	May 1589 ACA/17 f.195	Margt. Prior	West Mersea	a witch; she says that only her enemies think this; denied to P/4
1,059	June 1589 ACA/18 f.39ᵛ	Margery Banby (w/Edward)	Kelvedon	a witch; next court
1,060	Nov. 1589 ACA/18 f.80	wife of —— Wilcockes	Cressing	a sorceress, using sieve and shears to know if baby will be male or female and to locate lost goods (three witnesses named); next court
1,061	Nov. 1589 ACA/18 f.80	Agnes Browne	Cressing	as above, same witnesses; next court
1,062	Dec. 1589 ACA/18 f.92ᵛ	George Haven	Coggeshall	a witch; stands ex.
1,063	Jan. 1590 ACA/18 f.114ᵛ	Church-wardens of	Coggeshall	for not presenting 'one Margarett ——'in their last presentment as a a witch; warned to present her
1,064	March. 1590 ACA/18 f.132ᵛ	John Wade and wife	„	for making a magic ointment to cure their children's sickness; admitted they did it on advice of Mr. Shereman of Colchester, physician; next court with Shereman
1,065	March 1590 ACA/18 f.138ᵛ	Thos. Browninge/ Browne	Coggeshall	'seekinge helpe to Witches'; dismissed
1,066	March 1590 ACA/18 f.138ᵛ	John Badlye	Coggeshall	„ „ „ „ „
1,067	March 1590 ACA/18 f.139	Thos. Browne and wife	„	„ „ „ „ „
1,068	March 1590 ACA/18 f.139	wife of Leonard	Coggeshall	„ „ „ „ „
1 069	March 1590 ACA/18 f.139	Margt. Foster	Coggeshall	a witch, 'she is at Maldon'

No.	Date/Source	Name	Village	Offence/Process
1,070	March 1590 ACA/17 f.332ᵛ	Jn. Church and wife	Fordham	use witchcraft; cited, ex.
1,071	March 1590 ACA/17 f.332ᵛ	Robt. Wright and wife	,,	,, ,, ,,
1,072	Nov. 1590 ACA/19 f.88ᵛ	John Gyles	Wivenhoe	for sending his daughter to a cunning woman at 'newcastell'; next court
1,073	Apr. 1591 ACA/19 f.156ᵛ	Thos. Harvy	East Mersea	sought help for himself and others at 'one Creek of Cobduck in Suff[olk]'; admits, to confess
1,074	Apr. 1591 ACA/19 f.157ᵛ	Eliz. Maun	West Mersea	a witch; next court
1,075	Apr. 1591 ACA/19 f.157ᵛ	Margt. Wiseman	,, and Bradwell	a witch, daughter of Eliz., above; now (cf. Maldon) at Bradwell-iuxta-Mare; next court
1,076	July 1591 ACA/19 f.201	(John) Churche	Fordham	use witchcraft; stands ex.
1,077	July 1591 ACA/19 f.201	wife of Robt. Wright	,,	,, ,, ,,
1,078	July 1591 ACA/19 f.201	Alice Jenitas (widow)	Alresford	a witch; next court
1,079	Nov. 1591 ACA/19 f.240ᵛ	John Carter	Weeley	for boasting himself able to find lost goods by spells; denied, dismissed
1,080	Nov. 1591 ACA/19 f.240ᵛ	—— Bryant	,,	for using sorcery under the guise of surgery; dismissed
1,081	Dec. 1591 ACA/19 f.258ᵛ	Margt. Coalle (w/Joseph)	Frating	a witch; denied to P/5
1,082	Dec. 1591 ACA/19 f.270	Agnes Heard	Wivenhoe	a witch; next court
1,083	March 1592 ACA/20 f.179	Amos Manship	Colne Engaine	going to a cunning woman at or near Feering
1,084	June 1592 ACA/19 f.367ᵛ	Anne Heard	Little Oakley	a witch, long-suspected; stands ex., next court
1,085	June 1594 ACA/22 f.100	Widow Howe	Tolleshunt Knights (Bushes)	a witch; denied to P/5
1,086	July 1594 ACA/21 f.253	Margt. Clarke	Tendring	a witch and a 'woman of filthey behaviour'; denied to P/4
1,087	July 1594 ACA/21 f.253	Mary Bright	,,	a witch, mother of Margt. Clarke (above); denied to P/4
1,088	June 1595 ACA/21 f.390ᵛ	Alice Tibbould	Little Bromley	a scold, slanderer, and resorted to cunning men for help; stands ex., cited

No.	Date/Source	Name	Village	Offence/Process
1,089	July 1595 ACA/22 f.187ᵛ	Alice Marshall	Stisted	said to have used 'Loving powder' make a man love her; next court
1,090	July 1595 ACA/23 f.68	Eliz. Woodborne (w/Thos.)	Clavering	a witch; next court
1,091	Oct. 1596 ACA/23 f.122	wife of Jn. Rawe	Ashdon	a witch; next court
1,092	June 1597 ACA/22 f.271ᵛ	John Manning and wife	Tolleshunt Knights	for not receiving Communion, John replied that Smith's wife called his wife, 'being an old woman', 'Witche and bytche', so that he and his wife could not receive; to receive Communion
1,093	Oct. 1597 ACA/23 f.177ᵛ	Augustin Elliott	Great Chishall	called Margery Marshall whore and witch, admits, but says it was 'uppon iust causes'; to be reconciled
1,094	Apr. 1598 ACA/22 f.325ᵛ	Christian Hunt	Tollesbury	a witch; next court
1,095	May 1598 ACA/24 f.115ᵛ	Joan Roothe	Great Bentley	a witch and scolded in the church; next court
1,096	May 1598 ACA/24 f.120ᵛ	William Ruffle	Lawford	sent his wife to a cunning man, 'Goodin of Colchester', about his stolen horse; also, being a church-warden, failed to make present-ments and for attempted incontin-nency; next court
1,097	May 1598 ACA/24 f.122ᵛ	Joan Rothe	Great Bentley	a witch and scolder (to confess for scolding); said to be 'free of witchery'
1,098	Aug. 1598 ACA/23 f.212	Anne Rawe	Ashdon	a witch; stands ex., cited
1,099	Aug. 1598 ACA/23 f.212	Mary Rawe	Ashdon	a witch; stands ex., cited
1,100	July 1599 ACA/25 f.50	Edmund Crosse	Goldhanger	called Mary Hatchman whore and witch; stands ex., cited
1,101	July 1600 ACA/24 f.296	Widow Howgrave	Abberton	a witch and continually absent from church
1,102	Apr. 1601 ACA/24 f.361ᵛ	—— Hugrave	,,	,, ,, ,, ,, dismissed
1,103	July 1601 ACA/24 f.382	David Tarver	Little Oakley	a slanderer and called the wife of James Bean a witch and fought with another woman; denied to P/5, then admits, penance
1,104	Dec. 1606 ACA/29 f.284	Mary Woodward	Ramsey	a witch; P/4 failed to confess
1,105	Nov. 1609 ACA/32 f.126ᵛ	Alice Potchys (widow)	(Stisted)	a witch; dismissed

No.	Date/Source	Name	Village	Offence/Process
1,106	Apr. 1611 ACA/32 f.255	Anne Harvy (w/Thos.)	Colne Engaine	a slanderous person, calling Cicely Lepingwell a witch; churchwardens to certify detection
1,107	May 1611 ACA/32 f.262ᵛ	,,	,,	a slanderous person, calling Cicely Lepingwell a witch; churchwardens, ex.
1,108	Dec. 1588 ACD/1 f.36ᵛ, 37ᵛ	various (see across)	Witham	Wm. Roman of Witham, yeoman, deposed that Eliz. Harris, wife of George, was believed to have bewitched the child of Robt. Armond and had been tried at the Assizes. Jn. Barker of Witham corroborated this and said that he had heard that Armond went for help for his sick child to a cunning woman near Stifford

Commissary Court records at E.R.O.

1,111	1618 ABD/1 f.170	various (see across)	Danbury	in libel case between Susan Spilman and Edward Saffold, Jn. Newton of Danbury deposed that Saffold said that there 'was an old witch' who came to his house when he was out and hanged his dog, implying that Susan Spilman was the witch

Consistory Court records

1,112	Nov. 1575 DL/C 212 f.156ᵛ–157ᵛ, f.160	various	Little Saling	Wm. Bendlowes and Henry Smith both deposed that Jn. Reynoldes and his wife libelled Jn. Kirkham by alledging that he was a witch and had bewitched Reynolde's wife (who lay 'sick and full of blisters') and daughter: Kirkham, like Smith, was a servant of Bendlowes, Jn. Maryan deposed that Thomas Wood and his wife Alice libelled Margery Kirkham in saying that she had bewitched their child, suddenly sick.
1,113	July 1584 DL/C/301 f.29ᵛ	—— Joyce	Stanford Rivers	had been ordered to undergo public penance and to 'p[ro]test that she will not meddle with sorcery and witchcraft'; to certify of penance
1,114	Oct. 1584 DL/C/301 f.18ᵛ	Eliz. Morsby and daughter	Great Chesterford	stands excommunicated for witchcraft

No.	Date/Source	Name	Village	Offence/Process
1,115	Oct. 1584 DL/C/301 f.22ᵛ	Henry Gower (cleric)	Quendon	dwells in Quendon, having no living and a suspected 'charmer or sorcerer' who 'deceaveth many people'
1,116	Oct. 1584 DL/C/301 f.23ᵛ	Alice Bolton (wife)	St. Osyth	a witch; already imprisoned
		wife of Cooke		a witch; dead
		Eliz. Lomley		a witch; denied the detection; dismissed because a faulty detection and because she alleged 'that she hath byn convented and clered for it by the temporal magistra[te]'
1,117	March 1602 DL/C/303 f.236	Thos. Welles and wife Katherine	Birdbrook	witches
1,118	March 1602 DL/C/303 f.246	wife of Robt. Ager	Stebbing	a witch; on 31 May Robt. Ager certified that she had done penance 'for bewitching of women'; therefore dismissed
1,119	March 1602 DL/C/303 f. 246ᵛ	Barbara Pond (w/Edward)	„	a witch; next court
1,120	March 1602 DL/C/303 f.255ᵛ	Thos. Maunde	Great Dunmow	commonly thought a wizard, he replied that some people who came to him he sent to 'one Brite', now deceased, to be examined
1,121	March 1602 DL/C/303 f.260ᵛ	George Taylor	Thaxted	using sorcery to tell where lost goods were, 'deceavinge divers people'; ex.
1,122	March 1602 DL/C/303 f.301ᵛ	wife of Austyn Houlder	Beaumont	a witch, bound over by Mr. Pirton, J.P., to the next Assizes; 'mortua as she went to the sises'
1,123	March 1602 DL/C/303 f.338ᵛ	wife of John Frauncis	Hockley	a witch; stands ex.
1,124	March 1602 DL/C/303 f.359	William Burles	Black Notley	resorted to sorcerers; had left Notley; stands ex.
1,125	May 1602 DL/C/303 f.409ᵛ	Barbara Pound (w/Edward)	Stebbing	a witch, churchwardens said 'that Barbara Pond falling out with one of her neighbors she sayd it had byn better for her she had delt so w[i]th her wherupon the woman fell lame and p[er]swaded her self she was bewiched by her the same Barbara Pond'; the suspicion

No.	Date/Source	Name	Village	Offence/Process
				occurred at midsummer and Barbara hence claimed the 'benefitt of the p[ar]don'; dismissed
1,126	Dec. 1631 DL/C/319 f.29ᵛ	Edmund Rowlande	Stifford	a physician without licence and suspected to work 'by witchcraft' for the last seven years; unable to produce licence; penance
1,127	Apr. 1622 DL/C/325 f.25	Alice Soles (w/Jn.)	Leigh	a sorceress; she said she had been questioned by justices of the peace, therefore ordered to bring a certificate of such questioning

Records in transit, temporarily deposited at the P.R.O.

No.	Date/Source	Name	Village	Offence/Process
1,128	Sept. 1561 Archdeaconry of Essex Act Book, Sept. 1561– Apr. 1562. no foliation; court at Raileigh, Sept. 13, 1561	Churchwardens of Shopland		presented for 'myntenans of sorcery', having approved of the act of Margt. Hosie, who burnt a calf 'in witchcrafte to p[re]serve the slyenck [sic]', and who said in court that 'she was a honest wooman who can not be paid'; to pay 6d. to the poor, and dismissed
1,129	Dec. 1574 Fragment of Consistory Court (1574) Correction Book; no foliation; court at Chelmsford, Dec. 17, 1574	Thomas Smith	Earls Colne	for conjuring, and teaching without a licence; denied the charges; to stop teaching until he produced a licence and certificate from his neighbours
1,130	Dec. 1574 (as above case)	Alice Reade	Lawford	for using a 'sieve and shears' to find lost goods; to be examined at the next court
1,131	Hilary 1579 Consistory Court Deposition Book, Apr. 28, 1578–15 Nov. 1580. no foliation, Hilary 3, 1579	Brigitte Bradye	Doddinghurst	Wm. Waylet deposed how B. Bradye asked where a woman who had been mad ('dryven abowt the towne with a ratt or a moale') was; the woman, Alice Clement, replied 'Naye it was neither ratt nor Moale: but sutch an old witch as thow art:' Thomas Fisher of London also heard this slander
1,132	March 1605 Commisary Court Correction Book, from March 1605, f.1	Margt. Prentize (w/Thos.)	Little Burstead	a witch and 'a Rayler Curser and scoulder, and is said to be a rayler againste the marriage of ministers'; to attend Mr. Bockman 'to be taught her dutie'
1,133	March 1605 as above, f.16	Christine Fulton (widow)	Upminster	a witch; (note: 'to be heard of Justices')

No.	Date/Source	Name	Village	Offence/Process
1,134	March 1605 as above, f.55ᵛ	John Comines and wife	Great Parndon	'sorcery or witchcraft'; John said that he was bound to appear at the Assizes, therefore ordered to 'be instructed in the principles of Religion' (at f.251 brings certificate of honest behaviour)
1,135	March 1605 as above, f.69	Eliz. Chapman (widow)	Ugley	disturbed minister when he was reading the psalms by shouting at him 'to leave of[f] his witchery coniuration and sorcery'; she also struck him.
1,136	March 1605 as above, f.119	William Duffield	Great Waltham	a user of 'witchcraft' and resorted to similar witches for advice and help.
1,137	March 1605 as above, f.127ᵛ	—— Hingson (widow)	Rochford	a witch
1,138	March 1605 as above f.202	Richard Banckes	Earls Colne	for sorcery

BOROUGH COURT PROSECUTIONS

Only seven of the cases from Borough Court records are known to have been printed before. Ewen included cases 1,165 and 1,176 from Colchester in his list of Essex cases (the Ewen references are given under the cases). Cases 1,142 and 1,143 are described and partially printed in the *Essex Review*, xvi (1907), pp. 68ff., 161–2. Case 1,175 was reprinted in the *Essex Notebook and Suffolk Gleaner* (Colchester, May 1885, No. 8), p. 88. Case 1,141 and a presentment at Maldon in connexion with case 807 are printed in *Shirburn Ballads, 1585–1616*, ed. Andrew Clark (Oxford, 1907), p. 153.

The location and nature of these records are described in the Bibliography. In the Harwich and Colchester prosecutions the date in the column 'Date/ Source' is that of the sitting of the court (with the documentary reference below). The date under 'Offence/Process' is that of the supposed offence.

'S.R.' in the Colchester prosecutions is an abbreviation for Sessions Roll. 'g.c.' stands for gaol calendar; 'f.' for folio; 'm.' for membrane. For other abbreviations, see the introduction to the Assize abstracts, p. 254 above.

Maldon

No.	Date/Source	Name	Offence/Process
1,141	1572 D/B 3 1/6 f.149ᵛ	Alice Chaundeler	indictment for bewitching a child to death, exactly as in case 67
1,142	1591 D/B 3 1/8 f.23, 23ᵛ, 87ᵛ	Edmund Hunt	examination of Hunt for searching for lost treasure at Beeligh Abbey. He consulted Thomas Collyne, who

No.	Date/Source	Name	Offence/Process
1,143	1592 D/B 3, 1/8, f.39ᵛ, 34, 38, 41, 53ᵛ	Margt. Wiseman	suggested that he took a piece of earth to Dr. Dee; Hunt also procured parchment with magical drawings on it. George Oder was also examined concerning the affair recognizances of a number of men and women to appear to witness against Margaret concerning her witchcraft, and recognizances taken of others to ensure her good behaviour; details concerning her witchcraft, which included a description of a magical broom which swept on its own

Harwich

No.	Date/Source	Name	Offence/Process
1,144	Apr. 1601 98/14 f.1	Eliz. Hudson (spinster)	on 20 Nov. 1598 at Harwich bewitched Wm. Charnoll, son of Richard C., of H., taylor, so that he died on 25 Nov., to be hanged
1,145	Apr. 1601 98/14 f.1ᵛ	„ „ „	on 6 Jan. 1601 at H. bewitched Margt. Maynard, daughter of Walter M. of H., sailor, who died on 25th of same month; confesses guilt; to be hanged
1,146	Apr. 1601 98/14 f.2	Eliz. Hanby (widow)	on 18 June 1598, at H., bewitched Judith Blabbe, daughter of Wm. B. of H., mariner, who died on 8 Aug. following; denied; guilty; to be executed
1,147	Aug. 1601 98/14 f.2ᵛ	Alice Babbe (widow)	on 19 March 1601 bewitched Alice Taylor, daughter of Jn. T. of H., who died on 24th of the same month; denied; guilty; to be executed
1,148	Aug. 1601 98/14 f.3	Eliz. Hankinson (spinster)	on 19 May 1601 bewitched Katherine Lawrence, daughter of Jn. L. of H., inholder, who died on 22nd of the same month; she also bewitched Jn. Ingate, son of Jn. I. of H., mariner, who languished from 6 to 9 Aug. 1600, when he died; confessed; guilty; to be executed
1,149	Aug. 1601 98/14 f.3ᵛ	Margt. Grove (w/Jn., tailor)	on 12 Dec. 1602 bewitched Jn. Wolnaughe, son of Nicholas W. of H., mariner, who died the same day; confessed; to be executed

No.	Date/Source	Name	Offence/Process
1,150	Aug. 1605 98/14 f.15ᵛ	Mary Harte (spinster)	on 4 July 1605 bewitched 7 lb. of meat worth 11*d.* of the goods of Robt. Smarte of Dovercourt, which putrified ('*putrificat fetide*'); denied; not guilty; acquitted
1,151	Sept. 1606 98/14 f.17ᵛ, 18, 19	„ „ „	inquisition and indictment: on 24 Feb. 1582 [*sic*] bewitched Jn. Graye of H., sailor, who died on 9 March following; on 3 March 1605 at H. bewitched Ursula Man, wife of Jn. M. of H., mariner, who died on 22 July following; guilty; to be executed
1,152	Oct. 1609 98/14 f.40ᵛ	Thos. Barneby	he appeared personally and was exonerated from suspicion of felony and witchcraft
1,153	Oct. 1609 98/14 f.41, 41ᵛ	Cecily and Peter Wigborough	six people, three men and three women, bound to give evidence against Cecily and Peter for witchcraft
1,154	Jan. 1610 98/14 f.41ᵛ, 42	„ „ (shoemaker)	inquisition on oaths of seventeen men that: Peter W. of H. on 25 Nov. 1609 bewitched Jn. Ponder of H., sailor, who died on 5 Dec. following; and Cecily W. his wife, on 8 Nov. 1609 bewitched Robt. Braxted, son of Robt. of H., a mariner, who languished to the present; both deny; neither guilty
1,155	Dec. 1611 98/14 f.50	„ „ „ „	on 10 Sept. 1611 bewitched Eliz. Skynner, wife of Wm. S. of H., sailor, who was lamed and wasted
1,156	March 1612 98/14 f.51ᵛ, 52, 53ᵛ	„ „ „ „	inquisition on oath of various that Cecilia Wigborow on 20 May 1611 bewitched Eliz. Thorne of H., who languished to 10 Dec. following; not guilty
1,157	Aug. 1615 98/14 f.61	Margt. Buller (widow)	committed to gaol of Harwich; Wm. Derifall bound to give evidence against Margt. for bewitching his wife Eliz. to death
1,158	Sept. 1615 98/14 f.61ᵛ	„ of Dovercourt	inquisition on oaths of several who say that on 26 June, 1615 Margt. bewitched Eliz. Derifall, who died on following 4 July; denied; not guilty
1,159	Feb. 1618 98/14 f.67ᵛ	Anne Buller	Wm. Derifall and Wm. Camper to appear against Anne

No.	Date/Source	Name	Offence/Process
1,160	Sept. 1619 98/14 f.68	Margt. Buller	indicted for murder and witchcraft on body of Christopher Derifall; guilty; to be executed; and also for the same on Jn. Camper
1,161	July 1618 29/4, 29/10	Anne Buller	Wm. Camper to frame an indictment against Anne for bewitching his son Jn. to death; likewise Wm. Derifall, his brother Christopher having been bewitched
1,162	July 1618 133/2	„ „	very detailed deposition of Wm. Camper concerning the bewitching of his son John. Includes details of the familiar and nature of the illness (contortions).
1,163	Aug. 1633 65/7	Jane Wiggins	examination of Thomazine, wife of Richard Hedge, who accused Jane of diverse attacks on the lives and property of various; includes details of familiars and the quarrels which led to witchcraft

Colchester

No.	Date/Source	Name	Offence/Process
1,164	Apr. 1576 S.R. 18 Eliz. g.c. and m.12	Ethelreda Pilgrim (spinster)	in prison for suspicion of witchery; Ethelreda, of St. Mary C. on 29 Oct. 1575 bewitched Joan Masselyne, wife of Wm. M. of C., butcher, who died on 12 Dec.; true bill; not guilty
1,165	1582–3 Ewen, II, p. 429	Margt. Holbeye	indicted for bewitching Eliz. Pickas; imprisoned for a year
1,165b	Apr. 1585 S.R. 27 Eliz. g.c. and m.4, 15	Margt. Holbeye (spinster)	in gaol for 'witchery'; various women bound to give evidence against her; on 2 July 1582 bewitched Susan Pikas of C., spinster, who was wasted and consumed; true bill; guilty; year's imprisonment. On 2 July 1584 bewitched Wm. Goonbye, who died on 6 Dec. following, true bill; not guilty
1,166	Apr. 1585 S.R. 27 Eliz.	Henry and Alice Driver	prisoners on bail; Henry and Alice Driver; various bound to give evidence against them for witchcraft
1,167	Apr. 1585 S.R. 27 Eliz. g.c., m.11	Katherine Reve (spinster)	on bail; various to give evidence against Katherine, of St. James, C.; on 26 Feb. 1584 bewitched Helen Brownsmyth, wife of Andrew of C.

No.	Date/Source	Name	Offence/Process
			currier, who was tormented to 10 Jan. following; guilty; imprisoned one year
1,168	July 1592 S.R. 34 Eliz. m.8	Alice Driver (widow)	in gaol; on 3 Aug. 1591 bewitched Anne Ostelyn, daughter of Eliz., who died on following 7 Aug.; true bill; not guilty
1,169	July 1592 S.R. 34 Eliz. m.2 Ewen, I, p. 284	Margt. Rand (widow)	on bail; various to give evidence against her; jury say bill of presentment a true one, therefore indicted that on 28 Nov. 1591 she bewitched Judith Lingwood, wife of Jn. L. of C., tailor, who languished until 7 Dec. following; not guilty
1,170	May 1593 (10th) Examination Book, 1588–1500, no foliation	„ „ „	examination of Susan Compstone; told how Lingwood's wife scratched Widow Rand on the face and a horseshoe was nailed to the threshhold and the witch pushed over it
1,171	Apr. 1599 S.R. 41 Eliz.	Eliz. Shymell (spinster)	on bail; on 1 Apr. 1599 bewitched one cow worth 20s. and one pig worth 10s. of Philip Smyth; they died; true bill, not guilty
1,172	21 Apr. 1599 Examination Book, 1588–1600, no foliation	Eliz. Shymell (w/Edward)	examined concerning her relations with various suspected victims of her witchcraft, includes a reference to 'Robyn the devill'; mark of Eliz. four men bound for her appearance at court
1,173	26 May 1599 Examination Book, 1588–1600, no foliation	Parnella Abbott (of Greenstead)	detailed examinations of four men and a woman, including Wm. Denman, incumbent of Greenstead, as well as Parnella herself. Descriptions of various quarrels and injuries supposedly connected by witchcraft. Parnella had killed several men and been suspected as a witch for over twenty years. One victim went to 'Anne Cryx of New Castle' for a remedy after being bewitched. Parnella told how Alexander Bradock, surgeon of Colchester, asked her to keep a familiar for him, and Marcellus Goodwyn, physician of the same town, 'did Clapp two Clawes to this examynates head'

No.	Date/Source	Name	Offence/Process
1,174	Apr. 1600 S.R. Eliz. 42 g.c. and m.11	Petronella Abbott (spinster)	in gaol; various bound to give evidence against her, including Jn. Dyxson of Greenstead, labourer; on 10 Apr. 1599 bewitched Susan Dyxson, daughter of Jn., who died on 10 May following, not guilty
1,175	June 1651 Corporation Records (see introduction)	Margt. Burgis (w/Thos.)	information of three men of Horndon-on-the-Hill about the suspected bewitching of a man by Margt.
1,176	1651 Ewen, I, p. 285	John Lock	for using 'witchcraft' to discover the lost yarn of Wm. Fayrcloth

PROSECUTIONS IN CENTRAL RECORDS

All the central sources from which the following cases are taken are located at the P.R.O. Cases 1,182 and 1,183 are printed with comments,, in C. L. Ewen, *Witchcraft in the Star Chamber* (n.p., 1938), pp. 15, 55–6. Case 1,195 is printed on pp. 9–10 of the same pamphlet by Ewen. Ewen I,, pp. 282–3 also printed cases 1,198, 1,200, 1,202 from the *Acts of the Privy Council*. Case 1,196 is discussed by G. L. Kittredge in *Harvard Studies and Notes in Philology and Literature*, xvi (Harvard, 1934), pp. 97–101.

Star Chamber

No.	Date/Source	Name/Village	Offence/Process
1,181	Oct. 1606 St. Cha. 8 58/5	Edwin Hadslye of Willingale Doe	among those accused of deer-stealing and assault in the park of Lord Morley, and a 'Comon Coniurer'; article 12 inquired whether he offered information about the other deer-thieves, obtained from his magic glass, in exchange for his release
1,182	1606 St. Cha. 8 207/21	Richard Cradock, clerk, and others	accused by Jn. Mountford, Vicar of Radwinter, of conjuring up false spirits in the church and churchyard in an attempt to secure possession
1,183	1621–1 St. Cha. 8 32/13	Katherine Malpas of West Ham	counterfeited possession with an evil spirit and caused goodwives Hedlyn and White to be taken for witches. Mr. Jennings, Vicar at Westham, and Master Holbrooke, the preacher there, prayed for the possessed girl. Dr. Francklin of

No.	Date/Source	Name/Village	Offence/Process
			Ratcliffe, a user of 'sawcerie', was employed and given 20s. The girl was examined in 1622 by King James
1,184	1621–3 St. Cha. 8 213/7	Anne Mortlake of Birdbrook	accused of procuring a sorcerer (Widow Chapman) to drive her husband mad so that she obtained his property and he wandered around as 'Mad Mortlake'

King's Bench

No.	Date/Source	Name/Village	Offence/Process
1,185	1578 K.B.9 647 m.237	Katherine Howe	committed to gaol for *maleficii* and died in prison on 4 June 1578
1,186	1583 K.B.9 658 m.369	Joan Maidston	committed to gaol for 'fascination' and died there of plague on 20 Apr. 1583
1,187	1587 K.B.9 668 m.274	Lettice Harris	probably a witch: died of plague in Colchester Gaol, 7 March 1587. The following year Eliz. Harris of Witham was tried as a witch; see case 262
1,188	1587 K.B.9 668 m.277	Eliz. Jackson	probably a witch, since she was one of seven people appearing in a gaol delivery roll, six of whom are known to have been witches; died of plague, 7 March
1,189	1589 K.B.9 676 m.230	Joan Adcock	probably a witch, since she immediately follows the known witch Agnes Mose, and an Alice Adcock was accused of witchcraft at the next Assizes, case 307; died of plague, 28 Oct. 1589
1,190	1589 K.B.9 676 m.231	Francisca Upney	probably a witch and the daughter of the witch Joan Uptney of Dagenham (cases 296, 297) who confessed (1589 Pamphlet, sig. B) to having two daughters who were witches; the other was probably Alice Upney, delivered according to the gaol calendar of the 1589 Trinity Assizes
1,191	1593 K.B.9 683 m.152	Joan Grine	imprisoned for suspected 'fascination' and died of plague on 5 Apr. 1592
1,192	1596 K.B.9 690 m.285	Joan Luckyn	imprisoned for 'fascination' and died on 4 Dec. 1595 of plague
1,193	1596 K.B.9 690 m.283	Joan Gardiner alias Webb	imprisoned for 'fascination'; died on 9 Dec. 1595 of plague

No.	Date/Source	Name/Village	Offence/Process
1,194	1596 K.B.9 690 m.289	Mary Luckyn	imprisoned for *maleficii*; died of plague on 18 Dec. 1595
1,195	1612 K.B.27 1435 m.392	Alice Arthur (widow), Chelmsford	she complained that Robt. Fuller slandered her by saying 'she is a witche and hath bewitched my childe'; damages claimed, £40. Robert pleaded not guilty; no verdict

State papers

1,196	Apr. 1561 St. Pap. 12/16 f.117, 120	Jn. Devon alias Cox	for holding masses in Essex (at Newhall) and for love magic at Winchester
1,197	Sept. 1577 St. Pap. 12/186 f.221–5	Rob.t Mantell	examination concerning his escape from Colchester Gaol and of Drs. Elkes and Spacie about treasure-seeking, having a familiar in a ring and using alchemy, in Essex and London

Privy Council Acts

1,198	Aug. 1577 Acts P.C.n.s. ix, pp. 391–2, x, pp. 62–3	Henry Chitham of Great Bardfield	suspected of coining money and conjuring
1,199	May 1580 Acts P.C.n.s. xii, pp. 23–4	Various	Ralph Spacy of Southminster and Thos. Lovekin, —— Warner, —— Constance, to be apprehended for conjuring
1,200	May 1580 Acts P.C.n.s. xii, p. 34	Humfrey Poles of Maldon	to be apprehended for conjuring
1,201	July 1580 Acts P.C. n.s. xii, p. 102	'one Randell'	that the boy accomplice of Randell, committed with him for conjuring, should be set free at the next Assizes
1,202	Nov. 1580 Acts P.C. n.s. xii, pp. 251–2	Nicholas Johnson of Woodham Mortimer	accused of sorcery, making a wax image of the Queen; bailed to next Assizes
1,203	1580–1 Acts P.C. n.s. xii, pp. 29, 353–4	Robt. Mantell/Bloise	concerning his escape from prison, treason, and sorcery of his accomplices (cf. also P.R.O. Assizes 35/23 Hilary, Nos. 48, 49)

Contemporary literary references to prosecutions

1,204   Apr.–May 1570, John Strype, *Life of Sir Thomas Smith* (1820), pp. 97–100. Sir Thos. Smith examined witnesses concerning Malter's wife of Theydon Mount, and

Anne Vicars of Navestock; various charges including bewitching animals and humans and having familiars, also details of counter-witchcraft activity and of a visit to a cunning man, 'one Cobham of Romford'.

1,205   Apr. 1602, John Darrell, *A Survey of Certaine Dialogical Discourses* (1602), p. 54. Alice Bentley, tried at the Quarter Sessions at Saffron Walden, 13 Apr. 1602, for bewitching Susan Boyton, who was possessed.

Miscellaneous references

1,206   2 June 1568. Pardon for John Wentworth, late of Little Horkesley, Armigerous, for Thomas Bridge, yeoman, late of Little Horkesley, and for Robert Ellys, late of White Notley, yeoman, for all conjurations of evil spirits committed before the present date. *Cal. Patent Rolls. Eliz. I, iv, 1566–1569* (1964), p. 169.

1,207   1633–47. There are a number of references to Essex witchcraft in the Ashmole MS. deposited at the Bodleian Library, Oxford. Of the three cases, (*b*) is especially long. References between 1633 and 1641 were found in Richard Napier's astrological practice-book, which was continued by his successor, Sir Richard Napier. Cases between 1645 and 1647 appear in the first three volumes of 'Figures set upon Horary Questions by Mr. William Lilly'.

1,207*a*   18 August 1634. Eliz. Wilkins and Emma Taylor, her daughter, were suspected of witchcraft in another county, and it was suspected that the latter had travelled into Essex. There is no reference in known Essex prosecutions to either of these women. Ashmole MS. 412, fol. 153.

1,207*b*   There are numerous references to the bewitching of Elinor Aylet of Magdalen Laver Hall in Little Laver. She was the wife of John Aylet, Lord of the Manor of Magdalen Laver (Morant, *Essex*, ii, 142).

Ashmole MS. 412, fol. 13^v: 23 Oct. 1633
    Mrs. Elinor Aylet of Aythorpe Roothing was supposedly bewitched by Eliz. Spacy and goody Mathewe. Also mentioned were Jane Lasco and her daughter, Jane Case of Magdalen Laver; Rebecca Write, Jone Dowsit, and Parnel Sharpe, all of Aythorpe Roothing. In this, as in most of the references, there are various astrological calculations.

Ibid., fol. 16: 26 Oct. 1633
    E.A., now said to be of Magdalen Laver, was 'troubled w[i]th a soden lossenes' which first occurred on her husband's death. 'Elisab Spacie' is written above the diagram.

Ibid., fol. 19^v: 17 Oct. 1633 [*sic*]
    'Eliz. Spacy of High Roding appeared plainly to her in her sleep this nighte and then not 2 or 3 dayes after.'

Ibid., fol. 117: 7 April 1634
    E.A. suspects witchcraft: 'her husband selfe and family have bin much tormented' and her cattle die, give no milk, or kick down the pails.

Ibid., fol. 125: 23 April 1634
E.A. desires to visit Napier.

Ibid., fol. 141^v: 10 June 1634
    E.A. 'sorely tormented and vexed with a company of witches' and 'feares they will worke her End'; her son and cows both attacked and she is feverish and 'something comes like a fly roaringe and Bussing about her'.

Ibid., fol. 146: 9 July 1634

E.A. came to Napier. The following names are listed: Elizabeth Spacy of High Roding and Rebecca, Richard Pavitt and wife of Leaden Rooding, Parnel Sharpe, An Mathew of Harlow, Jeffery Holmes and Joane and her mother, Joane Dowsett. E.A. was 'very much troubled in her head and a dazling in her Eyes'; her urine was good, but had 'a great white sedement'; she fainted often and did not sleep well. She was first ill in childbed, but had had nine children since. Her husband, daughter, and cows also attacked.

Ibid., fol. 153ᵛ: — 1634

Two of those E.A. suspected 'lay about her house' and would not go away until they had spoken to her or her husband; she refused to see them. The two suspects were 'Somes his wife and her mother'.

Ibid., fol. 157: 7 Oct. 1634

E.A. was taken with a fainting fit and flushed all over her body. She suspects Elizabeth Spacy most. Her daughter of five years has a running sore on her back and her son of six 'was taken in the night and his eye lids drawn all awry and divers little knobbs like warts on his eye lids'.

Ibid., fol. 175ᵛ: 19 Feb. 1635

E.A. sent a letter.

Ibid., fol. 279: 12 April 1639

E.A. again very sick with her old fainting fits. Much 'troubled with a cold in her stomache and with a swellinge in her Belly and sick at her heart'; 'hath sometymes a dry tickling Coffe'; 'a Burneinge heate at her backe very paynefull'; 'he[r] Courses stayd for 6 weekes and then she came down and she was very ill after the stay[ing]' 'cannot sleep'.

Ibid., fol. 282ᵛ: 19 May 1639

E.A. very sick and 'they feare she could not live till morneinge'; cannot sleep and sick and fainting.

Ibid., fol. 292ᵛ: 3 March 1640

A list of medicines for E.A.

Ashmole MS. 184, inside the back cover: no date, *c*.1645

Mention of Mrs Aylett of Magdalen Laver Hall.

Ashmole MS. 178, fol. 31; 1645

'A House and Grounds bewitched in Essex', 'Maudlin hall in Essex: in Little Laver', 'John Aylett. Ellinor'.

Ashmole MS. 185, fol. 270ᵛ: 26 April 1647

E.A. of 'Maudlin Hall' bewitched; medicines including 'duobus nailes'.

1,207c In a number of the references in case 1207*b* there is, alongside, a reference to another, though possibly connected, case. This concerned Faith Say or Sage of High Laver. The first known reference to this case occurred on 7 April 1634 (Ashmole MS. 412, fol. 117) where 'Faythe Saye for the like strong p[re]sumptions of witchcraft' is appended to the case of Elinor Aylett. On 7 July following (ibid., fol. 146ᵛ) her cattle, butter, cheese, and beer were said to have been attacked by witches. Powder, ointment for the udders of the cows and a parchment to be hung in a barrel were prescribed. At an unspecified date later in the same year (ibid., fol. 153ᵛ) her milk, cheese, and beer had been cured, but her husband 'for a great payne in his back feares those ill people'. On 7 October (ibid., fol. 157) her husband was still sick and she herself suffered from 'a litenes in her head and a payne in her Teeth and a trembling at her heart'. She was still receiving treatment on 9 Feb. 1635 (ibid., fol

175ᵛ). It is possible that a reference to 'Goodwife Faith saith ye old woeman nowe ill' inside the back cover of Ashmole MS. 184 (1645) is to the same case.

Cases 1,208–1,220: Suspected Witches named in Depositions, but not in Indictments

1,208   The mother of Elizabeth Lowys of Great Waltham. See case 861.

1,209   Eve (mother) of Hatfield Peverel who taught Eliz. Frauncis her witchcraft. 1566 Pamphlet, p. 318.

1,210   Elizabeth Lorde, widow, of Hatfield Peverel. She bewitched Goodman Some and Jone Roberts. 1579 Pamphlet, sig. Aiiiiᵛ.

1,211   Margery Sammon of St. Osithes, various acts of witchcraft (cf. Assizes 35/36/T, g.c.). 1582 Pamphlet, sigs. A5, C4, C4ᵛ

1,212   Henry Celles of Little Clapton, various acts of witchcraft. 1582 Pamphlet, sigs. C8, D, Dᵛ, D3.

1,213   Joan Robinson of Walton, various acts of witchcraft. 1582 Pamphlet, sigs. F5ᵛ–F8.

1,214   Elizabeth Ewstace of Thorpe, various acts of witchcraft. (cf. Gaol Calendar, case 168). 1582 Pamphlet, sigs. C7, D7ᵛ, E4, E6.

1,215   Elizabeth Motte of Heningham Sible uses a familiar. 1589 Pamphlet, sig. B2ᵛ.

1,216   Elizabeth Whale of Heningham Sible, uses a familiar. 1589 Pamphlet, sig. B2ᵛ.

1,217   Elizabeth Clarke's mother (Bedingfield?) and kinsfolk of Manningtree; previously executed. 1645 Pamphlet, p. 1.

1,218   Judith Moone of Thorpe has the marks of a witch. 1645 Pamphlet, p. 25.

1,219   Sarah Burton imprisoned at Harwich for witchcraft. 1645 Pamphlet, p. 28.

1,220   Goodwife Hagtree had an 'imp' fifteen years before. 1645 Pamphlet, p. 29.

840   Case 840 is so curious that it merits further discussion. A number of the families involved, the Ayletts, Maxies, and Alstons, were prominent gentry families and are easily located in Morant, *Essex*. The exact nature of what was supposed to have occurred is obscure, as is the connexion with the village witchcraft with which the records primarily deal. Those implicated sent a petition to the Justices of the Peace (E.R.O. Q/SBa 2/56–8) stating that the charges of 'Coniuracon, Theft, Whordome and many other misdemean[ou]rs' were false. The first part of the deposition of Martha Hurrell will be enough to show the extraordinary allegations. The full account is contained in E.R.O., Q/SR, 324/118:

> She deposeth that betweene Easter and Mich[ae]lmas 1643 . . . Mr. Robert Aylett and Mr Tho Ailett, Mr James Richardson, Sarah Fletcher, Abraham Rich, Jo: Drake, Jo: Dier (all of Stistead), Lambert Smith, and the Coniurer, that went in black Apparrell, of a browne haire, and a blackish beard, a man of a middle size (and various others, named) . . . had half a dozen meetings. At her M[aste]rs twice and att Wm Drakes half a score times, and att Sr Wm Maxies house and att my La[dy] Edens once or twice, and they rode to Sr Wms and my Ladies, and once att Sr Martin Lumelyes . . . and these meetings were alwaies in the night. . . . And w[hen] they thus mett they went into the bed chambers of those p[er]sons att whose houses they mett, sometimes, and att her Mrs. they tooke M[ist]ris Drurie out of her bed and carried her into the hall chamber and there the Conjurer and

Henry had the use of her bodie, and Henry first, once a piece, and then the[y] fetcht her husband and laid by her, and then Eliz. Waite and Sarah Fletcher, and then they kissed him and puld up his shirt, and took up their Coates, and lay downe on the top of him, and they said that he did them some good. . . .

Among the other activities were stealing clothes and money, banquettings where they 'feasted and had fidlers from Coggishall and Sr Wm Maxies maid plaid on the virginalls', and some conjuring. 'Sir Wm. Maxies man did conjure by making a cirle in her Mrs hall and setting up 3 candles w[hi]ch burnt blue and w[he]n they put them out they did it [wi]th milk and soote'.
(Punctuation is slightly modified to make the sense clearer.)

861   *Depositions written at the end of an Archdeaconry Act Book* (E.R.O., D/AEA/2). The first person to be accused of witchcraft in Essex after the Witchcraft Statute of 1563 was Elizabeth Lowys. She was found guilty at the Summer Assizes, but pleaded pregnancy. A month before the Assizes she was questioned at the Archdeaconry Court. Her deposition and those of witnesses have survived at the end of the Act Book. They are unique and of considerable interest, especially because they are the earliest qualitative evidence for witchcraft beliefs in Essex. They show, among other things, the type of neighbourly quarrelling that surrounded witchcraft accusations. For these reasons, the depositions have been fully transcribed, with only punctuation slightly modified. Miss Tessa Ward of Chelmsford very kindly helped to transcribe the difficult script (cf. cases 3–5, 861, pp. 255, 278, above).

(1) Henry Geale, aged eighty or thereabouts, of Waltham Magna, where he had lived six or seven years, being examined, said:

'Firste that John Lewys and ollif his daughter aboute this tyme ii yeres had stolen a capon of this depo[n]ent, and when she came to demaund yt he denied yt utterlie, tyll at the last, when he sawe this depo[nent] wolld goe farther, he confessed yt and offered hym monye, but noo certein some. And [he had] solld yt to one Mary Barnard, Prowes wife sistar w[hi]ch capon the said Lewys fetched againe. He wold have d[elivere]d yt on a mud wall, but this depo[nen]t refused so to doo and will hym to come into this depon[ent] house. For this depo[nent] had be[n]e to see Tho Gryges [the] constable, who willed hym to sende for som[e] other man at the reseipt of the capon. And after the d[elivery] of the said capon at the p[er]swacyon of Tho Wygnoll. The said Gryges wif[e], who was godmother to ollif Lowys (who holpid her father to stele the capon), said to ollif "Thou art my goddaught[er] and suerlie, if th[e]y parents will not convert thee, I will", and soo then and there she bete her.

'This the capon de[livere]d, they fell in talke. The said wignoll said to the said John Lowys in this wise. "Fye for shame Lowys, beinge an old man willt not leve thy pilferinge? For thirty y[er]es past my father toke a handsawe out of thy hous." Then said Lowys, "I praie yow end this matter and I will nev[er] do so more." To whome againe the said Wignall saide, "Thow hast ben a prettie man in thy daies." "Ye" said Lowes "I may thanke my wif of this my Lamenes for soo she hathe bewyched me lame, and then I sent for the conynge woman of Wytham and she told me yt was my wifes doinge."

'And then and there Lowys wif and her mother fell at variac[o]ns, and for her p[ar]t she the said Lowis wif, being werie of the exercysinge of her wytcherie because her mother was strong[e]r in bewytchinge then she was, said she wollde devoure her sellf; and uppon that her husband, beinge in feare of her, beinge in the stret, went home and cominge home she was hanged in the hous. She hanged herself still [*sic*] she were sterke dede. And h[e]r husbande cut the rope. And beinge relieved, Tho Wignall and other[s] demaunded of her whye she did so; she said she dyd yt to the [e]nd her husbande and mother shulld be hanged because her mother was the strong[e]r wytche.

'Mr Warter has the examining.'

(2) Philippa Geale, aged thirty-two of Great Waltham, being examined, said:

'That Elizabeth Lewys, wife of John Lowys, and this depo[nen]t fell at varia[c]-ons for takynge in of worke, in that the said Lewys wif went to John Barnard's wif and said that this depo[nen]t wolld spyn no more of her worke. Thereuppon at the next meatynge they fell out. And this depo[nen]t tollde her that she lied and had tollde a wronge tale. And, amonge other talke, this deponent saiethe that she said "yf it be as folke saye, thow art a wytche". To whome the said Lewys wif aunswered, "yf I be a wyche the dyvell thee twytche". And ymmediatly upon that this depo[nen]t fell on a grete quyvering and quakeringe. And this was don about Satirday aboutes five yeres past. And soo after that [she] went home, continuynge soo till wednesdaie, at w[hi]ch daie she fell downe ded, and was so sick fourteen daies yt no bodie thought shee wolld have lyved. And then her neighbors sent for the preistes, to whome she utterid all. And then he sent for the said Lewys wif, threatenynge her if this depo[nen]t died she shulld be brent [i.e. burnt], and after her comynge this depo[nen]t mended.

'And otherwise she knows nothing.'

(3) Agnes Devenyshe, aged forty-seven, of Waltham, where she had resided eight years, deposed that:

'she hathe herde a comon brute [i.e. rumour] that Lewys wif ys a wytche. Item, that about M[ar]ch last, gooinge to Comes house, she wente to the said Lowys wiffes hous, and then they talked about a sore arme of hers. And then she [i.e. Eliz. Lowys] counselled her to goo to a woman under Munckewoode. And goynge thith[e]r, the folkes tolld her husbande and her that she was a wychte.

'It[em]. the saide Lewys wif did then and there aske her how Johnson drink did worke. And she this deponent aunswerid that yt was as yt did. Then the said Lewys wif said, "lett hym com and speke w[]ith me".

'It[em]. that this depo[nen]t goynge to her for monnye, viz. vi*s* viii*d* whiche she collde not spare, and aft[e]r that she had two piges and one of them sodenlie died, and the other ev[er] pyned tyll she was fayne to sell yt. And she judgeth that yt is the doinge of the said Lowys wiff. And then she this depo[nen]r fell sicke, w[i]th her husband and child w[i]th all, in[?] pain and grief.

'Item. that on[e] maye even, being at Canell[es] hous, John Canell his chillde being sicke, [it] laye w[i]th the neck clene awrye, the face und[er] the lift [*sic*] shollder, and the right arme drawen w[i]th the hande clene backwarde and up-warde, the shullder pynt before the brest pight [*sic*], the bodie lyinge from yt an oth[er]waie, not right but wrythinge, and the right legge clene backwarde behinde the boddie—contrarie to all nature; as they suppose the verye doinge of the said Lowys wif.

'And otherwise she knows nothing to depose.'

(4) Lewys wif, being examined, said:

'Whether or when she was in her garden or y[ar]de.
'She replied "that she hathe a v[ar]de and in yt yerbes."

'It[em]. how many tymes she hathe lien flatt or knelid in the yarde. She saithe she neve[r] knelid or laye flatt in the y[ar]de.

'Item. whether she in the y[ar]de or hous knelinge standing or lyinge flatt spake theis wordes, viz. Christ my christ, yf thow be a saviour come down[e] and avenge me of my enemys, or elles thow shall not be a saviouf. Denies.

'It[em]. whether she confess[e]d that she killed a Lamb by wytcherye, yelld "might yt chene [*sic*], must yt be fed w[i]th the mete of childrene?" when yt was a fedinge w[i]th mylke and whitebrede. She admitted that she said that she cam[e] unto the hous where a woman was feadinge a Lambe w[i]th mylk and whitebredde and spake "what, must yt be fed w[i]th whitebredde and mylke?", and that then the woman putt upp the Lambe, And the next daie yt diedd [b]y eatinge w[i]th whitebredde and mylke ov[er] muche.

'It[em]. whether she was a doer in the hurting of Gregorie Canells chillde. Denied and said "that she was noo doer of yt".

'It[em]. Whether she was ev[er] at Maplestead. She says "she was nev[er] ther, but her husband hathe sent some thether."

'It[em]. Whether she counselled Canell to goo to the Woman of Paswykke for the childes recov[er]ie. She replies "that she willed his wif to goo thithere aboutes the chillde."

'It[em]. that her daughters, Anne, Allice, and Ollyf, were at home w[i]th her sins [i.e. since] the corte and dwell in the hundred, and were at home seven daies comynge on the tuesdaie and went on the tuisdaie. And [she] sent for them becaus she was in troble, to have them praie for her, by Henrey Lewgarr. And after, she confessed that she sent for them by Lewgar, and when they cam[e] she said, "children I am broght out of my good name to an yll." The [e]lldest said "o mother, I am sorie that we ar[e] com[e] to this lamentacton."

'Item. yt she nev[er] talk w[i]th them in a chambere; and at there dep[ar]ting she gave them gods blessinge.

'It[em]. her oth[er] daughters were at home sins her troble—Phillice and Jone. Gregory Canell affirms that his childe sykened the mundaie afore the Corte. And, after the Corte, the saide Childe died, beinge soo difformyd as nev[er] was sene, viz. the right arme tirnynge clene contrarie, and the legg contrarie to that, and rysinge double to the hed of the chillde.'

(5) 'Henry Lewgar, aged thirty, deposed that:

'at or going to ch[u]rch Lewys wif gave hym viii*d* to goo fetche her daughters in dengye hall and in that town; and that she knew p[er]fytley that her daughter was at dengye hall, and one dwellinge w[i]the Clarke and th[e] other dwelling w[i]th reynold. And comynge first to Annie, said in the kychin in the hall house to her, and said to her that y[ou]r frether [*sic*] and mother praied her to com[e] to them. And th[e] other at Reynolds in the hall. And he laye at his brothers to Sudmyster. And to the thirde he and [the] other sister went, to Clarkes, and soo they cam w[i]th hym to little Waltham. And Ollif cam to Walltham and then in a fellde p[ar]ted from her.

'It[er]m that he hathe herd by talke that she hathe been suspect of wytcherie ev[er]ie four yeres.

'It[em]. that he cam[e] to Wignalls hous the night before he went, and went into the house to have his counsell before he went for them. And said, "Mother Lowe hereth me to go for her daughters."

'It[em] that she nev[er] taught them anie of her arte or cunyng.'

Appendix 2

Definitions of witchcraft

Recent historians of English witchcraft have had considerable difficulty in their attempts to define the basic terminology.[1] Similarly, there is no unanimity among anthropologists. The classic distinction between 'witchcraft' and 'sorcery' in Africa was first outlined by Professor Evans-Pritchard in the following words:

> Azande believe that some people are witches and can injure them in virtue of an inherent quality. A witch performs no rite, utters no spell, and possesses no medicines. An act of witchcraft is a psychic act. They believe also that sorcerers may do them ill by performing magic rites with bad medicines.[2]

The distinction here is between different types of means: the end is similar. Both witches and sorcerers injure people. Among the Azande a person *is* a witch. Witchcraft is an inherent quality, whereas sorcerers *act* in a certain way. Sorcerers are conscious of their activities, whereas witches, whose power is internal, may not be aware that they are witches until they are accused. While the witch is the vehicle for a power greater than herself, often the unwilling agent of vast evil forces, the sorcerer controls the power inherent in certain 'medicines' or other objects. Although both are driven by antisocial feelings, the witch is permanently malicious, having inherited her power or been taught it very early in life, while the sorcerer is only dangerous at specific times and acquires the power of evil later in life by a more self-conscious transmission.

Unfortunately, these analytic distinctions have not always worked when applied to societies other than the Azande. Thus, in Cewa society, there are 'sorcerers' who always use outward medicines or gestures and are conscious agents, but who, like 'witches', are permanently evil and learn their evil power early in life.[3] Even the Azande themselves do not have 'witches' by all these criteria: people are not permanently motivated by witchcraft, but only on specific occasions.[4] There have been other criticisms of the whole distinction,[5] yet it has been found a useful tool in the analysis of witchcraft beliefs in Tudor and Stuart Essex. We may therefore ask to what extent people distinguished between various types of 'witchcraft' and how far there were generally accepted definitions.

Examination of historical definitions on the basis of the above distinctions immediately reveals that there was immense confusion and variation. There are a number of obvious reasons for this. Some authorities based their definitions on the works of Continental demonologists; others on the opinions of country folk. Opinions of witchcraft changed between 1560 and 1680. Attitudes differed between social and religious groups. An illustration of the way in which a number of opposing concepts were subsumed under the word 'witchcraft' occurs in the work of the Kentish squire, Reginald Scot. 'Witchcraft', he said, was both good and bad in its effects, both inward and outward in its means, at least in the 'estimation of the vulgar people'. 'The effect and end' of witchcraft was 'sometimes evill, as when thereby man or beast, grasse, trees, or corne, &c., is hurt: sometimes good, as whereby sicke folkes are healed, theeves bewraied [*sic*], and true men come to their goods, &c.' Thus a person who cured an animal by magical means was, in common parlance, a 'witch'. Likewise, although outward rituals and medicines were used, inherent power of a personal kind was also needed. 'The matter and instruments, wherewith it is accomplished, are words, charmes, signes, images, characters, &c.'—external qualities. But their power depended on a certain personality. 'The which words although any other creature doo pronounce, in maner and forme as they doo, leaving out no circumstance requisite or usuall for that action: yet none is said to have the grace or gift to performe the matter, except she be a witch.'[6] A person *was* a witch and also acted as a witch.

Other writers did not agree with Scot that the 'vulgar people' did not distinguish between types of witchcraft. In fact, it was just such a tendency to make a distinction between the 'good' and the 'bad' witch that angered John Gaule. As he wrote in the middle of the seventeenth century:

According to the vulgar conceit, distinction is usually made betwixt the White and the Blacke Witch: the Good and the Bad Witch. The Bad Witch, they are wont to call him or her, that works Malefice or Mischiefe to the Bodies of Men or Beasts: The good Witch they count him or her that helps to reveale, prevent or remove the same.[7]

The Witchcraft Statutes also distinguished between different ends. The punishments for attempting to find lost goods, for instance, were different from those for trying to kill someone by witchcraft. Yet the Statutes, by including both offences, blurred the differences. Thus a 'good witch' in popular estimation might, theoretically, be executed just like a 'bad witch'.

There seems to have been, in fact, a constant struggle between those who wished to differentiate and those who wished to amalgamate. On the one hand, there were those who wished to punish equally all who used 'magical' power, irrespective of their ends, and irrespective of the degree of their control over such power. For them all 'superstition', especially that emanating from Rome, was 'witchcraft'.[8] For them the words 'witch' and 'conjurer' were synonyms.[9] On the other hand, these were those who wished to differentiate 'good' and 'bad' witches by their effects, and 'witches' and 'conjurers' by their degree of control over their power. The first of these distinctions we have seen in the passage by John Gaule quoted above. The second can be illustrated by the words of Sir Edward Coke:

A Conjurer is he that by the holy and powerful names of God invokes and conjures the Devill to consult with him, or to do some act. A Witch is a person, that hath a conference with the Devill, to consult with him or to do some act.[10]

The conjurer commands; the witch obeys.[11]

Two conclusions emerge from this short discussion of definitions of terminology. The first is that, although anthropologists have provided some useful analytic distinctions, these do not really help in a number of societies. The second is that words like 'witchcraft' and 'sorcery' were used in a number of different senses in seventeenth-century England. To avoid confusion, therefore, words have been used as indicated on p. 3, above, and illustrated in Fig. 1. Contrasting means and ends, 'witchcraft' is predominantly the pursuit of harmful ends by implicit/internal means. 'Sorcery' combines harmful ends with explicit means. 'White witchcraft' pursues beneficial ends by explicit means.

NOTES

1. K. M. Briggs, *Pale Hecate's Team* (1962), p. 3, discusses various definitions and suggests the effects of definitional differences among historians. Among other recent discussions, those of C. L. Ewen (Ewen, I), pp. 21–4, and G. Parrinder, *Witchcraft* (Pelican edn., 1958), pp. 8–13, are the most helpful.
2. Evans-Pritchard (1937), p. 21.
3. Marwick (1965), pp. 81–2, discusses the inapplicability of the 'witchcraft/sorcery' distinction in the Cewa setting.
4. 'A Zande is interested in witchcraft only as an agent on definite occasions . . . and not as a permanent condition of individuals', Evans-Pritchard (1937), p. 26.
5. One of the most forceful of the attacks on the widespread use of such a distinction was made by V. W. Turner, 'Witchcraft and Sorcery: Taxonomy versus Dynamics', *Africa*, xxxiv, No. 4 (1964), pp. 319–24.
6. Scot, *Discovery*, p. 389.
7. Gaule, *Select Cases*, p. 30.
8. For instance, see Perkins, *Damned Art*, pp. 150–2, 167.
9. Ady, *Candle*, pp. 63–4.
10. Edward Coke, *Third Part of the Institutes of Lawes of England* (1644), p. 44.
11. As Sir Walter Raleigh, echoing James I, put it (*History of the World* (1614), I, xi, 6, p. 209).

Bibliography

A. MANUSCRIPT SOURCES

I. ESSEX RECORD OFFICE

The Essex sources are described in F. G. Emmison, *Guide to the Essex Record Office* (Colchester, 1946–8), Parts 1, 2. Those records found most useful for the study of witchcraft prosecutions are listed in section (*a*) below. The sources used for the reconstruction of the social background to prosecutions in a sample three villages (as described in Ch. 6) are grouped in section (b). + against a source not in section (*b*) indicates that it was also used for the three-village study. For example, Quarter Sessions material was useful both as a source for witchcraft prosecutions and for its references to events in Hatfield Peverel, Boreham, and Little Baddow.

Undoubtedly the most important single source for witchcraft accusations are the Act Books of the Essex and Colchester Archdeaconry courts. Also of major importance are the Quarter Sessions records, and Maldon Borough records.

(a) *Witchcraft sources*

Ecclesiastical records

Archdeaconry of Essex
+ Act Books, 1560–1671   D/AEA/1–44
+ Deposition Books, 1576–1630   D/AED/1–5, 8–10
   Cause Books, 1581–1623   D/AEC/1–8
   Visitation Books, 1565, 1614   D/AEV/1, 5

Archdeaconry of Colchester
+ Act Books, 1540–1666   D/ACA/1–55
+ Deposition Books, 1587–1641   D/ACD/1–7
   Cause Books, 1588–1623   D/ACC/1–10
   Visitation Book, 1586–8   D/ACV/1

Archdeaconry of Middlesex
   Acts/Visitations, 1662–80   D/AMV/1–6

Bishop of London's Consistory Court
   Visitations, 1625–9, 1634–9   D/ALV/1, 2

Bishop of London's Commissary in Essex and Herts
    Act Books, 1616–68   D/ABA/1–12
    Depositions, 1618–42   D/ABD/1–8
    Miscellaneous, 1631–80   D/AXD/1–3

Quarter Sessions records:
    + Rolls, 1556–1680   Q/SR/1–441
      Bundles, 1610–80   Q/SBa/1–2
      Order Books, 1652–80   Q/SO/1, 2
      Minute Book, 1632–43   Q/SMg/1–5
      Estreats of Fines, 1626–49   Q/SPe/1–4

Maldon Borough records:
    + Court Books, 1557–1623   D/B/3/1/5–10
      Court Papers, 1594–5   D/B/3/3/65

Transcripts at the E.R.O.
    Essex Ship Money 1637,   T/A/42
    Diary of Ralph Josselin   T/B/9/1

Miscellaneous notes on witchcraft—of little value
    An essay on Matthew Hopkins   T/P/51/3
    Ducking of witches at Kelvedon   T/P/58
    Witchcraft in the eastern counties   T/Z/11/62, 79
    Witchcraft at Little Dunmow   T/P/107/1
    Burial of reputed witch, 1755   D/P/36/1/3
    A Colchester witch, 1747   D/DRg/4/57
    Notes on Manningtree witchcraft   T/P/114/9
    Notes on witchcraft   T/P/156/11

(b) *Sources for the study of Hatfield Peverel, Boreham, and Little Baddow, 1560–1603*

As well as the sources listed below, all references in other sections of the Bibliography with + against them were used in the three-village study.

Wills:
    Wills for Hatfield Peverel and Boreham between 1540 and 1610, as indexed and listed in *Wills at Chelmsford, 1400–1619*, ed. F. G. Emmison (Index Library, 78, 1958).

Parish registers:
    Boreham register, 1560–1603   D/P/29/1/1
    Little Baddow register, 1560–1603   D/P/35/1/1

Boreham accounts:
    Churchwardens and collectors for the poor,
      1565–1603   D/P/29/5

Hatfield Peverel, manorial:
   Mugdon Hall, court book, 1499–1558   D/DBd/M4
   Mugdon Hall, survey, 1589   D/DBd/M6/1, 2
   Hatfield Peverel, court roll, 1553–1603   D/DBr/M50

2. PUBLIC RECORD OFFICE

Assize records:
   + Home Circuit Indictments, 1559–1680   Assizes 35/1–121

King's Bench:
   + Ancient Indictments, 1560–1603,
       1645–7   K.B. 9/597–712, 830–9
     Controlment Rolls, 1582, 1647   K.B. 29/216, 296

Star Chamber:
   Proceedings, James I   St. Ch. 8
(Unfortunately the Elizabethan Star Chamber Proceedings have not yet been calendared. A search of the only thirty-one bundles (St. Ch. 7) which have been calendared, and of ten original bundles (St. Ch. 5/A. 1–9), revealed no cases of witchcraft. At present, therefore, it seems unlikely that a search for witchcraft cases in the 972 Elizabethan bundles would repay the labour involved. If cases appear in the Elizabethan records at roughly the same intervals as those in the Jacobean, we could only expect one Essex case every eighty or more bundles. No pre-1560 cases were discovered in *Select Cases in the Star Chamber, 1477–1544*, ed. I. S. Leadam (Selden Soc., xvi, xxv, 1903, 1911), or in the P.R.O. *Lists and Indexes* (xiii, 1901), which is a calendar of proceedings, 1485–1558).

Exchequer records:
   + Lay Subsidy Rolls, 1524–99   E/179/108–11

Ecclesiastical records:
   (These are on temporary deposit at the P.R.O. while awaiting transfer to
   the Guildhall Library).
   Archdeaconry of Essex Act Book, 1561–2   Uncatalogued
   Fragment of Consistory Court of London Correction Book, 1574   „
   Consistory Court (London) Deposition Book, 1578–80   „
   Commissary Court (London) Correction Book, 1588–93   „
   Consistory Court (London) Correction Book, 1589–90   „
   Commissary Court (London) Correction Book, 1605   „
   Commissary Court (London) Correction Book, 1619–20   „

3. LONDON COUNTY RECORD OFFICE

Certain volumes of ecclesiastical records were unfit for production, as specified below. When these have been repaired, additional cases of Essex witchcraft are almost certain to appear.

The series entitled 'Miscellaneous Books' comes closest to the E.R.O. 'Act' books and is the most useful source for the historian of witchcraft.

Consistory Court of the Bishop of London:
    Act Books, 1570–3, 1577–9, 1626–8   DL/C/8, 10, 24
    Assignation Book, 1638–40   DL/C/89
    Deposition Books, 1566–1625   DL/C/210–12, 221–4, 227–9,
        (those for 1586–1611, 1617–20
        were unfit for production)
    Miscellaneous Books, 1583–1683   DL/C/300–28 (vols. 300, 302,
        307, 313 were unfit for
        production)
    Personal Answer Book, 1617–20   DL/C/192
+ Wills, 1547–1627   DL/C/418

4. COLCHESTER BOROUGH RECORDS (Town Hall, Colchester)
Colchester Borough Court:
    Sessions rolls, 1562–1601   No catalogue mark (only
        13/43 years have rolls)
    Sessions rolls, 1605–20   No catalogue mark (only
        11/15 years have rolls)
    Books of examinations and recognizances
    1581–1600   7c, 8c

5. HARWICH BOROUGH RECORDS (Town Hall, Harwich)
Harwich Borough Court:
    Sessions of the Peace, 1601–39   98/14
    Miscellaneous memoranda and files of
    proceedings   29/4, 29/8, 29/10, 37/2, 65/7,
        133/12

6. BODLEIAN LIBRARY, OXFORD
Ashmole Manuscripts:
    178, 184, 185   Figures set by Mr. William Lilly upon Horary
        Vols. I–III (1644–7)   Questions,
    412   Mr. Richard Napier's Practice-book, 1633–5 continued by
        Sir Richard Napier, his successor, to 1641
    421 (fol. 170a)   Letter from Mathias Evans to Richard Napier in 1621
        concerning conjuring books

7. PRINCIPAL PROBATE REGISTRY (Somerset House, Strand, London)
Wills relating to the parishioners of Hatfield Peverel and Boreham, 1560–1604

8. HOUSE OF LORDS RECORD OFFICE
Pardon of Essex witches   House of Lords, Main Papers
    10 March 1645–6

9. DR. WILLIAMS LIBRARY (14 Gordon Square, London)
+ *The Seconde Parte of a Register*

B. PRINTED SOURCES*

I. PRIMARY SOURCES

(a) *Contemporary pamphlets on Essex witchcraft†*

1566 Pamphlet
The Examination and Confession of Certain Wytches at Chensford in the Countie of Essex before the Queens maiesties Judges, the xxvi day of July Anno 1566 (1566; the only copy is in the Lambeth Palace Library: it is largely reprinted in Ewen, I, pp. 317–24, and references in the text refer to Ewen's numbering, since the original numbering is confused).

1579 Pamphlet
A Detection of damnable driftes, practized by three Witches arraigned at Chelmisforde in Essex, at the late Assizes there holden, whiche were executed in Aprill. 1579 (1579; there is a copy in the British Museum, and selections are printed in Ewen, II, pp. 149–51).

1582 Pamphlet
A True and Just Recorde of the Information, Examination and Confession of all the Witches, taken at S. Oses in the countie of Essex (1582; abstracts are printed in Ewen, II, pp. 155–63, and there is a microfilm copy in the Bodleian Library, Oxford, Films S.T.C., 1,014), by W.W.

1589 Pamphlet
The Apprehension and Confession of three notorious Witches. Arraigned and by Iustice condemned and executed at Chelmesforde, in the Countye of Essex, the 5. day of Iylue, last past. 1589 (1589; the only copy is in the Lambeth Palace Library; abstracts are printed in Ewen, II, pp.167–8: there is a microfilm copy in the Bodleian Library, Oxford, in Films S.T.C., 952).

1645 Pamphlet
A True and Exact Relation of the Several Informations, Examinations, and Confessions of the late Witches, arraigned and executed in the county of Essex (1645; there are several copies and abstracts are printed in Ewen, II, pp. 262–77).

One other pamphlet relating to Essex witchcraft exists, but has not been used as a source, since it neither adds to our information nor seems to be accurate. It is *The Full Tryals, Examination, and Condemnation of Four Notorious Witches, At the Assizes held at Worcester, on Tuesday the 4th of March* (London, printed by I.W., n.d.). Some of it appears to be based on the 1645 Essex Pamphlet, but there are added details. The witches Rebecca West, Margaret Landish, Susan Cock, and Rose Hallybread featured in the Essex trials, but there is no mention of their victims, Obadiah Peak, Abraham Chad, or Elin Shearcroft. Nor is there any 'Preston' in Essex. The pamphleteer states that Rebecca West and Rose Hallybread were burnt at the stake and 'Dyed very Stubborn', although we know from other records that Rebecca West was reprieved and Rose Hallybread died in gaol (see cases 607, 648c). It seems, in fact, as if the pamphlet was a later

* The place of publication is London unless otherwise stated. Titles are abbreviated.
† The contents and accuracy of the pamphlets are discussed in Ch. 5, above.

fabrication based on the Essex Pamphlet of 1645 and, possibly, o. account from another county. It is difficult to see why the trial should h located at Worcester.

(b) *Contemporary books on law and witchcraft*

ADY, Thomas, *A Candle in the Dark: or, A Treatise Concerning the Nature of Witches and Witchcraft* (1656).

BERNARD, Richard, *A Guide to Grand Jury Men* (1627).

CASAUBON, Meric, *Of Credulity and Incredulity in things Natural, Civil and Divine* (1672).

CLARK, William, *True Relation of one Mʳˢ Jane Farrer's of Stebbin in Essex, being possess'd with the Devil* (1710).

COKE, Sir Edward, *Third Part of the Institutes of the Laws of England* (1644), pp. 44-7.

COOPER, Thomas, *The Mystery of Witchcraft* (1617).

COTTA, John, *A Short Discovery of the Unobserved Dangers of Several Sorts of Ignorant and Unconsiderate Practisers of Physicke in England* (1612).

— *The Triall of Witch-craft* (1616).

DALTON, Michael, *The Countrey Justice* (1618).

ENGLAND, Church of, Visitation Articles.

(On p. 313 above, evidence from a number of visitation articles for archdeaconries within the county of Essex was cited. These articles are located as follows. I am indebted to the respective librarians for information concerning the articles in their possession. The 'S.T.C.' numbers refer to the numbers in *A Short-title Catalogue of Books Printed in England . . . 1475-1640*, compiled by A. W. Pollard and G. R. Redgrave (1926), or to the additions to the S.T.C. being made under the direction of Miss K. F. Pantzer of Harvard University.)

	S.T.C. number	Location
Middlesex Archdeaconry:		
1582	10,275	Bodleian Library, Oxford
Essex Archdeaconry:		
1610	10,198	Archbishop Marsh's Library, Dublin
1615	10,198.5	Trinity College, Dublin
1635	10,199	University Library, Cambridge
1636	10,199.5	Trinity College, Dublin
1639	10,201	University Library, Cambridge
1672	—	Bodleian Library, Oxford
Colchester Archdeaconry:		
1607	10,188.5	Folger Shakespeare Library, Washington, D.C.
1631	10,189	Archbishop Marsh's Library, Dublin
1633	10,189.5	Plume Library, Maldon, Essex

FILMER, Sir Robert, *An Advertisement to the Jury-Men of England, Touching Witches* (1653).

GAULE, John, *Select Cases of Conscience Touching Witches and Witchcrafts* (1646).

— *The Mag-Astro-Mancer, or the Magicall-Astrological-Diviner Posed, and Puzzled* (1652).

GIFFORD, George, *A Discourse of the Subtill Practises of Devilles by Witches and Sorcerers* (1587).

— *A Dialogue Concerning Witches and Witchcrafts* (1593).

GLANVIL, Joseph, *Some Philosophical Considerations Touching the Being of Witches and Witchcraft* (1667).

HOPKINS, Matthew, *The Discovery of Witches* (1647). The 1928 edition by M. Summers was used throughout.

HUTCHINSON, Francis, *An Historical Essay Concerning Witchcraft* (1718).

JORDEN, Edward, *A Briefe Discourse of a Disease Called the Suffocation of the Mother* (1603).

LAMBARD, William, *Eirenarcha: or of the Office of the Justices of Peace* (1582).

MORE, Henry, *An Antidote Against Atheism* (1655), Book 3.

PECK, Francis, *Desiderata Curiosa* (1779), ii, 146–7.

PERKINS, William, *A Discourse of the Damned Art of Witchcraft* (Cambridge, 1608).

R.B., *The Kingdom of Darkness* (1688).

SCOT, Reginald, *The Discoverie of Witchcraft* (1584). All page references are to the 1964 reprint; Preface by H. R. Williamson.

STEARNE, John, *A Confirmation and Discovery of Witchcraft* (1648).

STRYPE, John, *The Life of Sir Thomas Smith* (1820), pp. 97–100.

SWAN, John, *A True and Brefe Report of Mary Glovers Vexation* (1603).

(c) *Other printed source material*

A number of witchcraft cases were discovered in the printed records of counties other than Essex. These are listed below, with page references, in the texts marked with an asterisk.

Acts of the Privy Council, 1542–1631

*ATKINSON, J. C., (ed.), *Quarter Sessions Records, 1605–1791* (North Riding Rec. Soc., 1884–92), i, 58, 213; iii, 177, 181; iv, 20; v, 259; ix, 6.

*BLAGG, T. M., (ed.), *Nottinghamshire Presentments Bill of 1587* (Thoroton Soc., Records Series, 11, 1945), pp. 22, 36.

*BUND, J. W., (ed.), *Worcestershire County Records: Calendar of Quarter Sessions Papers, 1591–1643* (Worcs. County Council, 1900), p.492.

Calendar of State Papers, Domestic, 1547–1660.

CLARK, A., (ed.), *Shirburn Ballads, 1585–1616* (Oxford, 1907), p. 153.

— *Lincoln Diocese Documents, 1450–1544* (1914), pp. 108–10.

*COPNALL, H. H. (ed.), *Nottinghamshire County Records: Notes and Extracts, 17th Century* (Nottingham, 1915), p. 45.

*COX, J. C. (ed.), *Three Centuries of Derbyshire Annals* (1890), ii, 88–90.

*CUNNINGTON, B. H. (ed.), *Records of the County of Wilts* (Devizes, 1932), pp. 61–2, 70, 75, 82, 156, 219, 225, 227, 242, 247, 278–82.

CUTTS, E. L., 'Curious Extracts from a MS. Diary of the Time of James II', *Trans. Essex Arch. Soc.*, i (1858), pp. 126–7.

GILBERT, W., 'Witchcraft in Essex', *Trans. Essex Arch. Soc.*, n.s. xi (1911), pp. 211–16.

HALE, William, *A Series of Precedents and Proceedings in Criminal Causes, 1475–1640* (1847).

*HAMILTON, G. H., and AUBREY, E. R. (eds.), *Books of Examinations and Depositions, 1570–1594* (Southampton Rec. Soc., 1914), pp. 158–9.

*HARBIN, H. E. BATES, and DAWES, M. (eds.), *Quarter Sessions Records for the County of Somerset, 1606–1677* (Somerset Rec. Soc., 1907–19), xxiii, 96–7; xxviii, pp.lv–lvi, 206, 331–2, 362, 369.

*HARDY, W. J. (ed.), *Hertford County Records, 1581–1894* (Hertford, 1905–10), i, 3–4, 13, 126–7, 137, 267–8, 275.

*HARDY, W. LE (ed.), *County of Middlesex, Calendar to the Sessions Records, 1612–1618* (Middlesex Rec. Soc., n.s. i–iv, 1935–41), i, 190–1, 199, 264, 365, 372, 376–7, 409; ii, 20, 45, 242, 279–80; iii, 16, 265, 306; iv, 133, 303, 309.

**Historical Manuscripts Commission, Various I* (1901), p. 283. (A Worcestershire case.)

**Historical Manuscripts Commission, Various I* (1901), pp. 86–7, 120, 127, 128, 129, 147, 150–1, 160–1. (Wiltshire cases).

**Historical Manuscripts Commission, Appendix to 9th Report* (1883), p.325. (A West Riding case.)

*JAMES, D. E. HOWELL (ed.), *Norfolk Quarter Sessions Order Book, 1650–7* (Norfolk Rec. Soc., 26, 1955), pp. 39, 93.

*JOHNSTONE, H. (ed.), *Churchwarden's Presentments, part 1, Archdeaconry of Chichester, 1621–1670* (Sussex Rec. Office, 49, 1947), pp. 82, 92.

KENNEDY, W. P. M. (ed.), *Elizabethan Episcopal Administration* (Alcuin Club Collections, xxvi, xxvii, 1924). Includes witchcraft visitation articles.

— and FRERE, W. H. (eds.), *Visitation Articles and Injunctions of the Period of the Reformation* (Alcuin Club Collections, xiv–xvi, 1910).

KNAPPEN, M. M. (ed.), *Two Elizabethan Puritan Diaries* (Chicago, 1933). (The diary of Richard Rogers of Essex is one.)

*LISTER, J. (ed.), *West Riding Sessions Rolls, 1598–1602* (Yorks. Arch. Soc., Record Series, iii, 1888), pp. 79, 147.

*LONGSTAFFE, W. H. D. (ed.), *The Acts of the High Commission Court within the Diocese of Durham, 1626–1639* (Surtees Soc., 34, 1857), pp. 34–42.

*PEYTON, S. A. (ed.), *Churchwarden's Presentments in the Oxfordshire Peculiars of Dorchester, Thame and Banbury* (Oxford Rec. Soc., 10, 1928), pp. lxi, 264, 294–5, 299.

*— *Minutes of Proceedings in Quarter Sessions, Parts of Kesteven, 1674–1695* (Lincs. Rec. Soc., 25, 1931), p. 119.

*PURVIS, J. S., *Tudor Parish Documents of the Diocese of York* (Cambridge, 1948), pp. 198–9.

↙*RAINE, J. (ed.), *Depositions and other Ecclesiastical Proceedings from the Courts of Durham, Extending from 1311 to the Reign of Elizabeth* (Surtees Soc., 21, 1845), pp. 27, 29, 33, 84, 99–100, 117, 247, 251–2, 313, 318.

*THOMPSON, A. H. (ed.), *Visitations in the Diocese of Lincoln, 1517–1531* (Lincs. Rec. Soc., 33, 1940), pp. xlix–l.

USHER, R. G. (ed.), *The Presbyterian Movement in the Reign of Queen Elizabeth, as Illustrated in the Minute Book of the Dedham Classis, 1582–9* (Camden Soc., 3rd ser., viii, 1905).

*WAKE, J. (ed.), *Quarter Sessions Records of the County of Northampton, 1630–1658* (Northants. Rec. Soc., i, 1924), p. 224.

*WILLIAMS, J. F. (ed.), *Bishop Redman's Visitation, 1597* (Norfolk Rec. Soc., xviii, 1946), p. 26.

*WILLIS, A. J. (ed.), *Winchester Consistory Court Depositions, 1561–1602* (Winchester, 1960), pp. 25–7.

2. SECONDARY SOURCES

(a) *History of witchcraft*

The majority of the works cited are on English witchcraft. The material in Lea and Robbins listed below, and especially the comprehensive bibliography in the latter, serve as an introduction to European witchcraft. Undoubtedly the most useful accounts of English witchcraft are provided by Ewen, Kittredge, and Notestein. The history of witchcraft generates considerable emotion; scepticism is necessary when reading a number of the works listed, especially those by Murray, Parrinder, and Trevor Davies. The work by K. M. Briggs not only provides a charming account of the literary background to prosecutions, but also includes an excellent bibliography on English witchcraft.

ANON., Removal of supposed skeleton of St. Osithes witch in 1963, *East Essex Gazette*, 19 April 1957 and 15 November 1963.

BRIGGS, K. M., *Pale Hecate's Team* (1962).

DAVIES, R. TREVOR, *Four Centuries of Witch Beliefs* (1947).

EVERARD, S., 'Oliver Cromwell and Black Magic', *Occult Review*, April 1936, pp. 84–92.

EWEN, C. L., *Witch Hunting and Witch Trials* (1929). (This work is referred to as Ewen, I).

— *Witchcraft and Demonianism* (1933). (Referred to as Ewen, II).

— *The Trials of John Lowes, Clerk* (n.p., 1937).

— *Some Witchcraft Criticisms* (n.p., 1938).

— *Witchcraft in the Star Chamber* (n.p., 1938).

— *Witchcraft in the Norfolk Circuit* (n.p., 1939).

— 'Robert Ratcliffe, 5th Earl of Sussex: Witchcraft Accusations', *Trans. Essex Arch. Soc.*, n.s. xxii (1936–40), pp. 232–8.

GRAY, I., 'Footnote to an Alchemist' *Cambridge Review*, 68, No. 1,658 (1946), pp. 172–4. (On an Essex cunning man.)

KITTREDGE, G. L., *Witchcraft in Old and New England* (New York, 1929).

LEA, H. C., *Materials Toward a History of Witchcraft*. Arranged and edited by A. C. Howland (Philadelphia, 1939), 3 vols.

MAPLE, E., *The Dark World of Witches* (1962). (Although sensational in style, it is largely based on Essex evidence. Ch. 10 is especially useful.)

MERRIFIELD, R., 'The Use of Bellarmines as Witch Bottles', *Guildhall Miscellany*, i, No. 3 (1954), pp. 3–15.

MURRAY, M. A., *The Witch-Cult in Western Europe* (Oxford, 1921).

NEILL, W. N., 'The Professional Pricker and His Test for Witchcraft', *Scottish Hist. Review*, 19 (1922), pp. 205–13. (Although about Scottish witch-hunters, this article makes a useful comparison with the Essex witch-hunter Matthew Hopkins.)

NOTESTEIN, W., *History of Witchcraft in England, 1558–1718* (Washington, 1911; reprinted New York, 1965).

PARRINDER, G., *Witchcraft* (Pelican edn., 1958).

ROBBINS, R. H., *The Encyclopaedia of Witchcraft and Demonology* (1959).

ROSE, E. E., *A Razor for a Goat* (Toronto, 1962).

ROSS, C., 'Calvinism and the Witchcraft Prosecution in England', *Jnl. of the Presbyterian Hist. Soc. of England*, xii, No. 1 (1960), pp. 22–7.

SMEDLEY, N., and OWLES, E., 'More Suffolk Witch Bottles', *Proc. Suffolk Inst. of Archaeology*, xxx, pt. 1 (1964), pp. 83–93.

SMITH, E., 'Witchcraft and Superstition' in *Memorials of Old Essex*, ed. A. C. Kelway (1908).

TEALL, J. L., 'Witchcraft and Calvinism in Elizabethan England', *Jnl. of the History of Ideas*, 23 (1962), pp. 22–36.

TREVOR-ROPER, H. R., 'The European Witch-craze of the Sixteenth and Seventeenth Centuries', *Religion, the Reformation and Social Change; and Other Essays* (1967), ch. 3.

VAUGHAN, E., 'Witchcraft in the Eastern Counties', *Home Counties Magazine*, xii (1910), pp. 247–50.

(b) *History of Essex*

ANGLIN, J. P., 'The Court of the Archdeacon of Essex, 1571–1609: An Institutional and Social Study'. (Univ. of California Ph.D. thesis, 1965.)

AUSTEN, F. W., *Rectors of Two Essex Parishes and their Times* (Colchester, 1943), pp. 50–3. (A Stock witch.)

BERRIDGE, J., 'Little Baddow in the Middle Ages' and in the sixteenth and seventeenth centuries, *Essex Review*, xliii, 12–21, 101–10; xlv, 194–200; xlvi, 103–9; xlviii, 22–8, 97–101, 132–40 (1934–9).

COLES, R., 'Past History of the Forest of Essex', *Essex Naturalist*, xxiv (1932–5), pp. 115–33.

— 'Enclosures: Essex Agriculture, 1500–1900', *Essex Naturalist*, xxvi (1937–40), pp. 2–25.

COLLINSON, P., 'The Puritan Classical Movement in the Reign of Elizabeth I' (London Univ. Ph.D. thesis, 1957.)

— *The Elizabethan Puritan Movement* (1967).

DAVIDS, T. W., *Annals of Evangelical Nonconformity in the County of Essex, from the Time of Wycliffe to the Restoration* (1863).

EMMISON, F. G., 'The Care of the Poor in Elizabethan Essex', *Essex Review*, lxii, No. 248 (1953), pp. 7–28.

HOPE, T. M., *The Township of Hatfield Peverel* (Chelmsford, 1930).

HULL, F., 'Agriculture and Rural Society in Essex, 1560–1640.' (London Univ. Ph.D. thesis, 1950.)

MORANT, P., *The History and Antiquities of the County of Essex* (1816), 2 vols.

NEWCOURT, R., *Repertorium Ecclesiasticum Parochiale Londinense* (1708–10), 2 vols.

O'DWYER, M., 'Catholic Recusants in Essex, *c.* 1580–1600'. (London Univ. M.A. thesis, 1960).

PILGRIM, J. E., 'The Rise of the "New Draperies" in Essex', *Univ. of Birmingham Hist. Jnl.*, vii (1958–9), pp. 36–59.

PRESSEY, W. J., 'Records of the Archdeaconries of Essex and Colchester', *Trans. Essex Arch. Soc.*, n.s. xix (1927–30), pp. 1–20.

QUINTRELL, B. W., 'The Government of the County of Essex, 1603–42' (London Univ. Ph.D. thesis, 1965).

SMITH, H., *The Ecclesiastical History of Essex* (n.d.).

— *The Victoria County History of Essex* (1903–1966), 5 vols.

(c) *Anthropological works on witchcraft*

(Because of the method of footnoting adopted in the text, whereby anthropological works are abbreviated to name of author, date, page, the following section of the Bibliography indicates the date of publication immediatcly after the author's name.)

DOUGLAS, M. (1966), *Purity and Danger*, ch. 6.

— (1967), 'Witch Beliefs in Central Africa', *Africa*, xxxvii, No. 1, pp. 72–80.

EVANS-PRITCHARD, E. E. (1937), *Witchcraft, Oracles, and Magic among the Azande* (Oxford).

— (1951), *Social Anthrolopogy*, pp. 98–102.

FIELD, M. J., (1960), *Search for Security*, Part 1.

FORTES, M. (1949), *The Web of Kinship among the Tallensi*, pp. 32–5.

GLUCKMAN, M. (1963), *Custom and Conflict in Africa* (Oxford), ch. 4.

— (1965), *Politics Law, and Ritual in Tribunal Society* (Oxford), ch. 6.

KLUCKHOHN, C. (1944), *Navaho Witchcraft* (Papers of the Peabody Museum, Harvard University, xxii, No. 2, Cambridge, Mass.).

KRIGE, E. J., and J. D. (1943), *The Realm of a Rain-Queen*, ch. 14.

LIENHARDT, G. (1951), 'Some Notions of Witchcraft among the Dinka', *Africa*, xxi, No. 4, pp. 303–18.

MARWICK, M. G. (1950), 'Another Modern Anti-Witchcraft Movement in East Central Africa', *Africa*, xx, No. 2, pp. 100–12.

MARWICK, M. G. (1952), 'The Social Context of Cewa Witch Beliefs', *Africa*, xxii, No. 2, pp. 120–35, and No. 3, pp. 215–33.
— (1965), *Sorcery in its Social Setting* (Manchester).
MAYER, P. (1954), *Witches* (Grahamstown).
MIDDLETON, J., and WINTER, E. H. (eds.) (1963), *Witchcraft and Sorcery in East Africa*.
NADEL, S. F. (1952), 'Witchcraft in Four African Societies', *American Anthropologist*, 54, pp. 18–29.
— (1954), *Nupe Religion*, ch. 6.
SENTER, D. (1947), 'Witches and Psychiatrists', *Psychiatry*, 10, pp. 49–56.
TURNER, V. W. (1957), *Schism and Continuity in an African Society* (Manchester).
— (1964), 'Witchcraft and Sorcery: Taxonomy versus Dynamics', *Africa*, xxxiv, No. 4, pp. 314–24.
WHITE, C. M. N. (1961), *Elements in Luvale Beliefs and Rituals* (Manchester). ch. 5.
WILSON, M. (1951), 'Witch Beliefs and Social Structure', *American Jnl. o, Sociology*, 56, No. 4, pp. 307–13.

Place index of Essex witchcraft references

Every witchcraft reference, prosecution or otherwise, where a place is named, is included. Each reference is marked on Map 1. The letter and number in parentheses immediately after the place-name refer to the square in which the village is located on Map 1. The numbers which follow the parentheses are those assigned to cases in Appendix 1. A date followed by P represents a reference in the witchcraft pamphlet of that year. The letters or numbers in parentheses after the pamphlet date indicate the exact location of the reference within the pamphlet.

For example, if one were interested in the village of Alresford the procedure would be as follows. In the place index one would find that Alresford was in square F3 on Map 1. On the map there are three crosses to represent the three witchcraft references in cases 648(b), 1,078, and p. 15–17 in the 1645 Pamphlet. The full titles of pamphlets are given on p. xx above.

Only villages with witchcraft references are included.

Lambourne (B5), 120, 532–6, 1579P (Bi^v)
Langdon Hills (C5), 923
Langham (F2), 613–14, 648, 648(*f*), 1,046
Laver, High (B3), 1,207
— Little (B3), 1,207
— Magdalen (B4), 1,207
Lawford (F2), 193–5, 595, 607–9, 1,096, 1,130, 1645P (1–15)
Layer-de-la-Haye (E3), 1,013–14
Layer Marney (E3), 839
Leigh (D5), 621–3, 885, 1,127
Leighs, Great (D3), 200–1, 555–8
— Little (C3), 545–6
Lexden (E2), 1,028
Littlebury (B1), 1579P (A7)
Loughton (A4), 300, 942

Maldon (D4), 67–9, 119, 870, 947, 949, 1,141–3, 1,197, 1,200, 1579P (Avi)
Manningtree (F2), 400–2, 602–4, 625, 626–8, 649, 793, 1645P (1–15)
Maplestead, Great (D2), 228–30, 1589P (A3)
Mersea, East (F3), 212–13, 814, 1,073
— West (F3), 1,058, 1,074–5
Messing (E3), 251
Mistley. *See* Manningtree
Moulsham. *See* Chelmsford
Mucking (C6), 976

Navestock (B4), 528–30, 657–61, 1,204
Nazeing (A4), 977–9
Nevendon (D5), 712
Newport (B2), 459, 675
Norton, Cold (D4), 981
Notley, Black (D3), 434–5, 456–8, 1,124
— White (D3), 1,206

Oakley, Great (G2), 269, 1,049
— Little (G2), 167, 1,084, 1,103, 1589P (E6–F4)
Ockendon, North (B5), 197–9, 510–11, 809
— South (C6), 537, 904, 908, 910
Ongar, Chipping (B4), 898
— High (B4), 913
Orsett (C6), 745–6
Osyth, St. *See* St. Osyth

Panfield (D2), 440
Parndon, Great (A4), 1,134

Pattiswick (D2), 493–6, 1,041, 1,043, 1,045
Purleigh (D4), 421–2, 829–30, 957

Quendon (B2), 845–6, 1,115

Radwinter (C1), 1,182
Rainham (B6), 100, 882, 984
Ramsey (G2), 429–30, 642–6, 1,012, 1,104, 1582P (E6*v*), 1645P (26–9)
Rayleigh (D5), 872, 951
Rettendon (D4), 403, 982
Rickling (B2), 554, 846
Ridgewell (D1), 70–1, 650, 748(*b*), 798
Rivenhall (D3), 1645P (12)
Rochford (D5), 64(*b*), 926, 928, 1,137
Romford (B5), 880, 887, 906–7, 911, 944–5, 1,204
Roothing (Roding),
— Aythorpe (B3), 1,207
— Beauchamp (B3), 956
— High (C3), 95–6, 1,207
— Leaden (B3), 1,207
— White (B3), 8
Roydon (A4), 108(*c*), 834

Saffron Walden. *See* Walden
St. Osyth (G3), 155–7, 160–5, 169, 174, 196, 202, 226–7, 605–6, 639–41, 648(*c*),
    814, 1,047, 1,116, 1582 P(*passim*), 1645P (29–33)
Salcott (alias S. Wigborough) (E3), 1,048
Saling, Great (C2), 450–1
— Little (alias Bardfield) (C2), 1,112
Sampford, Great (C1), 245–6, 1,053
— Little (C2), 242–4
Shalford (C2), 445, 567–8
Shenfield (C5), 133–5
Shopland (E5), 1,128
Springfield (D4), 563, 868–9, 877–8
Stambourne (C1), 748, 748(*b*)
Stambridge, Great (E5), 902, 909, 931
Stanford-le-Hope (C6), 985
Stanford Rivers (B4), 237–9, 815, 914, 956, 1,113
Stapleford Tawney (B4), 754(*b*)
Stebbing (C2), 189–91, 335–6, 347–8, 410, 711, 813, 823, 849, 1,118–19, 1,125
Steeple (E4), 864–5
Stifford (C5), 958, 1,108, 1,126
Stisted (D2), 143–5, 285–91, 507, 840, 1,089, 1,105, 1589P (Aiii)
Stock (C4), 108, 804–5, 891, 905
Stondon Massey (B4), 986

Index